Language and Identity
in a Multilingual, Migrating World

SIL International®

Publications in Sociolinguistics 9

Publications in Sociolinguistics is a serial publication of SIL International®. The series is a venue for works covering a broad range of topics in sociolinguistics. While most volumes are authored by members of SIL, suitable works by others will also form part of the series.

Series Editor
Susan McQuay

Editorial Staff
Gene Burnham, Editor
Susan McQuay, Proofreader
Eric Kindberg, Proofreader

Production Staff
Priscilla Higby, Compositor
Barbara Alber, Graphic Designer

Cover photograph: Background Image by Med Ahabchane from Pixabay. Reflection Image by Prithpal Bhatia from Pixabay. Image modified by Barbara Alber.

Map on page 219 © Stephen Watters. Map on page 298 © SIL International®. Map on page 299 © John R. Watters.

Language and Identity
in a Multilingual, Migrating World

Edited by J. Stephen Quakenbush and Gary F. Simons

SIL International®
Dallas, Texas

© 2021 by SIL International®

Library of Congress Control Number: 2022940608
ISBN-978-1-55671-455-9 (pbk)
ISBN-978-1-55671-501-3 (ePub)
ISSN 1091-9074

All rights reserved

No part of this publication may be reproduced, stored in a retrieval system, or transmitted in any form or by any means—electronic, mechanical, photocopy, recording, or otherwise—without the express permission of SIL International®. However, short passages, generally understood to be within the limits of fair use, may be quoted without written permission.

Data and materials collected by researchers in an era before documentation of permission was standardized may be included in this publication. SIL makes diligent efforts to identify and acknowledge sources and to obtain appropriate permissions wherever possible, acting in good faith and on the best information available at the time of publication.

Copies of this and other publications of SIL International® may be obtained through distributors such as Amazon, Barnes & Noble, other worldwide distributors and, for select volumes, sil.org/resources/publications:

SIL International Publications
7500 W. Camp Wisdom Road
Dallas, TX 75236-5629 USA

General inquiry: publications_intl@sil.org

Pending order inquiry: sales@sil.org
publications.sil.org

Contents

1 Introduction   1
   1.1 Part One: Understanding Multiples   2
   1.2 Part Two: Varying Contexts   3
   1.3 Part Three: Heart Matters   4
   1.4 Part Four: Descriptive Studies   5
   1.5 Afterword   6
   References   6

Part One, Understanding Multiples   9

2 Identity Choices of Minoritized Communities: Testing the Identity Construction Factors   11
   2.1 Defining who we are   11
   2.2 The Identity Construction Factors (ICF)   12
   2.3 How the ICF relates to identity choices   21
   2.4 Two case studies   24
   2.5 Applying the ICF to the case studies   26
   2.6 Critiquing the ICF approach   28
   2.7 Practical application of the ICF   30
   References   31

3 Remembering Ethnicity: The Role of Language in the Construction of Identity   35
   3.1 Introduction   35
   3.2 The role of language as one among multiple markers of ethnic identity   37
   3.3 Identities and languages in contact   40
   3.4 Sustaining the memory of a heritage identity   42
   3.5 Strategies for preserving the memory of an ethnic identity   48
   3.6 Emerging identities, emerging languages   49
   3.7 Conclusions   51
   References   51

4 The Dynamics of Identity: How Migration and Diaspora Impact Identity and Multilingualism   55
   4.1 Introduction   55
   4.2 Superdiversity   56
   4.3 The value of a model and the Perceived Benefit Model   57
   4.4 The importance of identity, affiliation, and solidarity   59
   4.5 Appropriate consideration of identity   60
   4.6 Conclusion   62
   References   62

5 Identity and Melting Pots: Negotiating Identity by Resisting or Pursuing Accommodation — 65
   5.1 Introduction — 65
   5.2 Historical overview of the Frisians — 66
   5.3 Frisians and accommodation — 70
   5.4 Theoretical foundation — 72
   5.5 Connecting practice to ideal — 73
   5.6 Frysk and "Language of the Heart" — 74
   5.7 Language and identity — 75
   5.8 Conclusion — 77
   References — 77

Part Two, Varying Contexts — 81

6 New Urban Varieties in Africa and the Identities That Go with Them — 83
   6.1 The linguistic context — 84
   6.2 A typology of urban African varieties — 85
   6.3 Language development and hybrid language practices — 94
   6.4 Urban identities — 95
   6.5 Conclusion: Urban language varieties and identities that do not self identify — 96
   References — 97

7 Trans-languaging, Identity, and Education in Our Multilingual World — 101
   7.1 Introduction — 101
   7.2 Multilingualism: Two kinds, but a continuum between the two — 102
   7.3 Multilingualism from a multilingual perspective — 103
   7.4 Multilingualism and mother tongue — 104
   7.5 Trans-languaging as effective linguistic performance — 105
   7.6 Trans-languaging and complex and fluid identity — 108
   7.7 Implications of trans-languaging in education — 110
   7.8 Conclusion — 111
   Appendix: Transcription Conventions — 112
   References — 113

8 Identity and Diaspora: Making Personal Identity Claims through Relational Networks — 115
   8.1 Introduction — 115
   8.2 Defining identity and diaspora — 116
   8.3 Language use by transnationals and translocals — 117
   8.4 Territory and transnationals and translocals — 118
   8.5 Relational networks and identity claims within diasporas — 119
   8.6 Living as transnationals and translocals — 121
   8.7 Conclusion — 122
   References — 123

9 Hidden Language, Hidden Identity: Identity Issues of Refugees from Minority Language Groups — 125
   9.1 Introduction — 125
   9.2 My personal journey — 126
   9.3 Definitions of identity, ethnicity, and refugee — 127
   9.4 Experiences impacting identity issues of the refugee — 129
   9.5 Language and identity — 136

9.6 Rebuilding identity	140
9.7 Conclusion	141
Appendix: Data Summary	142
Appendix: Interview Questions	144
References	144

10 African Cross-Border Languages: Might or Plight? 147
    10.1 Context and rationale for researching cross-border languages   147
    10.2 Describing the cross-border language situation of Africa   148
    10.3 The vitality of Africa's vehicular cross-border languages, and their impact on identity and language shift   151
    10.4 The vitality of Africa's limited cross-border languages, and their impact on language shift and development   155
    10.5 Understanding the implications for development of cross-border languages   159
    10.6 Summary and conclusion   161
    References   162

Part Three, Heart Matters 163

11 "Heart Language" as a Technical Term: A Critical Review 165
    11.1 SIL's historical language ideology   165
    11.2 Searching for the origins of "heart language"   167
    11.3 Fitting terminology to audience   169
    11.4 Perpetuating a monolingual bias   173
    11.5 Hindering academic discourse   174
    11.6 Conclusion   175
    References   175

12 L1 and L2 Comprehension and Emotional Impact among Early Proficient Bilinguals 177
    12.1 Introduction   178
    12.2 Comprehension   179
    12.3 Impact   182
    12.4 Conclusion   187
    References   188

13 When None of My Heart Languages Is My Mother Tongue 191
    13.1 Introduction   191
    13.2 Comprehension   194
    13.3 Intuitive impact   195
    13.4 Social capital   197
    13.5 Case studies and application   199
    13.6 Conclusion   202
    References   203

14 Reflections on "Language of the Heart" or "Acquired Reflex Language" 207
    14.1 Reflections   207
    14.2 Notes relative to theoretical models   210
    References   212

Part Four, Descriptive Studies — 213

15 Linguistic Identity and Dialect Diversity: A Conundrum with Regard to Magar Kham — 215
- 15.1 Introduction — 215
- 15.2 Linguistic diversity among the Magar Kham — 218
- 15.3 Ethnic identity as a foil of linguistic diversity — 220
- 15.4 Responses to linguistic diversity — 226
- 15.5 Magar Kham: A family of languages or dialects — 228
- 15.6 Magar Kham aspirations — 229
- 15.7 Lack of fit — 231
- 15.8 Summary — 233
- References — 234

16 Hiding Your Identity: The Case of Talysh — 237
- 16.1 Introduction — 237
- 16.2 The Talysh community — 238
- 16.3 The Lezgi and Pamiri communities — 242
- 16.4 Talysh revisited — 248
- 16.5 Implications — 250
- References — 254

17 Language Choice and Language Attitudes in Identity Formation among the Roma of Sadova — 259
- 17.1 Aims — 259
- 17.2 Background — 259
- 17.3 Research questions — 261
- 17.4 Theoretical background — 261
- 17.5 Methodology — 264
- 17.6 Questionnaire results — 265
- 17.7 Discussion of interview results in combination with other observations — 268
- 17.8 Implications for language development work — 271
- References — 272

18 Ethnolinguistic Landscapes of Madagascar: Surviving a Century of Erosive Language Policies — 275
- 18.1 Imagine the scene — 275
- 18.2 Language development in Madagascar — 277
- 18.3 Language ecology — 279
- 18.4 Sociolinguistics and language policies in Madagascar — 283
- 18.5 Diglossia — 284
- 18.6 Views of ethnicity, ethnolinguistic vitality, and Ethnolinguistic Identity Theory — 285
- 18.7 Applying Ethnolinguistic Identity Theory to the case of language maintenance in Madagascar — 287
- 18.8 Conclusion — 289
- References — 290

19 Multilingualism, Urbanization, and Identity among the Ejagham Speaking People — 295
- 19.1 Introductory and theoretical comments — 295
- 19.2 Profile of the Ejagham community — 297
- 19.3 Nodes of convergence — 301

19.4 Eastern Ejagham region relative to multilingualism and urbanization	302
19.5 Western Ejagham region relative to multilingualism and urbanization	304
19.6 Ejagham and education	309
19.7 Diaspora relative to multilingualism and urbanization	310
19.8 Conclusion	313
References	313
20 *Ethnologue* as a Sourcebook for Mapping Multilingualism: The Case of Sango	**315**
20.1 The changing role of *Ethnologue* in a multilingual world	315
20.2 Mapping the range of L2 use	316
20.3 Mapping the degree of L2 use	318
20.4 Identity and the spread of Sango	321
20.5 Conclusion	322
References	322
Afterword	**325**
21 The Research Agenda Going Forward	**327**
References	329
Contributors	**331**

1
Introduction

J. Stephen Quakenbush and Gary F. Simons

The relationship between language and identity is complex and varied, and even more so in our highly multilingual, massively migrating world. Advances in technology and travel have brought speakers of local languages into contact with languages of wider communication—not to mention each other—as they physically spread around the globe to an extent unimagined in previous eras. The result is a constantly changing ecology of languages. In such a changing environment, ethnolinguistic minorities negotiate and manage their identities and participation in broader society to a great degree through the languages they choose to add to or delete from their repertoire. Sometimes language choices are intentional and constitute obvious markers of emerging identities. Sometimes choices are less conscious, and the speakers themselves may not even be aware of the extent to which language shift is taking place in their community. Sometimes language choices are forced, such as when a refugee must learn a new language to survive in a completely new context. In every case, the choices made are important both for the future of the speakers and for the sustainability of the language varieties involved.

The theme that consistently emerges in this collection of papers is that "Multilingualisms vary." Given such variation, how can those from essentially monochromatic, monolingual backgrounds begin to appreciate the colorful multilingual realities of the majority world? It was this question that led to the first symposium to be sponsored by the Pike Center for Integrative Scholarship (pikecenter.org).[1] With the theme "Language and Identity in a Multilingual, Migrating World," the symposium was held May 10–15, 2018, in Penang, Malaysia, in the context of an International Language Assessment Conference also sponsored by SIL International. The resulting papers are presented here in four parts. The first part focuses on different models for understanding the dynamics of multiples—multiple languages, multiple identities, and the relationship between the two. The second part looks at varying social and geographic contexts of multilingualism, including urban, diaspora, refugee, and cross-border settings. The third part examines the history and adequacy of the term "heart language" as it has come to be used especially by organizations and practitioners of Bible translation in the West. The fourth part describes a range of particular multilingual situations in South Asia, Central Asia,

---

[1] The Pike Center Symposium Series falls under the Thought Leadership program of the Pike Center. Its purpose is to convene scholars and other thought leaders in the movement of language development and Bible translation to work on advancing knowledge in key problem areas and to set the agenda for further research.

Europe, Madagascar and Africa. The fourth part also provides an example of how language maps can more accurately portray multilingual situations by showing information on languages that are spoken as second or additional languages.

Finally, the concluding chapter of this volume seeks to build on the contributions of the overall symposium by suggesting a research agenda for furthering our understanding of language and identity in our multilingual, migrating world.

1.1 Part One: Understanding Multiples

Part One explores different models for analyzing how individuals and communities manage the multiple languages they speak and the multiple identities they claim.[2] Based on his previous research and incorporating insights from various models, Dave Eberhard proposes a helpful and comprehensive list of six factors that limit the "Identity Choices of Minoritized Communities." Focusing on minority communities that either have undergone or are currently undergoing significant language shift, he applies these Identity Construction Factors to the Mamaindê of Brazil and to an indigenous band in Oklahoma (USA). He concludes that all six factors are relevant, but need to be weighted according to context and interpreted from an emic perspective. An emic perspective is sought through exploring a community's *narrative identity* and the *dominant scripts* that they tell about their collective experience.

In "Remembering Ethnicity," Paul Lewis examines the interplay of language and identity and how these relate to knowledge bases. In the case of all three, ethnolinguistic communities in contact with others are faced with options ranging from keeping the ingroup through isolation and boundary-keeping, to adding the outgroup through compartmentalizing or hybridizing, to more complete assimilation with the outgroup. Lewis considers objective and subjective definitions of identity, focusing on language as one among multiple markers of ethnic identity. Noting that identity can be maintained even when languages shift, he argues that ingroup identity is still the foundational piece for maintaining both language and ingroup knowledge.

Mark Karan's "Dynamics of Identity" applies the Perceived Benefit Model (see Karan 2001) to explain how minority language communities make language choices in an environment of superdiversity. He notes that a major factor determining whether a minority group maintains its language and identity is the degree to which it feels threatened, arguing that the more threatened a group feels, the more likely it is that they will hold on to their language and identity. Ironically, then, a minority group's ethnic language and identity are most in danger when they feel the most safe.

Jaap Feenstra's contribution on "Identity and Melting Pots" is an often autobiographical account of his experience moving in and out of different languages and communities. Based on his own Frisian heritage, his wife's upbringing in Malaysia, and their experience living in the Tlicho community of Northwest Territories, Canada, Feenstra explores the interplay between language and identity. Appealing to Communication Accommodation Theory (Giles 2016) and adding an example from the literature on the Navajo [nav] language situation (House 2002), Feenstra builds the case that language choices are examples of accommodation (or nonaccommodation), and that it takes intentional effort to maintain an ethnic language together with a language of wider communication in order to be "strong

---

[2] "Multiple" here means simply "more than one."

like two people." Feenstra also touches on the notion of "heart language," one which is examined more fully in Part Three.

1.2 Part Two: Varying Contexts

Part Two contains descriptions of varying contexts of multilingualism: namely urban, diaspora, refugee, and cross-border contexts. Maik Gibson's "New Urban Varieties in Africa, and the Identities that Go with Them" highlights language varieties and practices in urban settings that defy easy description. Gibson proposes a typology of contact language varieties including: creoles and pidgins, urban dialects, youth jargons, and "hybridized (youth) language practices." A well-known example of the last category would be Sheng of Nairobi, a constantly changing language practice associated with a modern Nairobi identity. He concludes that just as new languages reflect new identities, hybrid languages reflect hybrid identities.

Sangsok Son examines the language practices of school children in Delhi, India, in his paper on "Trans-languaging, Identity, and Education in Our Multilingual World." Trans-languaging represents a paradigm shift in how language is viewed—as "the deployment of a speaker's full linguistic repertoire without regard for watchful adherence to the socially and politically defined boundaries of *named* languages" (Otheguy, Garcia, and Reid 2015). Building on the work of Indian scholars (compare Mohanty 2006), Son asks the important question of "How does one become multilingual?" and distinguishes between "grassroots multilingualism" (languages acquired naturally and simultaneously from childhood) versus "elite multilingualism" (additional languages typically acquired later and through formal education).

Janet McLarren and Mary McLendon take us into a world that transcends geopolitical borders in their paper, "Identity and Diaspora." Building on the literature as well as their fieldwork near Charlotte, North Carolina, the authors describe how individuals living in diaspora communities construct their own identities in social and cultural contexts more tied to social networks than to territory or language. "Transnationals" claim identity with multiple groups—from the homeland, the host country, and from the diaspora populations of which they are a part. In this way, transnationals become important mediators of the homeland to the world, and of the world to the homeland.

In "Hidden Language, Hidden Identity," Sunny Hong takes us into the experience of refugees from ethnic minority backgrounds. From interviews among refugees resettled in the Dallas-Fort Worth area, Hong illustrates the unique challenges faced by minority refugees with regard to keeping, claiming, or even communicating their homeland identities. Circumstances of loss, suffering, trauma, and liminality make even more difficult the language and identity choices they face, whether they attempt to assimilate to a host country culture, to counter-assimilate and hold ever more tightly to their own language and ethnicity, or to construct a new transnational identity.

Scott Smith focuses on another kind of situation where languages are spoken across geopolitical boundaries—in this case not so much due to migration, but rather due to how those borders were drawn by colonial powers in the first place. In "African Cross-Border Languages: Might or Plight?" Smith undertakes an overall description of cross-border languages in Africa, making use of the African Academy of Language's distinction between "vehicular" versus "limited" ethnic languages. He notes that the average number of speakers for "limited" cross-border languages (two million) is four times that of African languages overall (half a million), while vehicular cross-border languages have twenty times that number (ten million). He posits that the increasing use of vehicular languages signifies a shift toward urban and national identities, and that it is the increasing use of these vehicular languages that constitutes the most serious threat to the sustainability of Africa's many ethnic languages.

1.3 Part Three: Heart Matters

Part Three explores the history of the term "heart language" among practitioners and supporters of Bible translation, teasing apart its different components and evaluating their usefulness and testing the limits of their applicability. In "Heart Language as a Technical Term: A Critical Review," Gary Simons investigates the history of the term, focusing on how it has been used to communicate the need for Bible translation to a Christian audience. Essentially replacing the concept of "mother tongue," the term has been used for designating the (singular) language that is best suited for communicating with clarity and impact. Simons argues that a continued unexamined use of the term promotes what is essentially a monolingual perspective on language, and hinders productive academic discourse in the quest for understanding multilingual realities.

Kyle Harris considers two key phenomena associated with the notion of heart language in his paper, "L1 and L2 Comprehension and Emotional Impact among Early Proficient Bilinguals." He specifically asks whether L1 (a language learned first and in the home) offers communicative and emotive advantages over L2 (second or other languages that also become part of person's repertoire). Based on the Critical Period Hypothesis,[3] Harris concludes that those who begin learning an L2 after the age of five to seven will likely never achieve native speaker proficiency in that language, and thus the L1 should offer some advantage in terms of comprehension. Similarly, research suggests that L1 typically has greater emotional impact than L2 in cases of sequential bilingualism, where L2 is learned later. However, research does not support either greater comprehension or greater emotional impact for L1 over L2 in the case of "early proficient bilinguals" who acquire more than one language from early childhood in an emotionally rich social context. Here again, we see that multilingualisms vary.

In his paper "When None of My Heart Languages is My Mother Tongue," Daniel Paul delves yet deeper into the concept of heart language, and addresses the question of why some languages communicate more effectively and with greater impact than others in a given community. He makes a distinction between conscious, rational thought and subconscious intuition, and argues that speech communities will benefit most from information couched in speech varieties which have a high potential for intuitive response and are sufficiently comprehensible. Paul employs the concept of social capital from the field of sociology (Coleman 1988) to illustrate how "bridging" and "bonding" social capital apply differently in two case studies. He concludes that the speech varieties best suited to language development are those which a

---

[3] Here is the definition from his paper in this volume: "The idea of a critical period for language learning was introduced by Penfield and Roberts (1959) and further developed by Lenneberg (1967). The Critical Period Hypothesis (CPH), as it is commonly understood today, states that humans possess a heightened sensitivity and ability to learn languages during a bounded period early in life."

community's members are using to promote social capital amongst the groups in which they desire to be insiders.

John Watters reflects personally and poetically on the metaphor of heart language, stating that it captures "the point of convergence between emotion, authenticity, intentionality, veracity, well-being, security, and existential presence." Through a series of vignettes, Watters paints a picture of the role of "home languages" for individuals with differing life experiences. He offers "acquired reflex language" as a possible alternative to the term "heart language," and briefly considers, from a more scientific perspective, what biological and social realities might correspond with languages that "touch the deepest part of our being."

1.4 Part Four: Descriptive Studies

Part Four of this volume contains six descriptive studies of particular language situations. Stephen Watters describes the case of the Magar Kham [kjl] of Nepal as one characterized by "Linguistic Identity and Dialect Diversity." The number of languages recognized by the government of Nepal has gone from 58 in the 1950s, to a low of 17 in the 1970s, to a high of 123 in 2011. Clearly, there are varying views on how to characterize the ethnic languages of Nepal, and they are not all based on observable linguistic diversity. Watters points out that whereas the Magar Kham people speak what might be considered four or five different languages based on linguistic diversity alone, Magar Kham activists insist that there is only one Magar Kham people and one Magar Kham language.

John M. Clifton and Calvin Tiessen describe a situation of being "Hiding Your Identity: The Case of Talysh." Clifton and Tiessen argue that identity can shift over time, vary through a language group, and not be linked exclusively to a particular language. One can become multilingual for pragmatic reasons, without necessarily being willing to take on a new identity in the process. Talysh people typically speak Azerbaijani [aze] to a high degree of proficiency, and even self-identify to Azerbaijanis as being Azerbaijani. However, speaking Talysh [tly] to their fellow Talysh speakers is an important marker of ingroup identity, even if that identity is largely hidden to the outside world. The authors conclude that Talysh people exemplify dual identity, as reported elsewhere in the literature on the experience of some Spanish-English bilinguals as well as some African Americans.

Marlute van Dam presents a window onto "Language Choice and Language Attitude in Identity Formation among the Roma of Sadova," based on three years of participant observation in the community. She also conducted twenty-five interviews with Roma living in Sadova at the time and four others living elsewhere at the time but with connections to Sadova. Results of the interviews were then discussed with members of this highly mobile community to get insider interpretations of the data. Van Dam notes a not uncommon finding in sociolinguistic studies that reported attitudes about language do not always match patterns of actual use. Although Roma people report positive feelings toward their Romani [ruo] language and characterize Romanian as a language for use with outsiders, Romanian remains the preferred language in a number of domains even in Roma-only situations.

Leoni Bouwer describes a situation of considerable ethnolinguistic diversity in "Linguistic Landscapes of Madagascar: Surviving a Century of Erosive Language Policies." Government policy for the past hundred years has been to use either French [fra], "official" Malagasy [mlg], or a combination of the two for government and education, and the view of the dominant society is that official Malagasy is the language of all Malagasy people. Bouwer employs concepts from Ethnolinguistic Identity Theory (Giles and Johnson 1987) as a basis for interpreting her own research, which shows that official Malagasy does not extend well beyond the central highlands, and that elsewhere various local languages are preferred by local communities.

John Watters presents a case study on "Multilingualism, Urbanization, and Identity among the Ejagham Speaking People of Cameroon and Nigeria." Multilingualism is widespread among the Ejagham people, with many speaking three languages. Ejagham [etu] language and cultural identity are closely associated, although Watters gives an example of one group which claims Ejagham identity but speaks Kenyang [ken] instead of Ejagham. Urbanization is more of a factor in the western region (Nigeria), with very little influence on the eastern region (Cameroon). Watters reports that Ejaghams tend to resist larger ethnic languages such as Igbo, preferring Pidgin [pcm] as a language of wider communication. Children born in the Ejagham diaspora do not generally learn to speak their heritage language.

In *"Ethnologue as a Sourcebook for Mapping Multilingualism: The Case of Sango,"* Kenneth Olson and Gary Simons point out that the basic research question for *Ethnologue* has shifted from "What are all the languages spoken in the world?" to "What is the global language ecology?" *Ethnologue* has always focused on such issues as language name, places spoken, number of speakers and notable dialects. *Ethnologue* now further enriches our understanding of multilingual ecologies by including information on a language's domains of use, what kind of institutional support the language receives, and what other languages its speakers use. The authors illustrate how the latter information can be used to create a map depicting the extent to which Sango [sag] is used as a second language across the Central African Republic—in turn, giving a picture as to additional identities (associated with that second language) that are potentially open.

1.5 Afterword

The book concludes with an afterword about "The Research Agenda Going Forward." Part of the format of a Pike Center symposium is for the participants to make note of open research questions that arise out of the various presentations and then to work toward developing a consensus on an agenda for further research. Five areas of priority research were identified, namely: patterns of societal and individual multilingualism, the nature of identity shift and how it relates to language shift, how language development impacts identity, late acquisition of heritage languages, and optimal scale in language development efforts.

It is the sincere hope of the editors and authors that this collection of papers will make a significant contribution to scholarly research on language and identity, spurring further research that will yield greater insight especially into how these issues are lived and experienced by speakers of minority languages, and ultimately resulting in benefit to speakers of those many, beautiful, and varied languages.

References

Coleman, James S. 1988. Social capital in the creation of human capital. *American Journal of Sociology* 94:95–120.

Giles, Howard, ed. 2016. *Communication accommodation theory: Negotiating personal relationships and social identities across contexts*. Cambridge, UK: Cambridge University Press.

Giles, Howard, and Patricia Johnson. 1987. Ethnolinguistic identity theory: A social psychological approach to language maintenance. *International Journal of the Sociology of Language* 68:69–100.

House, Debra. 2002. *Language shift among the Navajos: Identity politics and cultural continuity*. Tucson: University of Arizona Press.

Karan, Mark E. 2001. *The dynamics of Sango language spread*. Publications in Sociolinguistics 7. Dallas, TX: SIL International.

Lenneberg, E. H. 1967. The biological foundations of language. *Hospital Practice* 2(12):59–67. DOI: doi.org/10.1080/21548331.1967.11707799/.

Mohanty, Ajit K. 2006. Multilingualism of the unequals and predicaments of education in India: Mother tongue or other tongue? In Ofelia García, Tove Skutnabb-Kangas, and María Torres-Guzmán (eds.), *Imagining multilingual schools: Languages in education and glocalization*, 262–283. Linguistic Diversity and Language Rights 2. Clevedon, UK: Multilingual Matters.

Otheguy, Ricardo, Ofelia García, and Wallis Reid. 2015. Clarifying trans-languaging and deconstructing named languages: A perspective from linguistics. *Applied Linguistics Review* 6(3):281–307.

Penfield, Wilder, and Lamar Roberts. 1959. *Speech and brain-mechanisms*. Princeton, NJ: Princeton University Press.

Part One
Understanding Multiples

2
Identity Choices of Minoritized Communities: Testing the Identity Construction Factors

David Eberhard

Abstract. This study revisits a recent proposal (Eberhard 2018) that identifies a set of factors that influence the identity choices of minoritized language communities in stages of language shift. Although not referred to as such in the original work, the factors are recast here as the Identity Construction Factors (ICF) proposal. These factors are applied to two new case studies, the Mamaindê of Brazil and an indigenous band in Oklahoma. A critique of that application demonstrates a need for weighted factors and an emic perspective. To ensure an emic perspective this proposal adds the notion of dominant scripts. This last addition is based on the notion of identity as narrative (Ricoeur 1991), capturing the stories communities and individuals tell themselves to make sense of their own group history and identity. This perspective of narrative provides additional insights regarding the limitations placed upon the identity choices of minoritized peoples. In the conclusion I touch on whether such a direction of inquiry holds promise for practical fieldwork and methodology in community-based language development.

2.1 Defining who we are

Minoritized communities who find themselves in a state of language shift will sooner or later come face to face with the question of group identity: "Who are we?" Such a question does not lend itself to empirical study because "Who are we?" is not an empirical question. It is a communal question that finds itself in a mutual dependency with a more personal question: "Who am I?" One cannot be answered without the other. In spite of the epistemological difficulties, practitioners of minority language development are beginning to take this question seriously because the answer to it will most certainly affect future language behavior, particularly when the level of language loss has already been severe. Communities in such situations often find that the future answers to their identity questions will be limited or constrained in various ways—we cannot always be whoever we would like to be, or perhaps not in the way we would like. In a previous study (Eberhard 2018), I sketched out what I believed to be the most influential factors that constrain the identity choices of communities undergoing language shift. In this study, I will apply those same factors (in a revised form) to two new case studies, critique that application, and modify it with new insights, coming up with a more robust and balanced approach to the study of identity within minoritized peoples.

Scholars interested in understanding the behavior of human collectivities, or rather, of individuals in human collectives, agree that studying the identities that drive that behavior remains an essential task. Precisely because of its non-empirical nature, identity has been described from a diversity of perspectives or lenses that both complicate and enrich. Some of the better known perspectives on identity in modern times include such notions as *innate* versus *constructed* (Goffman 1959), *habitus* (Bourdieu 1977), *acts of identity* (Le Page and Tabouret-Keller 1985), *individual* versus *group, single* versus *multiple* versus *hybrid* identity (Tajfel and Turner 1986), and the more recent expressions of identity embedded within the notions of *imagined communities* (Anderson 1991), *narrative identity* (Ricoeur 1991; McAdams 1993), *personal* versus *enacted* versus *relational* versus *communal* identity (Hecht 1993), *positionings* (Harré and Langenhove 1999), *subjectivities* (Solomon 2005), and a resurgent interest in *chronotopes* (Hammack 2010; Bakhtin 1981). All of the above have been useful in furthering our understandings of identity in general. None has been completely satisfying for the purposes at hand.

The definition I will be using for group identity is similar to the one found in Eberhard (2018), based partly on the work of Le Page and Tabouret-Keller (1985) and their *acts of identity*. This is the notion that we construct our group identity by a myriad of individual daily acts, such that our acts (including but not exclusive to language) demonstrate who we are. This view will be strengthened in the current study with the interdisciplinary concept of *narrative identity* (Ricoeur 1991; McAdams 1993), an approach developed by thinkers in the fields of philosophy, psychology, sociology, and sociolinguistics which has proved to be extremely insightful in identity studies in more recent years. The importance of adding the concept of narrative to this definition will become clear later in the paper. My revised definition, then, is as follows:

> **Group identity:** the perception of group belonging constructed by members of a particular community through the experience of a shared narrative, together with the internally accepted markers of that belonging.

The scope of this paper will be limited. Instead of tackling group identity in general, it will focus on the group identity choices of those minority language communities who are either undergoing or have already undergone extreme language shift.

2.2   The Identity Construction Factors (ICF)

The Identity Construction Factors (ICF) is a proposal. This proposal claims that there exists a set of social factors (either internal or external to the community) which act as major influences on the identity choices of minoritized people when their languages are in stages of shift. While these factors cannot predict the identity choices a community will make, they can encourage or discourage such choices. Communities may, of course, resist these pressures and construct an identity that runs counter to these influences. They may also prefer to construct multiple identities. But the assumption in this study is that a choice that runs counter to the majority of these societal factors is not the norm, and if we want to understand the tendencies of minority peoples in such scenarios, accounting for the trends is the place to start.

In a preliminary investigation into the identity choices of minoritized communities (Eberhard 2018), I identified what I believed to be the most influential factors behind these choices. Some of these factors were borrowed from other sources, and some were proposals of my own. All of them were chosen because of their particular relevance in language shift situations, a relevance that has become increasingly evident in my observations and discussions with over sixty endangered language communities on five continents over the past twenty-eight years. I refer to those factors here as the *Identity Construction Factors,* or the ICF for short.[1] While the original list had eight factors, I have condensed them down to six for the purposes of this study.

1. Perceived Benefits of Xish
2. Obligatory Identity Markers of Xish
3. Collective Grievances of Xish[2]
4. Perceived Benefits of Yish
5. Permeability of Yish
6. Repertoire of Yish

My use of Xish and Yish throughout this paper is taken and modified from Fishman's (1991) original usage. While Fishman applies the term "Xish" to any minority language, and "Yish" to any majority language, I will be using these terms as handy labels for whole societies, not just their languages. Thus, *Xish* here will be equivalent to "minority society" and *Yish* will refer to "majority society." Within Yish I also include either national or large regional cultures.

To better understand how the ICF works, it is helpful to divide these factors into two categories—internal factors and external factors. The internal ones are those that arise from traits within the local community, while external ones derive from social pressures present in the broader ecology. More importantly, the internal factors encourage an Xish identity while the external ones encourage a Yish identity.

Factors that encourage Xish
- Perceived Benefits of Xish
- Obligatory Identity Markers of Xish
- Collective Grievances of Xish

Factors that encourage Yish
- Perceived Benefits of Yish
- Permeability of Yish
- Repertoire of Yish

The following is a complete summary of these six factors, each illustrated by an example. This next section borrows considerably from the original text in Eberhard

---

[1] One would expect that some of these six factors would also apply to the identity choices of other human collectives besides minority groups experiencing language shift. But our focus here is on the latter.

[2] I have made a small modification to the original list in Eberhard 2018 by changing the label of the last constraint from Conflict to Collective Grievances. This aligns with Fishman and Garcia (2010:160) who point out that the "language and ethnicity link is strongest where it is energized by collective grievances between apparently contrasted collectivities." Changing the label of this constraint broadens its scope, enabling it to apply to other types of mistreatment that do not specifically include conflict.

(2018) where the interested reader can go for further evidence, background literature, and extended discussions of each factor. We start with the factors which encourage Xish, and then move on to those which encourage Yish.

2.2.1 Factors that encourage Xish

The subsections below describe those factors within a particular minority community that reinforce the group's ethnic identity, facilitating the maintenance of membership within that group and accentuating its boundaries. These factors are: Perceived Benefits of Xish, Obligatory Identity Markers of Xish, and Collective Grievances of Xish.

2.2.1.1 Perceived benefits of Xish

Perceived benefits is a way of talking about the positive rewards of any particular social behavior from the perspective of those who practice it. The word "perceived" indicates that the benefits may or may not be actual. What is important is that they are *believed* to be so. The perceived benefits of using one language over another are considered by many to be the major cause of language shift. This basic insight was developed further into the Perceived Benefit Model by Karan (2000). While Karan applied his model to language, I will borrow his term and apply it to identity, as I also believe such value judgements of benefit are powerful factors that affect the identity choices of members of minority groups.[3]

While the benefits of Yish will be taken up in a later section, I will first apply this notion to the benefits of Xish society, and by extension, to the identity that goes with it. The primary motivation for hanging on to an Xish identity (or a portion of it) in a changing world has to do with the perception that there are continued internal benefits that such an identity can still provide for the Xish community. Preserving traditional land, treasured cultural practices, and the artifacts of those practices are among the visible benefits. The continued use of traditional artistic and religious expressions can be viewed as aesthetic and spiritual benefits.[4] Maintaining familiar

---

[3] By applying Perceived Benefits analysis to identities (and not languages), we are getting closer to the actual choices made by individuals, as identity choices are typically more conscious than language choices. Language shift is thus the result of more foundational identity choices, which are often driven by the perceived benefits of each identity. In this study I make a deliberate distinction between the benefits of languages and the benefits of social identities because my observations show that minoritized communities often separate the two. When groups embrace their Xish roots as a major portion of their identity, but do not speak the Xish language, then we must have a way to assess the perceived benefits of a society and its associated identity as separate from those of language.

[4] A word should be said regarding the sacred and its role in group identity. Karan (2000) includes religious beliefs as one of his perceived benefits. I would like to go a step further and suggest that in many communities a traditional religion (or an adopted one) is not just perceived as a pragmatic good, as the other perceived benefits are, but as the highest good, and as such becomes regarded as a "sacred motif." Religion becomes a distinctive feature or dominant idea within a culture when it is adopted by communal consensus and claims the total allegiance of a whole community. Such motifs are nonnegotiable. This shared sense of what is sacred and what is not binds people together and creates one of the strongest foundations for identity. Numerous things can hold the power of sacred motifs, such as: sacred texts, sacred places/buildings/land, sacred deity, sacred beliefs,

social values, a familiar worldview, and useful bodies of knowledge are possible psychological benefits. A clear sense of one's history, a solidarity with one's ancestral or ethnic group, and the ability to facilitate intergenerational communication provide crucial social or relational benefits. Referring to linguistic benefits, Fishman (2001:22) makes a powerful defense of the "intangible" values of Xish, reminding us that its weakness is its strength. The very qualities of minority culture that are economically unimportant may be those that are communally the most significant.

There are some minority communities who persist in hanging on to a traditional identity in difficult environments that are not favorable to Xish. In such cases, the above benefits of Xish identity do not seem reasonable (at least to outsiders), particularly in the face of Yish benefits that are abundant and accessible and overpowering. It can even appear that such communities are making this choice against all odds. Paulston (1994:16) describes this amazing quality of resilience (or even resistance) as one of *ethnic stubbornness*.[5] The Gavião de Rondonia in west-central Brazil (personal observation) come to mind as supreme examples of this fascinating ethnic trait. The Zoró [gvo] and the Suruí, both closely related to Gavião in all other apparent respects, exhibit no such feature, and are shifting rapidly to a Brazilian identity. While ethnic stubbornness seems most applicable to groups who have maintained both their language and identity, it might also be applied (to a lesser degree) to groups who have lost their language but insist on preserving their traditional identity.

Any perceived benefits of an Xish identity reinforce a community's hold on Xish.

2.2.1.2 Obligatory identity markers of Xish

Le Page and Tabouret-Keller's (1985) *acts of identity* provides an initial base for exploring what constitutes group belonging within individual communities. In Eberhard (2018), I proposed that such acts of identity (or identity markers) are of two types: *active* identity markers and *passive* identity markers.

> **Typical active identity markers:** way of life, occupation, dress, food, religion, language, ceremonies, music/art forms, marriage patterns/restrictions, residence in Xish area, accent in L2, values, beliefs, social

---

sacred values, sacred images, sacred artifacts, sacred monarchy, etc. One clear example of a sacred motif is that of *aliyah,* "going up" to Israel, where the sacredness with which the land of Palestine was held within the Jewish diaspora, and the communal aspiration to return to that sacred space was eventually the basis for immigration to Palestine and the re-creation of the Jewish language and state. An entire national identity was born from this "sacred motif." (See the Wikipedia article on "Aliyah," https://en.wikipedia.org/wiki/Aliyah, for a number of references.) Since I borrow the idea of perceived benefits from Karan (2000), I will respect his inclusion of religion within the Perceived Benefits Model. But an argument could easily be made that due to its unique power within human collectives, "sacred motif" differs from more pragmatic benefits and should be considered as a separate influencer of identity in its own right within the ICF proposal. As such, it would require adding two new factors to the list, Sacred Motifs of Xish and Sacred Motifs of Yish, depending on the origin of the religion, each with its own possible values of strong sacred motifs, weak sacred motifs, or no sacred motifs.

[5]This is similar to the discussions of "change resistant cultures" in anthropology; see Oliver 1965.

networks, traditional authority, artifacts, material culture, visits to heartland.

Typical passive identity markers: shared history/ancestry, mother's/father's ethnicity, clan, land ownership, physical characteristics, existence of some speakers of Xish language, knowledge that Xish language exists, percent of bloodline.

Among their multitudinous acts of identity, both active and passive, communities often establish norms in regards to which one (or more) of these markers constitutes the final boundary marker of Xish, that is, the minimal requirement of an Xish identity when all else is gone. When groups have lost most of their traditional world, this is the identifier that still tells them and others who they are, delineating ingroups from outgroups. In Barth's words (1969:38), "Ethnic boundaries are maintained ... by a limited set of cultural features." Such boundary markers differ from culture to culture and may even vary across time within the same culture. I will refer to these special boundary symbols as a community's *obligatory identity markers*.

When a community's obligatory identity markers are active ones, they require more participation in everyday life and set a higher bar for Xish identity. Passive markers, on the other hand, require less participation and thus set a lower bar for Xish identity. In spite of the qualitative differences involved, identities based on active markers are often less salient and less emotive in the minds of a community than those based mostly on passive markers. This is because the awareness of identity loss (and the emotional response that accompanies it) typically grows as the prospects for maintaining that identity wane (Eberhard 2018:34–35).

Claims that point to the existence of such obligatory markers can be found throughout the sociolinguistic literature. According to Dorais (2010), the obligatory markers for the Inuit of Canada appear to be: (1) having Inuit parents, and (2) practicing an Inuit way of life. It should be noted that their language, Inuktitut, is not endangered like the rest of the languages in this study. It functions as an official language within its territory, with 90% of the population speaking it. They have managed to maintain strong language vitality in a part of the world where many languages are fading fast.

> The majority of the Inuit interviewed stated that language was extremely important for their sense of belonging to their Inuit identity. But when asked if it was imperative for group belonging, they said no, if one lost the Inuktitut language but either *had Inuit parents and/or continued to live as an Inuit,* that person would still be an Inuit, just a "bad little Inuk." ... In the eyes of the Inuit, one specific village of Inuit, the Mackenzie Inuvialuit, still remain fully Inuit, even if they have now lost their language (Dorais 2010:296–297; emphasis added).

When obligatory identity markers are present within a community, they reinforce traditional identity. When they are absent, Xish identity is severely limited.

2.2.1.3 Collective grievances of Xish

Collective grievances are the list of wrongs suffered by a group that are preserved in the communal memory (see Fishman and Garcia 2010:160). These are the consequences of injustices of all sizes, from laws that discriminate or oppress, to bloodshed and armed conflict. Such mistreatment may come from any group that is stronger—either from the national culture, a large regional ethnic group, one's stronger neighbors, or even from an internal variety of Xish that is ethnically related but at odds with the community in question. All of the above evoke grievances that can reside in the communal psyche of minorities for generations, solidifying barriers between ingroups and outgroups. The path chosen in responding to these grievances most certainly impacts the future identities of the communities affected.

Of the more well-known demonstrations of minority grievances in recent years have been the continual attempts on the part of the Catalan to secede from Spain. The most recent attempts were held via referendums in October 2014, and then again in October 2017 (Connolly 2017). But the origin of anti-Castilian sentiment in Catalonia is deep seated and goes as far back as the Reapers War (*Revolta dels Segadors*) in 1640, when the harsh treatment of Catalan communities at the hands of occupying Castilian troops caused a Catalan uprising (Guibernau 2000:1002). The national hymn of Catalonia, *Els Segadors*, immortalized this event, and the ancient grievance remains a part of their oral tradition. Catalonia's unique separatist identity is thus based on much more than current politics, finding its roots in communal remembering of what the Catalan consider to be long-standing political wrongs suffered at the hands of their rulers in Madrid.[6]

Collective grievances, when present, are some of the strongest possible influences that can be experienced by an Xish community. These events influence towards maintaining Xish identity. If Xish suffer an injustice at the hands of Yish, this constitutes an *external grievance*, and the boundary between Xish and Yish identity becomes highly delineated. If, on the other hand, they suffer an injustice at the hands of a related Xish group, then an *internal grievance* has occurred, and the response is to highlight their own uniqueness as a different type of Xish, or possibly as the only legitimate type of Xish. Either way, communal remembrance of being wronged strengthens one's particular variety of Xish. The fresher that memory, the stronger the identity.

An extreme type of collective grievance is found in certain parts of the world. I refer to this as *forced identity*—where a Yish identity is forced upon Xish groups by Yish authorities, or by the members of a larger regional group over them. Instead of simply being mistreated or pushed away by Yish, Xish is told—"You must become one of us." The expression of the smaller Xish identity is banned in public and no safe means of protesting these grievances is available. It may or may not involve conflict. Forced identity may take the form of a government limiting the number of ethnic groups it will recognize within its borders. It may also be the result of situations where a larger group which speaks a language of wider communication (LWC) is attempting to control the allegiance of smaller groups they consider under them. The end result of such Yish policies, however, typically fosters multiple identities on the part of the Xish group. In such cases a submissive Yish identity is adopted

---

[6] Fishman and Garcia (2010) remind us that while participating simultaneously in minority identities and larger identities are natural human behaviors, we must be careful how we manage the power that is latent in each of these group "belongings." "Negative consequences may flow from any human dimension that becomes a basis of collective behavior, be it class, gender, age, religion, race, or ethnicity. … Our commonalities and differences occur simultaneously, the one leading to the acquisition of lingua francas and the other leading to language loyalty within particular ethnolinguistic traditions. Both tendencies represent worthy characteristics of human social behavior and correspond to deeply ingrained human needs. Any frictions they cause must be arbitrated" Fishman and Garcia (2010:160).

by Xish as a survival mechanism to placate Yish authorities—claiming allegiance to Yish in public, learning the obligatory Yish narrative, and adopting a minimal set of Yish identity markers. But this is often a fairly weak identity. Behind that thin Yish veneer, typically there will also be a covert Xish identity which is silently nurtured until such time as it is allowed expression.

Many of my linguistic students at a northern Thai university hailed from various countries of Southeast Asia and were mother tongue speakers of numerous minority languages. In several cases, the small ethnic tribes these students came from were dominated by larger regional groups whose languages were used as LWCs.[7] These regional powers had a history of attempting to suppress any formal expression of smaller Xish identity within their area of dominance, instead insisting that everyone in their region, regardless of ethnicity or mother tongue, are speakers of the LWC and part of the LWC identity. Students mentioned that the production of vernacular orthographies is prohibited by force, and any literature found in these smaller Xish languages is burned. Academics are sued for giving a talk on their own minority language. These are forms of forced identity.

The unique conditions of forced identity, where an overt Yish identity is coupled with a covert Xish identity, makes Xish language (and identity) development virtually impossible. Fanning the flames of an Xish identity in such cases could be disastrous for the community. In such situations communities may survive best by waiting for more opportune times to express who they are.

Forced identity thus has multiple effects on a community. The pressure from Yish to force ethnic groups beneath them to abandon all forms of Xish identity markers limits what the Xish communities can do in public. However, it is also an incentive prompting two courses of action: it motivates Xish members to claim an overt (and feigned) Yish identity for fear of reprisal while strengthening their desire to foster a covert Xish identity as a means of solidarity within their ethnic group.

2.2.2 Factors that encourage Yish

The subsections below describe those external factors that influence a minority community to move towards a Yish identity.

2.2.2.1 Perceived benefits of Yish

According to Karan (2000:68–70), the benefits of Yish language can be categorized under the following headings: communicative motivation, economic motivation, social motivation, and religious motivation. Improved education and better health services are also common benefits of Yish. The perceived benefits of Yish society and its associated identity are similar to the above. When contact between Xish and Yish cultures begins to change Xish lifestyles via the aforementioned factors, the standards and values of Xish society may become harder to satisfy, while a new set of Yish-related values becomes more appealing and even more attainable (see Barth 1969:25). This cost/benefit negotiation is the driving force of language, culture, and identity shift. Joseph (2004:23) helps us to appreciate this process:

> Most of those giving up their traditional language are ... doing so as part of constructing an identity for themselves that is bound up with a conception of modernity.

---

[7] I refrain from giving details to protect the students.

The relative size gap between Xish and Yish cultures will influence the assessment of such benefits. Wherever there are language ecologies where Yish culture is not well developed, or is limited in size and depth, the benefits gained from Xish communities shifting to a Yish identity may not be sufficient for the price that must be paid. In such cases Xish communities may switch to Yish language but choose to remain Xish in identity. Many language groups in the Sepik of Papua New Guinea come to mind in this regard. The relatively modest benefits of becoming a part of Papua New Guinea national culture are not that far removed from the original benefits of Xish, and they certainly cannot compare to the benefits of becoming a part of, for example, Thai national culture or Brazilian national culture. The latter have monolithic cultural footprints. The options available to minority groups in these different language ecologies influence (but do not determine) the identity choices they make. Thus we find that most Sepik groups are choosing to keep their identity, even after losing their language (Eberhard 2015), while a significant percentage of minority groups in Thailand and Brazil are choosing to shift completely to a Yish identity.

The perceived benefits of a Yish identity influence a community towards Yish.

2.2.2.2 *Permeability of Yish*

Permeability is a way of measuring the ease with which outsiders of any group can cross boundaries and become insiders. This concept was developed by Giles and Johnson (1987) in their Ethnolinguistic Identity Theory. I will use it here to refer specifically to the ease with which members of an Xish language community may integrate into and become members of Yish society and take on a Yish identity. It is measured on a continuum from impermeable (or low permeability), where there is little chance of integration, to somewhat permeable, to permeable (or high permeability), where integration is facilitated and expected. It is thus a measurement of social effort. A useful metaphor here is that of an *identity wall*, highlighting the relative difficulty of assimilation instead of measuring the relative ease. A high identity wall would correlate with low permeability, and a low identity wall with high permeability.

Examples of permeable or somewhat permeable dominant societies are the Brazilian culture in Brazil and the Thai culture in Thailand.[8] Brazil is for the most part somewhat permeable, with a history of gradually assimilating minorities who over several generations have become a part of the fabric of society. Many indigenous peoples (such as the Tupinamba) are now extinct due to this assimilation process.[9] Some current groups who have recently undergone a complete integration into the vast Brazilian world in the span of two or three generations are the Torá (Anonby 2015:47) and the Sabanê (personal observation).

Thai culture is for the most part highly permeable. Smalley (1994:346) describes the Thai as a culture where "ethnic categories are generally centered rather than bounded, so ethnic boundaries are not only porous, but also non-exclusive."

---

[8]"Enter Malay and go downstream" is a translation of a popular Indonesian idiom used in the past to express the ease with which minority groups could become a part of the larger society (K. Anderbeck, personal communication, 2015). How much this continues to be the case in Indonesia today is an issue open for debate.

[9]Other groups became extinct due to warfare, genocide, and the many fatal epidemics unwittingly introduced into their communities by the *branco* "white person."

Incorporation is the primary way of unifying the diversity of language and ethnicity in Thailand. Minority groups who have migrated to Thailand and succumbed to the strong Thai identity include the urban Tai Lue, the Thai Yai, the Mon, and the Northern Khmer. Even the powerful Chinese language and culture has bowed to the Thai world and most Chinese descendants in Thailand are now more Thai than Chinese (Smalley 1994:3,173).[10]

Permeability of Yish, however, can be affected by social distance.[11] This is the degree of perceived gap between Xish and Yish cultures. This gap is measured on a continuum via the labels Narrow, Moderate, and Wide. The *social distance* scale can be applicable to characteristics of all sorts: linguistic, cultural, ethnic, religious, and ideological, among others. Specifically, I propose that in most language ecologies, Yish is more permeable to minority groups when the social gap between Xish and Yish is narrow. It is less permeable when the gap is wide. Perceiving others as similar to ourselves makes us more readily disposed to allow them to be part of our ingroup.

Within a particular Yish society, permeability can vary greatly depending on the Xish group under consideration, and the social distance involved. The cases of the Pattani Malay in Thailand (living on the border of Malaysia) and to a lesser degree the Hmong (originally from Laos) are considered to be bounded identities that are fundamentally distinct from a national feeling of Thai-ness (Smalley 1994). This leads to less permeable group boundaries, and ways of behaving towards them that differ from the ways that Thais acts towards other ethnicities within their borders. Most of the northern hill tribe ethnicities, on the other hand, have some affinity to the traditional Thai world both linguistically and socially, and thus tend to meet less resistance when integrating into Thai culture. The social distance scale is therefore significant in Thailand, a fact that is corroborated by Smalley (1994:238-254, 328-329).

Permeable Yish influences towards Yish identity, whereas Impermeable Yish discourages acceptance into Yish. Permeability itself can be further affected by social distance, where a narrow social gap facilitates membership within Yish, and a wide social gap hinders such membership.

2.2.2.3 *Repertoire of Yish*

The repertoire factor is a linguistic one. I have proposed it as a result of observing how the language patterns of numerous minority language communities in different parts of the world are related to the language repertoires of the majority communities surrounding them. This linguistic trait of the larger language ecology can potentially affect identity, as the loss of a minority language often (but not always) precedes the loss of a particular identity. The two values within this factor are: monolingual Yish and multilingual Yish.

---

[10] If hill-tribe ethnic groups want to incorporate and become Thai, they must register for the first time with the government. In the process they will be asked their religion. If they say they worship spirits, they are told that is not a religion and they are simply registered as Buddhists. The process is done. Barriers are eliminated. (Smalley 1994:348)

[11] The permeability of Yish is enhanced when certain opportunities present themselves to members of Xish. These are such things as social "doorways" within Yish (opportunities for Xish individuals within Yish society for accommodation, employment, and education), mixed marriages between Xish and Yish individuals, and the proximity of Xish communities to Yish urban centers.

Monolingual Yish describes a majority culture where monolingualism is the norm. In such language ecologies, there is a social expectation to speak only the Yish language, and a stigma is attached to speaking anything else. This works as an incentive towards Yish, where wider cultural norms influence smaller communities to leave behind their L1 and shift completely to L2. The opposite scenario, multilingual Yish, is characterized by a multilingual majority speaking more than one language as a norm. This scenario does not appear to result in any stigmatized behavior. Minority groups can either shift to Yish or remain bilingual in both Xish and Yish, without any social pressure either way.

Brazil and Thailand are once again useful for illustration. They both have language ecologies with a single, pervasive Yish language and culture. Minority groups who want to adopt a larger identity within these two countries have only one prestige language to choose from, Brazilian Portuguese or Thai. Such monopolizing languages, and the identities that accompany them, are hard for minorities to resist. The monolithic nature of these national identities, with a single language or a single religion or both, also contribute to their size, power, and influence over minority groups. The maintaining of diverse ethnic identities that go beyond regional differences is discouraged, and consequently minorities tend to lose their traditional identities with greater speed.

Some countries, on the other hand, such as Nigeria and the Philippines, have developed a plurality within Yish. The existence of more than one large ethnic or linguistic bloc necessarily brings diversity at the regional and country-wide level. In Nigeria the prime examples are Hausa, Yoruba, and Igbo; in the Philippines, we have Tagalog, Ilocano, Bikol, Cebuano, and Hiligaynon as a few examples of the larger LWCs. Besides national citizenship, several regional-wide identities are thus possible. Minorities, when observing the power relations of those above them in their language ecology, see a number of players on the national and regional stage. This may or may not develop into more identity options for the minority groups, but it certainly does temper the identity expectations at the higher levels. In such ecologies, it is not only permitted but in many cases expected that one would not only have a national identity, but also a separate ethnic and regional identity. And each of these identities would be customarily linked to a distinct language. This openness to pluralism allows the minority identities to survive alongside much larger regional or national ones. The diversity at the local level reflects in some sense the diversity at the higher levels.

The social norms of monolingual Yish societies pressure Xish communities towards abandoning the Xish language and shifting to Yish, whereas the influence of a multilingual Yish culture results in a general tolerance of minorities who speak Yish with or without the abandonment of Xish. The general premise behind this factor is that when monolingualism is the expected norm in Yish culture, not only is there a pressure for minority groups to move from Xish to Yish language, but there is also a pressure to move from Xish to Yish identity.

2.3 How the ICF relates to identity choices

The group identities of minoritized communities can be viewed as choices along a continuum between the Xish and Yish worlds. Each of the above factors is intrinsically linked to a single identity at either end of this continuum, either Xish or Yish, as indicated in the name of the factor itself. When these factors are applied to a particular community, the sociolinguistic context triggers one of several possible values. These values include options such as "present" versus "absent," "many" versus "some" versus "none," or specific terms related to the factor at hand. Charted on the continuum, the results of each of these values either encourages an identity choice in the direction associated with that factor (towards Xish or Yish), or, if the factor is absent, it has no effect on the identity choice. This central position along the identity continuum indicates that either Xish or Yish identity is equally likely, or the identity in focus is discouraged, yet nothing is implied about the opposing identity in relation to this particular factor. Where this is the case, it is almost certain that there will be a parallel factor influencing in the opposite direction.

Table 1a and table 1b identify the various possible values for each factor, and the influence of each of those values in terms of the identity choices for the communities involved. Care should be taken to remember that these are influences rather than predictions of such choices. Some minoritized communities may decide to resist these influences. The majority, however, find themselves deeply affected by these powerful forces.

Table 1a. The ICF with factors that encourage **Xish** identity

Factor	Possible values	Description	Influence on identity
1. Perceived benefits of Xish	Many	Many of these: traditional homeland; valued cultural practices, artifacts, traditional arts, traditional religion; familiar social values and worldview; useful bodies of knowledge; a sense of history; solidarity with ethnic group; a language that facilitates inter-generational communication	Encourages Xish
	Some	A few of the above	Moderately encourages Xish
	None	No perceived benefits of Xish	Discourages Xish
2. Obligatory identity markers of Xish	Present	Active markers: way of life, occupation, dress, food, religion, language, ceremonies, music, art forms, marriage patterns, residence in Xish area, accent in L2, values, beliefs, social networks, traditional authority, material culture, visits of heartland	Presence of many active markers that require participation in everyday life strongly encourage Xish (with low saliency)
		Passive markers: shared history/ancestry, mother's/father's ethnicity, clan, land ownership, physical characteristics, existence of some speakers of Xish language, knowledge that Xish language exists,	Presence of mostly passive markers)or a few active markers with low participation in everyday life) moderately encourages Xish

Factor	Possible values	Description	Influence on identity
		percentage of blood-line	(with high saliency)
	Absent	No obligatory markers present	Discourages Xish
3. Collective grievances of Xish	External grievances	Based on perceived wrongs suffered at the hands of Yish	Encourages Xish
	Internal grievances	Based on perceived wrongs suffered at the hands of a related group of Xish	Encourages one's own kind of Xish
	Forced identity	Yish community forces Xish community to renounce Xish (and to publicly assert Yish identity)	Encourages Xish as covert ID (while encouraging Yish as overt feigned ID)
	None	There are no collective grievances	Neutral—accommodates Xish or Yish

Table 1b. The ICF with factors that encourage **Yish** identity

Factor	Possible values	Description	Influence on identity
4. Perceived benefits of Yish	Many	Many of these: Education, employment, medical care, national culture, material culture, entertainment, technology	Encourages Yish identity
	Some	A few of these: Education, employment, medical care, national culture, material culture, entertainment, technology	Moderately encourages Yish
	None	No perceived benefits of Yish	Discourages Yish
5. Permeability of Yish	Permeable	Integration into Yish possible in first generation	Encourages Yish
	Somewhat permeable	Integration into Yish possible in second or third generation (through education, employment, religious affiliation, intermarriage, language learning, etc.)	Moderately encourages Yish identity (further influenced by social distance)
	Impermeable	No integration possible	Discourages Yish
6. Repertoire of Yish	Monolingual Yish	Yish community is mostly monolingual	Encourages Yish language and identity, discourages Xish
	Multilingual Yish	Yish community is mostly multilingual	Neutral- accommodates Xish, Yish or both

The final outcome in terms of influence is the cumulative effect of these six factors. The juxtaposition of these factors helps to explain the complex choices of minority peoples who sometimes claim an Xish identity and at other times a Yish identity, or even a hybrid form in between. Also note that the values assigned to each factor are not quantifiable in any empirical way. They are subjective assessments which require an informed evaluator and are only meant to be understood in relative terms.

2.4 Two case studies

This section follows the journey of two communities in their various attempts to sometimes grow closer to Yish and sometimes distance themselves from the outside world, all the while attempting to maintain a sense of group identity.

2.4.1 Cabixi Mamaindê

The Cabixi are part of the Mamaindê language community of west-central Brazil.[12] They reside on the banks of the Cabixi river in a single village, and number approximately forty individuals. They are a bilingual community, but are experiencing an acceleration in language shift, where the youngest speakers of the traditional Mamaindê language are eighteen years of age. This puts them currently at the initial stages of EGIDS level 7,[13] where all the adults are fluent in the L1, but the children do not speak it. The Cabixi community is distinct from the other three villages in the Mamaindê language group which are still at level 6a (where all persons of all ages still speak the language).

Their path to language shift began when a Mamaindê woman from the central village of Capitão Pedro married a man from the neighboring Parecis tribe. As her husband never learned the Mamaindê language, they lived in the nearby town of Vilhena where Portuguese became their family language. From this mixed marriage five children were born. All of them (four girls and one boy) were raised in the town of Vilhena and spoke fluent Portuguese. They eventually married Mamaindê spouses and moved back to the Mamaindê area, where they learned Mamaindê in their new Mamaindê homes at differing levels of success, although none of them became fluent. This little group of mixed blood siblings, four sisters and one brother, formed a tight nucleus that would one day form the basis for the new village of Cabixi. Two significant events marked the trajectory of this group.

Various conflicts between these individuals (or their spouses) and the rest of the Mamaindê community ensued. These conflicts grew until one day one of the men in this family was responsible for the accidental killing of the village chief during a hunting expedition. He fled the community, but the conflict between the rest of the family and the Mamaindê grew until it was insupportable. In appropriate Mamaindê

---

[12]Data on the Mamaindê community is based on the author's eighteen years of research among them. The last two trips were in 2015 and 2017.

[13]This refers to a level of language vitality as measured on the EGIDS, or the Extended Graded Intergenerational Disruption Scale (Lewis and Simons 2016:80–81). EGIDS level 7 applies to situations where only adults speak the language. Moving down the scale towards weaker vitality we come to level 8a, where the only speakers are those over childbearing age, and level 8b, where the only speakers are elderly members of the community with limited chances to use the language. See Lewis and Simons (2016) for the complete description of the scale.

fashion, this group of siblings resolved the conflict by moving their respective families to a new location on the reserve where they founded the Cabixi village.

At first, life on the Cabixi was much harder than it was in the main village. They had no fields and no dependable food source. They found themselves isolated and access to the Brazilian town of Vilhena was even harder than it was in the main Mamaindê village. But over time, they overcame these difficulties and their village began to grow. Access to town was facilitated by the purchase of boats and motorbikes. The mother of the sibling group still lived in Vilhena, and they began to show up and visit her house with more frequency. Those who were parents began to leave their children for long periods with their grandmother in Vilhena to study. Because of their schooling in Vilhena, and the increased amount of Portuguese spoken by the parents in the Cabixi, the children that were born after the move to the Cabixi became monolingual in Portuguese, albeit a marked style of Portuguese. Some of the adults began taking adult education classes in town to try to get jobs. A growing number of them now hold government jobs to serve their community in the village in the areas of basic education and health. But other than the grandmother, only one family has been successful in renting a house in Vilhena. This couple moves back and forth between their house in the village and their house in town, and they let their house in town be used by the Cabixi youth as a halfway house for those who are in town to study. The Cabixi village continues to be a place where members of the community return after spending extended periods in town.

Due to all the years the youth spend studying in town, there is a noticeable difference between the behavior of the adults and that of the children. While both young and old alike have borrowed heavily from Western culture, the adults prefer to live in the village more than the town, while the youth prefer the opposite. Regardless of whether they speak the heritage language or not, I have witnessed those who live on the fringes of Mamaindê identity be accepted as Mamaindê as long as they are descendants from at least one Mamaindê parent, return to the tribal village from time to time to renew their ties with their homeland, and participate in the traditional female rites of passage that continue to be held whenever girls reach puberty.

2.4.2 An Oklahoma community

This North American Indian group was originally from a different part of the country and moved to Oklahoma.[14] They have felt mistreated by the white man for centuries. They also have internal conflicts. A long history of disputes between three bands of their tribe goes back to the early 1800s and continues to the present. These disputes have caused deep fissures in a once united indigenous people, resulting in three separate identities, three separate names, and three separate tribes federally recognized by the US government. Today, in the band that I was privileged to visit, the youngest fluent speakers are mostly over fifty years of age, meaning that not only has the intergenerational transmission between parents and children broken down, but the parents themselves do not speak the language. In the informed estimate of the leadership, only 30% of those over fifty still speak the language and only 5% of those between thirty and fifty speak it. This puts the language vitality of the group

---

[14] This group remains unnamed due to a pledge of confidentiality. Data for this section comes from personal interviews I participated in with the Principal Chief and tribal council, March 24–25, 2018.

at EGIDS 8a, where only the grandparents or older are fluent speakers. Due to the widely dispersed nature of the community (most of them do not have neighbors who are community members), even those elders who are fluent are finding fewer opportunities to use the language on a daily basis.

Any individual is allowed to claim this particular Indian identity as long as they satisfy the one-fourth blood quantum. The leaders also emphasized that other important characteristics of belonging to their people include a natural spirituality and adherence to a right path in all doing and being. This particular band was never allotted a reservation but was instead awarded a small amount of federal trust land for their tribal headquarters. As a result, the vast majority of families in this band do not live on land set aside for them, but instead live in farmland, neighborhoods, towns, and cities interspersed with the rest of the citizens of Oklahoma. Most of their neighbors will not be from their own heritage community. Their cultural and social bonds are much looser as a result.

2.5 Applying the ICF to the case studies

Below I use a grid to apply the six factors of the ICF to the above two communities. While the results in the grids are not to be taken in an empirical way, they are meant to give some indication of which direction a community may be heading by identifying what is helping or hindering the construction or maintenance of a given identity. By comparing the factors that are influencing two different communities, this grid enables a rough understanding of the different influences the communities are under and their possible future choices in terms of identity. We begin by applying the ICF to the Mamaindê community, as shown in table 2.

Table 2. ICF grid for the Mamaindê community

Factor	Value	Influence on identity
1. Perceived benefits of Xish	Some benefits — Solidarity with group, elders, history, land and food	Moderately encourages Xish identity
2. Obligatory markers of Xish	Present — Active: participation in puberty rites, sporadic returns to the village. Passive: Descent from at least one Mamaindê parent.	Moderately encourages Xish identity
3. Collective grievances of Xish	Internal grievances	Encourages own kind of Xish identity
4. Perceived benefits of Yish	Many benefits — Education, employment, medical care, national culture, material culture, entertainment, technology	Encourages Yish identity
5. Permeability of Yish	Somewhat permeable — Second or third generation, through education, through employment	Moderately encourages Yish identity, but social distance between the Mamaindê and Brazilian society is wide, making the Yish world even less accessible.
6. Repertoire of Yish	Monolingual Yish	Encourages Yish, and discourages Xish identity

The Mamaindê community ICF grid shows that three of the six factors seem to be influencing a shift towards Yish (Perceived Benefits of Yish, Permeability of Yish, and Repertoire of Yish). But one of those factors, the permeability factor, only slightly influences in that direction as Brazil is only somewhat permeable, meaning that practically speaking this entry into the Yish world is possible but slow. Indigenous peoples who want to be accepted as Brazilian need to find a way to support themselves while they establish a home in (or marry into) a Brazilian community. Only then will their children (second generation) be able to speak Portuguese without any difference from their peers, acquire jobs where they can be independent of village life, and be embraced as fully Brazilian. A further challenge to permeability is the rather wide social distance between present day Mamaindê society and present day Brazilian society. These worlds are quite far apart in many aspects, but the Mamaindê youth are knocking on that door. The other factors on the grid (Perceived Benefits of Xish, Obligatory Markers of Xish, and Collective Grievances of Xish) indicate that while the general move in the Cabixi may be towards a stronger Yish identity, there are still significant incentives to maintaining an Xish identity. Furthermore, the continued presence and practice of cultural markers that remind them of their Xish roots will enable them to remain grounded in their Xish identity for the foreseeable future.

The case of the Oklahoma community is different. This is shown in table 3. Most of the families in this community live among the Yish population, have jobs alongside the Yish, and send their children to Yish schools. This pattern has been ongoing for multiple generations. The influence from their heritage identity is weaker and less tangible and is based mainly on the importance of a connection to elders, to the group, to their history, and to their spiritual roots. This translates into a present-day social distance between Xish and Yish that is quite narrow, not nearly as wide as the gap experienced by the Mamaindê. Three of the ICF factors (Perceived Benefits of Yish, Permeability of Yish, and the absence of Pluralistic Yish) thus point towards the stronger influence of Yish identity, while the other three factors encourage them to maintain an Xish identity. A simple summation of factors does not allow one to conclude which identity is strongest. However, we will see in the following section that the influence of the Collective Grievances factor, when present, can outweigh the others and reinforce the ongoing maintenance of a strong Xish identity for a considerable period of time.

Table 3. ICF grid for an Oklahoma community

Factor	Value	Influence on identity
1. Perceived benefits of Xish	Some benefits — Solidarity with group, elders, history	Moderately encourages Xish identity
2. Obligatory markers of Xish	Present — Passive: ¼ blood quantum	Moderately promotes Xish identity
3. Collective grievances of Xish	Internal and external grievances	Encourages own kind of Xish identity
4. Perceived benefits of Yish	Many benefits — Employment, education, medical care, access to national culture, material culture, entertainment, technology	Encourages Yish identity
5. Permeability of Yish	Permeable	Encourages Yish identity, social distance is narrow

Factor	Value	Influence on identity
		and thus presents a negligible barrier
6. Repertoire of Yish	Monolingual Yish	Encourages Yish identity, discourages Xish

2.6 Critiquing the ICF approach

The ICF approach as it was originally conceived is but a beginning. In this section I will propose some improvements to the model.

One of the glaring omissions is the notion of weight. The six factors are not ranked in any way. Some of these would inherently be more influential than others, such as collective grievances (with forced identity). The model does not yet show this. In a given community with different social dynamics, it is also possible that any of the other factors may be more impactful than the rest, while others may be present but have very little impact. This notion of weight conditioned by culture needs to be captured in some way for this approach to be useful. For instance, in the Oklahoma community, the six factors taken together would suggest that the overall influence towards Yish identity would be more prominent than the influence towards their Indian identity. However, the collective grievances this community has suffered both at the hands of Yish in the 1800s and at the hands of a neighboring band in recent years has made their particular variety of Xish much more salient. Although they now live and work among non-Indians, and although the majority of them do not speak any of the heritage language, their claim to Xish identity appears to be just as strong as ever. The ICF would need to include a way to represent the weight of the more critical factors, such as collective grievances, allowing them more influence on the final analysis, and this assessment of weight would need to be made by the members of the community themselves.

A second critique is that these factors are all fairly objective or *etic*. This information can be obtained by an observant outsider, or by the outsider asking the right questions. There is little in the way of an *emic* perspective here. The subjective voice of the community, and of the individual in the community, is missing (this critique agrees with Lewis, chapter 3 this volume, who makes a case for the need for subjective approaches to identity over objective ones). I sketch out below a way forward by adopting the notion of *narrative* as a foundational concept in our analysis of how identity is constructed.

2.6.1 Narrative identity

The emic corrective to this approach is to ground the analysis on the notion of narrative. More recent studies on identity have been based on Ricoeur's (1991) work on narrative, who identified it as the process by which we construct who we are. McAdams (2008:242) speaks of one's *narrative identity* as "an individual's internalized, evolving, and integrative story of the self." These are "stories we construct to make sense of our lives." Narratives also serve the important function of inherently situating people's identity in time and space (crucial elements in the study of *chronotopes* (see Bakhtin 1981)).

I believe this emphasis on narrative to be insightful not only for capturing the essence of individual identity, but also of group identity, recognizing that human collectives also build their own narratives which tell them who they are and who they are not. Choosing what to remember and what to forget are important elements of a group's sense of belonging, and it is through this selective communal remembering that the constructed nature of identity becomes most evident. As a former Poet Laureate reminds us: "Deciding to remember, and what to remember, is how we decide who we are" (Pinsky 1999:70).

Hammack (2010:178) claims that narrative identity is both individual and collective and is best assessed via a two-step process: (1) the telling of a life story; (2) historical and ethnographic analysis. As part of the second step, a group narrative that captures the group identity is told by a member of the group. This story can then be compared to an individual's life story to see how they have internalized any components of the group narrative. Borrowing from Hammack, I propose complementing the ICF approach with Hammack's process of narrative analysis to construct a more balanced model. This extra lens will be extremely useful to get at things we would not access otherwise if we only used a list of etic criteria.

2.6.2 Dominant scripts

Once we begin to approach group identity as a narrative, as a story, one conditioning factor becomes relevant. I will refer to this as the dominant scripts factor. *Dominant scripts* are the set of optional scripts within the group narrative that members are allowed to choose from to construct their own narratives. These scripts "can be identified in cultural products and discourse (e.g., media, literature, film, textbooks)" and contain "collective storylines that range from a group's history to notions of what it means to inhabit a particular social category" (Hammack 2010).

The presence of these dominant scripts in an individual's narrative confirms or strengthens their group allegiance. Note that the notion of dominant scripts is based on the claim that agency in our identity is limited. One cannot be whomever one wants to be and still inhabit a specific social group. Individuals have a limited number of canonical forms to choose from in a given cultural or group setting (Sarbin 1986:8; Bruner 1987:15).

An example of how dominant scripts influence identity comes from the Oklahoma indigenous community described above. Their ancestors suffered through the boarding school experience, the prohibition against speaking their language, and the long fight to gain their civil rights. Recently, they have been in numerous cases of litigation with their neighbors, a related band. In every single interview with individuals of the tribal council, when we asked about their own personal story, elements of these collective grievances would be expressed. Likewise, the notions of spirituality and following a "right path" or "right way" were pointed out as group values. In subsequent interviews, individuals referred to these values in their life stories and how they themselves are attempting to live them out in some way. Several of them were language teachers who commented on their goal as teachers to instruct in the "right path," or in a way that harmonized with their traditions.

Both of the above scenarios where individuals' life stories mentioned themes from the group narrative (collective grievances and the importance of spirituality and the right path) are examples of dominant scripts. The individuals interviewed were thus following accepted storylines. To speak of one's personal identity without referring to any of the dominant scripts is to cast doubt on one's membership in a group.

2.7 Practical application of the ICF

In conclusion, I will cover some possibilities for the practical application of the ICF model within community-based language development strategies. These ideas attempt to point a possible way forward when addressing the following methodological challenges: identifying multiple and hybrid identities, assessing narrative identity, and ensuring community ownership.

2.7.1 Multiple and hybrid identities

As a first practical consideration, I will comment on a possible approach to assess the presence and extent of multiple identities. If we look at obligatory markers, we can typically find that in groups where the obligatory markers of Xish are all active markers (such as fluency in the traditional language, or a traditional way of life), any secondary Yish identity in their identity repertoire will most likely be smaller than their Xish identity. Whereas, when the obligatory markers of Xish are all passive markers, then the presence of a second and significant Yish identity within that group is more likely. Which one is more significant or salient to the community is a separate question, and will likely depend on social context and history, but the presence of a second Yish identity in these latter cases is usually clear.

A second way in which the ICF can be used to show multiple identities is if the overall influence of these six factors seems divided, with a significant number pointing towards Xish and a significant number pointing towards Yish. In such cases, these split influences could be signs that both identities are present in equal degrees within the community, or that a hybrid identity has developed (one that incorporates elements of both Xish and Yish into a new identity—Zish).

2.7.2 Using ICF and narrative to assess ethnic identity

Perhaps the most practical use for the ICF would be to facilitate the assessment of the strength of ethnic identities. By determining how well group and individual narratives compare to the results of the ICF should give some indication as to the direction and strength of the identity in question. The more these results coincide, the more confidence we can have in our analysis. Complementing the ICF model with narrative analysis can indicate how influential a particular group identity is in the life stories that group members tell themselves. This in itself could be helpful information to those involved in community-based language development in situations where the development goal is sustainable identity (see Lewis and Simons 2016).

A possible preliminary attempt at combining the ICF with a narrative approach for assessing the strength of ethnic identity might involve the following six steps:

1. Community answers questions to elicit values for all ICF factors.
2. Community ranks these factors by weight and influence.
3. Intermediate analysis determines outcomes of the weighted ICF factors.
4. Community uses a timeline activity to tell the group story.
5. Community individuals of all ages are asked to tell their own story.
6. Comparative analysis puts narrative and ICF factors together in a final step.

The above approach would need to be fleshed out and tested. Whether or not the ICF could or should be the basis for a more comprehensive methodology of identity assessment is still an open question. I believe, however, that complementing the model with the notions of *narrative identity* and *dominant scripts* make it more robust.

Although moving towards narrative makes the journey messier and less empirical than where it started, I am convinced it takes us closer to the essence of identity.

2.7.3 Community-based identity assessment

In the end, communities must have ownership of their own identity assessment process. Only they can be the ones who will determine which factors are more salient and carry more weight. Only they know the communal narrative, and the dominant scripts that are a part of their lives. If the ICF is ever to be applied in some way among minoritized groups, it will be more accurate if the assessment is conducted by community leaders themselves (while guided by specialists in the ICF as needed, specialists who are willing to walk with the community along their identity journey).

References

Anderson, Benedict R. 1991. *Imagined communities: reflections on the origin and spread of nationalism*. London: Verso.

Anonby, Stan. 2015. The Extended Graded Intergenerational Disruption Scale applied in Brazil. In M. Paul Lewis and Gary F. Simons (eds.), *Ecological perspectives on language endangerment: Applying the Sustainable Use Model for language development*, 35–56. Dallas, TX: SIL International. leanpub.com/ecologicalperspectives/.

Bakhtin, Mikhail. 1981. *The dialogic imagination: Four essays*. Edited by Michael Holquist. Translated by Caryl Emerson and Michael Holquist. University of Texas Press Slavic Series 1. Austin, TX: UT Press. (Original work published as a whole in 1975, portions in 1935–1941.)

Barth, Fredrik. 1969. *Ethnic groups and boundaries*. Boston: Little, Brown, and Company.

Bourdieu, Pierre. 1977. *Outline of a theory of practice*. Translated by Richard Nice. Cambridge Studies in Social and Cultural Anthropology 16. Cambridge: Cambridge University Press.

Bruner, J. 1987. Life as narrative. *Social Research* 54:11–32.

Connolly, Kevin. 2017. Catalan political landscape as divided as ever. Accessed March 18, 2018. bbc.com/news/world-europe-42433670/.

Dorais, Louis-Jacques. 2010. *The language of the Inuit: Syntax, semantics and society in the Arctic*. McGill-Queen's Native and Northern Series 58. Montreal: McGill-Queen's University Press.

Eberhard, David M. 2015. Report on SUM workshop, Sepik and Highlands, PNG. SIL archives. Ms.

Eberhard, David M. 2018. Language shift and identity: Exploring factors which condition identity when a traditional language is lost. *MANUSYA: Journal of Humanities* 21(2):27–51.

Fishman, Joshua A. 1991. *Reversing language shift: Theoretical and empirical foundations of assistance to threatened languages*. Clevedon, UK: Multilingual Matters.

Fishman, Joshua. A. 2001. Why is it so hard to save a threatened language? In Joshua A. Fishman (ed.), *Can threatened languages be saved*, 1–22. Clevedon, UK: Multilingual Matters.

Fishman, Joshua A., and Ofelia García, eds. 2010. *Handbook of language and ethnic identity: Disciplinary and regional perspectives*. Vol. 1. Second edition. Oxford: Oxford University Press.

Giles, Howard, and Patricia Johnson. 1987. Ethnolinguistic identity theory: A social psychological approach to language maintenance. *International Journal of the Sociology of Language* 68:69–100.

Goffman, Erving. 1959. *The presentation of self in everyday life*. New York: Doubleday.

Guibernau, Montserrat. 2000. Nationalism and intellectuals in nations without states: The Catalan case. *Political Studies* 48(5):989–1005.

Hammack, Phillip L. 2010. Identity as burden or benefit? Youth, historical narrative, and the legacy of political conflict. *Human development* 53:173–201. DOI:10.1159/000320045/.

Harré, R., and L. Van Langenhove. 1999. *Positioning theory: Moral contexts of intentional action*. Oxford: Blackwell.

Hecht, Michael L. 1993. 2002—a research odyssey: Toward the development of a communication theory of identity. *Communication Monographs* 60:1, 76–82. DOI:10.1080/03637759309376297/.

Joseph, John E. 2004. *Language and identity: National, ethnic, religious*. Basingstoke, UK: Palgrave Macmillan.

Karan, Mark E. 2000. Motivations: Language vitality assessments using the Perceived Benefit Model of language shift. In M. Paul Lewis and Gloria Kendall (eds.), *Assessing ethnolinguistic vitality: Theory and practice*, 65–78. Dallas, TX: SIL International.

Le Page, Robert B., and Andrée Tabouret-Keller. 1985. *Acts of identity: Creole-based approaches to language and ethnicity*. Cambridge: Cambridge University Press.

Lewis, M. Paul, and Gary F. Simons. 2010. Assessing endangerment: Expanding Fishman's GIDS. *Revue Roumaine de Linguistique* 55(2):103–120.

Lewis, M. Paul, and Gary F. Simons. 2016. *Sustaining language use: Perspectives on community-based language development*. Publications in Ethnography 42. Dallas, TX: SIL International.

McAdams, Dan P. 1993. *The stories we live by: Personal myths and the making of the self*. New York: Guilford.

McAdams, Dan P. 2008. Personal narratives and the life story. In Oliver P. John, Richard W. Robins, and Lawrence A. Pervin (eds.), *Handbook of personality: Theory and research*, 242–264. New York: Guilford.

Oliver, S. C. 1965. Individuality, freedom of choice, and cultural flexibility of the Kamba. *American Anthropologist* 67:421–428. DOI: dx.doi.org/10.1525/aa.1965.67.2.02a00100/.

Paulston, Christina Bratt. 1994. *Linguistic minorities in multilingual settings: Implications for language policies*. Studies in Bilingualism 4. Amsterdam: John Benjamins.

Pinsky, Robert. 1999. Poetry and American memory. *Atlantic Monthly*, October 1999, 60–70.

Ricoeur, Paul. 1991. Narrative identity. *Philosophy Today* 35(1):73–81. DOI: dx.doi.org/10.5840/philtoday199135136/.

Sarbin, Theodore R. 1986. The narrative as a root metaphor for psychology. In Theodore R. Sarbin (ed.), *Narrative psychology: The storied nature of human conduct*, 3–21. New York: Praeger.

Smalley, William A. 1994. *Linguistic diversity and national unity: Language ecology in Thailand*. Chicago, IL: University of Chicago Press.

Solomon, Robert C. 2005. Subjectivity. In Ted Honderich (ed.), *Oxford companion to philosophy*, 900. Oxford: Oxford University Press.

Tajfel, Henri, and John C. Turner. 1986. The social identity theory of intergroup behavior. In Stephen Worchel and William G. Austin (eds.), *Psychology of intergroup relations*, 7–24. Chicago, IL: Nelson-Hall.

3
Remembering Ethnicity: The Role of Language in the Construction of Identity

M. Paul Lewis

Abstract. Sociologists of language and linguistic anthropologists have focused their attention on the relationship of language to ethnicity and, increasingly over the last three decades, on issues of language and identity shift and death. As globalization continues apace, most communities are exposed to and have significant levels of contact and interaction with others who have different, and even multiple, identities. This paper explores the role of language and languages in negotiating these contacts. The functions of multiple languages within a community's linguistic repertoire in transmitting the memory of an ethnic identity are considered along with the roles of various modes of language use: oral, written, and digital. The paper examines various community postures towards identity maintenance and construction. A hierarchy which takes identity to be foundational is proposed and the concepts of language, domains of use (bodies of knowledge), and modalities of use are explored as a framework for constructing individual and group identities.[1]

3.1 Introduction

Sociologists of language and linguistic anthropologists have focused their attention on the relationship between language and ethnic identity and, increasingly over the last three decades, on issues of language and identity shift and death, the loss of language and identity.

In this paper, I examine the ways in which language is used for identity construction and maintenance and the ways in which language itself is shaped by identities, either remembered, current, or emerging. I propose that individuals and groups in contact deal with multiple identities, multiple knowledge bases, and multiple languages, some of which may be only remembered, some current and active, and others which may be emerging and in flux as they do so. I identify

---

[1] An earlier version of this paper was presented at the Public Memory and Ethnicity conference at York Center for Public Memory, Lewis and Clark College, Portland, OR, in October 2007, a gathering primarily made up of historians. This updated and expanded version has benefited from comments given at that conference and additional thought and research during the decade since then, and especially from the editors of this volume.

language as a primary, though not the only, means by which identity and knowledge are remembered and transmitted from one generation to another.

Identity has been approached from two perspectives: the objectivist and the subjectivist (Ross 1979). Briefly described, the objectivist view is that identity is derived from the collection of behaviors that have come to be associated with a particular group. These behaviors define the identity. As behaviors change, are added, or abandoned, the identity is modified as well. Identity, for the objectivist, *is* the collection of observable behaviors. Ross (1979:4) describes the objectivist view as being "less likely to fall prey to mysticism, romanticism, and vagueness" and providing "clear-cut empirical referents that simplify the task of comparative research." The major critique of this view is that it is focused on "secondary rather than primary factors" (Connor 1972 as cited by Ross 1979:4).

In contrast, the subjectivist approach understands identity to be distinct from and ontologically prior to the behaviors which are associated with it. Identity is understood as a more basic sense of collective consciousness which is the source of the behaviors which both internally unify and externally separate the group from all other groups (Garvin and Mathiot 1956). According to this view, the visible behaviors which represent the identity are changeable or even disposable. They serve as symbols of the more basic sense of identity and of group solidarity and oneness. From this perspective, observable behaviors are expressions of solidarity and distinctiveness which are continuously being tailored and customized to fit the changing context. Bastide (1978:391) describes it in this way: "Codes, religious institutions, dance steps, and family forms are no more than a language by means of which consciousness, individual or collective, expresses itself." The subjectivist view sees that awareness of a distinctive identity as being more or less constant but continuously being expressed through a changing set of contextually constructed unifying and separating identity markers. Identities are constructed in one context but then reconstructed in various ways as their environment changes. Identities can also emerge, especially in situations of heightened contact, sometimes taking the form of what Maher (2005:86) describes as *metroethnicity*, "an ethnicity that is urban(e), ambiguous and lightly worn." Both of these types of constructed identities and their representations will be considered in this paper.

Cultural markers of identity according to this view are sets of distinguishing behaviors that through repetition and common use become sedimented over time and become very closely associated with a particular sense of identity. While this relationship may be very strong, the external markers of identity are not the same as the identity itself. Just as fashions change, tastes change, and innovations come and go, so the specific markers of identity can be acquired and shed as groups adapt and interact with each other and with their changing environment. The fundamental basis of identity is the desire to unify around perceived similarities and to separate from the "other." The markers of identity can and will change over time as various "others" are encountered and come into contrastive focus. A collective identity is constructed when a group unifies around a set of artifacts and behaviors, including shared bodies of knowledge, that distinguish them from all others.

Another theoretical distinction that has been made is between group identity and individual identity. Group identity, which is largely what is in focus in the objective and subjective framings of identity, is in large part constructed on the basis of ethnicity. One way to understand ethnicity is in terms of real or imagined shared ancestry and bloodlines, a history of co-location, and a shared lore regarding origins and cosmology. These often form the basis for the construction of an ethnic identity and are largely backward looking—relating "at however distant a remove, to an observably real past" (Edwards 1985:10). This group awareness provides a sociohistorical map where differences between groups are accounted for, boundaries are drawn, and similarities across those boundaries are explained. For this discussion, individual identity is treated as the extent to which an individual participates in and appropriates the markers of ethnic identity along with a variety of other more immediate contextual factors which shape the individual's self-representation. Roccas and Brewer (2002) provide a useful taxonomy of how individuals manage their ingroup memberships which parallels in significant ways the identity, knowledge, and language management strategies described below.

These theoretical distinctions (objectivist versus subjectivist) may seem moot, since an internal sense of identity is itself constructed and is marked by and only observable through the overt behaviors associated with it. Nevertheless, I argue here that the conceptualization of identity as ontologically prior to its behavioral markers is a heuristic that leads us to a better understanding of how group identity can be remembered, retained, and reinvented dynamically over time and in social space through the acts of identity repeatedly and widely engaged in by individuals. This understanding provides a framework for collaborative interventions with those members of threatened or emerging collectivities who wish to celebrate and memorialize their heritage, or newly minted identities, knowledge bases, and languages.

3.2 The role of language as one among multiple markers of ethnic identity

Language is one very significant marker of identity. A particular language, or set of linguistic behaviors, may come to be closely associated with a particular identity so much so that at times the language and the identity are seen as one or are named interchangeably (Eastman and Reese 1981). From the point of view of ethnic identity it does not make any difference whether we know, speak, or just claim an ethnically related language as long as there is one that we can somehow associate with. The general case is that there is a set of linguistic behaviors that are so closely associated with a particular identity and which have become so conventionalized and sedimented that we can call that set the language of a recognized ethnic identity.

Such a set of conventionalized linguistic behaviors can serve as a marker of an individual's identity whether or not the individual has competence in the language or even regularly uses it. For example, when it suits me, I can self-identify as a Welshman even though I know no more than ten words in Welsh. It suffices that I simply remember Welsh as a language which represents a group identity with which I willingly associate as the language of my father and of his forebears and as a marker of a contrastive identity that I wish to perpetuate. There are, of course, other cultural markers of Welsh ethnicity that I also embrace (and remember more than practice) such as the celebration of St. David's Day (March 1st), the preparation and consumption of Welsh cakes using my grandmother's recipe, and the celebration of Welsh performing arts at the *eisteddfod* and *gymanfu ganu*,[2] neither of which have I

---

[2]The *eisteddfod* is a celebration of Welsh arts including concerts, poetry, and literary performances. The *gymanfu ganu* is a festival of congregational singing with large groups gathering to sing in four-part harmony.

participated in or even attended. In spite of this obviously less than full use of the markers of my heritage identity, I remember them and appropriate them as markers of a Welsh-American ethnic identity. Ross (1979:3–4) describes this subjectivist approach to identity in the following terms: "An individual can speak an alien tongue, change his clothes, and abandon or modify old rituals without necessarily losing his sense of ethnic identification."

3.2.1 The role of language in constructing and maintaining ethnic identity

In addition to marking a remembered, existing, or emerging identity, language also has an important role in constructing and maintaining ethnic identity. While I cling to and remember my Welsh heritage, I don't dress like a Welshman (few modern Welsh people do), I only rarely eat like a Welshman, and I most certainly don't talk like a Welshman—neither through the use of Welsh nor even thr
ough the use of Welsh-accented English. When I visited Wales a few years ago, it was abundantly clear to all that I am, for all intents and purposes, an American.

If I want to project my Welsh, or even less ambitiously my Welsh-American, identity, I need to make use of the markers of that identity. I need to take on those external markers associated with Welshness and make use of them in a way that will both unite me with those who share that identity and, perhaps more importantly, at the same time separate me from all others who have the misfortune not to have been born in Wales or be descended from those who were.

Language thus plays a significant role in the projection of ethnic identity. It is through language and the way I use my linguistic repertoire (among other identity markers) that I am able to signal to others who I am, or at least, who I want them to think I am. Every utterance becomes, as Le Page and Tabouret-Keller (1985) have termed it, an act of identity.

The concept of focused and diffuse identities, introduced by Le Page and Tabouret-Keller (1985) helps us understand a bit better the ways in which speakers manipulate language and linguistic features to dynamically construct an almost infinite variety of nuanced representations of their multiple and overlapping identities, both ethnic and intra-ethnic, in each context in which they find themselves. A more focused identity is represented and projected through the increased use of distinguishing behaviors, including linguistic behaviors, that are associated with that identity. A more diffuse identity will be less clearly marked and so projected less strongly. It is this more-or-less focused sense of who one is (or who one wants to be) that shapes our utterances through choice of linguistic code, selection of lexical items, and adaptation of accent.

Much of this manipulation of linguistic markers may be unconscious, though it can also be consciously manipulated. Bakhtin's notion of heteroglossia (Bakhtin 1981, 1993) is one example of how linguistic behavior is used to project a contrastive identity and ideological orientation. In such cases, the identity projection is contrastive, that is, its focus is on who or what I am not. This heteroglossic use of language as a marker of contrastive identity is considered further below.

3.2.2 The role of ethnicity in the construction and maintenance of language

The converse of the use of language to construct a remembered or current ethnic identity is the function of identity in shaping and constructing language. Ethnolinguistic Identity Theory developed by Giles and others (Giles 1970, 1977,

1979, 1980; Giles, Bourhis, and Taylor 1977; Giles et al. 1991) emphasizes the notion that individuals perceive themselves as being members of a group and define their social identity in terms of their group membership(s). Each individual attempts to maintain (or achieve) a positive social identity by emphasizing the characteristics of their group which will be evaluated positively both by other members of the group and by others. Language is an obvious group characteristic and the ingroup/outgroup distinction is an important factor in affecting how individuals use their language.

As described above, speakers project their identity, in part, through language. They shape their linguistic production to best represent themselves in terms of their focused identities. Le Page and Tabouret-Keller (1985) describe this process for Central American creoles in which speakers were observed to adapt their speech to approximate the standard dominant language more closely in some contexts and to diverge sharply from that same standard in other contexts. This range of variation, well-known to creolists, is called the "creole continuum" with the most divergent forms identified as the *basilect* and the most similar to standard English (or any more dominant language according to each context) called the *acrolect*. Most speakers generally communicate using forms somewhere between those two extremes and so speak some form of a *mesolect* most of the time. What Le Page and Tabouret-Keller describe is how speakers freely and at will alter their speech to be more like the acrolect when the projection of that identity suits them or more like the basilect when the particular context motivates them to do so. Similar patterns of language use as identity projection have been observed in patterns of code switching and code mixing. This variation has less to do with proficiency in the standard or second language or with the level of education of the speakers than it does with the identity in focus that the speaker wishes to project at a particular time.

The classic example of the effect of group identity on language variation is the study of Martha's Vineyard English carried out by William Labov (1972). He identified a pattern of vowel raising which characterized the speech of the residents of the island. By observing their language use systematically, Labov determined that this particular phonological variant had been introduced and gradually grown to become widely used by residents of Martha's Vineyard as they increasingly wished to distinguish themselves from the growing numbers of tourists and summer-only visitors. While there are recognizable phonological patterns that this change in pronunciation follows, its primary motivation is the expression of a particular distinctive identity. It is a kind of not-so-secret code by which long-term residents of Martha's Vineyard can identify themselves to each other and differentiate themselves from outsiders.

These are the dynamics behind the maintenance of most regional and social class dialects and accents as well. With the homogenizing presence of broadcast media and the promotion of standardized languages in formal educational systems, the loss of regionalisms and social dialects would seem inevitable. Yet, these varieties persist. While many learn to erase their accents as they reach higher levels of education and move away from home, family, and friends, most can just as easily slip back into their regional variety when they return to visit or when they encounter a friend from home in a far away place.

While linguistic features can and will change over time, it is the underlying identity that is being expressed, now through one set of symbols and eventually through another, that motivates what Labov identified for historical and comparative linguists as sound change in progress. We should expect that this process of innovation and dispersal applies not only to phonological changes but to morphosyntax and semantics as well.

3.3 Identities and languages in contact

As a result of globalization, most communities are exposed to and have significant levels of contact and interaction with others who have different, and even multiple, identities. With the concepts of language and identity in mind, it is important to consider the dynamics of identity and language contact and the implications of that contact for how heritage ethnic identities can be remembered and the role of language in preserving and representing that memory. In addition, higher levels of contact lead to the emergence of new identities and with them new forms of language to mark them.

3.3.1 Multiple identities, multiple languages, multiple knowledge bases

Groups with different ethnic identities in contact with each other are immediately confronted with the differences and inequalities that exist between them. Some groups are more numerous, more powerful, and therefore in most cases, more prestigious. While efforts may be made simultaneously to identify (or imagine) and remark on similarities and shared features, it is the differences which most often motivate strategic patterns of identity negotiation.

Inevitably the attraction of that power and prestige will begin to erode the value attached to the less powerful and less prestigious identities. Identity revolves around who wants to be in relationship with whom and what those relationships will look like. "Understanding the structure of multiple social identities is important because representations of one's ingroups have effects not only on the self-concept but also on the nature of relationships between self and others" (Roccas and Brewer 2002:88). In some cases, less powerful groups in these sorts of contact situations engage in efforts to maintain not only their core identity but also to reinforce and strengthen their boundaries so that passage from one identity to another is made difficult. One of the effects of globalization, however, seems to be an increased facility to migrate among and to mix identities.

Where once a single set of linguistic features functioned as a marker of identity, in such contact situations, multiple linguistic sets come to serve as markers of the multiple identities. The language use patterns come to resemble much more closely the patterns of the creole continuum with mixing and hybridization of linguistic features resulting in a rich and highly nuanced array of linguistic resources that can serve as representations of those multiple identities. Sometimes the identity in focus is more basilectal. Sometimes it is more acrolectal. In between there is a bewildering array of hybridized mesolectal forms.

Just as there are multiple identities and multiple linguistic forms in play, so there are multiple knowledge bases which must be considered. With each focused identity, whether remembered, current, or emerging, there is an associated body of history, lore, and other shared bodies of knowledge that serve as markers of that identity. Who we are (our ethnic identity) is shaped by our knowledge of where we came from, who our forebears were, and how we got here. There is a shared body of knowledge regarding the environment and our relationship to it. We share cosmological, medical, agricultural, and technological knowledge that represent the way in which we as a group have interacted with our world. At the same time, people with such a shared ethnic identity are increasingly in contact with others who have different cosmologies, histories, and technologies that are associated with their identities. Migration and urbanization place different groups in closer proximity to each other. Different knowledge bases are more and more accessible to others. As minoritized groups take advantage of digital media as well as other channels of communication to promote their own identity, they also are exposed to these alternative identities and to the languages and knowledge bases associated with them.

This situation represents a huge expansion of opportunity for preservation of distinct identities and their associated languages but simultaneously presents a significant threat to smaller, less powerful, and less obviously rewarding identities. In linguistics, language endangerment has come to the fore as a major area of concern. The core of my argument here is that the loss of languages is a symptom rather than the cause of the loss of ethnic identity. The loss of a language and the loss of the knowledge that a particular set of linguistic forms encodes represents the Alzheimerization of an ethnic identity—a gradual forgetting of group identity as bits and pieces of it are irretrievably lost.

This diachronic perspective on identity and language maintenance can be complemented by a continuum of synchronic responses to intergroup contact. Ross (1979) proposed that there is a continuum of such responses shaped by the social organization and level of identity mobilization or activism of communities. In Ross's model, communal groups, with "little incentive to subjectively differentiate a collective we from an external they" (Ross 1979:5) constitute one end of that continuum and contrast with "minority groups" with more activist orientations towards identity and language maintenance (cf. Lewis 1993; Paulston 1987, 2000 for applications of an expanded version of this continuum).

3.3.2 The functions of multiple languages in transmitting the memory of an ethnic identity

Within this array of parameters of contact, language plays a particularly important role not only as a symbol of identity, as described above, but also as a means of transmission of identity and of the knowledge associated with a given identity. Language is the medium of public memory. Certainly there are other nonverbal channels by which the memory of a shared identity can be preserved and transmitted (such as cuisine, dress, visual arts or dance, ceremonies, and monuments) but the narrative that makes sense of those nonverbal semiotic systems can only be expressed in words. The dilemma that each minority ethnic community faces is the decision regarding the linguistic repertoire they will use to preserve and transmit the shared group memory of identity and knowledge.

In addition to the words and structures of language, the modalities of language—oral, written, and, increasingly, digital use—are also significant.[3] There is considerable evidence that the differences are more than technological. One uses the technology of orthographies and the by-products of orthographies—paper, pencil, clay tablet, stylus, typewriter, printing press, computers, LCD displays, laser printers, etc.—and the other uses the vocal tract and kinesthetic, gestural, and proxemic strategies

---

[3] Quakenbush (personal communication) suggests that a set of overlapping parameters along the lines of "embodied (spoken or signed)" vs. "disembodied (written)," "real-time" vs. "recorded," and "in-person" vs. "mediated" would be a more revealing way of classifying modalities than the more common tripartite distinction of "oral-written-digital."

(augmented occasionally by public address systems, recording technologies, radio, television, and the like). There is a growing body of work on the interaction between the forms of language and discourse that are used in various digital representations of language. Just as different linguistic codes are associated with a particular identity, so the modality of those languages comes to be associated with an identity and thus is manipulable as a means of identity projection as well.

Modality plays a significant role in the preservation of the public memory of an ethnic identity. The oral modality, though simpler, less technologically dependent, and largely dependent on memory, has generally been considered ephemeral, restricted in its reach either geographically or socially, and thus less permanent and less sustainable. The written modality, though more dependent on technology (and formal education), is seen as more permanent, more extensible, and more sustainable as an aid to public memory. These assertions have, with good reason, been questioned. It is not clear, and more likely is a prejudice of the literate, that the more highly technological modalities have greater durability and thus are more sustainable. Oral knowledge transmission, in fact, has quite a good track record in preserving the memory of an identity over very long periods of time.

3.4 Sustaining the memory of a heritage identity

A frequently used dictum is that the key to the preservation of a heritage identity is the enshrinement of that identity in literature written in the language most closely associated with it. Lewis and Simons (2016) propose that the preservation of identity depends first and foundationally on the creation of space for that identity through reinforcement of the values and beliefs and of the rewards and benefits associated with that identity. With that in place, language policy and practice that preserves the oral use of the language is the next brick in the wall of heritage identity preservation. With oral transmission secure, the development of the language for written uses can become a useful tool in the preservation of the heritage identity. Without a secure identity and vibrant oral use, the preservation of heritage knowledge by writing it in the heritage language is primarily an exercise in documentation. While a noble and useful endeavor, documentation alone will not achieve the goal of ongoing transmission of a heritage identity. Those who currently associate with that identity and the language it is expressed in will, within a few generations, have moved on to another identity and its associated language and knowledge bases in the extreme case, or to another set of associated markers of that identity including a new language in less dire cases.

It is a strong and vibrant focused identity that produces oral language usage that is authentic and that will be remembered and transmitted without conscious effort. Lacking a focused identity, oral language use will begin to shrink and become more and more ritualized. It will preserve the memory of the identity but only with conscious effort as ritual phrases, aphorisms, stories, and lore are learned and drilled and recited almost for their own sake. With focused identity, and authentic oral language use, the production of written literature follows naturally as an additional means of remembering, celebrating, expanding, and developing "who we are" as a group and as individuals.

Without vibrant oral transmission, written use of language for the preservation of the memory of an ethnic identity serves a function similar to that of a photo album. Over time the details behind each picture become more and more vague and eventually the memory of who that is a picture of or when that vacation trip happened is lost. The Rosetta Stone (or even a thousand similar artifacts) provides us with a window into the ancient world but it is hardly an adequate basis for the ancient classical cultures it enshrines to be revived and carried on.

While all of these pieces can fall into place simultaneously and in any order chronologically (written literature serving in many cases as a way to restore a positive evaluation of an identity, for example), they are logically and conceptually hierarchically ordered. Simply producing written materials will not ensure the preservation of an identity. But the loss of a focused identity inevitably leads to the failure of literacy to take root or be sustained and will ultimately lead to the demise of oral language use as well.

3.4.1 Sustainable identity

If minority groups are dealing with multiple identities, knowing the general nature of how those identities can be negotiated will be important for the preservation of an identity and for remembering it from generation to generation. There are four identity configurations that are likely to remain stable over a long period of time.

Maintenance of ingroup identity. A group may choose to maintain only a single, traditional identity. This would be the case in situations where a community is isolated either by circumstance, or intentionally, by the will of others or by their own choice. In most cases where a single internal identity is being maintained in today's world of frequent intergroup contact, a heavy intentional investment is required. The isolated, unreachable, and untouched community is increasingly rare.

Where intentional isolation is opted for, group boundaries will tend to be strong and impermeable. The stability of this configuration depends greatly on the ability of the group to maintain and enforce its isolation. Contact with outsiders and exposure to a different set of values can erode the internal identity and destabilize this configuration. Successful examples of such isolation are few and even those which are often cited as representatives of exclusive ingroup identity maintenance face continuing erosion which must be dealt with by ever renewed efforts and continuous reinforcement. Frequently mentioned examples of this orientation are the Old Order Amish or the Hasidic Jews in the United States. Both groups minimize the amount of contact they have with outsiders and reinforce their distinctive identities using multiple markers—dress, religion, language—of that distinctiveness. This strategy corresponds in general terms to what Roccas and Brewer call *dominance*, a configuration where "individuals adopt one primary group identification to which all other potential group identities are subordinated" (Roccas and Brewer 2002:90).[4]

Compartmentalization of multiple identities. A group may choose to adopt multiple identities, keeping them compartmentalized with relatively rigid boundaries between them. One way in which this can happen is through the *addition* of identities. Thus a group may maintain its traditional ingroup identity and at the same time adopt external innovations or technologies and participate in those fully at different times and in different settings.

This represents a kind of *compartmentalization* of identity with certain activities being conducted based on an internal, traditional, or heritage identity and other

---

[4] Roccas and Brewer (2002) identify a smaller, more particularistic configuration, *intersection*, which describes sub-group memberships within an ethnic identity group. For example, female lawyers, or Persian-speaking taxi drivers in Washington, DC, are examples of intersecting identity features which characterize this level of ingroup membership.

activities carried out in a completely external identity orientation. Roccas and Brewer (2002:90) describe this as "a process of differentiation and isolation." Bastide (1978:168) refers to this "principle of compartmentalization" in analyzing the changing situation of African slaves in Brazil: who "escaped the law of marginalization by erecting an almost impassable barrier between his two conflicting inner worlds, which allowed him to maintain a dual loyalty to often contradictory values." In some cases this dual identity may be split socially across generations with older folks maintaining the traditional ways and younger people accepting external innovations and participating in the outside world. "With compartmentalization, social identities are context specific or situation specific" (Roccas and Brewer 2002:90).

While individuals can move between these two worlds, the two identity orientations are clearly distinct and maintained as being different from each other. In some cases the two orientations contradict each other—for example, simultaneously holding two contradictory understandings of cosmology (the earth orbits the sun, the sun rides its chariot across the sky).

If the old ways die with the older generation, then identity shift has taken place and the traditional identity becomes no more than a memory. In some cases, age-grading can be observed. It is often the norm that young people, as they grow older, become the maintainers of the old ways leaving the new ways to their children who then become those who participate in and take on the outgroup identity. This may be accompanied by patterns of emigration and return (often between rural and urban settings) at different stages in life. In still other cases, the majority of the population of all generations may move freely between the two worlds of identity. Lewis (2001) describes this pattern as observed in Sacapulas, a town in Guatemala, where the general pattern was for young people to leave town to take jobs in the capital city. There they participated in urban life. Later in life, they returned to Sacapulas to resume their roles, now as elders, in the community.

Hybridization of identities. Another way in which a group can manipulate multiple identities is through *hybridization*. This will occur where both young and old maintain some traditional identity features while adapting and incorporating some external features as well. This is a process of change, however, and is not a stable configuration. Homi Bhabha (1990) talks about this phenomenon, calling it the "third space." Both the internal identity features and the external ones are modified and blended. Neither identity orientation remains "pure." While the distinction between ingroup and outgroup is still present, the internal is a modified ingroup identity and the external is a modified outgroup identity. Roccas and Brewer (2002:91) identify this strategy as *merger*, where "nonconvergent group memberships are simultaneously recognized and embraced in their most inclusive form" and "social identity transcends single categorical divisions between people."

In some settings, one generation may be practicing the compartmentalization of identities while the next is hybridizing (i.e., in a dynamic process of change). Others in the society may be assimilating to the external identity entirely.

Assimilation of identity. A group may adopt the outgroup identity and drop their heritage identity all together. Alternatively, a new identity may emerge as the result of the hybridization process. While some traditional features may be retained or adapted, new features "borrowed" from other groups may also be incorporated into the behavioral repertoire of individuals and, eventually, an entire ethnic community. Many immigrant groups experience this transition over several generations, gradually losing the traditional markers of their distinctive ethnic identity and assimilating more and more with the dominant group around them (which is simultaneously changing over time as a result of contact). The memory of the heritage identity may linger for many generations but other than a few relic representations of it (a particular ethnic food, some specialized vocabulary, etc.) the group identity becomes that of the dominant society.

This configuration, a "new" single identity configuration, may be stable and may remain so until there is contact with some other, perhaps more powerful and prestigious, group and the process of compartmentalization, hybridization, or assimilation begins again. Over a long period of time, a group may undergo multiple shifts in identity in this way. What's more, with the changing fortunes of dominant and less-dominant groups, the process might even reverse itself or come full circle as a previously waning identity regains strength, reasserts, and, often, reconstructs itself.

This representation of the process of identity contact is a significant oversimplification. It represents the process of change only from the perspective of the subordinate identity adapting to and assimilating with the more dominant one. It does not take into account that at the same time as the subordinate group is adding or hybridizing with another identity, the superordinate group is also adapting and may add or hybridize features taken from the subordinate, and other groups with which it is in contact. Sometimes these appropriated identity markers are intentionally or unintentionally pejorative (or may be taken that way) but as they gain currency, in what sociolinguists have called "covert prestige" (Labov 1966; Trudgill 1972, 1983) in the dominant society, they become more acceptable. The growth of "faux Spanish" in North America among monolingual English speakers is an example of this phenomenon.[5]

These stable configurations should be seen as stopping points on a continuum of identity remembrance. The monocultural heritage identity may gradually give way to a multicultural compartmentalized or hybridized identity which may eventually turn into a new monocultural assimilated identity with little or no memory of earlier times.

3.4.2 Sustainable language use configurations

If identity is foundational, then language use should parallel and reflect the underlying identity configuration. When there are multiple languages present in a community, whether there are significant numbers of bilinguals or not, those languages often become closely associated with particular uses or functions which are themselves associated with one or more of the identities of community members. *Diglossia* (Ferguson 1959; Fishman 1965, 1967) is the term used to refer to the state of affairs where community members have associated a particular language with a particular set of activities.[6] While diglossia is not always present where there are multiple languages in close proximity to each other, it is the tendency of human societies

---

[5] I use the term "faux Spanish" to describe the appropriation of Spanish words and phrases by English speakers based on a stereotypical representation of the Hispanic identity and language. These loans are most often mispronounced and misused and may be calques of similar English expressions. A commonly heard example is the expression: "No problemo!"

[6] Functional compartmentalization is often described in terms of "domains of use" which are constellations of topic, location, and participants with which a particular language becomes associated. In practice these domains become conventionalized and labeled as Home or Church or School because in the majority of cases those locations involve

to seek this kind of compartmentalization so that speakers know which language to use in any particular setting. In its strongest form, diglossia represents an almost watertight compartmentalization of language functions. One language variety and only one is used for each function and all members of the community know what those functional assignments are. While not all may be able to use the appropriate language for those functions because of their lack of bilingual proficiency, they know which language ought to be used. Because of this tendency, diglossia is considered to be a very stable configuration. Communities where diglossia has been established are often examples of stable language maintenance over very long periods of time. "Stable multilingualism" is a term that has also been used to describe this state of affairs (Lewis and Simons 2016).

In many contact situations where bilingual proficiency is increasing or newly acquired, some of the clear-cut compartmentalization may be breaking down or beginning to "leak." This represents the beginning of the loss of diglossia and a destabilization of the situation. The consequences of "leaky diglossia" (Fasold 1984) can range from a reconfiguration of language use patterns to complete language shift. Thus the absence or presence (and the relative strength) of diglossia is an important factor to be considered in examining how the memory of a heritage identity will be transmitted.

The languages in a multilingual society are almost always associated with groups that have different degrees of power and prestige. Thus, as a shorthand method of describing this relationship between the languages, one variety is called the High (H) variety and the other is called the Low (L) variety. There are three stable language configurations:

Monolingual L. This is the situation of the relatively isolated monolingual community which functions almost exclusively in their single language—the language most closely associated with their heritage identity. Though there may be other languages in use with recognized functional assignments within the larger context, most members of the community have little or no proficiency in them. Fishman (1967) described this kind of situation as diglossia without bilingualism. This language use configuration closely parallels the Maintenance of Ingroup Identity configuration of the preceding section.

Diglossic L and H. This is the situation where there are multiple languages in use within the community, diglossia is present so the speakers have a clear sense of which language to use in which domain of use, and significant segments of the population have relatively high levels of proficiency in all of the language varieties. Thus speakers can readily switch from one language to another as they go from one domain to another in their daily activities. In Fishman's (1967) terms, this is diglossia with bilingualism. This language use configuration closely parallels the Compartmentalization of Multiple Identities configuration.

Monolingual H. This situation is similar to the Monolingual L situation described above except that the speakers have proficiency in the H variety and not the L. This may be the situation of the dominant language group with a minority language community close by. It may also be the situation of a language community that has shifted from its heritage language to the dominant language. Because of the social dynamics and the perceived lack of rewards and advantages derived from being

---

a recognized set of participants talking most often in a particular language about an expected topic.

associated with L, few speakers will be highly motivated to acquire (or maintain) L. Generally, any remaining speakers of L are expected to acquire and use H with little accommodation in the other direction. This is a reestablishment of diglossia without bilingualism in Fishman's (1967) taxonomy. This language use configuration closely parallels the Assimilation of Identity configuration.

As can be seen, the common feature of these stable language configurations is the presence of the clear association of the language use functions with one or more of the identities available to individuals. Where that compartmentalized assignment of language functions has not been achieved, the situation is likely to be in transition. The process of reconfiguring the diglossic assignment of functions may also parallel the Hybridization of Identities configuration (in Fishman's terms, bilingualism without diglossia).

3.4.3 Sustainable knowledge base configurations

It is not only language that transmits and marks identity; it is the information and knowledge that language communicates. So, in addition to the identity configurations and the language configurations, we can also talk about knowledge base configurations. Ethnic groups are dealing with both their inside or heritage knowledge which connects them with their heritage identity and with outside knowledge which connects them with the "other" with whom they are in increasing contact.

The four stable knowledge base configurations parallel and are associated with the identity and language use configurations:

Ingroup knowledge only. This represents the increasingly rare situation of isolated minority language communities with little or no contact with outsiders. Where contact exists there may be an ideological rejection of that outside knowledge. In some cases, there may be no access to the outside knowledge either because of lack of communications infrastructure (roads, schools, market towns, etc.) or because of the lack of communicative tools (shared language, interpreters, knowledge brokers, etc.). Some groups develop an ideological rejection of outside knowledge because of these lacks in access and opportunity. Sometimes the ideological rejection inhibits the development of access and opportunity. This situation remains stable as long as the isolation is maintained. When contact increases and when communications infrastructure and tools are developed, it becomes increasingly difficult for a community to maintain only their traditional knowledge.

Compartmentalized knowledge. In this situation, community members acquire knowledge from both sets. As with identity and language, they may acquire this knowledge additively, essentially keeping the multiple bodies of knowledge separate and unintegrated. For example, they may operate simultaneously using traditional medicine and Western medicine. They may use one body of knowledge to solve some problems and another to solve others.

Hybridized knowledge. Alternatively, they may hybridize the two bodies of knowledge reinterpreting heritage categories in terms of newly learned scientific categories, or vice versa. In religion, they may syncretize, assigning new names to old gods, or ascribing heritage characteristics to outside deities.

Assimilated outgroup knowledge. Some communities abandon their heritage knowledge altogether and acquire and use outgroup (or hybridized) knowledge exclusively. They may retain some features of their heritage knowledge as relics of the past but these are primarily nostalgic or symbolic in nature. An example of this maintenance of relic knowledge is the still commonly held belief that "catching a chill" will result in a viral infection generally known as "the common cold."

3.5 Strategies for preserving the memory of an ethnic identity

The key issue in preserving the memory of an ethnic identity is how innovations derived from contact with the outside will be managed. Below I briefly describe four possible approaches in terms of the concepts of traditional versus outside identities, languages, and knowledge bases.

3.5.1 Keeping the ingroup

The preservation of the memory of an identity depends heavily on the maintenance of the traditional ingroup identity. The maintenance of group solidarity and unity is fundamental. In this effort, language is an important mnemonic device. Like the acronyms we memorize before tests, mnemonic devices only help us if we remember what they stand for. And it is here that the use of writing to preserve the memory of antiquated forms can best be seen. In the worst case scenario, with an identity that is nearly gone, oral use of the associated language variety is also fading, and only the written records remain to remind us of and link us to that past.

3.5.2 Compartmentalizing

Probably the most critical area of negotiation for a minoritized ethnicity is how it will deal with outsiders and with the markers of outside identity while maintaining inside identity markers. Physical isolation, as a means of maintaining the boundaries between the inside and the outside is one strategy that is increasingly more difficult to achieve. A strategy of addition, keeping the ingroup and adding from the outgroup in a distinct compartment, may well be an ideal, but is no less difficult a strategy. So, Japanese graduate students studying linguistics in English at American universities talk about linguistics in English and may continue to do so even when they return to Japan.

This represents to a great extent the area of work that those of us working in language development are concerned with. As outgroup knowledge is introduced it must be dealt with both linguistically and socially. One alternative is to transmit new knowledge in the outgroup language, as described above, establishing a new compartmentalized domain of use. Another way to deal with new bodies of knowledge is to borrow, transliterate, and assimilate key terminology to make it possible to discuss parts of a new knowledge base in the ingroup language. A third alternative is to actually develop terms in the ingroup language that represent the concepts authentically. This is the realm of translation in the deepest sense—not only taking external forms and exchanging them for internal forms but taking outgroup knowledge and transforming it into knowledge that is authentically part of "who we are."

3.5.3 Hybridizing

A heritage ingroup identity can also be preserved and retained in altered forms. Since according to the subjectivist view, identity is the sense of belonging to a group, that sense can be retained even while all of the markers of that identity—the external behaviors associated with it—are gradually replaced. Thus, clothing can change. It is the same identity but now wearing Levi's or Wrangler. Food can change. Along with our traditional ethnic dishes, we now eat McDonald's Ramadan Mexican Combo Pita Plates from time to time. And languages can be changed. Instead of Catawba or Miami or Apache or Nahuatl, we now speak some other language, perhaps with a distinctive identity-revealing accent. We are still (more or less) who we were, we just mark that identity with different external behaviors.

I would argue that to the extent that a distinct identity is maintained there will be distinctions retained (or constructed) in the mode of dress, the kind of food eaten, or the language spoken, or all of the above. Though some Native Americans have shifted to English, many speak a particular variety of English that identifies them as Native Americans. Distinctive identity is always marked externally in some way.

3.5.4 Expressing the traditional to the other

Finally there is the question of how a traditional ingroup identity can be expressed to outsiders in a way that will make sense to them. Some groups choose not to make their identity, language, and knowledge available to others. Most minoritized groups, however, struggle with the task of self-representation and with efforts to gain recognition and to be heard. Generally they are laboring against negative attitudes, inequalities, and the hegemonic devaluation of who they are. As a result they are pressured to abandon the traditional and with it their language and their knowledge bases. The result is an identity not only abandoned but forgotten. Should they not choose the route of assimilation, however, the issues become the same as those faced in the processes of addition and compartmentalization.

Translation of identity, language, and knowledge becomes the focus and the key to not only maintaining but spreading the memory of an ethnicity.

3.6 Emerging identities, emerging languages

Perhaps it is here that it would be helpful to apply these concepts to the phenomenon of emerging languages, or more precisely, emerging identities marked by their own distinctive forms of speech. There is much current interest in the notion of hybridized identities, the results of increasing contact between groups of people, and the mixing or acquisition of identity markers among those who are in such situations of heightened contact. Most often, however, this interest focuses on code-switching, mixed language phenomena, and the use of nonstandardized styles and registers as acts of identity, as described above.

As much as linguistics has struggled to define the notion of "a language" as distinct from any other language, there is an increasing focus on the emergence of linguistic codes which approach the level of being "separate languages" but which, not unexpectedly, draw on the linguistic resources of high-contact environments in much the same way as pidgins and creoles but without many of the same contextual factors which have been considered to be the incubators of pidginization.

In some cases, these emerging languages represent the "vulgarization" of dominant national and international languages. The many varieties of English which embody local identities and language histories are most often cited as the best examples of these emerging nonstandardized but clearly identifiable "X-lish" varieties (Spanglish, Singlish, Malaylish, Chinglish, etc.). This is a process that parallels the development of the Romance languages from the colloquial Latin spoken in the outlying regions of the Roman Empire. This process is one with which we are familiar and which we can understand in terms of social and geographic variation.

More difficult to account for are those emerging varieties that are sometimes referred to as urban languages where the provenance of the emerging forms is not always entirely clear or is so diverse as to make the construction of a genetic family tree near to impossible. While Singlish can be clearly identified as having English as its matrix variety, the provenance of Sheng in Nairobi is not nearly so obvious. These newly emerging urban varieties seem much less stable, continuously morphing, and so internally diverse that intelligibility among those who are users of the varieties may be limited or even temporary. These are the varieties where the role of identity in constructing language can be most plainly seen.

Without knowing enough about any of these emerging urban languages to be able to make any strong claims, I would propose that a couple of generalizations merit further examination and testing:

- Urban languages emerge in situations of superdiversity where multiple ethnic groups and languages are in continuous contact, yet no single identity among those which are nondominant can claim priority. This accounts for Maher's (2005:86) characterization of "metroethnicity" as being "a 'shifting-sands ethnicity', driven not by the demands of ethnic orthodoxy or powerful loyalty to a particular ethnic or historical tradition. It is an ethnicity invoked rather by an appeal to other cultural demands." Betawi [bew], a Malay-based creole that emerged in the nineteenth century may be an example of the appropriation of a linguistic variety for just such purposes. *Ethnologue* (Simons and Fennig 2018) reports that the speaker population for Betawi may be imprecise "due to [the] vague ethnic and linguistic definition of 'Betawi'." Though the language of a "historic identity," it has been reported that many users of Betawi are from the rising Jakarta urban elite who find it to be "cool" (Yunita Susanto, personal communication). *Ethnologue* describes it as "the Low language in a diglossic situation but possessed of covert prestige when used by the upper classes."
- Some urban languages emerge as counter-identity markers. They serve to counter the dominant identity. This reflects Garvin and Mathiot's (1956) notion of the unifying and separatist functions of language. While in most cases the unifying function is what we take note of, in these emerging languages, we might do well to focus on the separatist function. To use an urban vernacular is to define oneself negatively. "I am not one of them" (and perhaps not one of any of "them"). Sheng speakers, for example, may not have a cohesive socioeconomic, racial, ethnic, religious, or political profile, but Sheng marks an identity that is NOT the establishment. The multiple and changing character of the variety reflects that nonhomogeneous but distinctive identity (Bosire 2006, Samper 2002). Sheng's close association with and frequent usage of hip-hop genres and discursive styles further serves to mark it as a variety of counter-cultural resistance, thus focusing on the covert prestige of the variety (Alim et al. 2008).

In contrast, Maher (2005) asserts that it is the "coolness" factor that is primary in the selection of some urban identity markers. "In the liberated, cool metroethnic both language and speaker are an aesthetic subject; language a lovely accessory not a perfectly formed object from an ethnic tradition" (Maher 2014:2). To cite Maher (2005:86–87) again: "Metroethnicity is a light touch. Metroethnicity is relativistic. It discards the truth claims of traditional ethnicity. It is a restructuring. Metroethnicity involves a critique of ethnicity."

So it seems that there are two types of emerging identity and language phenomena: (1) those like Sheng which are primarily focused on the separatist, counter-cultural manipulation of identity and language, and (2) those like Betawi, which represent the "coolness" of an elite urban identity. Both are examples of hybridization but provide us examples of that process at work in very different socioeconomic milieus.

3.7 Conclusions

Given the complexities that minority ethnic groups deal with in regard to multiple identities, multiple languages, and multiple knowledge bases, and the hierarchical nature of identity, orality, and literacy, we can begin to develop a model of the role of language in remembering ethnic identity.

I have described three analogous kinds of oppositions: ingroup and outgroup identity, ingroup and outgroup language (described as L and H), and ingroup and outgroup knowledge.

I have also argued that the foundational piece is identity, and ingroup identity in particular. In some cases, that identity may be almost entirely from the past and so rely heavily on mnemonic devices such as traditional celebrations and rituals to keep its memory alive. In other cases that identity may represent a continuous link from past to present and be actively engaged in creating its own future through developing and evolving styles, artistic works, and adaptive patterns of language and language use.

In addition, I have further argued that focused identity underlies vigorous and vibrant oral language use and that only then does the written use of the heritage language where it has not previously been present have a reasonable foundation for sustainable ongoing development and use.

References

Alim, H. Samy, Awad Ibrahim, and Alastair Pennycook. 2008. *Global linguistic flows: Hip hop cultures, youth identities, and the politics of language*. Milton Park, UK: Taylor & Francis e-Library. books.google.com/books?id = ffyOAgAAQBAJ/.

Bakhtin, M. M. 1981. *The dialogic imagination: Four essays*. Edited by Michael Holquist. Translated by Caryl Emerson and Michael Holquist. University of Texas Press Slavic Series 1. Austin, TX. (Original work published as a whole in 1975, portions in 1935–1941.)

Bakhtin, M. M. 1993. *Speech genres and other late essays*. Translated by Caryl Emerson and Michael Holquist. Edited by Vern W. McGee. University of Texas Press Slavic Series 8. Austin, TX.

Bastide, Roger. 1978. *The African religions of Brazil: Toward a sociology of the interpenetration of civilizations*. Translated by Helen Sebba. Johns Hopkins Studies in Atlantic History and Culture. Baltimore, MD: Johns Hopkins University Press.

Bhabha, Homi. 1990. The third space: Interview with Homi Bhabha. In Jonathan Rutherford (ed.), *Identity: Community, culture, difference*, 207–221. London: Lawrence and Wishart.

Bosire, Mokaya. 2006. Hybrid languages: The case of Sheng. In Olaoba F. Arasanyin and Michael A. Pemberton (eds.), *Selected Proceedings of the 36th Annual Conference on African Linguistics*, 185–193. Somerville, MA: Cascadilla Proceedings Project. lingref.com/cpp/acal/36/paper1423.pdf/.

Connor, Walker. 1972. Nation-building or nation-destroying?. *World Politics* 24: 319–350.

Eastman, Carole M., and T. C. Reese. 1981. Associated language: How language and ethnicity are related. *General Linguistics* 21(2):109–116.

Edwards, John. 1985. *Language, society and identity*. Oxford: Blackwell.

Fasold, Ralph W. 1984. *The sociolinguistics of society*. Language in Society 5. Oxford: Blackwell.

Ferguson, Charles A. 1959. Diglossia. *Word* 15:325–340.

Fishman, Joshua A. 1965. Who speaks what language to whom and when? *La Linguistique* 1(2):67–88.

Fishman, Joshua A. 1967. Bilingualism with and without diglossia; diglossia with and without bilingualism. *Journal of Social Issues* 23(2):29–38.

Garvin, Paul, and Madeleine Mathiot. 1956. The urbanization of the Guarani language. In Anthony F. C. Wallace (ed.), *Men and cultures: Selected papers from the Fifth International Congress of Anthropological and Ethnological Sciences*, 365–374. Philadelphia: University of Pennsylvania Press.

Giles, Howard. 1970. Evaluative reactions to accents. *Educational Review* 22(3): 211–227.

Giles, Howard, ed. 1977. *Language, ethnicity and intergroup relations*. European Monographs in Social Psychology 13. London: Academic Press.

Giles, Howard. 1979. Ethnicity markers in speech. In Klaus R. Scherer and Howard Giles (eds.), *Social markers in speech*, 251–290. Cambridge: Cambridge University Press.

Giles, Howard. 1980. Accommodation theory: Some new directions. In M. W. S. De Silva (ed.), *Aspects of linguistic behaviour: Festschrift R. B. Le Page*, 105–136. York, UK: Department of Language, University of York.

Giles, Howard, Nikolas Coupland, Angie Williams, and Laura Leets. 1991. Integrating theory in the study of minority languages. In Robert L. Cooper and Bernard Spolsky (eds.), *The influence of language on culture and thought: Essays in honor of Joshua A. Fishman's sixty-fifth birthday*, 113–136. Berlin: De Gruyter.

Giles, Howard, Richard Y. Bourhis, and Donald M. Taylor. 1977. Towards a theory of language in ethnic group relations. In Howard Giles (ed.), *Language, ethnicity and intergroup relations*, 307–348. London: Academic Press.

Labov, William. 1966. *The social stratification of English in New York City*. Washington, DC: Center for Applied Linguistics.

Labov, William. 1972. The social motivation of a sound change. *Word* 19:273–309.

Le Page, Robert B., and Andrée Tabouret-Keller. 1985. *Acts of identity: Creole-based approaches to language and ethnicity*. Cambridge: Cambridge University Press.

Lewis, M. Paul. 1993. Real men don't speak Quiché: Quiché ethnicity, Ki-che ethnic movement, K'iche' nationalism. *Language Problems and Language Planning* 17(1):37–54.

Lewis, M. Paul. 2001. *K'iche': A study in the sociology of language*. Publications in Sociolinguistics 6. Dallas, TX: SIL International.

Lewis, M. Paul, and Gary F. Simons. 2016. *Sustaining language use: Perspectives on community-based language development*. Publications in Ethnography 42. Dallas, TX: SIL International.

Maher, John C. 2005. Metroethnicity, language, and the principle of cool. *International Journal of the Sociology of Language* 175/176:83–102.

Maher, John C. 2014. Reversing language shift and revitalization: Ainu and the Celtic languages. *The Japanese Journal of Language in Society* 17(1):1–16.

Paulston, Christina Bratt. 1987. Catalan and Occitan: Comparative test cases for a theory of language maintenance and shift. *International Journal of the Sociology of Language* 63:31–62.

Paulston, Christina Bratt. 2000. Ethnicity, ethnic movements, and language maintenance. In Gloria Kindell and M. Paul Lewis (eds.), *Assessing ethnolinguistic vitality: Theory and practice*, 3:27–38. Dallas, TX: SIL International.

Roccas, Sonia, and Marilynn B. Brewer. 2002. Social identity complexity. *Personality and Social Psychology Review* 6(2):88–106.

Ross, J. A. 1979. Language and the mobilization of ethnic identity. In Howard Giles and Bernard Saint-Jacque (eds.), *Language and ethnic relations*, 1–13. Oxford: Pergamon.

Samper, David Arthur. 2002. Talking Sheng: The role of a hybrid language in the construction of identity and youth culture in Nairobi, Kenya. PhD dissertation. University of Pennsylvania. repository.upenn.edu/dissertations/AAI3043947/.

Simons, Gary F., and Charles D. Fennig, eds. 2018. *Ethnologue: Languages of the world*. Twenty-first edition. Dallas, TX: SIL International. Accessed 27 April 2018. ethnologue.com/language/bew/.

Trudgill, Peter. 1972. Sex, covert prestige and linguistic change in the urban British English of Norwich. *Language in Society* 1:179–195.

Trudgill, Peter. 1983. *On dialect*. Oxford: Blackwell.

4
The Dynamics of Identity: How Migration and Diaspora Impact Identity and Multilingualism

Mark E. Karan

Abstract. This paper demonstrates that identity is a pivotal factor in motivating the preservation of nondominant languages. First, superdiversity, which is becoming more and more of a language landscape norm, is discussed, showing that multilingualism, diglossia, urbanization, migration, and refugee situations are becoming more and more prevalent. A good understanding of the dynamics of languages and multilingualism is called for. The Perceived Benefit Model (Karan 2001) is useful in understanding and discussing these dynamics. Identity, affiliation, and solidarity are presented as related concepts, and demonstrated to be key in providing motivations crucial to the maintenance of nondominant languages, within the framework of the Perceived Benefit Model. Practical implications of the role of identity in the maintenance of nondominant languages are discussed.

4.1 Introduction

We are living and working more and more in a multilingual and migrating world resulting in great changes in our language-related world. These changes have to do with a trending shift from a prior norm where languages were distributed geographically and were, in most cases, the normative language used within the geographical divisions, to a new norm where multilingualism, diglossia, and mixed populations, though always a part of our language-related world, are now the new norm in most urban situations and a growing number of rural situations. Globalization processes and forces, such as more open borders and improved transportation and communication, are impacting our language-related world. These concepts will be discussed below in the section on superdiversity.

This paper will attempt to demonstrate that identity is a pivotal factor, if not the key factor, in shaping our emerging language-related world. Identity and affiliation are the pivotal factors in motivating the continued use of minoritized or nondominant languages in multilingual situations. Any change that involves languages or language use has identity, affiliation, and solidarity implications. Most language development related activities, ranging from trying to maintain a language to encouraging culturally appropriate music with local language lyrics in religious exercises, are attempts to change the status quo that require understanding and working with the dynamics of language and identity.

The dynamics of something involve the inner workings and motivational structures of how and why something works the way it does, based on the underpinning foundations of how and why things are as they are. Discussions of dynamics often include models, which are useful to the degree that they represent and explain why things are as they are and why things work as they do. Thus models are evaluated by their effectiveness in being both explanatory and predictive. The Perceived Benefit Model, introduced by Karan (2001), helps explain how life and language works, and in this paper helps demonstrate how identity is a key or pivotal factor in understanding and working with languages in this multilingual, migrating world.

4.2 Superdiversity

Linguistics and sociolinguistics are fields where it has long been noted that a large percentage of the objects of our study, languages, are going extinct. This assumes that the languages are indeed the object of study. Meanwhile, in contrast to the loss of some languages, the number of people communicating with language is not at all decreasing, but rather increasing. Similarly, the degree of multilingualism in the world appears to be increasing rather than decreasing. The object of study of linguistics and sociolinguistics is perhaps better conceived as not simply languages, but rather human language—communication through speech.

There is a perceptible change in the object of study of linguistics and sociolinguistics, and it is not related simply to the fact that certain languages are going extinct. It is more related to the fact that the typical language landscapes of the past are not the typical language landscapes of the present (and expected future). In the past, there were many places (relatively self-contained geographical regions) where one language was predominantly used. People groups were separated by wars or geographical boundaries like oceans or mountains. Since language changes over time, geographically delineated languages developed and further diverged.

Much linguistics and sociolinguistic research in the past thus centered around language identification, genetic classification of languages, language surveys, and language mapping—activities based on the understanding that geographically defined languages were predominantly used in their respective geographic areas. The objects of study were the languages.

In the last fifty or sixty years, there have been extraordinary changes in linguascapes (language landscapes). Because of globalization due to advances in modern transportation, communication, and relative world peace and open borders, in most urban areas and in an increasing number of rural areas, the norm has changed from basically one language being used to a norm of mixed populations, multiple languages, and multilingualism, all influenced by urbanization and other forms of migration.

Vertovec (2007, 2010) coined the term *superdiversity* while studying the very fast demographic changes happening in London in the first part of this century. Superdiversity has to do with new increased levels of cultural diversity and patterns of speech, based on modern communication, transportation, and migration.

Blommaert and Rampton (2011:3) state:
> Over a period of several decades—and often emerging in response to issues predating superdiversity—there has been ongoing revision of fundamental ideas (a) about languages, (b) about language groups and speakers, and (c) about communication. Rather than working with homogeneity, stability and boundedness as the starting assumptions, mobility, mixing, political dynamics and historical embedding are now central concerns in the study of languages, language groups and communication.

This field of superdiversity is very much growing in popularity. Routledge recently published *The Routledge Handbook of Language and Superdiversity* (Creese and Blackledge 2018), which includes a good listing of the various works on the subject. Some, such as Czajka and de Haas (2014), argue that the concept of superdiversity is European based and ethnocentric, based on recent greater immigration into a diminishing number of smaller European countries, and that immigration and migration have always been major factors over most of the world.

Whatever view of superdiversity we take, that superdiversity is at a new all-time high, or that superdiversity has always been there and Westerners are only becoming more aware of it, we need to acknowledge that migration, urbanization, and prolonged refugee situations are very much part of our language-related world, and need to be considered in research. Languages do exist, but an insistence on maintaining languages as the sole objects of study for different sociolinguistic research will impede quality research. The field of superdiversity is as popular as it is because it is providing the needed research platform for understanding, discussing, and dealing with the dynamics of language in our increasingly complex linguascapes.

4.3 The value of a model and the Perceived Benefit Model

The theme of "Language and Identity in a Multilingual, Migrating World" can be understood as having to do with the role of identity as it relates to language in our multilingual, migrating world. What does identity do? How does it influence things? How strong a factor is it? I attempt to address these questions by my term "dynamics of identity." When dealing with the dynamics of something, what something does, how it influences other things, how strong a factor it is, it is often helpful to use a model of the dynamics, a model that explains why things work the way they do.

Models are often used to understand and explain difficult concepts and to make certain concepts more tangible (Coll, France, and Taylor 2005). Models are also used to make and test predictions. Thus a model is good and valuable to the extent that it is explanatory, predictive, testable, and applies in most if not all situations.

The model I build on in this study is the Perceived Benefit Model (Karan 2001). This model was developed during a study in the Central African Republic researching the spread of the Sango [sag] language. Over 700 subjects throughout the country were tested for their Sango ability using a sentence-repetition fluency test. The subjects also responded to a questionnaire where their social factors (age, education, ethnic group, occupation, etc.), their residence and travel history, their language repertoire, and what they thought different languages were good for were noted. The measured fluency in Sango was then compared with the different factors using a step-up, step-down multilinear linear regression to identify the strength of different factors' effect on Sango ability.

One of the findings of this study was that the same variation that Weinreich, Labov, and Herzog (1968) demonstrated to be present in language change situations was also present in the language shift situation involving Sango. Quantitative research demonstrated that certain social categories, such as women, the more educated, the upper classes, and the younger subjects, were more on the forefront of the change processes than men, lesser educated, lower classes, and older subjects in both language shift situations and language change situations. The same crossover pattern where the next to highest social class scored slightly higher than the highest class was also present in both. This basically confirmed that the same type of change processes that were operating in language change situations were operating in language shift situations. This insight was pivotal to the development of the Perceived Benefit Model.

Another major foundational element of the Perceived Benefit Model was Bourdieu's linguistic marketplace analogy and theory (Bourdieu 1982), where language is like a commodity and people gain that commodity by choosing to learn languages, and then spend that commodity by using those languages to get (purchase) what they desire (e.g., status, jobs, mates). The author prefers this analogy over ecology-based analogies such as Haugen's (1972:325–339) language ecology analogy because the linguistic marketplace analogy chooses the languages to be used by their usefulness and value to the user, while a metaphor based on ecologies would seem to imply an ecological niche or survival-of-the-fittest motivation for selecting which languages die out or grow stronger.

A third major foundational element of the Perceived Benefit Model was Edwards' (1985:98) observation of the importance of the whole motivational fabric of society in attempting to bring about language shift or maintenance. This argued strongly for a micro-societal approach to a model of language shift over a macro-societal approach. The macro-societal approach would look at major factors such as industrialization and urbanization as they influence language shift, while the micro-societal approach would see the change process as individuals, influenced by motivations, making decisions, where the conglomerate of the individual decisions made up the societal change.

Another foundational element of the Perceived Benefit Model was Labov's Martha's Vineyard study (1972), where he demonstrated that individuals who identified with the island, and who planned to stay on the island, exhibited more centralization of the vowels in the diphthongs studied. Basically, their speech was influenced by their individual identification and planned future choices. A component of the Perceived Benefit Model is that individuals make language choices based on the future they see for themselves and the good they feel those choices could help to bring about for their future selves and identities.

Yet another foundational element of the Perceived Benefit Model was Rogers' (1962) argument that diffusion of innovation often follows an S-shaped model. There are first a few innovators, then some early adopters, then many in an early majority, then many more in a late majority, then the few who lag behind. At first there is little change or shift, followed by much more in the middle, with slow change or shift again happening at the end of the innovation process.

The Perceived Benefit Model, developed in 2001, is applicable to both language change and language shift situations. It holds that individuals make language-related choices based on their perception of their personal benefit. The choices, either in learning or using a language, are made based on what is seen to bring the most benefit to the person. The benefit can be social identity or affiliation, power or prestige, or be communicative, economic, religious, or nationalistic. These motivations were later presented as a basic taxonomy of language choice motivations (Karan 2011).

In Karan (2011), the explanatory power of the model was demonstrated by showing how the model applied to various documented cases of language shift. The author maintains that this list is easily augmented by anyone who knows the details of a language shift or language change situation. Because of the explanatory power of the model, thinking about a shift or change situation in its context and in the context of the model (testing the model) most often provides a validation of the model through an observation that the model fits well with the situation; it explains well what happened.

4.4 The importance of identity, affiliation, and solidarity

Identity, affiliation, and solidarity are related concepts and phenomena. Identity has to do with how one sees oneself, who one sees oneself to be, what group is part of who one is. Affiliation has to do with the sense of belonging to that same group. And solidarity has to do with feelings and actions of oneness with that same group. This concept of identity, with its related affiliation and solidarity, is the main motivational force for the use and preservation of smaller, ethnic, minority, minoritized, nondominant languages. Karan and Corbett (2014) illustrate this dynamic through analyses of the Fur [fvr] language (2014:58–60), the Kichwas [qud] language (2014:60–61), and the Nenets [yrk] language (2014:58). This dynamic is further supported, as has been observed repeatedly by this author in many situations over more than thirty years in different parts of the world, where speakers of minoritized languages express the equivalent of: "We are X people. We belong to the X group. The X language is our language; thus, we must speak the X language" (2014:58).

In the taxonomy of motivations associated with the Perceived Benefit Model, the main motivational categories are: Communicative, Economic, Social Identity, Language Power and Prestige, Nationalistic and Political, and Religious (Karan 2011:140–3). Certain motivations are normally associated with larger, more dominant languages. These motivations are: Communicative, Economic, the Prestige-group-related and Solidarity-related subsets of Social Identity, Language Power and Prestige, and Nationalistic and Political motivations.

The motivations normally associated with the continued use or desired revitalization of smaller, less dominant languages are Communicative and the Solidarity-related subset of Social Identity (Karan and Corbett 2014). Communicative motivations are important to the use and maintenance of both dominant and less dominant languages. For the more dominant languages, Communicative motivations are normally in reference to the larger world, while for the less dominant languages, Communication motivation normally is in reference to ingroup members, often older, more monolingual relatives or community members.

Social Identity motivations are important in reference to both dominant and less dominant languages. For the more dominant languages, it is the Prestige-group-related and Solidarity-related subsets of Social Identity motivations. But for the less dominant languages, the Solidarity-related subset of Social Identity motivations is a very strong, if not crucial motivation.

The concept of the important role of identity in the maintenance of nondominant languages is not at all new. Fishman (1989:226) wrote about the importance of the "maintenance of intracultural boundaries." This is most likely referring to solidarity, or inclusive feelings associated with identity. He stated that this identity related solidarity "is crucial for intergenerational minority group mother tongue maintenance" (1989:226).

The general theme and focus of John Edwards' book, *Minority Languages and Group Identity: Cases and Categories* (2010), seems to be that alongside of communicative and instrumental functions, group identity is likely the "single most important aspect of human language" (2010:3).

Nguyen and Hamid (2016) studied the language attitudes, identity, and L1 maintenance of Vietnamese [vie] minority language speakers. They reported, "The students were found to have displayed the integrative orientation in valuing their L1, and the instrumental orientation in valuing Vietnamese and English" (2016:87). These results are consistent with the Perceived Benefit Model and other supporting evidence.

These solidarity-related assertions are easily tested, and the author encourages such testing. In cases where less dominant languages are being used, maintained, or revitalized alongside of larger more dominant languages, and where the motivations for using the less dominant language are known or testable, are or are not those motivations related to solidarity?

4.5 Appropriate consideration of identity

Recognizing that identity, with associated affiliation and solidarity, is an integral motivation to nondominant language use, and recognizing that we are living and working in a superdiverse world with much migration, multilingualism, and urbanization, it is appropriate to consider how migration, urbanization, and refugee situations affect and influence identity-based motivations. In general, migration, urbanization, and refugee situations have the potential to increase identity-based motivations, especially when those situations are viewed as a threat to the nondominant group identity.

The factor of *bounded solidarity* (Portes and Sensenbrenner 1993) is a relevant and important dynamic in creating or increasing identity-based motivations to use and preserve nondominant languages. Bounded solidarity is the feeling of unity that naturally and normally arises from real or perceived threats to the group in question. The recognition of a threat brings about internal trust and affiliation. When a group feels that they or their shared nondominant language is threatened, the result can be motivation to use, preserve, and defend that language, in order to preserve their identity (Karan 2011:148). Migration, urbanization, and refugee situations can naturally produce that threat to the new nondominant group or language created in the new destination linguascape.

Ehala and Zabrodskaja (2011) researched the impact of interethnic discordance on subjective ethnolinguistic vitality. They hypothesized and demonstrated that "high perceived interethnic discordance may enhance group vitality by reducing permeability of group boundaries and strengthening emotional attachment to the group by inducing identity threat" (Ehala and Zabrodskaja 2011:121). Language situation changes such as migration, urbanization, and refugee situations share similarities in that they create pockets or scatterings of people who have a shared identity and language in the midst of larger, more dominant groups of people who use different languages. When this happens, it often and naturally results in real or perceived threats to the nondominant language and group identity. The resulting bounded solidarity increases the motivation to use the nondominant language. This kind of motivation is clearly identity related.

It is worth noting here that the amount of motivation to use the nondominant language will be in proportion to the threat the nondominant community is feeling toward their community, ethnicity, or language. This is of interest, because it potentially provides dynamic motivational insight concerning the integration or non-integration of a smaller group and language into a more dominant group and language. The higher the perceived threat, the less integration, and conversely, the lower the perceived threat, the more integration. The knowledge of this dynamic could be of importance to language group leaders, planners, and governmental leaders interested in current and future linguistic landscapes. Lower levels of threat are conducive to integration.

If a group of planners and activists desire increased use of a nondominant language which is surrounded by a more dominant language, they may be able to induce an increase in identity-related motivations by focusing on the perceived threat felt by the nondominant group. If a group of planners desires that groups who are at odds with each other adopt a common written standard (as could be the situation in the case discussed by Stephen Watters, chapter 15 this volume), a useful approach might be to look at any potential intergroup misunderstandings or problems and work toward reconciliation before attempting to introduce the written standard. These are two examples of applications of the dynamic motivational insight concerning the integration or non-integration of a smaller group and language into a more dominant group and language. Many other possible applications exist.

In certain cases, environments created to encourage the use of nondominant languages have contributed to their decline, while actions taken to discourage nondominant languages provided the threat-based, identity-related motivations for their continued use. Eberhard (chapter 2 this volume), discusses Fishman and Garcia's (2010:160) collective grievances—communal memories of wrongs suffered. He states that "Collective grievances, when present, are some of the strongest possible influences … towards maintaining Xish identity." Pressure to adopt a dominant language in discouraging a nondominant language could create a "forced identity" type of collective grievance (Eberhard, chapter 2 this volume), which would push toward adopting the nondominant language identity. This is similar to, and would work in conjunction with, the concept of providing the bounded solidarity type of threat-based motivations for the continued use of the nondominant language. Encouraging the use of the dominant language can result in a forced-identity collective grievance and a threat-based identity motivation, both encouraging the use of the nondominant language. And encouraging the use of the nondominant language can cause a lessening of both the forced-identity collective grievance and the threat-based identity motivation.

Other factors that influence identity-based motivation are the passage of time and exposure to "the old country." Succeeding generations of a nondominant community living among a more dominant community will almost always have less contact with the nondominant language and culture, and more contact with the dominant language and culture. This typically results in less identity-based motivation to identify with the nondominant culture and less motivation to use the nondominant language. The younger generations, having had less exposure to the nondominant language and culture, will often adopt a main identity more associated with the dominant language and culture. They often have a greater appreciation for the advantages of assimilation into the larger language and culture. Thus, among displaced populations, motivations to use the nondominant language naturally decrease over time as the relative percentage of those who grew up in the "old country" situation decreases.

Given the insight that motivation actually works at the individual level rather than the community level, the Perceived Benefit Model helps to explain what is going on here since individuals in the generation that immigrated will have different motivations than their second- and third-generation descendants. Thus Perceived Benefit Model is useful in explaining the third-generation assimilation to dominant cultures that is very common in immigrant-rich countries. Younger generations, seeking their personal good and having grown up in different circumstances and environments from their parents and grandparents, would make language-related choices based on their own set of language-related motivations. As their identity-related motivations would be different from those of their parents and grandparents, their language-related choices would be different.

The Perceived Benefit Model, in conjunction with bounded solidarity, also helps explain why so many language groups become motivated to preserve or revive their language only when it is almost too late to do so. The threat of the impending language death provides the perceived threat that increases their identity-based motivation. The Perceived Benefit Model, in conjunction with bounded solidarity, would also be predictive in projecting that there will be future cases of both third-generation assimilation to dominant cultures and language groups only becoming interested in preserving or reviving their language when language death threatens.

4.6 Conclusion

Our language-related world has changed, and will continue to change. Migration, urbanization, and refugee situations bringing about a new superdiversity is our new reality. With this new reality we need to better understand how language use works, and why people make the language-related choices they do. In this paper, I attempt to apply the Perceived Benefit Model to explain how minority language communities make language choices in an environment of superdiversity, noting that a major factor determining whether a minority group maintains its language and identity is the degree to which it feels threatened. I argue that the more threatened a group feels, the more likely it is that they will hold on to their language and identity. Ironically, then, a minority group's ethnic language and identity are often most in danger when they feel the most safe. Further study is suggested into language planning ramifications of the complex relationship between language situation changes, bounded solidarity, the time factor, and identity-related motivational factors, in relation to this and other helpful models.

References

Blommaert, Jan, and Ben Rampton. 2011. Language and superdiversity. *Diversities* 13(2):1–21. Accessed April 6, 2018. unesdoc.unesco.org/images/0021/002147/214772e.pdf/.

Bourdieu, Pierre. 1982. *Ce que parler veut dire : L'économie des échanges linguistiques* [What it means to speak: The economy of the linguistic marketplace]. Paris: Fayard.

Coll, Richard K., Bev France, and Ian Taylor. 2005. The role of models and analogies in science education: Implications from research. *International Journal of Science Education* 27(2):183–198.

Creese, Angela, and Adrian Blackledge, eds. 2018. *The Routledge handbook of language and superdiversity*. Routledge Handbooks in Applied Linguistics. London.

Czajka, Mathias, and Hein de Haas. 2014. The globalization of migration: Has the world become more migratory? *International Migration Review* 48(2):283–323.

Edwards, John. 1985. *Language, society and identity*. Oxford: Blackwell.

Edwards, John. 2010. *Minority languages and group identity: Cases and categories*. IMPACT: Studies in Language, Culture and Society 27. Amsterdam: John Benjamins.

Ehala, Martin, and Anastassia Zabrodskaja. 2011. The impact of inter-ethnic discordance on subjective vitality perceptions. *Journal of Multilingual and Multicultural Development* 32(2):121–136.

Fishman, Joshua A. 1989. *Language and ethnicity in minority sociolinguistic perspective*. Clevedon, UK: Multilingual Matters.

Fishman, Joshua A., and Ofelia García, eds. 2010. *Handbook of language and ethnic identity: Disciplinary and regional perspectives*. Vol. 1. Second edition. Oxford: Oxford University Press.

Haugen, Einar. 1972. *The ecology of language: Essays by Einar Haugen*. Selected and edited by Anwar S. Dil. Stanford, CA: Stanford University Press.

Karan, Mark E. 2001. *The dynamics of Sango language spread*. Publications in Sociolinguistics 7. Dallas, TX: SIL International.

Karan, Mark E. 2011. Understanding and forecasting ethnolinguistic vitality. *Journal of Multilingual and Multicultural Development* 32(2):137–149.

Karan, Mark E., and Kerry M. Corbett. 2014. The importance of identity and affiliation in dialect standardization. In Carrie Dyck, Tania Granadillo, Keren Rice, and Jorge Emilio Rosés Labrada (eds.), *Dialogue on dialect standardization*, 55–62. Cambridge: Cambridge Scholars Publishing.

Labov, William. 1972. *Sociolinguistic patterns*. Philadelphia: University of Pennsylvania Press.

Nguyen, Trang Thi Thuy, and M. Obaidul Hamid. 2016. Language attitudes, identity and L1 maintenance: A qualitative study of Vietnamese ethnic minority students. *System* 61:87–97. Accessed April 6, 2018. DOI: 10.1016/j.system.2016.08.003/.

Portes, Alejandro, and Julia Sensenbrenner. 1993. Embeddedness and immigration: Notes on the social determinants of economic action. *American Journal of Sociology* 98:1320–1350.

Rogers, Everett M. 1962. *Diffusion of innovations*. Glencoe, IL: Free Press of Glencoe.

Vertovec, Steven. 2007. Super-diversity and its implications. *Ethnic and Racial Studies* 30:1024–1054.

Vertovec, Steven. 2010. Towards post-multiculturalism? Changing communities, conditions and contexts of diversity. *International Social Science Journal* 61: 83–95.

Weinreich, Uriel, William Labov, and Marvin I. Herzog. 1968. Empirical foundations for a theory of language change. In Winfred P. Lehmann and Yakov Malkiel (eds.), *Directions for historical linguistics: A symposium*, 97–195. Austin, TX: University of Texas Press.

5
Identity and Melting Pots: Negotiating Identity by Resisting or Pursuing Accommodation

Jaap Feenstra

Abstract. This essay is a composite of experience-based deduction as well as literature-based research—checking my assumptions and biases against validated work done by others. My wife grew up quintilingual, being regularly exposed to five languages, and I myself grew up bilingual, or trilingual if I include English. Both of us feel privileged to have lived in six different countries—including more than twenty years of living relatively close to the arctic circle and, currently, within an hour or two driving distance from the equator, on the island of Borneo in the Malaysian area where my wife grew up. In this paper I attempt to write about principles and lessons learned as they apply to multilingualism and maintaining identity. I make use of Giles' Communication Accommodation Theory to explore the dynamics of and motivations for choosing different languages, and give contrasting case studies of language use in Navajo [nav] and Tlicho [dgr] communities. I conclude that, with intentional effort, it is possible to manage multiple identities and to maintain the languages associated with those identities.

5.1 Introduction

In this section, I briefly sketch the linguistic histories of myself and my wife, which provide the foundation for observations made throughout the rest of this paper.

5.1.1 Multilingual backgrounds

I grew up in Witmarsum, a small rural community in the Dutch province of Friesland (or Fryslân), which happens to be the birthplace of the well-known sixteenth century Anabaptist leader, Menno Simons, as well as the workplace of a prominent seventeenth century Frisian poet, author, and language-activist, Gysbert Japix. My cultural and multilingual background is actually quite simple in comparison to the complexity in which, Morina, my Malaysian wife grew up. Her immediate family is very multiethnic representing a complicated "language ecology" (cf. Lewis and Simons 2016). Her parents, grandparents, aunts and uncles, or other relatives who looked after her during her early childhood, spoke a combined total of at least five different languages: Iban [iba] (her mother's first language), Tamil [tam] (her father's first language), Hokkien [nan], Bahasa Malay [zsm], and English [eng]. To add to our multilingual experience, for two decades both of us lived and worked in a First Nations setting in Canada, serving the Tlicho [dgr] community, in the Northwest Territories. In addition, we have had ample interaction with immigrant communities in Canada, notably Dutch [nld] and Filipino [fil].

5.1.2 Frysk and Dutch

During the last few centuries the province of Fryslân, where West Frisian, or Frysk [fry], is spoken, has been characterized by a "stable bilingualism" (cf. Lewis and Simons 2016). Such is the rural setting I grew up in. Frysk and Dutch harmoniously coexisted in my hometown of Witmarsum. From when I was small I interacted with people around me in Frysk while being daily exposed to Dutch through radio broadcasts, church services, newspapers, books, schooling, and so on. Dutch and Frisian clearly had distinct and complementary functions in my community, typical of a stable multilingualism.

5.1.3 Empirical account and research

My own multilingual experiences, as well as observing firsthand my wife's language experience, has helped me understand and empathize with the reality that people groups all over the world increasingly face—balancing language use and identity issues in complex and ever-shifting multilingual environments. In other words, this paper is partly an empirical or eyewitness account. However, to mitigate the danger that support for arguments I use become too anecdotal and subjective, I will bring in research and findings from relevant recent literature, mostly from Giles (2016) and Ehala (2018).

5.2 Historical overview of the Frisians

To give sufficient context to my experience I will give a brief overview of the sociolinguistic history of the Frisians and how they in their earlier territory have merged (or melted in) with the people around them—certainly in their language use. I will also attempt to explain how many Frisians, including myself, do not hold on to their traditional language, Frysk, as an inalienable and emblematic part of identity. I will seek to develop the thought that people and communities, through processes of accommodation, negotiate their identities, depending on their values, aspirations, contexts, and social encounters in general.

5.2.1 Historical territory

The Frisians have lived in the northwestern continental coastal areas of Europe from well before the Roman conquest (see map 1).

Around the year 12 BC the Frisians, as well as other Germanic nations north of the Rhine river, were conquered by the Romans. The Frisians revolted in 28 AD because of the heavy taxes the Romans exacted from them. Until around 700 AD the territory of the Frisians covered the northern stretch of what is now Flanders, much of the area of the current Dutch provinces—except for southern provinces of Noord Brabant and Limburg—and the western stretch of the northern peninsular part of Germany up to the current border with Denmark (Springer 1953).

Map 1. Historical territory of the Frisians

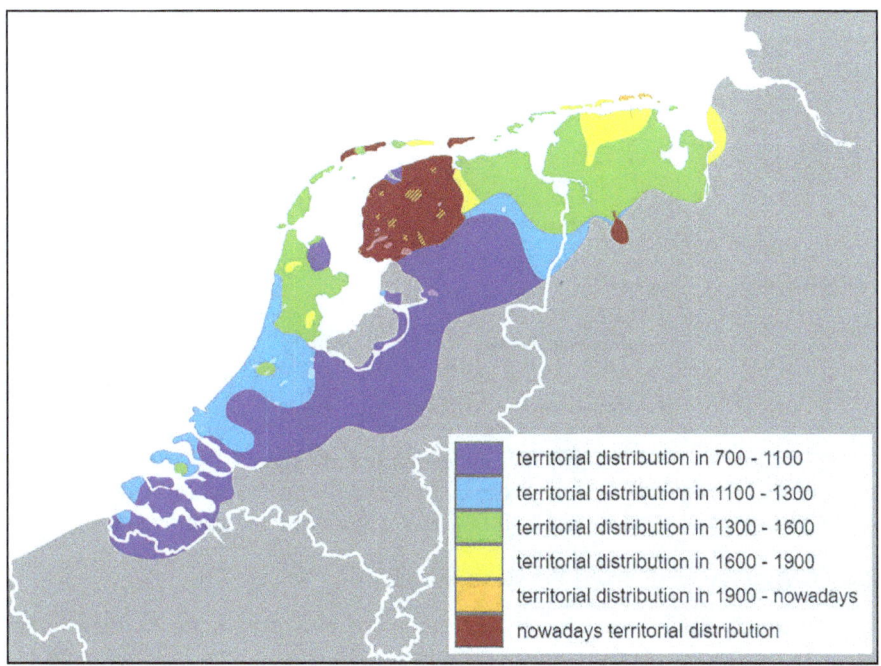

© 2017 Dmitry Lavrinenko. From Wikimedia Commons. CC BY-SA 4.0.
wikimedia.org/wiki/File:Frisian_language_area_history_map.svg/.

5.2.2 A North Sea Germanic language

Frysk is a North Sea Germanic language, also referred to as an Ingvaeonic language. Of all the Germanic languages, Frisian is historically the most closely related to English (see figure 1). However, in the sociolinguistic melting pots English has been significantly influenced by the Scandinavian languages and French while Frisian has adopted a substantial amount of its vocabulary from Dutch (Harbert 2007; de Vaan 2017).

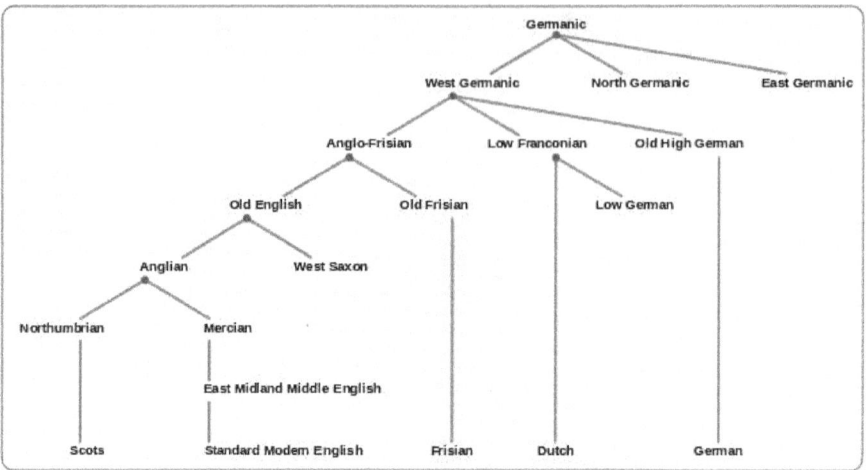

Figure 1. West Germanic languages.
© 2015 by Coran tek en. From Wikimedia Commons, CC BY-SA 4.0. commons.wikimedia.org/wiki/File:Westgermanic_English_tree.svg/.

5.2.3 Language shift from Frysk to Dutch

Over the centuries, Frisians have been adaptive and pragmatic in their view of language—or at least accommodating. Where Frysk was spoken in large parts of the Netherlands, it gradually was replaced by Dutch, or rather, Dutch dialects. According to de Vaan (2017), this possibly happened through a process of Dutch-speaking people moving into towns, gradually tipping the scales of balance to Dutch as the dominant language. Then, in turn, the rural areas would follow. Based on de Vaan's description, I have created a set of diagrams—figures 2a through 2d—that illustrate the proposed process.

Figure 2a begins with a set of communities that use L1, represented as blue dots. Through an immigration process, people who speak L2 move into the major communities, represented as pink dots in figure 2b. Figure 2c indicates that after some decades L2 has become dominant in the major communities, represented as red dots, and is starting to encroach on L1 in the smaller rural communities. After a generation or two, the shift from L1 to L2 is complete, as shown in figure 2d. A region such as West Friesland, an area in the northern part of the province of Noord Holland, was predominantly Frisian speaking. It is very well possible that as Dutch-speaking traders and craftsmen moved to the larger towns, their influence eventually tipped the sociolinguistic scales of balance away from Frysk to Dutch. This likely was an ongoing process spanning a number of decades, if not generations. Through a process of accommodation, Dutch—or an evolving Dutch dialect—became the language of wider communication. Over time, the process of attrition and accommodation affected the rural areas as well.

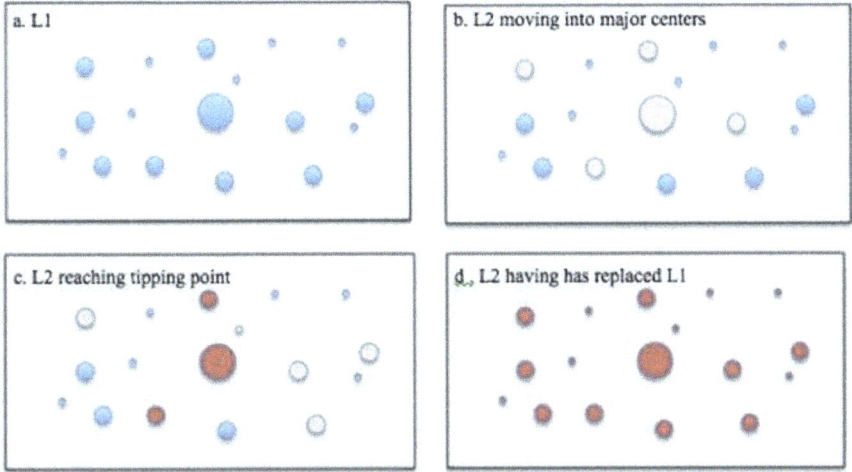

Figure 2. Conjecture of how language shift might happen.

5.2.4 Leeuwarden: The city with a world record number of names

This kind of scenario, of language shift first happening in the towns, also began—and can still be observed—in the area of the current province of Fryslân. The Frisian capital of Leeuwarden serves as an example of such a phenomenon. During the fifteenth and sixteenth centuries, through the influx of mostly Dutch-speaking people, Leeuwarden developed a hybrid language—called Stedsk or Stedsfrysk (translated, Town Frisian). A similar process took place in a number of other towns in the province such that the evolving languages in many towns have substantial overlap, even though they might well have developed independently. These hybrid languages are a composite in which the vocabulary is mostly Dutch while the phonology and syntax are mostly Frysk (Duijff 2002). Interestingly, the multilingual dynamics in the history of Leeuwarden are evidenced in the fact that, starting with the first written record from the year 1039 to the final standardization of the name in 1884, the city archives have accumulated no fewer than 225 different names for the city—enough to land the city a place in the *Guinness World Records* (MacEacheran 2018). It should be pointed out that the majority of those names are variations of pronunciation and spelling on either the Dutch name, Leeuwarden, or the Frisian name, Ljouwert, but the preponderance of names is undoubtedly reflective of the linguistic or dialectic diversity in this town—Frysk, Dutch, Stedsk, or the academic language of Latin.

5.2.5 Language activism

The history of Frysk shows that in such a sociolinguistic melting pot, identity negotiation is a never-ending process. And choosing to hold on to the minority language as an elective signal takes strong motivation and effort—it needs activists and champions. Gysbert Japix (1603–1666) was such a man for the Frisians. He was a seventeenth century teacher and poet who grew up in the town of Bolsward, some seven kilometers from Witmarsum, where I myself grew up. He even served as a school teacher in my home village (and is commemorated by a prominent sculpture). He noticed the language shift that started to happen all around him, became concerned, and ended up being a champion for Frysk. He raised awareness of the value of the language and the impending threat of Dutch taking over functions of the Frisian language. Japix's activism led to a strengthening of Frysk and a proliferation of its literature. Speaking Frisian clearly became an explicit identity marker. Japix embodied a growing determination among the Frisians in Fryslân to resist accommodating to the encroaching Dutch language. A similar language revival happened again in the nineteenth century, with three Halbertsma brothers as the activist leaders. And again in the twentieth century, a similar language revitalization took place (Sirkwy 2014).

5.3 Frisians and accommodation

5.3.1 Current sociolinguistic environment

Currently in the twenty-first century, the sociolinguistic environment of Frysk once again looks threatened in its survival. Many Frisians have moved away from Fryslân due to study, work, or relationships. Conversely, many people from near and distant provinces have moved into the Frisian-speaking part of the country—not simply to the larger towns but also to rural areas. It seems that Frysk is losing its value as a dominant, collective identity marker. As table 1 shows, based on research done in the mid- to late-1980s, approximately half the people living in Friesland have Frysk as their first language (Klinkenberg 2017). Interestingly, that percentage of speakers has stayed about the same over the last few decades, though Dutch has increased at the expense of regional dialects—the Frisian-Dutch hybrid languages. The percentage of parents who use Frysk as the language at home in their interaction with children is now reported to be 49% (2017:14).

Table 1. First language of people living in Fryslân

	Frisian	Dutch	Dialect	Other
1967	71%	13%	16%	Not tracked
1980	54%	31%	13%	Not tracked
1994	55%	28%	15%	2%
2007	54%	35%	10%	1%
2016	52%	36%	7%	5%

After Douwes et al. (2010) and Klinkenberg (2017).

We can see a shift, in particular, away from the mindset observed in the nineteenth century when Frisians were less accommodating to the use of other languages. According to Galema (1986), the numerous Frisians who moved to the United States during that time held onto their language and other cultural heritage into the third generation of emigrants, which Ehala (2018:27) implies is the general maximum length for intergenerational transfer. The trend of parents not speaking to their children in their heritage language is observable all over the world. My wife is working with the Bidayuh people in the Malaysian part of Borneo. The Bidayuh leaders have observed a similar trend in language shift. English and Bahasa Malay [zsm] are taking over home functions (Noeb and Ridu 2017).

5.3.2 Balancing Frysk and Dutch

The struggle of constant language and identity negotiation that the Frisians have gone through—and are still going through—is simply a consequence of any meeting and mixing of people speaking different languages. Multilingualism and negotiation of language function is a worldwide phenomenon—and given the speed of change and migrations of people, things are happening at an increasing speed, at an exponential rate. I would submit that whenever two people meet, a cultural negotiation starts, often within a framework of mutual accommodation. This happens in mannerisms, but especially in language. This takes place at an individual or micro level as well as at a group or macro level. People are social beings who accommodate and adapt. Numbers count, and it is often the smaller group that has to do most of the accommodation.

Frisians have woven Dutch and Frisian into their functional and social fabric. Even in an overall Frisian context, they may start a conversation with someone they don't know in Frysk, but when the person answers in Dutch, by far the majority of Frisians will switch to Dutch (Douwes 2010:21). When Frisian children go to school, they mostly open Dutch books. Those who attend church listen to Dutch sermons and homilies and sing Dutch hymns. By far the majority read Dutch books, including a Dutch Bible. Writing is mostly in Dutch, but according to the latest survey, about 19% feel they can write in Frysk. This indicates that proportionally more Frisians write Frysk today as compared to surveys dating as far back as 1967 (Klinkenberg 2017).

5.3.3 Accommodation as a value

From experience, I have observed numerous times how Frisians tend to accommodate to Dutch-speaking minorities or individuals in their community. For instance, if there is one person in a group of ten who does not understand Frysk, most Frisians will feel it appropriate (that is, socially correct) to adjust. Many would feel it is rude not to accommodate to those who do not understand Frysk. This does not at all seem to indicate a shame for the language, as the majority of Frisians—86% according to a 2008 survey—are proud of speaking Frysk (Douwes et al. 2010).

Based on personal observation, having emigrated from my home area to Canada, I know that Frisians—and the Dutch in general—have a strong value of accommodation to new settings. Though I myself am deeply grateful for my heritage, it did not keep me from moving away from a Frisian-speaking community and adopting English as my primary language of communication. Obviously there are other values that compete with giving priority to the mother tongue. The recent generations of Frisians who have emigrated seem pragmatic and adaptive. As a Frisian immigrant to Canada told me: "We simply wanted to assimilate"—which also meant that reading Dutch or Frisian soon was replaced by reading English. This expresses a strong value in the Netherlands at large, that we have to adapt in new settings. As Giles observes, nonaccomodation "can often be seen as threatening to the host community" (2016:4). This is true for the Dutch, including Frisians, who expect people coming to the Netherlands to culturally and linguistically adapt. They expect the same of themselves when they emigrate to countries such as Australia, Canada, or elsewhere.

5.4 Theoretical foundation

5.4.1 Communication Accommodation Theory

To aid us in generalizing lessons beyond the Frisian sociolinguistic situation, it may be helpful to look at the concept of accommodation. One of the most prominent and robust theories in this regard is the Communication Accommodation Theory (CAT), developed by Howard Giles and others beginning in the 1970s (Giles 2016). The theory focuses on how individuals adjust dialectic speech or the choice of language to accommodate their interlocutor. I observe this regularly with my very social and adaptive wife. Just by listening to the way she talks—irrespective of the content—I can determine whether she is talking to someone in Canada, England, or to a relative. She nearly always adjusts to dialectic features.

In addition to this foundational notion of accommodation as convergence, CAT also looks at "divergence and nonaccomodation as forms of social differentiation" (Giles 2016:3). In looking at resistance to accommodation, the inverted principles of pursuing accommodation may help in understanding group dynamics where there is a strong motivation for using the language(s) of wider communication. CAT considers the subjective aspects of language accommodation (or nonaccomodation). It takes into consideration "that speakers accommodate not where others are in any objective measurable sense but, rather, to where they are believed (or biasedly heard) to be communicatively" (Gallois, Weatherall, and Giles 2016:4). Finally, CAT also looks at the interaction between the younger and older generations. Researchers find that younger people tend to overaccommodate while older people tend to underaccommodate.

5.4.2 Relevance to multilingualism

CAT clearly has much to offer as a theoretical framework in better understanding accommodation in multilingual settings. The intergroup or contextual research that Giles and others describe (Giles 2016) is highly relevant for understanding social dynamics in multilingual settings. As Gallois, Weatherall, and Giles (2016) have observed, accommodation to a more prestigious language and nonaccommodation to a local language may be an identifier or a contrasting feature. They give the example of young people in Taiwan increasingly wanting to identify with the larger society by using Mandarin—who, whether consciously or not, "diverge from their own (older) family by not code-switching back to the local language" (Gallois, Weatherall, and Giles 2016:107).

People can intentionally disidentify with a language—that is, disassociate from it and from what they feel it stands for and how that might negatively reflect on them. I heard an emphatic account of such disidentification from a young woman who grew up in a Frisian-speaking family in Friesland. She recounted an excursion she and her siblings made with their parents. She told us that they visited the city of Amsterdam, but that she had refused to walk anywhere near her parents *because they kept talking to each other in Frisian* and she felt that was very embarrassing. She seemed to imply that using Frisian in a Dutch and a global city such as Amsterdam would make them look provincial and unsophisticated. As these two examples show, accommodation and nonaccommodation can be corollaries of identification and disidentification.

5.4.3 Discover the diversity of motivation

What is attractive about the CAT framework is that the concept of accommodation gives opportunity to discover a diversity of motivations. Identification (or conversely, disidentification) may be the underlying motivation. Or it may be knowledge transfer —something prominently described in the Sustainable Use Model (SUM) of Lewis and Simons (2016). The motivation for accommodating could be deceptive, for the purposes of fraudulent activity or spying, or it could represent a social gesture of respect or care, or yet again an adjustment made in the interest of economic advancement. CAT allows for the complexity of what drives people negatively or positively in their social interactions with others.

In their theoretical framework on sustainable language use, Lewis and Simons (2016) write about what they call "life-crucial knowledge" as being a strong motivational factor for language use. They write, "Both the formation of identity and the transmission of knowledge are mediated through language (among other means) and so local communities, as they negotiate multiple bodies of knowledge and multiple identities, often deal with multiple languages as well" (2016:93). Empirically, I recognize both aspects—identity and knowledge transfer—as a general and fairly encompassing way of framing concepts (in a theoretical construct). Indeed, it does fit my multilingual experience to a large degree. However, it seems that CAT covers a much broader range of motives as it "conceptualizes motivation as an emergent process that dynamically changes during the course of an interaction" (Dragojevic, Gasiorek, and Giles 2016:43).

"Speech communities" and individuals within them do not have uniform and static sets of values and motivations that are nicely layered in a hierarchical fashion. Accommodation in multilingual settings seems indeed an emergent process that can dynamically change. Though as linguists we might aspire for people to have their unique language at the top of their value hierarchy, the reality is that with many people this is simply not the case. Even if people might say their language, or their cultural heritage in general, is the most valuable to them, people do not necessarily act on what they believe is their highest value. This phenomenon is researched and described in depth by Robert House and others (2004) in their exhaustive "GLOBE Study of 62 Societies" (2004).

5.5 Connecting practice to ideal

5.5.1 Navajo

Debra House (2002) describes such a disconnect between the ideal and the practice in a book on language shift among the Navajos. She observed that "nearly every Navajo I talk to says that the Navajo language is crucial in maintaining Navajo culture and that both are part of a Navajo identity" (2002:vii), yet the language shift is accelerating. Elsewhere in her book she writes that the Navajo students she works with "speak quite favorably about the idea of living the traditional lifestyle of their ancestors, [but] I have no evidence that this positive attitude has actually translated to the practice of a purely traditional lifestyle by any of these students" (2002:88). In regard to language use, she writes that there is an ideological emphasis on "advancing Navajo culture and language knowledge and practice. The emphasis has been on image over substance; for the Navajo Nation as a whole, actual progress in halting or reversing language shift has been minimal. Each succeeding Navajo Nation language survey tells the tale" (2002:85). She puts forward the idea of an alternative to the competition between heritage and mainstream, "that elevates neither traditional Navajo nor American mainstream language and culture at the expense of the other" (2002:90). Essentially, she is encouraging a composite culture and language practice and argues that this would be consistent with the philosophical core of the Navajos.

5.5.2 "Strong Like Two People"

House's (2002) study and conclusions regarding Navajo, the biggest Athapaskan language, offer intriguing parallels for Tlicho, from the same language family. Since the early 1970s, the Tlicho have expressed a very similar philosophy—aspiring to a hybrid or composite culture. They have termed it "Strong Like Two People," a paraphrasing of a philosophical position that was "developed by Chief Jimmy Bruneau as a way to encourage Tlicho young people to embrace the benefits of the contemporary world while holding onto their own cultural heritage and traditions" (History.com n.d.). This is how they give both Tlicho culture and mainstream culture an acceptable place—embracing a part of the melting pot process, yet not accommodating completely in order to show their heritage and distinctiveness. Based on recent statistics, such a composite value-accommodation has worked well in the Tlicho setting. The statistics of Census Canada taken in 2011 and in 2016 prove that there is sustained bilingualism in the Tlicho communities. However, though the reported number of speakers increased between 2006 and 2011, there now is a reported drop in numbers between 2011 and 2016 (NWT Bureau of Statistics 2018). That shows that even the Tlicho are challenged to maintain the balance and to sustain the use of their traditional language.

5.5.3 Frisians finding balance

Ever since the sixteenth century the Frisians have had to find a similar way—"strong like two people"—to come to terms with the encroaching Dutch language. They somehow found a balance, and for generations have had well-functioning bilingualism. In the past sixty years the Frisian language has come under threat once again—maybe more than before. But through a composite process of accommodation to the Dutch language, as well as sufficient nonaccomodation, they have found a way to stop the attrition in numbers of speakers who claim Frysk as their first language, remaining above the 50% mark over the last fifty years (Douwes et al. 2010; Klinkenberg 2017). This is a significant accomplishment, considering the growing number of nonindigenous people who have come into the province of Fryslân. It must be pointed out that the hybrid languages—Stedsk, Bilts, and Stellingwerfs—show a proportionate decline. These languages show less than half the number of speakers they had in 1967 (see table 1, where they are listed as "Dialect").

5.6 Frysk and "Language of the Heart"

Let me briefly touch on accommodating through language to people's emotive side. It has been said that somehow the first language or mother tongue is as a rule more understandable, emotive, and intimate (cf. Harris, chapter 12 this volume). This notion of equating the first language with the "heart language" is problematic, however, as amply demonstrated by the research reported in the papers in this volume by Kyle Harris and Daniel Paul. From my own experience speaking Frysk and observing Frisians, I do not totally recognize such a concept. At best, I can say that use of Frysk gives a sense of a relationship, familiarity, and a common bond. But overall I question the validity of the concept of heart language. I would conjecture that many Frisians are best able to express their emotions in Dutch, as it is the default language they use to read, write, and text in. Let me give two anecdotal examples of Frisians not using their Frysk to express their intimate emotions.

5.6.1 "I Love You!"

During my late teens, a girl in a nearby village apparently was in love with me and sent me a note to say so. The note simply said, "I LOVE YOU!" She did not write it in Frysk, her first language, and she did not write it in Dutch, but she wrote it in English. That was at best her third language, but likely her primary one when listening to romantic pop music.

5.6.2 Eulogy in Dutch

A well-known Dutch national leader—who popularized the so-called *polder model*—grew up in my hometown of Witmarsum. Recently he was back for the funeral of his mother. Though he grew up speaking Frysk and had lived in Friesland into his adulthood (within a stone's throw of the commemorative sculpture of Gysbert Japix), he apologized for not giving a eulogy in Frysk but in Dutch. He explained that he had been away from Friesland for decades and felt he was able to express his emotions in Dutch better than in Frysk. Personally I recognize this as my own experience as well. Though English is my third language, having been away from the Netherlands and Fryslân for more than half my life, I feel that I can express my emotions best in English.

5.7 Language and identity

5.7.1 Balancing many identities

Just as people can be multilingual, perhaps balancing as many as five languages, so people can have multiple, if not numerous, identities. I am Frisian and I am happy with that, but I am also Dutch and I am happy with that, too. Yet I hold a Canadian passport and like to dangle luggage tags with a Canadian flag on my suitcases. People increasingly operate in complex social environments and have to balance their many identities. Their various identities may outnumber what their linguistic repertoire can handle, so people make choices about which languages they want to hold on to, and which ones they, consciously or not, will abandon. Ehala (2018) gives some intriguing treatment of multiple identities, referencing work done by Roccas and Brewer (2002) within the framework of Social Identity Complexity. According to Ehala, "people seek ways to reconcile their inconsistent perceptions, beliefs and collective identities" (2018:25). Figure 3 shows a categorization of ways in which people can hold two identities.

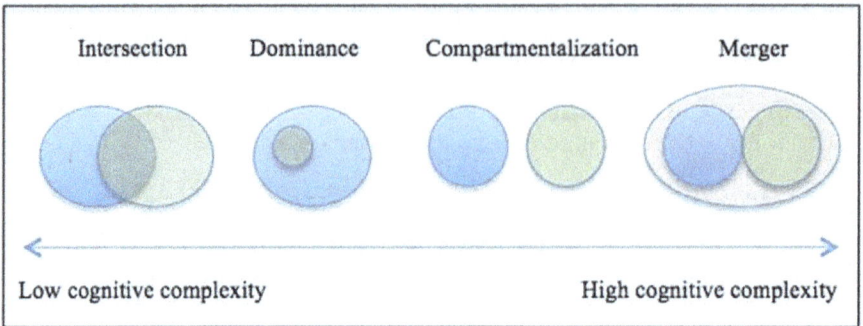

Figure 3. Ways of holding two identities. (After Ehala 2018, citing Roccas and Brewer 2002.)

5.7.2 Frisians and identity

Frisians—like Tlicho, Navajo, and most ethnolinguistic groups—have negotiated along the theoretic dimensions of low versus high cognitive complexity (see figure 3). Individual Frisians will be found at different points on this continuum as there is undoubtedly a significant difference between those who are living in rural areas, those who live in the larger towns, and those who have moved away from the province of Fryslân. The latter group will likely have a merged identity, while people in rural areas might take more explicit pride in being Frisian—showing a dominance of that identity over the other. I would venture to say that very few Frisians would disassociate from their Dutch identity. When traveling abroad, most would readily identify themselves as Dutch.

With regard to language as an emblem of identity, Frysk still plays a significant role in Frisian identity, as the Klinkenberg (2017) report shows. However, based upon my general knowledge and reading of the literature—in particular, based on Klinkenberg—Frisians have negotiated and adjusted their identity with or without Frysk. For a large area of the Netherlands where Frisian used to be spoken, that obviously resulted in Dutch (in its various dialects) gradually taking over as the dominant or only language. Or, to speak in terms that Pennycook (2010:3) uses, Frysk and Dutch were part of an amalgamative "language practice." Such practices resulted in Dutch as it is spoken today in these areas. Whether or not the Frisian language was an important part of their identity in days past we may never know, but their descendants use other values and emblems to express their identity.

For a substantial portion of people in Fryslân (46%), the language is clearly an emblematic part of their identity, especially those still living in the rural areas of origin—not simply an entrenched feature, something they are born with, but an explicitly elected feature. It is something that clearly and conscientiously is used to signal who they are (Ehala 2018). However, according to the latest survey by the Fryske Akademy—the institution that studies, guards and promotes the Frisian language—Frysk is not necessarily the primary emblem or indicator of identity (Klinkenberg 2017). This seemed to surprise the researchers. The majority of people indicated that being Frisian in origin, having Frisian blood, is what counts most. This corresponds with my personal feeling, as well. My overall heritage—Frisian at heart—seems to be what I treasure and hold on to. My Frisian surname and my place of birth I can always hold on to as identity signals. Though the Frisian language is important—I still speak it fluently—it is not the inalienable emblem of my *Frisianness*.

It is simply a negotiable part, using it when I can, but leaving it dormant when the situation seems to require accommodation to Dutch, English, or another language. I would echo what Ehala has written that people seem to implicitly practice "old-fashioned identity negotiation that searches for the optimum between societal needs and individual desires" (2018:13).

Interestingly enough, that is how many Jewish people see their identity as well—it is not physical appearance, religion, tradition, or language that determines their identity, but bloodline (Ehala 2018:87). Actually, any external appearance of what seem inherited distinguishing features can be deceptive. Ehala (2018) gives the example of Rachel Dolezal, a civil rights activist, who pretended to be African-American, but was actually of European descent.

5.7.3 Tlicho and identity

With the Tlicho people, things are much more pronounced and emblematic regarding what it means to be Tlicho. Though they clearly have embraced a composite culture —traditional and mainstream—they repeatedly bring up their origin, traditional culture, and language as the distinguishing characteristics. Those are the explicit, elective, or emblematic parts of who they are. They treasure them, celebrate them and invest in them (cf. Tlicho Community Service Agency 2005). The Tlicho people accommodate to the mainstream culture, but that accommodation has its limits. There is nonaccomodation as well—limits to how far the community will go in incorporating mainstream culture. Giles refers to such nonaccomodation as "forms of social differentiation" (2016:4). It seems that differentiation is often part of an identification construct.

5.8 Conclusion

Individuals, collectives, and ethnolinguistic communities all over the world have to negotiate their identities. Whether they are West Frisians living in Fryslân in the Netherlands, or Tlicho people living in the sparsely populated subarctic in the north of Canada, or Navajo people living in the southwestern part of the USA, or the Bidayuh people groups living on the island of Borneo, they are all surrounded—intermixed or an integral part of people who speak a language of wider communication, either the national language or one of its dialects. If they ignore such negotiation, either through unrealistic idealism concerning the primary place of their traditional language and culture, or through an implicit mental capitulation to the mainstream culture and language, they will amalgamate—in the melting pot—with the people around them. However, if they consciously and strategically seek to balance multiple identities through a process of accommodation and nonaccomodation, they will have a much better chance to sustain an intergenerational language transfer. The Tlicho have found a way to be "strong like two people" and the West Frisian have been able to maintain the linguistic emblem of Frysk over the last four centuries.

References

De Vaan, Michiel. 2017. *The dawn of Dutch: Language contact in the Western Low Countries before 1200*. NOWELE Supplement Series 30. Amsterdam, Netherlands: John Benjamins.

Douwes, Rynke, Marieke Hanenburg, and Barbara Lotti. 2010. *Languages and language education in Fryslân: The role and position of Frisian in the province of Fryslân and in Frisian education.* Leeuwarden, The Netherlands: Mercator Research Centre. Accessed April 26, 2018. mercator-research.eu/fileadmin/mercator/documents/publications/2010_Douwes_Hanenburg_en_Lotti_-_Language_and_language_education_in_Fryslan.pdf/.

Dragojevic, Marko, Jessica Gasiorek, and Howard Giles. 2016. Accommodative strategies as core of the theory. In Howard Giles (ed.), *Communication accommodation theory: Negotiating personal relationships and social identities across contexts*, 36–59. Cambridge, UK: Cambridge University Press.

Duijff, Pieter 2002. *Taal in stad en land: Fries en Stadsfries* [Frisian and Town Frisian: Language in the city and countryside]. The Hague: Sdu Uitgevers.

Ehala, Martin. 2018. *Signs of identity: The anatomy of belonging.* New York: Routledge.

Galema, A. 1986. "Forjit my net": Friese emigratie naar de Verenigde Staten aan het eind van de negentiende eeuw ["Forget me not": Frisian emigration to the United States at the end of the nineteenth century]. *Groniek* 96. Accessed March 20, 2018. rjh.ub.rug.nl/groniek/article/view/17416/14906/.

Gallois, Cindy, Ann Weatherall, and Howard Giles. 2016. CAT and talk in action. In Howard Giles (ed.), *Communication accommodation theory: Negotiating personal relationships and social identities across contexts*, 105–122. Cambridge: Cambridge University Press.

Giles, Howard, ed. 2016. *Communication accommodation theory: Negotiating personal relationships and social identities across contexts.* Cambridge: Cambridge University Press.

Harbert, Wayne. 2007. *The Germanic languages.* Cambridge Language Surveys. Cambridge: Cambridge University Press.

Haugen, Einar. 1972. The ecology of language. In Einar Haugen, *The ecology of language: Essays by Einar Haugen*, 325–39. Stanford, CA: Stanford University Press.

History.com. n.d. *Tlicho Nation educator's guide.* Accessed April 27, 2018. history.com/images/media/pdf/Tlicho-Nation_Study-Guide.pdf/.

House, Debra. 2002. *Language shift among the Navajos: Identity politics and cultural continuity.* Tucson: University of Arizona Press.

House, Robert J., Paul J. Hanges, Mansour Javidan, Peter W. Dorfman, and Vipin Gupta, eds. 2004. *Culture, leadership, and organizations: The GLOBE study of 62 societies.* Thousand Oaks, CA: Sage Publications.

Klinkenberg, Edwin. 2017. *Rapportaazje: Taalsosjologyske Survey: 'Taal yn Fryslân, de folgjende generaasjee'* [Report: Language Psychological Survey: Language in Friesland, the next generation]. Leeuwarden, Netherlands: Fryske Akademy.

Lewis, M. Paul, and Gary F. Simons. 2016. *Sustaining language use: Perspectives on community-based language development.* Publications in Ethnography 42. Dallas, TX: SIL International.

MacEacheran, Mike. 2018. The Dutch city with a constantly changing name. British Broadcasting Corporation. Accessed April 24, 2018. bbc.com/travel/story/20180423-the-dutch-city-with-a-constantly-changing-name/.

Noeb, Jonas, and Robert Sulis Ridu. 2017. Language development in Bidayuh: Past, present and future. In Marilina Bongarrá, Monique Arritt, and Florence G. Kayad (eds.), *Selected papers of the Bidayuh language development and preservation project*, 3–46. Kuching, Malaysia: Dayak Bidayuh National Association.

NWT Bureau of Statistics. 2018. Indigenous language as home language by community, 2006-2016. 2016 Census of Canada. Accessed December 21, 2021. statsnwt.ca/census/2016/.

Pennycook, Alastair. 2010. *Language as a local practice*. Abingdon, UK: Routledge.

Roccas, Sonia, and Marilynn B. Brewer. 2002. Social identity complexity. *Personality and Social Psychology Review* 6(2):88–106.

Springer, Lawrence A. 1953. Rome's contact with the Frisians. *The Classical Journal* 48(4):109–111.

Sirkwy.nl. 2014. *Gysbert Japix*. Leeuwarden, The Netherlands: Tresoar. Accessed April 26, 2018. sirkwy.frl/index.php/skriuwers-biografyen/36-g/356-gysbert-japix/.

Tlicho Community Service Agency. 2005. Strong like two people. Accessed April 27, 2018. vimeo.com/36572761/.

Van Hout, Roeland, and Uus Knops, eds. 1988. *Language attitudes in the Dutch language area*. Topics in Sociolinguistics 5. Dordrecht, Netherlands, and Providence, RI, USA: Foris Publications.

Part Two
Varying Contexts

6
New Urban Varieties in Africa and the Identities That Go with Them

Maik Gibson

Abstract. Many African cities, such as Nairobi, Juba, Johannesburg, Abidjan, Lubumbashi, and Yaoundé, have developed new language varieties and practices, which in some cases defy easy definition. In each city there is some degree of multilingualism, reflected in these language practices. Along with linguistic innovations, many urban dwellers are embracing hybridized identities, which reference both the local and the global, as does their speech. We propose categories reflecting different types of linguistic contact: creole, urban contact varieties, youth jargons, and hybrid language practices. We also examine urban identities in similar contexts, noting the common lack of clear naming practices for both the urban linguistic varieties and identities, with a particular focus on Nairobi, Kenya, and Bunia, DRC. While urban language varieties and identities are often not necessarily clearly named by the communities which embrace them, they are nonetheless observed in everyday behavior, and as such need to be considered when working on media products for these communities.

Many African cities represent relatively new and dynamic linguistic ecosystems (McLaughlin 2009; Beck 2010; Hurst 2017). By this we mean they can be seen as multilingual speech communities with shared patterns and evaluations of language choice and use, part of which is the use of new specifically urban varieties. These urban varieties all exhibit some evidence of language contact. Our overall goal is to outline something of the nature of these varieties, and then look at their links to urban identities. As these varieties exist within a fluid, multilingual environment, any names that refer to them within the community do not necessarily refer to a particular well-defined variety within that spectrum (Kube-Bath 2009; Gibson 2015), which adds to the complexity of their sociolinguistic analysis.

Given that linguistic choices often index choices concerning identity, we are confronted by a complex picture of both linguistic varieties and identities within the African city, on which we hope to throw some light in this chapter. For both language and identity, we find hybridity and fluidity, referencing both the local and the global. Furthermore, we find a lack of conventionalized names for these urban linguistic varieties and social identities—varieties and identities which are nonetheless recognized by those members. We are confronted by unnamed abstractions, which need to be understood if appropriate choices in language development interventions are to be made.

By looking especially at the linguistic situation in Nairobi, Kenya, with reference to other African cities, and examining some self-reported identities in Bunia, Democratic Republic of the Congo (DRC), we will try to represent something of this complexity, along with the link between the various types of urban linguistic varieties and the multiple identities that are at play.

6.1 The linguistic context

We first address the linguistic side of new varieties in African cities. Most, though not all, African cities are multilingual. And what we mean in this case is not merely that they are populated by people who speak a variety of languages, from different backgrounds (which they do), but that within the life of the city, different languages have different functions.[1] There is a shared repertoire of varieties, as well as knowledge and use of multiple other varieties which are not necessarily shared. This multilingualism itself is not the subject of this chapter, but provides the context for the varieties that we address here.

Most African cities have been sites of massive migration during the twentieth and twenty-first centuries. As they have brought together people from multiple and diverse linguistic backgrounds, the new urban dwellers have made use of whatever linguistic resources are available to them in order to communicate with their new neighbors, along with new cultural practices (McLaughlin 2009:1). For example, Swahili [swa] in Nairobi was not a first language for most of the founding African population, so it gained many L2 speakers, who changed the form of the language rapidly, whether through transfer from their own languages, or by some process of simplification (or a combination of these two). Thus contact varieties arose and became the effective vernaculars of the city. So we see that the massive population influx into the cities gave rise to extremely high levels of language contact, which in turn gave rise to contact varieties which are therefore widely divergent from the "original" varieties of those languages, and continue to bear the marks of this contact in different ways.

Before proceeding to give a brief typology of the kinds of varieties that have arisen in urban settings in Africa, we wish to set one of these urban centers against its broader sociolinguistic, multilingual context—in this case, Nairobi. There are speakers of many different languages living in Nairobi. But if we take the bird's eye view of Nairobi as a speech community, we see that varieties of both Swahili and English [eng] have functions that are city wide, and also have some level of shared evaluation and perceived appropriateness to different social contexts. While not all Nairobians have a high level of English, they recognize it, and may feel there are situations where speaking it would be appropriate. We find English in the classroom, in written official documents, in situations where power or education are communicated, while Swahili (in various guises) is used to express solidarity, and is the language of the market, the informal economy, and the *matatu* (minivans which serve as Nairobi's main means of public transport). Swahili is also found as the dominant language in many homes (Gibson 2012), as is English to a lesser extent among the more educated. Alongside these languages exists a plethora of other

---

[1]Usefully described by the concept of *sociolinguistic domains* in Fasold (1984:60).

languages such as Kikuyu [kik], Luo [luo], and Kamba [kam], which are used in many homes, but also find some more general functions in particular parts of town, for example in some churches. But unlike English and Swahili, there would be no expectation of using these languages outside a context dominated by members of these communities. A similar, but not identical, scenario would hold for African cities such Kinshasa (Lingala [lin] and French [fra]), Cape Town (Xhosa [xho], Afrikaans [afr], and English), Dakar (Wolof [wol] and French), and Lusaka (Bemba [bem] and English).

This multilingualism is the context in which the urban varieties have developed, and continue to develop. Not all the patterns of multilingualism are alike, and neither are the urban vernaculars alike, though they do have many things in common. The topic of this paper is, however, the nature of the urban vernaculars in these cities, rather than the patterns of multilingualism that exist.

In all cases, the history of the urban vernaculars has involved a significant level of language or dialect contact; the nature of this contact is presumably a factor in accounting for the different types of urban vernaculars. Their type, and thereby their relationship to other varieties of languages, in turn affects what challenges their variety faces when looking at opportunities for its use and development in contexts such as education, media, and literature. Along with language contact in their history, these varieties also generally exhibit some level of ongoing creative hybridity. An additional issue is that the urban context often gives rise to quite distinct youth styles, often based on these vernaculars. Where new varieties arise, they bring with them new opportunities for indexing identity.

6.2 A typology of urban African varieties

Having set the urban vernaculars in their broader social context, we attempt a typology of linguistic classification which reflects different types of social contact that have taken place (Trudgill 2011), and ongoing development. All typologies exhibit stress under the pressure of real data, but some of these distinctions are more easily understood than others. Here we present the categories of: (1) a creole (or pidgin), (2) an urban contact variety, (3) a youth jargon, and (4) a hybrid language practice. It will become clear that some of these overlap, which will drive us to further definition.

6.2.1 Creoles and pidgins (Juba Arabic, Nigerian Pidgin, Fanagalo)

The most extreme types of language contact lead to languages called pidgins and creoles. The traditional account of the genesis of pidgins is that they are based on an incompletely learned version of a language, which is then used as an interlanguage between different groups, none of whom use it as their first language. Oft-cited examples are the English-based pidgins (now creoles) of the Caribbean, where African slaves from multiple linguistic backgrounds resorted to using English words to communicate among themselves, along with grammatical features from West African languages as well as English. Once these speakers had children, these children used what was a second language for their parents as their first language—making it a creole, which would then develop a full range of grammatical features. Some pidgins never become home languages (and therefore creoles), so may continue to exist with limited vocabulary and grammatical structures (e.g., Fanagalo [fng]).

Typically, creoles involve a lexifier language, which provides most of the vocabulary, while the source of the grammatical structures is more controversial—there is still an open question on whether the grammatical structures of these languages were simplified (or follow typological universals more closely), or whether they reflect the home languages of the speakers of the developing pidgin. As creoles have their own linguistic structures, they are generally treated by linguists as independent languages, but this does not mean that they are necessarily conceptualized as such by their speakers. Some examples of creoles and pidgins in African contexts are Juba Arabic [pga], Nigerian Pidgin [pcm] (also known as Naija, which is actually a creole as it has many mother-tongue speakers), and Fanagalo (a pidgin used in South African mines, which never moved beyond pidgin status—its utility is now being reduced with Zulu [zul], Afrikaans [afr], and English taking over its previous functions).[2]

In Juba, South Sudan, and the southern provinces of that country, the dominant language of wider communication in speech is Juba Arabic. It uses primarily Arabic lexis, but Arabic grammatical features are largely absent—for example, verbal conjugation and tense/aspect marking is marked by explicit pronouns and particles, rather than prefixes and suffixes. Arabist Clive Holes states that "Juba Arabic and (Ki)Nubi [kcn] are virtually unrecognizable as varieties of any kind of Arabic" (2004:26)—Kinubi is the name for closely related varieties spoken, but not used in a vehicular fashion, by communities in Kenya and Uganda descended from nineteenth century Sudanese troops resettled in East Africa. One example will demonstrate something of the nature of Juba Arabic (Logworong n.d.):

Juba Arabic
Ita   gi   amulu   sunu   bukura?
2s   FUT   do   what   tomorrow?

Here all the lexical items are derived from Arabic. But the verb *amulu* would need to be marked for both person and tense/aspect in either Standard or spoken (Sudanese or otherwise) Arabic. We find an unchanging verb form in Juba Arabic, with the person marked by a compulsory pronoun (unlike in Arabic where its presence is optional) and the tense signaled by a particle. Despite the clear linguistic divergence from Arabic, many of its speakers do not see a clear distinction between it and spoken varieties of Sudanese Arabic, referring to it as a broken version of Arabic, rather than a separate language.

Juba Arabic shows all the signs of a complete grammatical restructuring, generally evidence of there being a very low number of first-language speakers of the lexifying language present in the initial community that spoke the language. The grammatical features are closer to that of the vernacular languages spoken in South Sudan, such as Bari [bfa].

Creoles are often considered by their speakers (and others) to be "broken" varieties of other languages (Arabic in this case and English for Nigerian Pidgin). But their structural differences, and lack of intelligibility with the lexifying language mean that linguists generally consider them to be separate languages. This level of difference from other languages means that they may be more easily recognized as separate languages by their speakers, which generally makes their use in writing more easily accepted in the society than for some of the language varieties described

---

[2] For an alternative account of creole genesis, see Mufwene (2008).

below. This is by no means a simple thing, but the greater the differences from varieties already used in writing, the greater the perceived benefits (Karan 2011) of urban language development. Both Juba Arabic and Naija have some use in church, and some Scriptures also exist. This does not mean that attitudes towards their use in writing are widely positive, or that it would be simple to introduce them into education. Structured and planned oral uses, on the other hand, would seem to be less challenged by negative attitudes towards them, as that is what they are primarily used for—speaking rather than writing. Social media and various forms of texting and messaging on mobile phones also seem to be places where the attitudinal barrier to writing is diminished (Gibson 2016), as they represent conversation more than prose.

6.2.2 Urban contact varieties (Dakar, Nairobi, Lubumbashi, Johannesburg)

What we refer to as urban contact varieties are found in multiple cities. We can cite examples such as Nairobi Swahili (Bosire 2006; Deen 2005), Lubumbashi Swahili (Ferrari et al. 2014), Town Bemba (Spitulnik 1998), Dakar Wolof (McLaughlin 2001), and Urban Xhosa (Thipa 1992). This is not an exhaustive list. Varieties known by names such as Sheng, Tsotsitaal, and Indoubil will be dealt with in the section on hybrid language practices.

While it is impossible to know every detail of the development of current varieties, these varieties would appear to have a different history from the creoles and pidgins briefly described above. Here the most likely scenario is that the founding community that formed the nucleus of the new urban community did include some speakers of the lexifying language, even if the majority came from other language backgrounds. Compared to creoles, the restructuring of these varieties has been relatively minor—most structures (e.g., verbal conjugation) remain more or less intact, though generally with a large amount of regularization of irregular patterns. Unsurprisingly, some varieties show more restructuring than others—for example, Lubumbashi Swahili has innovated more in terms of structure than Nairobi Swahili. The varieties lie on something of a continuum.

Despite this, these urban contact varieties are sometimes claimed to be creoles or pidgins, which are characterized by a phase, historically, where the variety spoken had no first-language users. Creoles tend to have innovative constructions in tense and aspect marking, but this is not the case here to the same extent as would hold for a creole. But justifying a clean break between creoles and these urban contact varieties is also difficult. We can refer to these urban contact varieties as creoloids (cf. Platt 1975; Trudgill 2011:67, 68)—a term which invokes the similarities with the emergence of creoles.

Creoloids are language varieties where there is significant contact-related regularization and simplification of paradigms, without a complete restructuring—it is theorized that this happens when there is a majority of L2 speakers using the variety for intercommunal communication, alongside an L1 minority who provide a model for how it is spoken. This would seem to be the case for the early days of Nairobi, for example, where many of the African servants of the colonists were Swahili-speakers, probably outnumbered by local populations of Kikuyu, Maasai, and others.

Rather than dwelling on histories which are varied, we will look at the current varieties being spoken. We use the term "urban contact varieties" rather than just "urban varieties" to underline the level of difference, as well as their history, invoking Trudgill's model of dialect contact (1986). For the moment we will defer discussion of whether they constitute separate languages, rather than being widely divergent varieties of more widespread languages. It is notable that these urban contact varieties often serve as the primary home language in cities, and that the standard languages to which they are related are not used as home languages, at least not in the cities of which we speak. In Nairobi people will often acknowledge that "better" Swahili is spoken at the coast, including Kenya's second city of Mombasa, where the variety spoken is less divergent from the standard variety in, for example, nominal class marking.

We offer one specific example of Nairobi Swahili from Bosire (2006:190) contrasted with the same sentence in Standard Swahili (glossing as in original).

Standard Swahili
u-me-vi-on-a   vi-tabu   vy-angu?
you-tense-cl.8-see-fv cl.8-book   cl.8-my
'Have you seen my books?'

Nairobi Swahili
u-me-on-a   vi-tabu   za-ngu?
you-tense-see-fv   cl.8-book   cl.10-my?
'Have you seen my books?'

There are two differences between the quoted sentences, both reflecting structural rather than lexical differences (which also exist). The first is in the verb, where in the standard variety there is an extra morpheme marking the class of the object (books), which is typically absent in spoken Nairobi Swahili. And we see that the final word, the marker of possession, is different: in Standard Swahili it is the same class marker as the head noun, but looks to be from a different class in the Nairobi version. What has in fact happened is that agreement of adjectives in Nairobi Swahili is based on semantics rather than the typical Bantu agreement system, with all plural inanimate nouns, as in this case, using the markers of what is otherwise known as Class 10. We see that the overall structure of the verb (its manner of marking, choice of prefixes and suffixes such as for person and tense/aspect) is broadly similar, but that the traditional Bantu classifier system has been reanalyzed as one which carries only distinctions of animacy and number.

One of the most complete descriptions of an urban contact variety is of Lubumbashi Swahili (Ferrari et al. 2014). One of the observations in this work (2014:7), which applies to many of these varieties, is "Ces parlers n'ont généralement pas de nom, seule leur forme la plus argotique en possédant un." [These speech varieties generally have no name, only their most slangy form possessing one.] Here we see another feature of these varieties, which is the incorporation of a great amount of vocabulary from other languages, especially the relevant colonial language, whether English or French. Some of the other differences that Ferrari and colleagues note are in the pronunciation of several phonemes, a different form for verbal first person marking *mi* (where both Standard and Nairobi Swahili have *ni*), directional particles that are not found in other Swahili varieties (such as *ku* 'to'), and more transparent numbers from twenty upwards (for example, *makumi mbili* 'two tens' rather than the opaque Arabic loans such as *ishirini*, which are used in Standard Swahili and in most East African varieties). We may suppose that Lubumbashi Swahili is somewhat further along the creoloid continuum than Nairobi Swahili. We see not only difference, but also some level of confirmation of Trudgill's (1986) *Dialects in Contact* model, which predicts that new dialects will level differences and be structurally simpler than the dialects of those who moved in (cf. Labov 1972).

The issues for using these varieties in education or Bible translations are perhaps more complicated than for the creole varieties, which are already relatively complex. This stems from the fact that these varieties tend to maintain some, if incomplete, level of intelligibility with the "standard" versions of their related languages, so that they are often recognized as "incorrect" versions of the standard. This can make the case for developing these varieties for written use weaker than for creoles, which are even more clearly different. Even where there is a policy, for example, of using Swahili in the schools, this will tend to be Standard Swahili, and much of the teaching is focused on learning the high, standard form of the language, correcting the "mistakes" of the local form (e.g., see Mbua 2009). However, Standard Swahili does not function as a valued high variety for Nairobi youth—this is a position occupied by English, so Swahili school classes neither result in many proficient users of Standard Swahili, nor in Swahili being used as a vehicle of self expression—from the very start of schooling, the substantial difference between the speaker's variety and the Standard is emphasized. While the use of the local variety in education might, other things being equal, constitute a useful innovation, it may be seen by some as an attempt to debase the language, and thus meet with strong resistance. The levels of challenge here vary with the levels of linguistic divergence from the standard, which as we have attempted to communicate, lie on a spectrum.

6.2.3 Youth jargon (Nouchi, Camfranglais)

Both the creoles and urban contact varieties described above are very much home languages—used by parents with their children, by children with other children, in the market, and on the street. What we describe here as youth jargons are more restricted in their domains of use, being styles or registers of speaking (we may invoke Hurst's [2009] term *stylect* here perhaps). And in these cases, both of the varieties described are based on French, and furthermore exist in cities which do not have city-wide African languages of wider communication in the same way that we find in Nairobi, Kinshasa, or Lusaka. However, both do use resources from African languages.

The varieties have names which are commonly used and recognized in the communities, unlike the general case for the urban contact varieties above. In Abidjan the variety is called Nouchi, and in Yaoundé we can speak of Camfranglais (neither variety is restricted solely to these cities). There is little evidence that these varieties are becoming established as separate languages, or are being used widely outside youth culture. They are often markers of solidarity, and may perhaps be part of a broader picture of factors giving rise to localized varieties of French. Again, we will have the briefest of looks at some data (from Kouega 2013:154, quoted by Vakunta 2014).

Camfranglais
Ma friend se call Suzy, elle me helep bad.
'My friend's name is Suzie; she helps me a lot.'

This example of Camfranglais is one which sticks to its naming—the overall structure of the sentence is French (use of the reflexive *se*, positioning of the object pronoun *me* before rather than after the noun). But within the sentence we see four words derived from English, including both verbs. *Helep*, rather than being borrowed directly from English, has been taken from Cameroonian Pidgin English, and the meaning of *bad*, rather than being negative, has undergone semantic inversion, a common feature of youth varieties note that words such as *sick* and *wicked* have undergone similar inversions in some varieties of youth English). In fact, borrowing in Camfranglais is not exclusively from English, but also extends to African languages, and the words which are borrowed are typically pronounced according to the phonologies of the source languages rather than of French.

Nouchi, like Camfranglais, is also a youth variety with French syntax, which borrows from a variety of languages, but its most recognized feature is its borrowing from other Ivorian languages, rather than other European languages, though such borrowing does also occur. The following example is from Ahua 2008:138).

Nouchi Abidjan
Le   mɔ̀gɔ́   veut   me   kpā.
the   chap   wants   me   take
'The chap (Jula) wants to take (source??) me.'

Here we see borrowing from one African language with the phonology—in particular here, the tone—intact, along with many neologisms and semantic shifts. The second non-French word in this example does not have an identifiable source—but this should not surprise us, as youth varieties are sources of great innovation. Youth registers have multiple associations, and often have a dual function—of increasing solidarity among the users, but also excluding others, for which the use of unfamiliar lexis can be a successful strategy. This is also often associated with criminality (where the desire to exclude others has an additional pragmatic driver), which is argued to be reason for jargons which can also be termed antilanguages (Halliday 1978), such as Cockney Rhyming Slang or Polari, identified with criminals and homosexuals respectively, but both providing some expressions to more widely used youth language.

Of course, youth jargons do not need to be based on European languages, but are also found as versions of urban varieties of African languages, such as Kirundi [run] in Bujumbura (e.g., Nassenstein 2017).

6.2.4 Hybrid language practices (Nairobi, Lubumbashi, Johannesburg)

The final category that we present is hybrid language practices (HLPs). It is perhaps the most difficult to define, and where there has been the least unanimity on how we should describe the varieties, or perhaps practices, outlined. In our discussion of urban contact varieties, we quoted Ferrari et al. (2014:7), "Ces parlers n'ont généralement pas de nom, seule leur forme la plus argotique en possédant un," focusing in effect on the first part of the quote, the fact that many of these varieties have no effective name. Now we turn to focus on the *plus argotique*—most "slangy"—end of the spectrum of varieties and practices found among urban youth. And these often do have names. The discussion of what is the nature of these varieties is complicated by what these names refer to—it is evident that different analyses of these varieties are to some extent due to the same label being attached to different parts of the spectrum of language varieties and practices. But it is also clear that any discussion needs to consider both the nature of the urban contact variety and the youth jargons described above—these HLPs may best be described as youth jargons with an urban contact variety base. However, in the literature we find one exemplar, Sheng, variously defined as an:

- independent language (Ferrari 2004; Rudd 2008; Kiessling and Mous 2004; Osinde and Abdulaziz 1997)
- example of hybridity (Bosire 2006)
- urban dialect of Swahili (Githiora 2002)

As stated above, the definitions of hybridity and urban dialect are both part of the picture as we represent it here.

The labels which are used to talk of these varieties are various—in Nairobi people talk of Sheng; in South Africa we hear of Tsotsitaal, Iscamtho [fly], and many other names; in DRC we read about (K)Indoubil and associated words. In each case there is, as Kiessling and Mous (2004) indicate, an identity signaled which is in opposition to broader societal norms—the varieties are not meant to carry formal prestige, but instead to signal a break from it. Part of that departure is the embracing of hybridity, of intentionally using vocabulary from different parts of the world—referencing both the local and the global, as neither one nor the other alone captures the identity to which the youth aspire. They are urban, African, connected both to the village and to the globe.

The labels, and the levels of difference, have led to claims that these labels represent independent languages, along with requests for ISO 639-3 codes.[3] In fact what constitutes a separate language is largely a social, as well as a linguistic, question, and is not the primary question for our purposes here, where we are asking questions about appropriate engagement with these varieties or practices for language development, how they index identity, and what types of identity they are linked with.

Having given the broad context, we aim to flesh it out with an example of Sheng from Nairobi, taken from *Shujjaz.FM*,[4] a Kenyan multiplatform communications channel, incorporating radio, social media, and a free comic, which uses Sheng as its primary medium. Here is the text from the title page from some years ago.

> *Wasee! Karibuni kwa site yangu ya nguvu! Hapa unaweza kuwa member wa Shujaaz.FM. Ji-register upate mambo fyam!*
>
> 'Dudes! Welcome to our site of strength. Here you can become a member of Shujaaz.FM. Register to get cool stuff.'

Overall the grammar and structure are of the urban contact variety Nairobi Swahili. An English eye will notice three English loanwords immediately—*site, member,* and *register*. The latter has the Swahili reflexive prefix *ji* attached, creating a hybrid word with English lexis, but Swahili morphology. There are also two specifically Sheng words—the initial *wasee* 'dudes' and the final *fyam* 'cool'. While the former word conforms to Swahili patterns (and looks suspiciously close to *wazee* 'old men'), the latter, with its final nasal, does not. But there is so much borrowing in Swahili from English in Nairobi, that it is quite common to have words ending in consonants. The origin of this word is unclear—as with Nouchi, some innovative lexis seems to

---

[3] See, for instance, recent requests to create codes for Town Nyanja iso639-3.sil.org/request/2016-023/ and Sheng iso639-3.sil.org/request/2016-034/.

[4] facebook.com/DJBoyie/

have no identifiable source in another language. Sheng words also often come from transformations of words by various strategies, e.g.,

- Swahili *fundi* ('artisan') > Sheng *ndifu* (by metathesis of syllables)
- English *father* > Sheng *fadhi*
- Swahili *matatu* ('minivan') > Sheng *mat/mao* (by shortening)
- or Swahili *matatu* ('minivan') > Sheng *mathri* (by taking the meaning of *tatu* in Swahili and translating it to English "three")
- or Swahili *matatu* ('minivan') > Sheng *jav*, short for "javelin," referring to the way the minivans are driven, then shortened.

New words are constantly coined, old ones replaced—this is part of the dynamic of varieties such as Sheng.

This has been but a brief linguistic overview of some Sheng data, but the morphosyntax is generally the same as that of everyday Nairobi Swahili, with particular words (and an openness to mixing in with English) signaling that this is no longer everyday Swahili, but represents this special youth code. Occasionally some plural morphology is borrowed from English (e.g., *ma-yuts* 'youths', with both Nairobi Swahili plural *ma-* and English *-s* on a naturalized form of "youth"). Some work has contrasted Sheng grammatical structures with those of Standard Swahili, and therefore claimed it is a separate system, but this ignores the swathes of population who speak with the same Nairobi Swahili morphosyntax as what is there defined as Sheng, but would never consider themselves speakers of Sheng. Gibson (2015) found that the defining characteristic of Sheng in the minds of Nairobians was the lexis chosen, and that Sheng was created by putting Sheng words into Nairobi Swahili. Indeed, just using a lot of English within the Swahili was not considered sufficient to brand speech as Sheng, even if this is typical of Sheng. It was for a similar context, urban Cape Town, that Hurst (2009) coined the word "stylect," to capture that the lexical innovation and mixing are part of a style which is recognized, but also to some extent a performance.

As mentioned above, one of the problems with talking about varieties such as Sheng truly is a problem of definition. It is a human tendency to take the most extreme version of something as its exemplar, and the prototypical meaning of a term is often the most distinctive from other words—and when discussing phenomena such as youth stylects, public discourse rarely takes time to carefully define its terms. For example, in his piece *Vile and Useless, Sheng Must Go,* Muganda (2013) writes, "Truth be written, sheng [sic] has no commercial value, is vile, despicable, uncouth, impolite and Kenya as a nation will never benefit from it in any way." While he does not mention criminality, we see that for the writer Sheng represents a lack of politeness. Muganda does mention the constantly changing vocabulary. Mugubi (2006), however, contests this type of definition of Sheng:

> Sheng was my first language back in the 1970s. It was the medium my family used best to communicate, and yet none of us knew the spelling of touting or drug peddling. It was also no secret code for deviance in our case.

It is clear from this that for Mugubi, associations of criminality (though evidently commonly invoked) are inaccurate. He seems to be using the term *Sheng* in a much broader sense, which we may refer to in our typology as better represented by *Nairobi Swahili*. But our aim here is not to "correct" him, but to understand how the term is used by different people in different contexts. We then read something of a justification for engagement with Sheng (or perhaps what we are calling Nairobi Swahili) in the following words taken from the same piece:

> Sheng transcends ethnic fences and therefore forges unity among the speakers. ... Yet, English and Kiswahili do not define who we are. Sheng, that blend of many of the languages prevalent in Kenya, is who we are. (Mugubi 2006)

In Gibson (2015), it was found that the term *Kiswahili* (Swahili for "Swahili") refers prototypically to Standard Swahili, the variety taught in school, and used in print. And Sheng generally stands for the other end of the spectrum, apart from for one interviewee, who claimed to use Sheng in his home life and whose definition of what constitutes Sheng was broader, along similar lines to that used by Mugubi above. In my own experience, I met Nairobians who would claim not to really speak Swahili, who I would then hear speaking what sounded like Swahili to me, and doing so quite fluently. What was being said (and a similar situation was also found in the south of DRC in Gibson 2018) was that people were admitting to not being able to control Standard Swahili sufficiently to be able to say that they were in fact speakers of Swahili. Some people, after having this pointed out to them, would then claim that it was Sheng that they spoke, but then would often add that it was not real Sheng. We can interpret this as their feeling some level of discomfort with defining their speech variety as either prototypical Swahili or prototypical Sheng—what we might call Nairobi Swahili. But in Nairobi there is no conventionalized way of talking of this variety—it can be described, but does not have a convenient label, as we have above quoted Ferrari et al. 2014 as saying for Lubumbashi Swahili. Similarly, Kube-Barth (2009:109) notes that the students she interviewed use the term *Nouchi* when referring to vernacular French spoken in Abidjan, rather than the youth style. Readers may find the following diagram helpful:

Lexicalized	Not lexicalized	Lexicalized
Kiswahili	(*Nairobi Swahili*)	**Sheng**

<————— - - - - —————————————>

What the diagram attempts to show is that there is a continuum of varieties and styles (though with something of a break between Standard Swahili—Kiswahili—and Nairobi Swahili on the left), with only two labels clearly defining the end points (Kiswahili on the left and Sheng on the right), while the main varieties used for everyday communication are not clearly labelled. Instead, speakers extend the meaning of either Sheng or Kiswahili to talk of the not lexicalized central space, while aware that this does not constitute an exemplar. When given some terminology to talk about three places on the continuum—the language of the street, the home, and the school—everybody interviewed in Gibson (2015) was able to identify the different varieties, and recognized them. This, however, leads to people who speak in essentially the same way as each other using different labels. In contexts such as this, asking someone "Is it Swahili or Sheng that you speak?" does not lead to good data, as it implies a clear-cut distinction which was not found to be present in Gibson (2015).

This situation is by no means unique to Nairobi or Kenya. We see much the same dynamic at play in South Africa in a provocatively titled paper by Mesthrie (2008), "I've been speaking Tsotsitaal all my life without knowing it," where he critiques the use of the label "Tsotsitaal" to refer to varieties which he describes as Urban

Xhosa, Urban Zulu, and so on. These terms, again, are used by linguists, but not by the speakers of these nonstandard urban varieties. The fact that Tsotsitaal can refer to language practices involving varieties based on Zulu, Xhosa, Sotho, or Swati weakens the claim that this constitutes a separate language—it's a nod to the style (the meaning of Tsotsitaal is effectively "gangster talk"). We find a similar pattern in DRC with Indoubil (though with a lower tendency to use the term for everyday speech), which can also apply to urban speech styles based on different languages—here Swahili and Lingala.

6.3 Language development and hybrid language practices

If HLPs are constantly changing, with innovation and change of vocabulary being rapid (it is certain that some of the Sheng terms I have introduced are already outdated), it seems valid to pose the question of whether these varieties are appropriate vehicles for language development—how could educational materials be prepared in them if they are so fluid and constantly changing, or books such as the Bible? Part of the definition of Sheng is that of an antilanguage, which resists conformity and formalization. And that is one of the problems with treating these practices themselves as separate languages, which otherwise might lead to recommendations of use in education and the written translations of the Bible. What may be intended in recommendations like these is the everyday Nairobi Swahili, which is on the other hand not what the name Sheng normally conjures up. The problem with arguing for engagement with something socially unlabeled, such as Nairobi Swahili, is that the name is not known to refer to something specific.

But a model for effective engagement does exist, and in what is properly, prototypically, Sheng, and that is *Shujaaz.FM,* the details of which are more fully outlined in Gibson (2013). *Shujaaz.FM* exists in several media—as a comic, on social media, on radio, and on YouTube. As Sheng is a vehicle of what is "cool," and not attached to the types of formal prestige associated with education, it is more strongly associated with speech, rather than writing. However, before the advent of the internet, comic books were one place where one was more likely to find representations of vernacular rather than formal speech. Back in 1959, Ferguson noted that in diglossic societies, while newspapers were generally in High varieties, the comics would be in the Low—the vernacular. And social and broadcast media are also appropriate places for the use of what are essentially vernacular (Low) varieties (Gibson 2016). *Shujaaz.FM*, with its multiplatform approach and ongoing engagement, may well be a good model for inspiring urban and youth focused language development efforts in environments suited to varieties which index solidarity rather than formality.

The idea of language development activities in varieties such as these is often misunderstood, with goals that seem fantastical. Setting up an education system, or translating a printed text such as a portion of the Bible for ongoing use would be ill advised for an HLP as the target variety of choice. This is not to discourage development efforts into the urban contact variety, if attitudes around its appropriateness could effectively be dealt with so that members of the community would happily use it for their material or spiritual needs.

Mugubi's (2006) comments on Sheng focus on its role in marking identity, rather than on it being needed for interethnic communication: "English and Kiswahili do not define who we are" and "Sheng, that blend of many of the languages prevalent in Kenya, is who we are." We could paraphrase these two quotes as stating that Sheng can be used for identificational purposes, referencing the urban, vernacular, identity. Any use of Sheng in print or online would need community support and constant updating on websites and in another media.

Shujaaz.FM, while using an urban variety, is actually targeted (and for development reasons—its primary support comes from international non government organizations) at rural youth. So while Sheng may be an urban vernacular, it indexes modernity and "street cool," which is sought after not just by urban youth, but their rural counterparts, too. Urban and rural contexts, while distinct, do not exist in a vacuum, and urban varieties will often both spread into and influence the countryside's speech, while rural patterns also enter the town with the continued inflow of people into the cities.

6.4 Urban identities

Identity is a complex construct, which is not one dimensional. For a fuller picture see the papers in part one of this volume. In a country such as Kenya, identities in addition to "African" that are commonly claimed are those of nationality ("Kenyan"), and then a host of different ethnic identities, such as Kikuyu, Kamba, or Luo. In some cases there is both a communal and a clan identity (e.g., both Luhya and Maragoli, which is constructed as one of the Luhya clans). These latter identities are often rooted in rural contexts, but do also continue to be relevant in the city (witness, for example, the interethnic violence in Nairobi after the 2007 presidential election, which was often articulated in terms of such identities).

However, just as we have seen urban language varieties that have no agreed autonym, there are signs that there are some meaningful urban identities that are not commonly conventionalized, but are nonetheless psychologically real, or at the very least recognizable. I will start with two accounts of conversations which demonstrate this, before moving to some empirical data from Bunia, DRC.

The first story comes from meeting a young Kenyan lady in the UK. I asked her where she was from, and her smile disappeared, and she looked down. She answered that her father was from Nyanza (in effect a way of saying she belongs to the Luo community, though there are other communities who make Nyanza province their home). The indirect reference to ethnicity is consistent with its being somewhat stigmatized. I noticed the discomfort, and clarified, asking where she had grown up—at which point her face brightened, and she told me she was from Westlands, a well-to-do suburb of Nairobi. A quick analysis would suggest that she was happy to identify as from Nairobi, but that the Luo identity was not especially relevant, and could be seen to evoke tribalism.

A similar story comes from a class in sociolinguistics in Nairobi, where the topic was language and identity. For some students in the class, the ethnic group they belonged to was a significant part of their identity. But one student, who had grown up in Nairobi in a family from the Kikuyu community, and who did not speak fluent Kikuyu, responded with some ambivalence to the question of whether she was a Kikuyu—answering along the lines of "I don't really speak Kikuyu, but I suppose I am Kikuyu," while looking uncomfortable with the question. When I asked her if she would consider herself a Nairobian, she smiled, and nodded saying words along the lines of "Oh yes, that's who I am."

These two anecdotes do not prove anything conclusively, but they do point to the fact that some urban dwellers in Nairobi do not forefront their ethnic identity—in both of the cases above, the individuals carry it, if with some reluctance. Neither of them would initially present themselves as a Nairobian, as that is not one of the available ethnic identities which are seen as mutually exclusive options, but a Nairobian identity is compatible with also being a member of an ethnic community. It does not fit in the normal categories of identities socially constructed in Kenya, but seems nonetheless to be what is indexed by some of the linguistic choices made in varieties such as Sheng. Just as Nairobi Swahili is socially recognized, but is not consistently named or foregrounded—so we also find that an urban identity is not foregrounded, but nonetheless recognized. This plays out in the development of new urban linguistic varieties, which are mainly disassociated from ethnic stereotypes associated in many minds with the countryside, rather than the city.

Turning from anecdotal data, we now present some empirical data from Gibson and Bagamba (2016), concerning urban children in Bunia, DRC, from the Northern Hema community. The children were asked what they felt their identity to be from the options given. The table found in (2016:357) is reproduced here as table 1.

Table 1. Identity perception by Northern Hema children living in Bunia

Age groups of children	Sample size	Inhabitant of Bunia	Hema living in Bunia	Northern Hema
5-9 year olds	61	74%	7%	20%
10-13 year olds	51	61%	8%	31%
14-18 year olds	38	45%	11%	45%

In that paper we also examine parents' language choices when talking with their children, and children's linguistic preferences (which have quite a high apparent correlation with children's perceived identities). We note that older children both identify more with the traditional ethnic identity than the younger children, and are stronger speakers of Baledha—the percentage figures are not identical, but there is more than a passing similarity. We are unable to judge from this data whether the ethnic identity and language are becoming less important with time, or whether the difference between children of different ages is because the children learn the ethnic language and adopt an ethnic identity later than acquiring Swahili. But there are two main points to take from this data, which are that many of the children (for whom constructions of identity may be less salient in any case), when given the choice, are happy to talk of themselves as urban, and that there seems to be some correlation between feelings of ethnic identity and the ability to speak the language in both the cases of Bunia and Nairobi. Of course, we know that there are many cases where identity does not necessarily shift when language does (e.g., in Irish, Welsh, and many Native American communities), but that does not negate the claim that there is often a correlation between language choice and strength of identity feeling. The data given here are consistent with the claim of the link between identity and language.

6.5 Conclusion: Urban language varieties and identities that do not self identify

We have noted that African cities have often developed urban contact varieties that are widely divergent from the vehicular language that provided most of their vocabulary, and that the varieties which dominate often have no name by which their speakers consistently refer to them. Alongside this the urban identity tends to assert itself indirectly, rather than definitively entering into national consciousness alongside the traditional ethnic communities. One of the significant ways, however, that these identities do announce themselves is through language, especially through hybridity—using linguistic resources which reference the local, the global (together referred to as the glocal), and also, as we have seen for Nouchi and Sheng, the brand new—words which have no obvious origin. That these communities have not felt the need to name the daily norm, but just the extreme ends of it, is interesting. We may see this change in the future, but the commonality of this absence—in Nairobi, Lubumbashi, and Johannesburg, to name but some examples—needs some level of explanation. What we have been able to offer is that, due to prototypes, varieties of language tend to be seen as extremes, or as maximally different from each other as possible. Middle ground is harder to speak of.

Yet, when it comes to language development, practitioners need to be able to identify particular varieties. And that is rendered more difficult when the labels are stretchy—one speaker might sometimes refer to their home variety (which perhaps only a linguist would name Nairobi Swahili) as Swahili, and in another instance might use the label Sheng to describe the same variety. When planning for language development it might be easier to talk of audiences, and how they will best engage, rather than necessarily focusing on a linguistic description. For example, when interviewing staff at *Shujaaz.FM* for Gibson (2013), I was told that the goal was not in and of itself to use Sheng, but to represent the way that the audience speaks, to represent the reality of Kenyan youth. As such, in certain contexts there would be more English, in others more traditional, less Shengy Swahili. The goal was therefore appropriateness, rather than being fixated on using one particular style or practice of language. This seems the best response when dealing with such varieties which are of necessity fluid and difficult to pin down.

References

Ahua, Blaise Mouchi. 2008. Mots, phrases et syntaxe du Nouchi. *Le français en Afrique* 23:135–150. unice.fr/ILF-CNRS/ofcaf/23/AHUA Blaise Mouchi.pdf/.

Beck, Rose Marie. 2010. Urban Languages in Africa. *Africa Spectrum: 50 Years of Independence in Africa* 45(3):11–41.

Bosire, Mokaya. 2006. Hybrid languages: The case of Sheng. In Olaoba F. Arasanyin and Michael A. Pemberton (eds.), *Selected proceedings of the 36th Annual Conference on African Linguistics*, 185–193. Somerville, MA: Cascadilla Proceedings Project. lingref.com/cpp/acal/36/paper1423.pdf.

Deen, Kamil Ud. 2005. *The acquisition of Swahili*. Language Acquisition and Language Disorders 40. Amsterdam: John Benjamins.

Fasold, Ralph W. 1984. *The sociolinguistics of society*. Language in Society 5. Oxford: Blackwell.

Ferguson, Charles A. 1959. Diglossia. *Word* 15:325–340.

Ferrari, Aurélia. 2004. Linguistic representations of Sheng, a new vernacular language spoken in Nairobi, Kenya. Paper given at Sociolinguistics Symposium 15, University of Newcastle-upon-Tyne, 1–4 April 2004.

Ferrari, Aurélia, Marcel Kalunga, and Georges Mulumbwa. 2014. *Le swahili de Lubumbashi: Grammaire, textes, lexique* [Swahili of Lubumbashi: Grammar, texts, lexicon]. Paris: Editions Karthala.

Gibson, Maik. 2012. Language shift in Nairobi. In M. Brenzinger and A.-M. Fehn (eds.), *Proceedings of the 6th World Congress of African Linguistics, Cologne, Germany, 17–21 August 2009*, 569–575. Cologne: Rüdiger Köppe.

Gibson, Maik. 2013. Urban Sheng as a hook for the message: The targeting of both urban and rural youth by Shujaaz.FM. Paper presented at African Urban and Youth Language Conference, Cape Town, July 2013.
Powerpoint: https://www.academia.edu/4181502
Video: youtube.com/watch?v=MJm3OdnIC_E/.

Gibson, Maik. 2015. The urban vernacular(s) of Nairobi: speakers' representations and beliefs about Swahili and Sheng. Paper given at Sociolinguistics Symposium 19, Berlin, August 2012. academia.edu/9756856/.

Gibson, Maik. 2016. Assessing digital vitality: Analytical and activist approaches. In Claudia Soria, Laurette Pretorius, Thierry Declerck, Joseph Mariani, Kevin Scannell, and Eveline Wandl-Vogt (eds.), *Proceedings of the LREC 2016 Workshop "CCURL 2016—Collaboration and Computing for Under-Resourced Languages: Towards an Alliance for Digital Language Diversity"*, 46–51. lrec-conf.org/proceedings/lrec2016/workshops/LREC2016Workshop-CCURL2016_Proceedings.pdf/.

Gibson, Maik. 2018. What counts as Swahili in the Democratic Republic of the Congo? Field researchers' attitudes in language-in-education research. Paper given at CIES conference, Mexico City, 28 March 2018. academia.edu/37086676/.

Gibson, Maik, and B. Araali Bagamba. 2016. Language shift and endangerment in urban and rural East Africa. In Luna Filipović and Martin Pütz (eds.), *Endangered languages and languages in danger: Issues of documentation, policy, and language rights*, 351–360. Amsterdam: John Benjamins.

Githiora, Chege. 2002. Sheng: Peer language, Swahili dialect or emerging creole? *Journal of African Cultural Studies* 15(2):159–181.

Halliday, M. A. K. 1978. Anti-languages. In M. A. K. Halliday (ed.), *Language as a social semiotic: The social interpretation of language and meaning*, 164–182. London: Edward Arnold.

Holes, Clive. 2004. *Modern Arabic: Structures, functions, and varieties*. Georgetown Classics in Arabic Languages and Linguistics. Washington, DC: Georgetown University Press.

Hurst, Ellen. 2009. Tsotsitaal, global culture and local style: Identity and recontextualisation in twenty-first century South African townships. *Social Dynamics* 35(2):244–257.

Hurst, Ellen. 2017. African (urban) youth languages. In *Oxford Research Encyclopedia of Linguistics*. dx.doi.org/10.1093/acrefore/9780199384655.013.157/.

Karan, Mark. 2011. Understanding and forecasting ethnolinguistic vitality. *Journal of Multilingual and Multicultural Development* 32(2):137–149.

Kiessling, Roland, and Maarten Mous. 2004. Urban youth languages in Africa. *Anthropological Linguistics* 46(3):303–341.

Kouega, Jean-Paul. 2013. *Camfranglais: A glossary of common words, phrases and usages*. LINCOM Studies in Pidgin and Creole Languages 13. Munich: LINCOM Europa.

Kube-Bath, Sabine. 2009. The multiple facets of the urban language form, Nouchi. In Fiona McLaughlin (ed.), *The languages of urban Africa*, 103-114.

Labov, William. 1972. *Sociolinguistic patterns*. Philadelphia, PA: University of Pennsylvania Press.

Logworong, Rombek. n.d. Juba Arabic verbs and phrases. scribd.com/doc/3751607/Juba-Arabic-Verbs-and-Phrases/.

Mbua, Abigael Wangari. 2009. An investigation into common Kiswahili grammatical errors related to noun classes, made by secondary school students in Nairobi: A case study of Dagoretti High School students. Unpublished project for MA in Linguistics, Nairobi Evangelical Graduate School of Theology.

McLaughlin, Fiona. 2001. Dakar Wolof and the configuration of an urban identity. *Journal of African Cultural Studies* 14(2):153–172.

McLaughlin, Fiona, ed. 2009. *The languages of urban Africa*. Advances in Sociolinguistics 54. London: Continuum.

Mesthrie, Rajend. 2008. "I've been speaking Tsotsitaal all my life without knowing it": Towards a unified account of Tsotsitaals in South Africa. In Miriam Meyerhoff and Naomi Nagy (eds.), *Social lives in language—Sociolinguistics and multilingual speech communities: Celebrating the work of Gillian Sankoff*, 95–109. Amsterdam: John Benjamins.

Muganda, Clay. 2013. Useless and vile, sheng must go. *Daily Nation*, February 19, 2013. nation.co.ke/Features/DN2/Useless-and-vile-sheng-must-go/-/957860/1697626/-/gmvqufz/-/index.html/.

Mugubi, John. 2006. Kenya: Sheng is the 'slanguage' of the future. *Daily Nation*, 6 October 2006. http://www.allafrica.com/stories/200610060018.html.

Mufwene, Salikoko S. 2008. *Language evolution: Contact, competition and change*. London: Continuum.

Nassenstein, Nico. 2017. Kirundi slang—youth identity and linguistic manipulations In A. E. Ebongue and E. Hurst (eds.), *Sociolinguistics in African contexts*, 247–267. New York: Springer.

Osinde, Kenneth, and Mohamed Abdulaziz. 1997. Sheng and Engsh: the development of mixed codes among the urban youth in Kenya. *International Journal of the Sociology of Language* 125:43–63.

Platt, John T. 1975. The Singapore English speech continuum and its basilect 'Singlish' as a 'creoloid'. *Anthropological Linguistics* 17(7):363–374.

Rudd, Philip W. 2008. Sheng: the mixed language of Nairobi. PhD dissertation. Ball State University, Muncie, IN.

Spitulnik, Debra. 1998. The language of the city: Town Bemba as urban hybridity. *Journal of Linguistic Anthropology* 8(1):30–59.

Thipa, H. M. 1992. The difference between urban and rural Xhosa varieties. *South African Journal of African Languages* 12(Supplement 1):77–90.

Trudgill, Peter. 1986. *Dialects in contact*. Language in Society 10. Oxford: Blackwell.

Trudgill, Peter. 2011. *Sociolinguistic typology: Social determinants of linguistic complexity*. Oxford: Oxford University Press.

Vakunta, Peter Wuteh. 2014. From Pidgin English to Camfranglais: Review of *Camfranglais: A glossary of common words, phrases and usages*, (2013) by Jean-Paul Kouega. *Panbazuka News*, February 12, 2014. pambazuka.org/arts/pidgin-english-camfranglais/.

7
Trans-languaging, Identity, and Education in Our Multilingual World

Sangsok Son

Abstract. This paper argues that trans-languagers should be looked at from a trans-languager's internal point of view. In order to understand how they trans-language and why, the emic point of view among trans-languagers is necessary. The author begins this article with the introduction of two different ways of becoming multilingual, i.e., elite multilingualism versus grassroots multilingualism, and describes the characteristics of grassroots multilingualism, which reflect the trans-languagers' linguistic practices in a more accurate way. He further contends that the complex nature of mother tongue cannot be clearly explained with the understanding of language as a static, separate. and fixed entity but makes more sense if language flows. As speakers trans-language across the fuzzy boundaries of languages, they continuously negotiate their identity from their identity repertoire. Gee's four different perspectives on identity are used to argue that a trans-languaging discourse between a teacher and a group of students is a space where both the teacher and the students construct, negotiate, and reconstruct their identities. Lastly, it is argued that trans-languaging practices of students should be used in classrooms in a strategic and purposeful way so that they can perform better in meeting curriculum requirements, both in terms of language specific performance and academic content knowledge.

7.1 Introduction

The world is changing rapidly. The de-territorialization of people is increasing as migration happens both domestically and cross-territorially. Urbanization increases both in the village as well as in the cities. Not only do people move to cities but "cities also move to the villages." While the global world is fast changing, it becomes more interconnected virtually as well as physically. As people are more mobile and borders more fuzzy, the understanding of language as distinct entities with clear boundaries among them has to be questioned (García and Seltzer 2016). Languages show porous boundaries and continue to converge on one another in fluid space (Agnihotri 2007). Languages flow. Linguistic practices of speakers are dynamic, complex, and fluid. Multilingual speakers add new language features to their existing language repertoire as they come into contact with others with different linguistic backgrounds. They use whichever linguistic features are available to them in interrelationship with other features according to the contingency of social life. They "trans-language."

In this paper I argue that in this postmodern global world, "trans-languaging" is the most effective kind of linguistic performance for communication and learning new things among societal or "grassroots" (Mohanty 2006) multilingual speakers, which may be performed freely using various features from different linguistic repertoires. Trans-languagers, moreover, are argued to constantly construct, negotiate, and reconstruct their identity through the trans-languaging process. The discussion on trans-languaging is preceded by the introduction of internal perspectives on multilingualism, mother tongue, and language, and followed by some implications of trans-languaging in education.

7.2 Multilingualism: Two kinds, but a continuum between the two

People may have different understandings of multilingualism according to how they themselves became multilingual. There may be two kinds of processes of how to become multilingual. One extreme case would be that people become multilingual through formal or nonformal education while living in a nearly monolingual society. They may learn new language(s) in a rather conscious way at different stages of their education while they continue to develop their home language(s). They learn other languages but scarcely have chances to use them outside the classroom where they learn those languages. So they usually use their home language in most of their daily lives unless they move to other linguistic communities where different languages are used. The other extreme case would be that people grow up in multilingual environments from their birth or childhood and develop more than one language unconsciously as they interact with others with different language backgrounds. They continue to use most of their linguistic repertoire in their normal life. The former become multilingual sequentially, one language after another, the latter do so simultaneously.

There may be various ways to become multilingual along the continuum between the two scenarios. One person may move along this continuum depending upon the different needs of using different languages and the degree of virtual or physical "investment" (Peirce 1997) required in learning them. As a Korean language speaker, I have learned English and Hindi at different stages of my education, but I had hardly any chance to use them, mostly using only Korean while I stayed in Korea where Korean is dominantly used. But I used all the linguistic repertoires of all three languages while staying in India for fifteen years, where I interacted with multilingual speakers with similar linguistic repertoires. In contrast to my case, multilingual people may migrate to rather monolingual countries or communities where a more prestigious language, such as English, is spoken and their existing multilingual repertoires may shrink due to less chance to use them than in their multilingual home countries. In the following section, some characteristics of multilingualism among those who become multilingual from birth, corresponding to the latter kind of process mentioned above, will be discussed from their internal and multilingual perspectives.

7.3 Multilingualism from a multilingual perspective

Multilingualism should be understood through a multilingual ethos and pluralistic stance rather than through a monistic perspective. This is because, as del Valle (2000:124) argues, linguistic frameworks that are designed to describe monoglossic communities do not fit into the description of the language situation of linguistically heteroglossic communities such as India. It is, therefore, problematic to apply monistic models to fluid multilingual situations (Agnihotri and Khanna 1997:17). Pattanayak (1981:xiv) rightly points out:

> ... the economics of monolingualism is such that two languages are a nuisance, three languages are uneconomic and many languages are absurd. But where many languages are a fact of life and a condition of existence, restrictions on the choice of languages is a nuisance and one language is not only uneconomic, but absurd.

Mohanty (2006) refers to monoglossic multilingualism as *elite multilingualism* and to heteroglossic multilingualism as *grassroots multilingualism*. He goes to great effort to describe grassroots multilingualism from a multilingual ethos and pluralistic and heteroglossic stance. He argues that multilingualism in India exhibits aspects of maintenance, complementarity among different languages, and multilingualism with multiple and fluid linguistic identities.

7.3.1 Widespread multilingualism at the grassroots level

Whereas multilingualism tends to be observed more in educated or elite communities in predominantly monolingual societies, Mohanty (2006) points out that Indian multilingualism is commonly observed at the grassroots level as well as among the educated class. When there are two or more languages in a person's or community's repertoire, they are likely to fulfill different functions (Agnihotri 1995:5) in different domains. In the everyday life of Indians, this helps individuals and communities at the grassroots levels to communicate among themselves and with members of other language communities. Such widespread grassroots multilingualism makes communication across the country possible because it constitutes "the first incremental step towards concentric layers of societal multilingualism" (Mohanty 2006:263).

7.3.2 Maintenance norm

Even when people are in contact with speakers of other languages, this does not necessarily lead to the loss of a lesser known language. While language shift may result from language contact in predominantly monolingual communities, minority languages in India have been maintained for many generations in spite of being in close contact with majority languages. Mohanty (2006) argues that the multilingual ethos and the noncompeting roles of languages support the idea that maintenance is the norm and shift is a deviation in the Indian subcontinent as he mentions below.

> In the Indian context, bilingualism (multilingualism) is an integrative and adaptive strategy for mother tongue maintenance and for a positive relationship with the wider society, which makes it a necessary step in the direction of multilingualism in India. (Mohanty 1994:5)

In spite of this maintenance norm, Mohanty (2006) observes that minority languages are subject to marginalization and often protect themselves from majority languages by shrinking their use only to the home or the religious domain. According to this observation, grassroots multilinguals are in need of other languages besides their minority language mainly used at home if they want to fully express themselves. Thus the relationship among the languages used by the grassroots multilinguals is complementary.

7.3.3 Complementarity of languages

In this way multiple languages spoken by one person are argued not to compete with one another but rather to function in a mutually complementary way (Mohanty 2006). One language is simply not enough for meeting all the communicative requirements of a speaker's social life; each language for a multilingual person is just part of his or her linguistic repertoire. This is true for the language that grassroots multilinguals first learn at home. All the languages in which a multilingual is competent are necessary for him or her to communicate with because this is how a multilingual is able to express himself or herself fully and why he or she has become multilingual. Languages complement one another not only across different domains but also within the same domain by the strategy of code-switching.

7.3.4 Multiplicity and fluidity of linguistic identities

Language is one marker of identity. Whenever people speak, they not only exchange information with others, but they also constantly convey a sense of who they are, being engaged in the process of identity construction and negotiation (Peirce 1997:410). Linguistic identity is observed more strongly than even religious identity in some cases in South Asia, such as with Bengali in Bangladesh and Tamil in Sri Lanka (Bhatia and Ritchie 2004:796). Furthermore, language speakers in India negotiate and extend their identities beyond a certain language. This is not only because they speak multiple languages but because they also have a flexible perception of languages and language boundaries, which leads to *fluidity of identity*. These multiple and fluid identities again affect the perceptions of their mother tongues and of language boundaries that are *porous* (Agnihotri 2009:270).

7.4 Multilingualism and mother tongue

If grassroots multilinguals freely use different languages and use code-switching as a norm, one may question what their mother tongue(s) is (are) among the several languages they know. Following the criteria developed by Skutnabb-Kangas (2007, 2008) to define mother tongue (MT), the conception of mother tongue is not as simple as the language that one learned first from his or her first caregivers. The language(s) one *learned first* (MT by origin) from their first caregivers is/are not always the same as the one(s) people *know the best* (MT by competence), *use the most* (MT by function), or *identify with* (MT by identification).

The complexity of defining mother tongue is exemplified by an empirical study (Son 2016). Most students from non-Hindi Indian language (NHIL) backgrounds have been analyzed as having several mother tongues depending upon different definition criteria. The majority of students in the Municipal Cooperation of Delhi School were found to have learned more than one language at home beginning from childhood (MT by origin). While all the students themselves from NHIL background in Central School identify with Hindi as their mother tongue (MT by internal identification), their teachers believe that their mother tongues are not Hindi but their respective NHIL (MT by external identification).

So which language is the MT of these children? Can we say that the NHIL they learned first is still their MT, even if most students of this group prefer speaking Hindi to their family members while their family members speak NHIL to them? Which language is the MT of the students who have learned Hindi and NHIL together from their childhood? What is their MT if there is a discrepancy between what the students themselves identify with as their MT and what their teachers perceive as the MT of the students? If we see language as separate and autonomous entities with clear boundaries between languages, it may be impossible to figure out which language is the MT of these children. Conceptions of language as a bounded entity fail to depict the complex linguistic practices of the grassroots multilingual (Creese and Blackledge 2015). Language is argued not to be a static and fixed structure but to be performance, practice, and action whose boundary is fluid (Fasold 1984) and porous. Language is performed and flows.

7.5 Trans-languaging as effective linguistic performance

In a setting like this, language is not a static structure; rather, people trans-language using various linguistic resources. When multilinguals trans-language, they "deploy their full linguistic repertoire without regard for watchful adherence to the socially and politically defined boundaries of *named* languages" (Otheguy, García, and Reid 2015), and in this way they communicate most powerfully and effectively. If they are permitted to use only limited linguistic features of their linguistic repertoire, even if those features are mostly from their so-called MT by origin (the language they learned first), they feel insufficient and limited in communication. Grosjean's (1994) pentathlon metaphor makes sense in this regard. The running speed of a pentathlete will never be as fast as that of a 100-meter runner, but he or she can perform best and accomplish the goal when all the five events are played in combination. Multilinguals are constrained and limited in languaging if they are allowed to use only part of their linguistic repertoire, even if that part mainly consists of their language of origin, or "mother tongue."

Recently when my parents-in-law visited me for a week to celebrate their birthdays, my fluency level in Korean was obviously less in dialoguing with them, who hardly understand English. There were many pauses while I tried to communicate only in Korean. I wish I could have used other linguistic features from other languages that I know in order to fully express my ideas and feelings. My Korean fluency has been shrinking since I left Korea two decades ago. Other linguistic features have been developing in interrelationship with Korean language features and some Korean language features have been used less due to more usage of linguistic features from other languages. When, however, I can use my full linguistic repertoires without any limitation, I can best communicate richly and effectively. So *trans-languaging* is proposed to be the best practice for enabling the most effective communication and learning of new concepts among multilinguals.

7.5.1 Trans-languaging and code-switching

If trans-languaging is seen from the perspective of code-switching (CS), trans-languaging includes the concept of CS but is not limited by it. People also trans-language even when they do not switch codes but use the linguistic repertoire of a single language. In this sense trans-languaging has both "monolingual" and "bilingual" modes (Grosjean 1994, 1998, 1999). To truly differentiate trans-languaging from CS, however, an epistemological shift is necessary as the two are understood from different paradigms. CS presupposes the existence of different languages as discrete and separate entities and looks at language as static and fixed structures, while trans-languaging transcends the socially named language labels and looks not at fixed structures of languages but rather at speakers and their linguistic performance. Trans-languaging starts from the language practices of multilingual people while CS starts from discrete languages (García 2012). Trans-languaging is not the random practice of a speaker's whole linguistic repertoire, but rather adjustment by using different linguistic features according to the contingency of the situation. Trans-languagers know when to voluntarily utilize or suppress which part of their linguistic repertoires depending upon the social context. But they should not be forced by others to limit their use of linguistic features. If I take the definition of CS which includes not only switching between languages but also between different *varieties* of the same language, all the people in this world trans-language whether they are "monolingual" or "multilingual." Trans-languaging, from this perspective, also transcends the difference between monolingual and multilingual. Both monolinguals and multilinguals are trans-languagers.

The excerpt below (from Son 2016) by a grade five teacher in Central School shows that CS as a framework for analysis has limitations in explaining the complexity of the discourse. The teachers were actually trans-languaging without regard for boundaries of named languages, English and Hindi. (See the appendix for the key to transcription conventions and the Hindi transliteration in Roman characters for the following excerpts.)

Excerpt 1.

T: Indefinite. Definite. Indefinite: that is not certain. Definite: that is certain. Ek AdmI jA rahA thA {A man was going}. wah AdmI kEsA thA, kahAN thA, kyA thA {How was that man, Where was that man, Who was that man}? koI matlab nahIN {Nobody knows}. Mere pAs ek pen hE {I have a pen}. I have a pen. I have an apple. Apple kis type kA hE {What kind of apple is this}? himAcal kA apple hE {Is this apple from Himachal Pradesh}? J.K. [Jammu and Kashmir] kA apple hE {Is this apple from Jammu and Kashmir}? Is kA nAm kyA hE {What is the name of this apple}? You can't say because it is some difficult. Simply 'a' and 'an' means one. 'a' and 'an' means one.

In the excerpt above, the general flow of inter-sentential CS can be depicted as follows:

English ("Indefinite. Definite. Indefinite: that is not certain. Definite: that is certain.") → Hindi ("Ek AdmI jA rahA thA. wah AdmI kEsA thA. kahAN thA. kyA thA. koI matlab nahIN. Mere pAs ek pen hE.") → English ("I have a pen. I have an apple.") → Hindi ("Apple kis type kA hE? himAcal kA apple hE? J.K. kA apple hE? Is kA nAm kyA hE?") → English ("You can't say because it is some difficult. Simply 'a' and 'an' means one. 'a' and 'an' means one.")

So one could argue that there are four instances of inter-sentential CS, i.e., English→Hindi, Hindi→English, English→Hindi, Hindi→English. It could also be said that there may be more than four instances of CS as some English words are borrowed and incorporated into Hindi sentences. If those borrowed words are counted as CS, the detailed CS flow including intra-sentential instances appears as follows and the frequency of CS is fourteen times.

> English ("Indefinite. Definite. Indefinite: that is not certain. Definite: that is certain.") → Hindi ("Ek AdmI jA rahA thA. wah AdmI kEsA thA. kahAN thA. kyA thA. koI matlab nahIN. Mere pAs ek") → English ("pen") → Hindi ("hE") → English ("I have a pen. I have an apple. Apple") → Hindi ("kis") → English ("type") → Hindi ("kA hE? himAcal kA") → English ("apple") → Hindi ("hE?") → English ("J.K.") → Hindi ("kA") → English ("apple") → Hindi ("hE? Is kA nAm kyA hE?") → English ("You can't say because it is some difficult. Simply 'a' and 'an' means one. 'a' and 'an' means one.")

Externally, this discourse is seen to have fourteen instances of CS, but from the teacher's internal point of view (García 2017), he freely trans-languages using his full linguistic repertoire without watchful adherence to the boundary of different named languages, Hindi and English.

7.5.2 Trans-languaging with strategies and purposes

In excerpt 2 below (from Son 2016) also supports that the teacher demonstrates trans-languaging as performance of a unitary linguistic repertoire, it further demonstrates that he trans-languages not in a random way, but in a strategic and purposeful way. In this trans-languaging discourse, different cohesive ties are found to be creatively used from different features across the boundary of Hindi and English. The teacher uses various cohesive ties from the two languages as if they are just one language, namely, a whole linguistic repertoire.

> **Excerpt 2.**
> T: file hotI hE {There is file}. THIk hE {All right}? ab sab se pahale edit [hotI hE is omitted here] {Now first of all [there is] edit }. What do you do with edit? edit kyA hotA hE {What is edit}? hE na, edit kA meaning bataIe {Look, tell me the meaning of edit}. What is meaning of edit?
> S: Sir, this option is used to close the open document.

In excerpt 2 it is observed that, as shown in table 1 below, all the academic terms, whether occurring as an English term or a Hindi phrase, are situated in the topic position. Thus, such terms as "file," "edit," "edit," and "edit kA meaning" all occur initially, while comments on these topics follow, and are expressed in Hindi ("hotI hE {is}," "[hotI hE {there is]}," "kyA hotA hE {what is}?," and "bataIe {tell me}"). As the academic terms are located in the topic position, they may receive more attention from the students; while they are elaborated in Hindi in the comment position so that the children can understand something in their stronger language, Hindi, about the topic expressed in English. And "kyA {what}" receives attention by being located in focus position within the comment, which makes students become more curious about what edit is all about. Thus topic-comment cohesive tie helps develop clear coherence in the children's minds. Therefore, trans-languaging does not mean that multilinguals mix their languages without order, but rather they trans-language in a sensible and reasoned way. Linguistic performance in this instance is based on a unitary repertoire as cohesive ties are made across the boundaries of Hindi and English.

Table 1. Topic-comment cohesive tie

Topic	Focus	Comment
file	**hotI hE**	
edit	**[hotI hE]**	
edit	**kyA hotA hE?**	
edit kA meaning	**batAie**	

7.5.3 Trans-languaging as a spinning top

Trans-languaging is like a striped multicolored spinning top when it is in motion, as in figure 1(b). The top is meant for spinning, so it is best appreciated when it spins. When it spins, it shows a mixture of the different colors that are on it; we cannot figure out which colors are combined to show the mixture. But we don't really need to know which colors are combined, because we enjoy the beauty of the mixture of different colors while it is spinning. We call it "alive" when the top spins. Likewise, multilinguals are best appreciated when they freely trans-language, using their whole linguistic repertoire across the boundaries of different named languages. However, we tend to look at the top when it is static, because we want to find out what kind of different colors are actually on it, as shown in figure 1(a). We want to know which languages are used when and we feel uncomfortable when trans-languagers mix different languages. But we need to feel uncomfortable in order for the multilinguals to feel comfortable while trans-languaging—we call it "dead" when the top does not move.

Figure 1. A spinning top: (a) At rest. (b) In motion.

7.6 Trans-languaging and complex and fluid identity

As the trans-languaging paradigm sees language not as a static and fixed structure or entity but as fluid and dynamic linguistic performance, trans-languagers are also argued to have fluid, complex, and dynamic identities. Identity needs to be understood not in terms of plurality but rather in terms of complexity and fluidity. While static aspects of identity such as gender, class, ethnicity, and so on are not denied—neither should fluid aspects of identity be ignored. The identity of trans-languagers is constructed, performed, and negotiated. Trans-languagers use their *linguistic repertoires*, employing or suppressing different features of their named languages in accordance with the different linguistic repertoires of their interlocutors. The same dynamic is argued to hold for identity. A speaker's *identity repertoire* (Creese and Blackledge 2015) is utilized in the complex and dynamic processes of identity negotiation in adapting to the contingencies of his or her social life. Communicative resources are used in constructing this identity repertoire, and the linguistic repertoires of trans-languagers are an important part of these communicative resources. Different features of linguistic repertoires can index various aspects of identity.

Gee's (2000) four ways of viewing identity are used here to study how teachers and students construct, negotiate, and reconstruct their identity as they trans-language using different linguistic features in the classroom. Gee describes the four perspectives on identity as being connected and interrelated like "four strands ... woven together" (Gee 2000:101) and thus difficult to isolate from one another. These four perspectives on identity are identified as the nature, institutional, discourse, and affinity perspectives.

The *nature perspective* (or N-Identity), as the person's essential state, is a description of "who I am." This identity is developed from forces like nature over which people have no control. For example, "A" is my blood type. Having blood type A is a state that I am in, and I have not done anything to make this so. But N-Identity gains its force as an identity through the influence of institutions, discourse, and affinity groups. In the case of the teachers in the Central school, they are male Indians. And the students in that school are either male or female Indians.

The second perspective on identity is the *institutional perspective* (or I-Identity). This identity is given or imposed by an institution or an authority, not by nature. Those male adult Indians are the *teachers* whose position is given by an authority (in this case, the board of Central School). And the boys and girls are *students* in that school.

Gee's third perspective is the *discursive identity* (or D-Identity). The source of this power is neither nature nor an institution, but stems from the discourse or dialogue of "rational" individuals. What Gee means by "rational" here is that others use reasons to identify someone as having a particular characteristic, rather than being forced to do so by rules, tradition, or institutional authority. One can understand a D-Identity as either an ascription or an achievement. An individual can intentionally seek to have others recognize him or her in a certain way (*achieved* D-Identity). On the other hand, a group of students may be recognized in some US schools as English language learners (ELLs) because of their N-Identity of Hispanic origin (*ascribed* D-Identity) even if there are various degrees or different levels of English proficiency among the ascribed ELLs, some of whom were born in the US and function in English as well as any other mother-tongue English speaking students.

The final perspective on identity is the *affinity perspective* (or A-Identity). People may actively choose to join an affinity group where they can share similar likes and dislikes and participate in activities that are characteristic of that group. Gee mentions that "for members of an affinity group, their allegiance is primarily to a set of common endeavors or practices and secondarily to other people in terms of shared culture or traits" (Gee 2000:105).

Now let us examine with this framework of identity, an excerpt from the Central school where the teacher and the students negotiate their identity.

Excerpt 3.

T: Have you seen this shape before? ham ne dekhe yah (teyas) {Have we seen this}? How many sides does it have? ismeN kitne sides hEN {How

many sides are in this}? ismeN to pANc, che sides hEN {There are five, six sides in this}. kyA, geometrical shape kyA hE {Which geometrical shape is this}? right circle hotA hE {There is a right circle}. gol hotE hEN {There are circles}. circle hotE hEN {There are circles}. car TUTeN hote hEN {There are four pieces}. [T talks to a S.] kyA karte hEN {What are you doing}? jyAdA bolne par piTAI karenge {If you talk a lot, I will spank on you}. [T talks back to the class] cAr koNe hEN to kyA bolenge {If there are four corners, what will they call it}? If you are having four corners, what will be the name of the shape?
S1: Sir, cArkON {four corners}?
T: **In English!**
S1: Sir, square?
T: No.
S2: And rectangle?
T: No.
S3: Sir, square?
T: Square is one of them. But the name is different. In Hindi cAturbut {Quadrangle}.

Both the teacher and the students have the same *N-Identity* as they were born as citizens of India who mostly trans-language across their linguistic repertoire. However, this N-Identity of both the teacher and the students are negotiated with *A-Identity* as all of them voluntarily chose this Central school for the teacher to teach major subjects such as Math in English and for the students to learn English. Their N-Identity as trans-languaging Indians is further negotiated by their respective *I-Identities*. The teacher with authority expects his students to improve their English by telling them to speak English and the students are expected to listen to their teacher's instruction to use English. At the same time, the teacher shows *achieved D-Identity* as a teacher who can fully use English and his students have *ascribed D-Identity* as students who need to learn their English. Interestingly, this process of identity negotiation is neither unidirectional (i.e., from N-Identity to others) nor sequential (i.e., successively one after another). The negotiation process is, rather, multidirectional and simultaneous. While the teacher instructs his students to use only English with his Institutional, Affinity, and Discursive identity, he himself trans-languages with his Nature identity both before and after giving the instruction. The students also negotiate their identity from all four perspectives as they interact with the teacher. Even if they hear from their teacher that they are not supposed to answer in Hindi, and so correct their performance from Hindi to English, they have heard and soon hear again their teacher speak in both languages. There is always a tension among the different perspectives of identity. This example shows that identity is not static or fixed but rather dynamic, complex, and fluid as people are always in the process of construction, negotiation, and reconstruction of identity.

7.7 Implications of trans-languaging in education

If students trans-language outside of the classroom as part of normal practice, strategies in the classroom should take advantage of this trans-languaging performance as a resource. Limiting language to one form or the other, and identities to one or the other fails to take into proper account the fluid language practices and fluid identities of multilingual students. Successful education programs will thus build off of what the learner already knows and is familiar with rather than restricting students to only a part of their linguistic repertoire.

If trans-languaging is not allowed in the classroom for grassroots multilingual students, it is like teaching in and assessing less than half of their linguistic repertoire, while students from dominant language backgrounds are learning and being assessed using most of their linguistic repertoire, as more often than not classroom transactions use most features of their linguistic repertoire (García, Ibarra Johnson, and Seltzer 2017; Otheguy, García, and Reid 2015). So allowing trans-languaging across a student's full linguistic repertoire is a matter of social justice and helps to make democratic classrooms, creating a more equal playing field.

While meeting the school standards is still a focus which usually requires linguistic proficiency in separate languages, it is crucial to allow the students to maximally use their whole linguistic repertoire during the process as needed. Trans-languaging in education does not mean randomly mixing languages. Trans-languaging in instruction means purposeful and strategic design of classroom space, lesson plans, and pedagogical methods where the full linguistic repertoires of students are welcomed (García, Ibarra Johnson, and Seltzer 2017). This kind of instructional design aligns with students' natural trans-languaging practices (García and Seltzer 2016) and puts students' general linguistic performance and language-specific performance at the center.

Trans-languaging exemplifies the Gutiérrez (2007) metaphor of windows and mirrors. Trans-languaging first *mirrors* what students are familiar with in terms of their linguistic performance, reflecting their existing knowledge of the world. Only then can trans-languaging open up *windows* for new knowledge of language and academic content, as are required by the school curriculum.

7.8 Conclusion

Trans-languagers should be looked at from a trans-languager's internal point of view; if we truly want to understand who trans-languagers are and how they trans-language and why, the *emic* point of view among trans-languagers is necessary. For this reason, I began this article with the introduction of two different ways of becoming multilingual in order to draw the reader's attention to the kind of multilingualism with which they are unfamiliar. I described the characteristics of grassroots multilingualism which have been pointed out by several Indian linguists (e.g., Mohanty, Agnihotri, and others), who themselves grew up as grassroots multilinguals and still live in a multilingual society. Subsequently, the traditional concept of mother tongue (MT) was argued to be insufficient to properly depict the linguistic performance of grassroots multilinguals. Students from the Municipal Cooperation of Delhi School show different interpretation as to what their MT is, depending on different criteria, namely, MT by origin, by function, by competence, or by identity. The complex nature of MT cannot be clearly explained with the understanding of language as a static, separate, and fixed entity. We must work from a different paradigm. This helps us to see how language flows and multilinguals trans-language.

Multilinguals perform best when their whole linguistic repertoire can be freely used. In other words, if they are constrained to use only part of their linguistic features, even if those features originate from their MT by origin, they cannot fully express themselves. They should not be forced by others to suppress a significant part of their language repertoire, but should voluntarily do so according to the contingencies of their social life. Three examples of classroom interaction were introduced to show how trans-languagers themselves communicate without watchful adherence to the boundary between named languages such as Hindi and English. As speakers trans-language across the fuzzy boundaries of languages, their identity is not static or fixed either. Trans-languagers continuously negotiate their identity from their identity repertoire. Gee's four different perspectives on identity were used to argue that a trans-languaging discourse between a teacher and a group of students is a space where both the teacher and the students construct, negotiate, and reconstruct their identities. Lastly, it was argued that trans-languaging practices of students should be used in classrooms in a strategic and purposeful way, both in instruction and assessment, so that students can perform better in meeting curriculum requirements both in terms of language-specific performance and acquisition of academic content knowledge. Trans-languaging not only enhances the educational performance of trans-languagers but it also creates greater equality among students.

Appendix: Transcription Conventions

Underlining	utterances in Hindi
[ ]	contextual information
( )	unintelligible items
(??)	items in doubt
..	short pause
...	longer pause
UPPERCASE	accentuation
(1)	1-second pause
(2)	2-second pause
=	speaking turn latched to a preceding one
::, :::, ::::	lengthening of sounds
/ /	simultaneous utterances
{ }	translation of Hindi into English
T	teacher
S	a student
Ss	students

Hindi Transliteration Conventions

Retroflex sounds are transliterated as capitals:
For example, TH for ठ, T for ट, D for ड, DH for ढ,
D for ड, N for ण, R for ड़, RH for ढ़

Big vowels (बड़ी मात्रा) are transliterated as capitals:
A for आ, E for ऐ, I for ई, O for औ, U for ऊ

Nasalization is transliterated by N:
mEN for मैं, meN for में, hEN for हैं

References

Agnihotri, Rama Kant. 1995. Multilingualism as a classroom resource. In Kathleen Heugh, Amanda Siegrühn, and Peter Plüddemann (eds.), *Multilingual education for South Africa*, 3–7. Johannesburg: Heinemann.

Agnihotri, Rama Kant. 2007. Identity and multilinguality: The case in India. In Amy B. M. Tsui and James W. Tollefson (eds.), *Language policy, culture, and identity in Asian contexts*, 185–204. Mahwah, NJ: Lawrence Erlbaum.

Agnihotri, Rama Kant. 2009. Multilinguality and a new world order. In Ajit K. Mohanty, Minati Panda, Robert Phillipson, and Tove Skutnabb-Kangas (eds.), *Multilingual education for social justice: Globalising the local*, 268–277. New Delhi: Orient Blackswan.

Agnihotri, Rama Kant, and Amrit Lal Khanna. 1997. *Problematizing English in India*. Research in Applied Linguistics Series 3. New Delhi: Sage Publication.

Bhatia, Tej K., and William C. Ritchie. 2004. Bilingualism in South Asia. In Tej K. Bhatia and William C. Ritchie (eds.), *The handbook of bilingualism*, 780–807. Malden, MA: Blackwell.

Creese, Angela, and Adrian Blackledge. 2015. Trans-languaging and identity in educational settings. *Annual Review of Applied Linguistics* 35:20–35.

Del Valle, José. 2000. Monoglossic policies for a heteroglossic culture: Misinterpreted multilingualism in modern Galicia. *Language and Communication* 20:105–132.

Fasold, Ralph W. 1984. *The sociolinguistics of society*. Language in Society 5. Oxford: Blackwell.

García, Ofelia. 2012. Theorizing trans-languaging for educators. In Christina Celic and Kate Seltzer, *Trans-languaging: A CUNY-NYSIEB guide for educators*. New York: The Graduate Center, The City University of New York. cuny-nysieb.org/.

García, Ofelia. 2017. Talk of Ofelia García on "Trans-languaging" during the Multilingualism and Diversity Lectures, June 2017. Stiftung Universität Hildesheim. youtube.com/watch?v=5l1CcrRrck0/.

García, Ofelia, and Kate Seltzer. 2016. The trans-languaging current in language education. In Bjorn Kindenberg (ed.), *Flerspråkighet som resurs* [Multilingualism as a resource], 19–30. Stockholm: Liber.

García, Ofelia, Susana Ibarra Johnson, and Kate Seltzer. 2017. *The trans-languaging classroom: Leveraging student bilingualism for learning*. Philadelphia: Caslon.

Gee, James Paul. 2000. Identity as an analytic lens for research and education. *Review of Research in Education* 25:99–125.

Grosjean, François. 1994. Individual bilingualism. In R. E. Asher (ed.), *The encyclopedia of language and linguistics*. Oxford: Pergamon.

Grosjean, François. 1998. Transfer and language mode. *Bilingualism: Language and cognition* 1(3):175–176.

Grosjean, François. 1999. Individual bilingualism. In Bernard Spolsky (ed.), *Concise encyclopedia of educational linguistics*. Oxford: Pergamon.

Gutiérrez, Rochelle. 2007. Context matters: Equity, success, and the future of mathematics education. In Teruni de Silva Lamberg and Lynda R. Wiest (eds.), *Proceedings of the 29th Annual Meeting of the North American Chapter of the International Group for the Psychology of Mathematics Education*, 1–18. Reno: University of Nevada.

Mohanty, Ajit K. 1994. *Bilingualism in a multilingual society: Psycho-social and pedagogical implications*. Mysore: Central Institute of Indian Languages.

Mohanty, Ajit K. 2006. Multilingualism of the unequals and predicaments of education in India: Mother tongue or other tongue? In Ofelia García, Tove Skutnabb-Kangas, and María Torres-Guzmán (eds.) 2009, *Imagining multilingual schools: Languages in education and glocalization*, 262–283. Linguistic Diversity and Language Rights 2. Clevedon, UK: Multilingual Matters.

Mohanty, Ajit K., Minati Panda, Robert Phillipson, and Tove Skutnabb-Kangas (eds.) *Multilingual education for social justice: Globalising the local*. New Delhi: Orient Blackswan.

Otheguy, Ricardo, Ofelia García, and Wallis Reid. 2015. Clarifying trans-languaging and deconstructing named languages: A perspective from linguistics. *Applied Linguistics Review* 6(3):281–307.

Pattanayak, Debi Prasanna. 1981. *Multilingualism and mother tongue education*. Delhi: Oxford University Press.

Peirce, Bonny Norton. 1997. Language, identity, and the ownership of English. *TESOL Quarterly* 31(3):409–429.

Peirce, Bonny Norton. 2010. Language and identity. In Nancy Hornberger and Sandra Lee McKay (eds.), *Sociolinguistics and Language Education*, 349–369. Clevedon, UK: Multilingual Matters.

Skutnabb-Kangas, Tove. 2007. *Bilingualism or not: The education of minorities*. New Delhi: Orient Black Swan.

Skutnabb-Kangas, Tove. 2008. *Linguistic genocide in education or worldwide diversity and human rights?* New Delhi: Orient Longman.

Son, Sangsok. 2016. *Negotiating classroom linguistic diversity: A study of teaching-learning strategies in multilingual classrooms in Delhi*. PhD dissertation. Zakir Husain Centre for Educational Studies. Jawaharlal Nehru University, New Delhi, India.

8
Identity and Diaspora: Making Personal Identity Claims through Relational Networks

Janet McLarren and Mary McLendon

Abstract. Traditional concepts of immigration and migration are insufficient in explaining behaviors and identities of diaspora populations in today's globalized world. Members of diaspora communities make ethnic and language identity claims through relational networks as they interact with multiple communities in different geographical locations. These claims are made by personal agency of individuals through interactions with others who make the same claims. The concept of transnationalism (Glick-Schiller et al. 1992), living in social spaces in multiple countries regardless of citizenship status, better captures diaspora self-identity, where members maintain connections of language and identity to their homeland communities while learning new languages and forming additional loyalties in the new host locations. Multiple language use reflects the plurality of communities in their lives. Language use is not the driving force in identity, rather identity choices are based on desires for recognition of belonging to a group. Taking seriously the identity claims of diaspora individuals means recognizing them as influential voices of the ethnic group.

8.1 Introduction

Ethnic groups are traditionally associated with language and territory. Yet in the globalized world of today, diaspora populations make ethnic identity claims through relational networks (Gilroy 1994) as they interact with multiple communities in numerous geographical locations. In this paper we examine how migrants make and maintain multiple identity claims in their lives. We argue that identity claims have more to do with individual choices of maintaining relational networks than with geographic or language origin.

Individuals, using personal agency, make identity claims through interactions with others who make the same claims. Agency can include choosing not to identify—as much as choosing to identify—with a given group. Identity is assigned by the groups that individuals associate with, and also chosen by the individuals themselves. People choose which groups they want to be part of in order to further their personal life goals and express this identity through practices recognized by others. They create and maintain relationships with certain individuals, wear certain clothes, speak certain languages, all as a means of being considered part of a group.

Mr. K told us that his father died recently in Tanzania.[1] Mr. K was born and brought up in Tanzania but had just begun a year-long assignment in the United States of America (US) with his American-born wife. He traveled back to Tanzania to attend his father's funeral and to visit his family there. When he presented his US passport on arrival in Tanzania, the immigration official asked why he had a US passport and not a Tanzanian one since his name and speech were Tanzanian. The official had assigned a Tanzanian identity to Mr K in spite of his US passport. It was only when Mr. K explained that his father had died, and he was visiting his family that the official allowed him to enter the country. Although Mr. K normally lives in Tanzania with his wife and daughter, they come to the US for year-long periods. He applied for American citizenship and received a US passport to facilitate travel with his family who all carry US passports. He now considers himself an American, too.

Mr. K makes multiple identity claims. He told us he is Sukuma [suk], though his family lives in Musoma, a city in the north outside the Sukuma homeland. The majority of the Sukuma migrated to the south within Tanzania. He is also currently part of the African diaspora in the United States. Gaining American citizenship and using a US passport is one expression of his identity claim as an American. As all of us, he has additional identities, such as father, husband, brother, etc. He demonstrates his various identities through different sets of practices applied according to the situation or group in which he identifies. He maintains relationships with people in all these groups.

Mr. K chose to seek and receive a US passport to make international travel with his wife and daughter easier. In doing so, he had to give up his Tanzanian passport, since Tanzanian law does not allow dual citizenship. He states this has been hard for him. He still claims identity with the Sukuma ethnic group as well as his Tanzanian heritage. In addition, he has taken on the identity of an American. These identities are expressed and reinforced through numerous actions on his part, including speech acts. He carries and uses a US passport to cross international borders. It is only a part of his American identity. He speaks in English for his work in the US, but speaks Kisukuma with his family of origin, both when physically present with them and through phone and internet connections.

Claiming multiple identities is a dynamic process where a person is not necessarily at ease with all the identities claimed. However making identity claims is an everyday function of relating to others and living out one's life.

8.2   Defining identity and diaspora

Identity is often defined differently depending on the discipline. Nation-states use various categories like race, gender, or location of residence. The *Ethnologue* uses linguistic and geographic parameters for identifying groups of people (Simons and Fennig 2018). The movements of people due to globalization bring a new dimension to identity formation, especially to identities of those who migrate to another location to live.

---

[1] The authors have chosen to use pseudonyms uniformly for all the examples from our data. The data was gathered primarily by interviews, with some participant observation.

In this paper we take an anthropological and social perspective, where identity is not a fixed aspect of an individual. "Rather, it is ... socially constituted, a reflexive, dynamic product of the social, historical and political contexts of an individual's lived experiences" (Hall 2013:31). Individuals construct their identities within a sociohistorical environment that influences the kinds of identities available to them—the social and cultural groups they are assigned to by others and those they purposefully participate in during their lives. Examples of groups include gender, ethnic origin, religion, and social class. These groups share practices, role expectations, and values in common with other members of the group and claim a common identity (Sökefeld 2001:532). Individuals make identity claims both orally and through their actions, by participating in the activities of the group in which they claim identity. They act out varying degrees of loyalty by how they follow the norms already established for the roles they exercise within the group.

The concept of diaspora also has more than one meaning, having changed with the postmodern turn in scholarly thinking. A traditional understanding of diaspora took the Jewish experience as the standard paradigm, emphasizing the loss of territory and isolation from the host culture (Hickman 2005). Yet the fact of moving from one location to another, though it involves some uprooting, need not imply isolation in the host community and rupture with the previous life. Some usages today expand the concept beyond usefulness, applying it to anyone who has moved residences even within the same city (Brubaker 2005). At a minimum, the term diaspora applies to anyone who lives outside their homeland. More useful definitions agree on certain characteristics including social relationships developed due to displacement, orientation to the homeland, and marking social boundaries beyond the locations they currently inhabit through continuing to claim identity with the ethnic group of the homeland (Brubaker 2005, Hickman 2005, Vertovek 1997). We define diaspora as groups of people who live outside the homeland, either in another part of the same nation-state or outside of it, who maintain loyalty to and make identity claims with those who still live in the homeland.

Identity construction is an ongoing process of forming and reforming multiple identities in response to the social and cultural situations people live in. Diasporas form when migrants from a given location act together to maintain their ethnic or identity boundaries relative to the homeland. The word diaspora itself invokes relational networks, relating to trans-cultural processes (Gilroy 2000:123). Ortiz (2015:9) defines ethnicity as a verb, because it is not static, rather "an ongoing movement of competing constructions of social identity." The competition doesn't mean constructions are always at odds, rather that they may not always be in harmony and some are more salient in a given situation. As migrants move between cultural contexts, they have a greater variety of identity options to choose from. Some migrants hold tightly to the identities they brought with them when they moved. Others find the new options so compelling that they leave behind any identities they previously held. Yet others choose to use both sets of identities and live them out in their multiple social environments.

8.3 Language use by transnationals and translocals

Ethnic groups are typically associated with language. Migrants may learn new languages to live more comfortably in the host country and at the same time maintain the language(s) of their homelands across distances through regular and frequent contact with people in the homeland and among other migrants from that homeland.

Travel and communication technology of today allow people living long distances apart to talk with and visit their families and friends all over the world. Many migrants we talked with told us they spoke almost daily with family who remained in the country they left, with visits back and forth between the two locations by both those who left and those who stayed. Many migrants today communicate frequently with the homeland groups they are part of and maintain pride in and identity with them. Glick-Schiller and her colleagues (1992) call this transnationalism, where activity of migrants in the affairs of groups in both the homeland and the host location show they identify with and are loyal to groups across national boundaries. But not all migrants express transnational behaviors.

Although language choice is a significant part of identity (Rosa and Trivedi 2017:332) and affects who is included in the relational networks, it is not the deciding factor in identity claims made by transnationals. Even when migrants lose language competence in the languages of the homeland, they may still make identity claims of belonging to the ethnic group. North African migrant women in southern France claimed both French and Arab or Berber identities whether or not they spoke or read these languages well (McLarren 2004). One young woman studied Arabic at the University of Marseille. Having grown up in France with parents who emigrated from Algeria, she said,

> "I want to be reconciled with the Arab world because I am an Arab. I carry it in my facial feathers, the color of my skin, my name, all of me. Others say it, too, so I do it to be comfortable within myself. And I am French, too." (Miss P)

These women took pride in this heritage and participated extensively in relational networks with others who shared this heritage.

Various interconnected factors influence language choice, such as which languages are spoken in the home, views about accents of the majority language held by the general public, and choices about identity formation (Hatoss et al. 2011). Each individual makes their own choice. Some people maintain their original language and use it in their homes. Several of the older ethnic women we met at churches spoke poor or no English. Some younger people spoke little or none of their parents' language, but other young people translated for their parents. Language maintenance is not equivalent to ethnic maintenance. One couple told us they spoke English at home with their children, yet the wife wore the traditional *shalwar kameez* at church. There seems to be no universal pattern of language use and choice among migrants. They make choices based on their situations and their own preferences.

8.4 Territory and transnationals and translocals

Loyalty to and identity with an ethnic group is not contingent on geography. Migration away from the traditional location is not always a one-way displacement with the intention of focusing on the new host location, in spite of political discourse about adaptation and integration (McLarren 2004; Lilomaiava-Doktor 2009). More and more, migrants are becoming transnationals or translocals,[2] active in the life of both the new location and their homeland (Pande 2017; Hatoss et al. 2011). Some

---

[2] A "transnational" is someone who acts transnationally. Glick-Schiller uses the term in her seminal paper of 1992. A "translocal" refers to someone who is displaced from their traditional territory but remains within national boundaries. See Greiner 2010.

literally live in both places. This is more than simply having homes in two locations. They "do not live between two places ... rather they remain firmly rooted in their identification with their place of origin" (Lilomaiava-Doktor 2009:7), even as they create new identities for themselves in the new location, just as Mr. K created his American identity in part by becoming an American citizen. Ukrainians in Canada lobbied the Canadian government for aid and intervention during the recent conflict between the Ukraine and Russia. Their loyalty to the Ukraine did not require a permanent return to the homeland, rather they took action for their homeland in the host land, extending their relational networks there. Some also went to the Ukraine to support and join the soldiers (MacKinnon 2015). Migrants develop relationships and networks in the new locations, while maintaining and strengthening those from the old locations (Hatoss 2003; Lee 2009). They build networks that join the two social environments, taking action and making decisions which span borders (Glick-Schiller et al. 1992).

Translocals are similar to transnationals but live within the same country as their homeland. Greiner (2010) describes the Kunene people of Namibia who live one period of their lives in the city, then return to the village to care for the farms when they are older. This happens within the same country, but the dual identity and loyalty acted out parallels transnationalism. Transnationals and translocals feel an affinity for and have emotional bonds with their place of origin (Glick-Schiller 2011; Nnaemeka 2007) while at the same time developing a love for the new location (Hatoss 2003).

Many ethnic groups have no national territory they call their own, yet they hold a strong identity as a group and are recognized as such by outsiders. The traditional territory they claim may cross boundaries of today's nations. The Hmong originated in China but moved south to Vietnam and Laos to avoid persecution. They also spread to Thailand before moving all over the world as displaced refugees from the war in Indochina in the mid-1900s (Lee 2007, 2009). The act of being called Hmong refugees by the United Nations means they are considered an ethnic group by the recognized nations of the world, regardless of their location. This also is true for the Kurds and Berbers whose traditional homelands include sections of multiple nation-states of today. The fact that the homeland areas cross national boundaries promotes different loyalties and ways of being a minority group. Despite these differences, activities of transnationals of these ethnic groups contribute significantly to a sense of united identity across national boundaries. The Kurdish diaspora has been active politically for the creation of a Kurdish nation since 1946. The Berber diaspora has been active in cultural and linguistic research and in making the Berber languages written (Bengio and Maddy-Weitzman 2013). Each of these three groups claims a common ethnic identity even while speaking more than one ethnic language within the group. Geography and language are only part of their identity.

8.5 Relational networks and identity claims within diasporas

People use personal agency to choose which identity or identities to claim, depending on who else is involved in the communication. When considering identity as an ongoing process of choosing how to relate to people around us as suggested earlier, we can move beyond the binary perspective of "us-them" (Glick-Schiller 2012). In every society, people use socially predefined identity categories such as race, origin, ethnicity, and language as the means to decide who is one of their group. This binary thinking is present in both the majority and minority groups, in both the host and migrant populations. However, these categories do not give a full picture of a person's identity.

People are connected to each other through shared knowledge, values, goals, and language, including specialized vocabulary. They claim to be part of a group, to identify with it by using the language and following the values, and working for the goals of the group regardless of their physical location (Lilomaiava-Doktor 2009). The group affirms their identity claim by accepting them, or it can also reject them and their claim.

People build relational networks within the groups in which they claim identity. Because they claim multiple identities, they build and maintain multiple networks. Some of these networks overlap, just as the groups they claim to be part of often overlap, but each one has unique values and expectations of its members. Mr. E is an engineer with the US space program in Florida. Originally from the Democratic Republic of the Congo (DRC), he was concerned that many of his friends and relatives had no means of income. Using networks he developed as a scientist in the US, he invited fellow professionals to help resource microloans to people from his homeland in DRC to buy livestock and seeds for farming. He served as the broker between those giving and receiving the loans. These two networks overlap in the realm of finance. Networks are built and maintained as a means of affirming unity and belonging with the group (Levitt 2004). Thus, transnationals experience "dual or multiple belongingness" (Pande 2017:34) not limited to a single group. The very act of participating in a relational network is itself an identity claim of belonging to that group.

By definition transnationals claim identity with homeland nationality and ethnic groups, as well as with the host nation and society. They express their loyalty to the homeland through various means: financial remittances, regular communication and visits, political action, and economic and spiritual aid (Addis 2012:967). The authors interviewed several individuals and groups in Charlotte, North Carolina, USA, and found all these types of involvement of migrants with their homeland communities. Mrs. S from Romania spoke with her parents and family there about once a day and took her daughter on a yearly visit to Romania. She also hosted her parents for a few months each year in her home in Charlotte. She also participated in the American church where she was a member, attending multiple meetings each week and joining others from the church in helping meet the needs of local homeless people.

One church, made up mostly of Malayalam migrants from India, also includes both non-Indian Americans and non-Malayalam Indian migrants. They told us some members joined a month-long mission in northern India sponsored by an English-speaking American church in Charlotte. The Malayalam diaspora has strong networks both with American churches in Charlotte and national churches in India.

A Korean church we visited went on a mission weekend joined by a Korean church in Washington, DC. Their identities as Romanian, Malayalam, and Korean are affirmed through the relational networks they maintain. These networks are not limited to the homeland and include transnationals living in other locations outside the homeland. The pastor of the Korean church is part of a mission network of churches among the Korean diaspora all over the world. Transnational networks can also involve social media. A quick internet search shows that many ethnic groups have websites and blogs, often with several different language options for users. They recognize and cater to the loyalty felt by migrants who don't speak the ethnic language but still want to identify with the group. Transnationals maintain relational networks with multiple communities located in multiple geographic locations.

8.6 Living as transnationals and translocals

Everyone has chosen identities for themselves and has refused identities assigned to them by others. Each identity involves a set of norms they conform to or seek to challenge. Living in social groups involves building relationships with others within the groups and using these relational networks to affirm the identity claims. Others also seek to assert identity claims on individuals which may not be accepted by the individual. For example, Miss R in France, interviewed by one author, had parents who were Algerians. She was born in France and considered herself French, not Algerian. She had never been to Algeria and had no known relatives there. Yet she was often treated with suspicion by European background French people, who assigned an Algerian identity to her despite her rejection of this identity claim.

Transnationals have created other options besides integration or assimilation into the host community, where this would mean abandoning the homeland country and community. Transnationals maintain relational networks with the home community as well as forming new networks among the host community. They engage economically and politically in the social life of both communities. Mr. S from the DRC has lived for over twenty-five years in the US, raising his children there. Over these years he has returned frequently to the DRC to work and has developed his relationship networks in both countries. He is fluent in several languages and is assisting in the development of his homeland language as one transnational activity. Claiming identity in the host country doesn't preclude rejecting one's identity with the homeland. Maintaining relational networks and loyalty to the homeland communities results in activity on their behalf.

Several nation states have recognized the value diaspora populations bring. They link two countries by taking identities from both. Canada and Australia celebrate the diversity and multiculturalism that diaspora populations bring. These countries encourage migrants to maintain their previous identities. They allow differences in dress such as Muslim women wearing a veil (McLarren 2004:86). Newland and Tanaka (2010) document the many ways transnationals have interacted with homeland communities in different spheres of social life: economic, educational, and networking. Many governments encourage migrants living outside the nation-state to vote in their homeland elections and to contribute more than money to the nation. Facebook has a page entitled "European Transnationals Initiative"[3] which encourages Europeans living in the United Kingdom to vote in their homeland elections. Transnationals participate as citizens in both nation-states where they claim identity.

Transnationals also contribute to multinational organizations or organizations with a multicultural workforce. Having relationships in very different kinds of groups strengthens the ability of transnationals to understand multiple points of view and enables them to bridge cultural gaps. Transnationals are bicultural, learning and valuing the social life of two cultures. They have a learned sensitivity to cultural contexts, important even for communicating nonculturally dependent knowledge and skills (Brannen 2004). Kane and Levina (2016) found that bicultural people who maintained identity with the homeland, who we are calling transnationals, functioned better as managers in multinational corporations. Their dual loyalty to home and host cultures benefits both home country staff and the company or

---

[3] See facebook.com/eurotransnationals/.

organization through their promotion of training in needed skills and engagement of significant stakeholders.

Transnationals also impact the broader societies in which they participate. They mediate knowledge and culture of their home communities to the rest of the world, enriching the cultural mix of the host lands. Ethnic music and foods find a new home. In England today, curry, brought by South Asians, is as ubiquitous as fish and chips. With the increase in number of people traveling, airline tickets to what used to be exotic places are cheaper, so more people travel to them. Increased exposure between cultures can bring greater good in the form of greater understanding between cultures as well as new challenges for both hosts and homelands. In our globalized world, ideas, goods, and people circulate and penetrate to unexpected places with sometimes unwelcome results. With the global migration crisis and increase in worldwide travel and communication, human trafficking of multiple kinds has burst on the world scene. Zimmerman and Kiss (2017) state:

> Irregular or illegal migration status can be used to threaten and coerce workers. Poor language skills can prevent migrant workers from understanding and negotiating employment terms and engaging in job training, and, importantly, it can hinder their understanding of local rights and assistance resources.

Migrants can be vulnerable to crime organizations that cross borders, often being deceived into thinking they're being recruited for legal employment to help their families. Isolating people from their communities and families can have dire consequences.

The ethnic group changes because of transnational involvement. We spoke with Mrs. D, a translocal in DRC. She is a member of the national parliament and is involved in empowering her ethnic group in the rural areas through language and economic development. She sold a piece of her property to buy a truck to transport agricultural goods from the rural areas to Kinshasa, the capital city. She is renovating property she has in the rural area to accommodate language development workers while they test the newly developed orthography and written materials of her homeland language. She hasn't lived in the rural region for years, yet has devoted her life to helping the people with whom she identifies. Transnationals and translocals not only make identity claims that are recognized by the homeland group, they also influence what happens in the homeland.

8.7 Conclusion

Not all networks which people participate in are contained within geographic boundaries since those who identify with each other don't always live in the same location. Identities are dynamic, in that they change with new experiences and through personal choice. In today's globalized world it is possible for diaspora populations to maintain their identity claims within the groups they leave behind when they migrate, while developing additional identities with the new people among whom they settle.

Transnationals claim identity in groups both in the homeland and the host location. Language use is not the driving force in identity, rather identity choices have to do with the desire to be recognized as belonging to a group. The concept of ethnicity is not dependent on geography. Transnationals and translocals who live outside the traditional territories and maintain relationships with those who remain in the homeland region often continue to make ethnic identity claims with their homeland group. Taking seriously the identity claims of diaspora individuals means recognizing them as influential voices of the ethnic group. They are tied to the homeland via networks of relationships independent of but related to language and territory.

References

Addis, Adeno. 2012. Imagining the homeland from afar: Community and peoplehood in the age of the diaspora. *Vanderbilt Journal of Transnational Law* 45:963–1041.

Bengio, Ofra, and Bruce Maddy-Weitzman. 2013. Mobilised diasporas: Kurdish and Berber movements in comparative perspective. *Kurdish Studies* 1(1):65–90.

Brannen, Mary Yoko. 2004. When Mickey loses face: Recontextualization, semantic fit, and the semiotics of foreignness. *Academy of Management Review* 29(4): 593–616.

Brubaker, Rogers. 2005. The 'diaspora' diaspora. *Ethnic and Racial Studies* 28(1): 1–19.

Gilroy, Paul. 1994. Diaspora. *Paragraph* 17(3):207–212.

Gilroy, Paul. 2000. *Against race: Imagining political culture beyond the color line.* Cambridge, MA: Belknap Press of Harvard University.

Glick-Schiller, Nina. 2011. Locality, globality, and the popularization of a diasporic consciousness: Learning from the Haitian case. In Regine O. Jackson (ed.), *Geographies of the Haitian diaspora*, xxi–xxix. New York: Routledge.

Glick-Schiller, Nina. 2012. Situating identities: Towards an identities studies without binaries of difference. *Identities: Global Studies in Culture and Power* 19(4):520–532.

Glick-Schiller, Nina, Linda Basch, and Cristina Blanc-Szanton. 1992. Transnationalism: A new analytic framework for understanding migration. *Annals of the New York Academy of Sciences* 645:1–24.

Greiner, Clemens. 2010. Patterns of translocality: Migration, livelihoods and identities in northwest Namibia. *Sociologus* 60(2):131–161.

Hall, Joan Kelly. 2013. *Teaching and researching: Language and culture.* Second edition. Applied Linguistics in Action Series. London: Routledge.

Hatoss, Anikó. 2003. Identity formation, cross-cultural attitudes and language maintenance in the Hungarian diaspora of Queensland. Paper presented at *Cultural Citizenship: Challenges of Globalisation: An Interdisciplinary Conference*, Melbourne, Australia, 5–7 December 2002. University of Southern Queensland ePrint. eprints.usq.edu.au/1158/1/Hatoss_Deakin_paper.pdf.

Hatoss, Anikó, Henriette van Rensburg, and Donna Starks. 2011. Finding one's own linguistic space: Views on English, Afrikaans and identity in a semi-urban Australian context. *Sociolinguistic Studies* 5:257–289.

Hickman, Mary J. 2005. Migration and diaspora. In Joe Cleary and Claire Connolly (eds.), *The Cambridge companion to modern Irish culture*, 118–136. Cambridge: Cambridge University Press.

Kane, Aimée A., and Natalia Levina. 2016. "Am I still one of them?": Bicultural immigrant managers navigating social identity threats when spanning global boundaries. *Journal of Management Studies* 54(4):540–577.

Lee, Gary Yai. 2007. Diaspora and the predicament of origins: Interrogating Hmong postcolonial history and identity. *Hmong Studies Journal* 8:1–19.

Lee, Sangmi. 2009. Searching for the Hmong people's ethnic homeland and multiple dimensions of transnational longing: From the viewpoint of the Hmong in Laos. *Hmong Studies Journal* 10:1–18.

Levitt, Peggy. 2004. Transnational migrants: When "home" means more than one country. *MPI ejournal*, Oct. 1, 2004. Accessed Nov 7, 2017. migrationpolicy.org/article/transnational-migrants-when-home-means-more-one-country/.

Lilomaiava-Doktor, Sa'iliemanu. 2009. Beyond "migration": Samoan population movement (Malaga) and the geography of social space (Va). *The Contemporary Pacific* 21(1):1–32.

MacKinnon, Mark. 2015. Bypassing official channels, Canada's Ukrainian diaspora finances and fights a war against Russia. *The Globe and Mail*, February 26, 2015, updated May 12, 2018. Accessed May 30, 2018. theglobeandmail.com/news/world/ukraine-canadas-unofficial-war/article23208129/.

McLarren, Janet. 2004. Identity and immigration among Maghrebi women in France. MA thesis. California State University at Los Angeles.

Newland, Kathleen, and Hiroyuki Tanaka. 2010. *Mobilizing diaspora entrepreneurship for development*. Washington, DC: Migration Policy Institute.

Nnaemeka, Obioma. 2007. Re-imagining the diaspora: History, responsibility, and commitment in an age of globalization. *Dialectical Anthropology* 31:127–141.

Ortiz, Louis Manuel. 2015. Being Nepali without Nepal: The imaginative process of ethnicity among the Nepali diaspora in Lancaster, PA. MA thesis. Eastern University, St. Davids, PA.

Pande, Amba. 2017. Diaspora: Identities, spaces and practices. In Nandini C. Sen (ed.), *Through the Diasporic Lens*, 27–37. New Delhi: Authors Press.

Rosa, Jonathan, and Sunny Trivedi. 2017. Diaspora and language. In *Routledge Handbook of Migration and Language*, 330–346. New York: Routledge.

Simons, Gary F., and Charles D. Fennig, eds. 2018. *Ethnologue: Languages of the world*. Twenty-first edition. Dallas, TX: SIL International. Accessed April 3, 2018. ethnologue.com/language/suk/.

Sökefeld, Martin. 2001. Reconsidering identity. *Anthropos* 96(2):527–544.

Vertovec, Steven. 1997. Three meanings of "diaspora," exemplified among South Asian religions. *Diaspora* 6(3):277–299.

Zimmerman, Cathy, and Ligia Kiss. 2017. Human trafficking and exploitation: A global health concern. *PLoS Med* 14(11):e1002437. November 22, 2017. Accessed May 23, 2018. https://doi.org/10.1371/journal.pmed.1002437/.

9
Hidden Language, Hidden Identity: Identity Issues of Refugees from Minority Language Groups

Sunny Hong

Abstract. Most people in minority groups around the world are usually powerless while they live in their home countries. When they become refugees, they become even more powerless, as they are forced to move from their homeland to live in foreign places. Along the way, they may suffer the loss of family members and experience the ravages of war or other catastrophes. Victims of social forces that they cannot change, they begin a journey of liminality and vulnerability, facing multiple new languages and cultures. Resettled refugees once again face many challenges to their identity due to social, economic, political, religious, linguistic, and cultural differences. Their identity is stripped from them as they live out of context. Much research has been done on refugee populations. However, most of it is has been done at a country level, failing to distinguish minority language groups and their unique challenges. This paper captures identity issues of minority language refugees by interviewing twenty-five refugees resettled in the area of Dallas and Fort Worth, Texas.

9.1 Introduction

People in minority groups around the world are usually powerless while living in their home countries. When these people become refugees, they are rendered even more powerless as they are forced to move from their homeland to a foreign country. Along the way, they may suffer the loss of family members, experience the ravages of war or ethnic cleansing, or witness many other catastrophes. During the course of these events, their identity—including cultural artifacts, practices, roles, and language—is stripped from them as they are forced to live in a different social context. They are deprived; they are the victims of social forces they cannot change or control; they are liminal and vulnerable; and they encounter unfamiliar languages. Much research has been carried out on refugees. However, most of the existing research is about refugees originating in and fleeing to particular countries, without recognizing the unique challenges of minority groups within those countries.

This paper aims to shed light on issues regarding identity that refugees from minority language groups face. Interviews were conducted with twenty-five people. Eight come from the Zotung Chin in Myanmar, three from the Zomi in Myanmar, three from the Jarai in Vietnam, seven from the Bembe in the Democratic Republic of the Congo, four from the Uduk in Sudan. Each of them were settled in the Dallas-Fort Worth area. Eight out of the twenty-five were women, and seventeen were men. All were born in their homeland; children who were born in a foreign country were not included. All of them were members of a Christian church; the interview participants were contacted through the churches. The interviews were conducted from January to March of 2018. Detailed information about the interview participants can be found in appendix A. The findings of this paper are based on the stories collected from these interviews.

9.2 My personal journey

After graduating from college, I emigrated from Korea to the United States of America (USA). For many years, I kept my Korean identity as I tried to learn English and adjust to the culture in the US. I heard the term "Korean-American" used for Korean immigrants to America, but I felt that the term was only appropriate for Koreans who had been born in America, and so it did not apply to me. Since I did not identify myself as a Korean-American, I did not like being called an Asian-American either. However, when I visited Korea, I realized that I was no longer culturally entirely Korean because of my exposure and adjustments to the US culture. While I do not have a problem with being called by my English name, Sunny, when among English speaking people, I want to be addressed appropriately among Korean-speaking Koreans, usually with a title, representing the Korean side of me. When a Korean-speaking Korean calls me Sunny, I feel that I am not being treated as a Korean. Especially when a younger Korean calls me Sunny, I feel that I am not being shown respect, because the person is omitting an honorific form that would show the respect that age differences require in Korean conversation.

Through a study of culture, I came to accept that my identity had become both Korean and American, and that I was truly a Korean-American, a hyphenated person, who is competent in both cultures in daily functioning (Chen 2014:2). After having accepted that identity, I then moved to the Philippines, where I lived for eight years. The people there accepted my Korean identity without any problem because of my physical traits, but they ignored the American part of my identity because of its invisibility. I had not been bothered by the Korean identification in the US because that was the only additional culture that needed to be explained. But in the Philippines, I realized that I could not be fully understood without the two layers of culture within me being recognized and accepted. After going through identity issues a couple of times and understanding similarities between my culture and Asian culture, I can extend my identity to accept being considered Asian-American as well, but I still feel that Korean-American is the best description of who I am. Fishman and García (2010:42) describe what I have been through when they explain how "the links between ethnic identity and language are socially constructed and change over time ... ethnic identities are formed or reshaped through dynamic processes of linguistic and cultural contact."

In terms of language, Korean [kor] is the language in which I think and express myself most easily. Even after more than three decades of living in the US, I struggle with expressing myself in English from time to time. However, sometimes I find that

I can use English words or phrases to express my thoughts or feelings even better than in Korean. English has become more than just an instrumental language to me. When I write in Korean first and translate into English, I find that what I have written becomes more expressive than if I had written in English first. When I write in English first and translate into Korean, the Korean becomes more logical than if I had written in Korean first. Korean focuses on being expressive and English on being logical; my linguistic identity is based on a combination of the two languages.

Immigration has changed the dynamics in my family relationships. When my family members flew from seven different countries for a family reunion in 2012, there was no common language for communication that everyone could understand. Translation between English and Korean was necessary to communicate among my family members.

As an immigrant, I have had to work through identity issues, but the challenges regarding identity are much greater for refugees. Both immigrants and refugees experience uprootedness, but for refugees, the uprooting is involuntary, urgent without time to plan and prepare, and usually accompanied by suffering.

9.3 Definitions of identity, ethnicity, and refugee

The definitions of identity, ethnicity, and refugee on which this paper is based are provided below.

9.3.1 Identity

Identity helps explain who a person is internally and externally in society. Identity is contextually determined, depending "essentially on circumstances and contrasts that play upon it, modify it, and create or recreate it" (Fishman and García 2010: xxviii). Identity is both individual and group oriented. Identity is an anchor that connects a person with a group. Edwards (2009:19) stated that:

> The essence of identity is similarity: things that are identical are the same, after all, and the word stems from the Latin *idem*. And this most basic sense is exactly what underpins the notion of identity as it applies to personality. It signifies the 'sameness' of an individual 'at all times or in all circumstances', as the dictionary tells us, the fact that a person is oneself and not someone else.

Categories based on similarities become markers of identity: race, language, religion, culture, age, artifacts, kinship, sex, social class, geography, and so on. Those similarities bring a sense of groupness.

Culture influences identity. In an individualistic culture, people find their identity primarily in the person, while in a collectivistic culture, people find their identity in a group. The desire or purpose of the group is more important than that of the individual in a collectivistic culture, and the group protects the members of the group. A member of the group cannot think of himself or herself apart from the group. All of the interviewees in this paper are from collectivistic cultures, and their identities are embedded in the group to which they belong.

9.3.2 Ethnicity

Among the markers of identity listed above, ethnicity encompasses multiple markers that provide a strong sense of solidarity.

> Importantly, ethnicity is only one of the multiple social categories to which someone can belong (Makihara 2010:35); attachments to kinship, race, color, culture, generation, language, socioeconomic class, religion, and country of origin are just some of the complex interconnected dimensions that make up a person's identity. (Hatoss 2013:156)

Personal identity is attached to ethnicity, and group membership to an ethnicity is not by choice but given at birth. Ethnicity is sustained by multiple markers that are constructed by racial, cultural, geographical, linguistic, and religious dimensions.

An ethnic minority group is a subset of a nation's ethnic makeup. It may or may not share the same markers with the ethnic majority group of the nation.

> 'Ethnic' tends to be reserved for groups that are at some level thought of as marked or 'other'. What happens as a result is that the terms 'ethnic' and 'ethnicity' typically only refer to minority groups. In short, groups we describe in terms of 'ethnicity' are very often the 'other'; invoking an oppositional relationship of a 'them' to an 'us'. (Mooney et al. 2011:134)

Because of the automatic connection made between "ethnic" and "minority" by the larger society, the power and status of an ethnic minority people group differ from that of the majority group. If the ethnic minority group has few markers in common with the majority group, and if they are oppressed by the majority group, they are likely to feel distant from the majority group. The participants of this research were already marginalized by the majority people group in their home countries before they became refugees, because of differences in looks, primary and secondary languages, accented speech of the official dominant language, and behaviors. An ethnic minority people group might choose to reinforce their ethnic identity and keep themselves apart, or they may desire to merge with the majority people group in order to obtain power and status. Because there are many interrelated factors, the identity issues of an ethnic minority group are complex. For people in an ethnic minority group who become refugees, identity issues become even more complex.

9.3.3 Refugee

According to the United Nations High Commissioner for Refugees, a refugee is "someone who is unable or unwilling to return to their country of origin owing to a well-founded fear of being persecuted for reasons of race, religion, nationality, membership of a particular social group, or political opinion" (UNHCR 2010:3). People who have experienced persecution and relocation from their home country due to reasons indicated above are categorized as refugees, but people who are displaced due to difficulties such as natural disasters are not.

From the time when refugees are uprooted until finally resettled, there are three stages that they go through which are identified by the place of residence. These places are: homeland, transitional country, and host country. Homeland indicates the place of origin or residence before the refugee is uprooted. Transitional country (or place) refers to any places a refugee stays temporarily after being uprooted until being resettled in the host country. Host country denotes the place where a refugee is finally resettled.

Life as a refugee begins once a person is uprooted from their home and moves to a transitional place, but their legal status as a refugee does not begin until they are considered to be a refugee by the United Nations. For refugees, the transitional stage ends when they are finally resettled in a host country. During the transitional time, some refugees may live in any place they can legally or illegally find to live, whether it is in their home country or, as happens more often, in a neighboring country, or in a refugee camp. One interview participant crossed a border five times, risking his life each time to stay in a neighboring country, because his life was not safe in his home country.

When refugees come to the US, they are classified differently from normal immigrants and receive benefits from the Office of Refugee Resettlement.[1] The average number of years that interview participants for this research had been refugees was 11 years, with a range of 0.75 to 42 years. Asian refugees (5.8 years) took significantly less time than the African refugees (17.6 years) to resettle. Their information can be found in appendix A.

9.4 Experiences impacting identity issues of the refugee

When people become refugees, they lose the customary things, people, and places they identify with and new unfamiliar things are added to their lives. This experience of significant loss and disruption has a major impact on their identity. This section describes some of the losses and new challenges experienced by the refugees who were interviewed.

9.4.1 Loss

Being a refugee means having lost home, job, financial resources, family members, language, culture, identity, status, future, memories, and normal life in the homeland. Some interviewees cannot visit their homeland because it is currently at war. While other immigrants to the US are free to visit their homeland, refugees cannot go back to their homeland until they have been given legal status in their host country. Even with a legal status, they may not be able to enter their home country either because they left it illegally or because they may not have the financial resources to do so. One interviewee shared his painful experience of being unable to visit his homeland when his father died because of his legal status. Refugees' family members in the homeland cannot visit them in the US, due to political or financial issues. Out of the twenty-five refugees interviewed, only two had been able to visit their homeland. The reason one of the two people went back to his homeland was to get married. Due to the inability to return, they lose a sense of connection to their homeland, which diminishes their social and cultural identity. Refugees deal with a sense of failure that comes from their loss and disconnectedness, and that sense of failure also impacts their identity. One Bembe man said, "I miss something, part of me. Uprooting is not easy" (B1).[2]

Because of the loss of family through war and relocation, some refugees congregate as a family even though they are not related by blood. Other families are not able to be located in the same place. One refugee married a woman he met in a transitional country, but his marriage had not been recognized in his home country. Not knowing how long the marriage issue would take, he decided to move to the US alone as a refugee and tried to sponsor his wife. However, because his marriage was

---

[1] See, for instance, *Eligibility for Benefits and Services*, refugeehealthta.org/access-to-care/eligibility-for-benefits-and-services. Accessed May 22, 2018.
[2] This and similar citations are anonymized references to the identity of the interviewee; consult appendix A to discover some basic information about each ot the interviewees.

not considered legal in his home country, he has not been able to bring his wife to the US for the past four years. In the US, he lives with a couple, whom he calls uncle and aunt. Another refugee was physically separated from his wife while fleeing from his country. In the meantime, his wife has remarried in their home country; their marriage was canceled as a result of his becoming a refugee.

When children of refugees lose their parents, they may live and move around with other adults whom they may call their parents. Four out of the twenty-five interviewees moved alone to the US. For refugees, the concept of family may not be based on traditional blood relations. Most interviewees have family members in several different countries: some live in the homeland, some are in a refugee camp in a transitional country, and some may have resettled in another host country.

When parents have to rely on their children to speak for them because of their lack of language and cultural skills, they feel that they are not able to protect their children and fulfill their role as parents. Parents experience loss of dignity resulting from those moments. Children may not be proud of their parents, because they cannot speak English with their friends or because they do not have a good education or a good occupation in the US. Children may become translators for their parents and sometimes even decision-makers because they understand the US culture and context better. Therefore, children become "adults" very early on. Because of role changes between parents and children, parents lament that they do not receive proper respect from their children and that their parental identity has been lost, even while they take pride in their children's ability to speak English.

The parents were devastated when their children reported them to authorities for practices considered normal back in the homeland, such as corporal punishment for the children's benefit. "I feel bad when my children make a decision. I did not come here to lose the culture, but I see that it is happening. I am not happy that my children are moving away from my culture" (U4). Parents may lose their children to the US culture unless the children are able to maintain both cultures.

In the refugees' homeland, men are the breadwinners. In the newly settled country, however, men may not be able to find a job, while women may be able to find one more easily. In this case, men experience a sense of a loss of dignity by not being able to provide for their families and live out their roles as fathers and husbands. "The social breakdown was explicitly acknowledged over and over again by the refugees" (Coker 2004:408).

When refugees move to a very different place culturally, one which devalues the things they consider important, their cultural identity is shattered.

> First, lamentations about the loss of cultural integrity were the most common complaints made by the Sudanese. Secondly, the refugees articulated these losses, more often than not, in terms of social representation and/or changes in the nature of social interaction. Loss of culture was the loss of the physical freedom to perform dances and traditional ceremonies. It involved changes in the way people spoke and dressed that were seen as rooted in the host country. It involved changes in the nature of people themselves so that they became 'foreign' and no longer provided the community support necessary to maintain unity in exile. As in the previous excerpt, these changes and losses were represented through physical appearance or contextualized as a breakdown in the fabric of society. The loss of rituals and traditions, morality, loyalty and trust in the family, the loss of children to Egyptian

culture, etc., were consistently invoked to express the loss of culture and self. (Coker 2004:409)

As soon as refugees move to a refugee camp, they lose freedom of movement, opportunities for employment, choice of where to live, and access to medical care. They feel exploited and lack basic needs for life. One interviewee experienced the deaths of his father, mother, uncle, and aunt at a refugee camp, but he was not able to do anything to help himself prevent the loss or to deal with it. When people from different countries gather in a refugee camp, there is no common history or cultural cohesiveness to create a sense of unity and community. One interviewee counted seventeen different languages spoken in one refugee camp. What bonded people together in the camps was their common experience of war, loss, confusion, mistreatment, and fighting for survival.

Most of the refugees interviewed had been farmers. Because of their close relationship with the land, a significant part of their identity was based on the land. In the US, farmers usually possess large portions of land and use many kinds of mechanical equipment for farming, while the refugees had previously done more physical labor on smaller plots of land in their homeland. It is not feasible for them to be farmers in the US, so most of them take whatever manual jobs are available that they do not necessarily enjoy in order to pay their bills. However, loss of land in itself brought about a loss of identity. Because they were no longer connected to the land in their homeland or in the US, they did not know who they were and lost their sense of dignity.

9.4.2 Trauma

The great dangers and harsh living conditions refugees experience lead to emotional instability and physical illness. "Trauma means living with the recurrent, tormenting memories of atrocities witnessed or borne. Memories infect victims' sleep with horrific nightmares, destroy relationships, inhibit capacity to work or study, torment their emotions, shatter their faith, and mutilate hope" (Langberg and Monroe 2016:471). One interviewee said, "I heard bombing and gunshots. I just ran and ran. I saw dead bodies all over the field. I just ran. I don't know why I was not shot and dead. It's been over thirty years but I still can remember, and I am traumatized by it. I cannot get rid of it" (J2).

Another interviewee shared her experience in a refugee camp. When the food came, people rushed in to get food but in their desperation, they trampled over each other and several people died. Witnessing such incidents traumatized her. Coping with trauma while adapting to a new language and culture can sometimes be too much for refugees to handle.

9.4.3 No sense of belonging

People from a collectivistic culture look for a group to belong to when they move to a new place. However, because they are settled in the US, the most individualistic culture in the world according to *Hofstede Insights*,[3] they are not able to find a group to belong to as in their homeland. Back in their homeland, people were used to gathering under a tree to converse with neighbors or to having tea together, instead of staying in their homes. In the US, people stay in their homes after work and do

---

[3] hofstede-insights.com/country-comparison/the-usa/.

not usually spend time getting to know their neighbors. Life in the US is very private and isolating to them. Refugees may never be able to find a group outside of their ethnic group to belong to in the US. This makes them feel that they are not part of the broader community or nation they live in.

9.4.4 Not identifiable

There were three different types of responses to the question on, "Where are you from?" The refugees from Africa had a clear identity, as Congolese or Sudanese, or even as Africans. The Congolese were proud of being Congolese because Congo has progressed well and has been influential on surrounding countries. One Bembe man said that it was animosity between two ethnic groups in Congo, and not Congo as a whole, that caused them to become refugees. An interviewee explained how ethnic groups in Congo understood their ethnicity and their national identity: "It is like an orange. It is an orange as a whole but inside the orange, there are small parts. So those small parts are the ethnic groups in Congo, and we are all Congolese" (B1).

However, other people groups had a different response. One Zomi interviewee from Myanmar said,

> When people have asked me where I was from, I say that I am from Dallas. [laughter] But if I could not say that I am from Dallas when people asked me in Dallas, then I asked them back, "Why do you want to know?" Unless I really need to say my ethnicity and my identity, I don't answer that question. However, I don't have hard feeling towards Burmese in the US. (Z2)

This particular answer showed the mindset of someone who does not want to identify himself as Burmese or Zomi. Because the government of Myanmar threatened his life, he does not want to be identified as Burmese. At the same time, he does not want to say he is Zomi because nobody in the US would recognize it. While he was living in his homeland, he was a member of a despised minority group. In the US, he is a refugee and a member of a group nobody knows about. No matter how he identifies himself, either by nationality or ethnicity, he cannot express who he really is because of his unknown tribal group or his desire not to be identified with the nation that he is from.

Another person answered the "where are you from" question as follows: "I answer that I am from Myanmar but I am not a Burmese. I am a Chin. Then I explain where the Chin are from. I don't say I am Zotung Chin because even other Chin people do not know Zotung Chin people" (C4). When asked about his identity, he had to respond by saying who he was not.

Unlike Africans with a strong national identity with their homeland, some non-Africans were unable to verbalize their identity as to who they are in the US society when asked about it during the interviews. They answered by saying who they were not, or that they were members of an ethnic group not known to most Americans. In contrast, refugees from majority people groups could clearly state the home country that they had come from without any hesitation.

Children of refugees may have been born in a refugee camp or in a foreign country and so have never been to the homeland of their parents. They may have learned the common language used at the refugee camp or foreign country rather than the language of their parents and so are unable to identify themselves with their parents' culture. However, they are required to state their nationality as that of their parents' country on legal forms. In such cases, the national identity that is given is misleading.

9.4.5 Normal becomes odd

One Bembe mother said,

> A skirt [a cloth wrapped around her waist] is a proper clothing for a lady, and it is not proper for a lady to wear pants in my homeland. In America, it is normal for the ladies to wear tight jean pants. It is horrible to me to see my daughter wearing pants. When I asked my daughter to wear a skirt, she protested that she would be treated weird at school because a wrapped skirt was not an expected outfit for a high school girl in America. (B6)

So, the norm in her homeland became odd in the US. And the experience turned out to be humiliating for both mother and daughter. When the mother sent the children's pictures to her sister in a refugee camp, her sister was upset to see her niece wearing tight jean pants. Her sister even made an international call to scold her and to tell her to properly teach her daughter. She agonized over this experience.

9.4.6 Power and liminality

Refugees are constantly moving from place to place until they are finally resettled in a host country. Even after resettlement, they have little control over how they choose to live. Liminality and powerlessness are two sides of the same coin for refugees. "Liminality" is a term used in anthropological literature to describe the state of being outside before coming through a rite of passage (Turner 1969:359). It is also used in migration literature to describe the state of being on the edges of society. The ambiguous status of refugees, treatment that they receive, and a lack of status or possessions all contribute to the liminality that refugees experience and endure. Uncertainty, vulnerability, and powerlessness are issues that refugees deal with constantly. Life is uncertain and out of context when refugees are displaced and uprooted from their homeland. Their life is marginalized and they are vulnerable to those around them who have power. "Lacking a firm ground on which to establish their identity as legal outsiders, they are liminal persons, open to exploitations from within and from without" (Coker 2004:402).

Minority people around the world live in a society that is controlled by the majority people and so must adapt to the rules of the majority. Furthermore, refugees depend on the United Nations or the transitional country to provide for their needs while they are being resettled. While they were living in the transitional country, some were harassed by the police or faced deportation. They were at the mercy of the transitional country, and they did not have political or social power.

> Refugees tend to be marginalized in their new societies; that is, to suffer from feelings of alienation and, more often than not, lower status than they had in their countries of origin. In such positions of liminality and marginality, all aspects of their lives are called into question, including ethnic and national identity, gender roles, social relationships, and socio-economic status. (Camino 1994:iv)

Since they have been treated as marginal people throughout their journey, when they are treated as normal persons, they feel special. "When someone greets me in America, that makes me feel [like] a human being. Those are healing words to me" (Z1). When she was paid during a job training in the US, she was very much surprised because she was used to not getting full compensation for her labors and could not claim her rights because of her legal status in the transitional country.

The "moving" aspect of refugees' lives highlights their liminality: "the refugee —a concept embodying displacement, whether viewed as a legal or sociological concept-is conceived of as a moving entity" (Tuitt 1999:107).

9.4.7 Technology

Most developed countries and major cities in less developed countries have internet access. However, small villages in less developed countries (primary places of origin for minority refugees) and refugee camps usually do not have internet access. Out of the twenty-five refugees interviewed, only one uses the internet to communicate with her family in other parts of the world not in their homeland. The other refugees buy a phone card to call their family back in the homeland or refugee camp. It was only a couple of years ago that their families started to even have phones. Sometimes the phone connection is not reliable. It is very expensive to call from the homeland; when families call from the homeland, they usually tell the refugees to call them back, so they will not have to foot the bill.

> African communities are on the unfavorable side of the 'digital divide'; they are even more disadvantaged when they lack literacy skills in English, the main language of the Internet (Osborn 2004). ... This digital divide, combined with a general decline of traditional social networks in modern society, poses challenges to immigrant communities as it is difficult for them to maintain their traditional ways of connectedness. (Hatoss 2013:221)

The various options of accessing the internet are not available to most refugees from minority groups. Many refugees from majority people groups and their families back home have internet access, so they can get up-to-date information about family and the situation in their home country. They leave their homeland with 24/7 connectivity via the internet. However, most refugees from minority people groups do not have the luxury of an internet connection, but they must rely on voice contacts through the phone. With a phone connection, they are not able to share video, pictures, or printed resources, so their ability to fully communicate with their family is limited.

Some effort has been made to connect groups of refugees through the internet. The Zomi people have developed a website to connect Zomis around the world to help them keep their culture, language, and identity alive. However, people back in the homeland cannot access the website simply because there is no internet access there.

> As diaspora communities become increasingly deterritorialized and "uprooted from time and space through communication technologies" (Bida 2009:33), new forms of diaspora, which I have termed "Cyberspora" or online diaspora, are developing. Appadurai (1996) used the terms "ethnoscapes," "technoscapes," "finanscapes," "mediascapes," and "ideoscapes" to describe the globalized reality, characterized by seminal shifts in the way contemporary communities experience time and space (Giddens 1991). Bernal (2006) reported how the Eritreans in diaspora

use the Internet as a transnational public sphere where they produce and debate narratives of history, culture, democracy and identity. (Hatoss 2013:217)

9.4.8 Oral versus literate culture

All the refugees interviewed come from oral cultures. At least ten out of the twenty-five interviewees never had formal education, and they did not know how to read or write. When I visited their churches, I discovered that some churches do not provide written lyrics for the songs because everyone sings from memory. Half of the churches did not hand out a printed order of service, and the people did not seem to pay much attention to the bulletin when they had one.

Some refugees who were illiterate learned how to write when they moved to a transitional country; they started to use a phone to send text messages, and they learned how to write through texting. People also learned how to read and write through the church, by reading the Bible and singing songs. Adult refugees who had never attended school before coming to the US had to learn how to flip the pages of a book and how to grip a pencil for the first time in their lives. They had to learn the importance of reading and writing and signing legal documents. They had to adjust to a literate culture.

9.4.9 Appearance issues

Some of the refugees' children were born in the US. For them, the US is their home and English is their mother tongue. Even though they learn about their parents' culture at home, they are Americans linguistically and culturally. But because of their physical appearance, they are sometimes considered to be foreigners. Also, refugees from Africa are mistaken as African-Americans. Because they have a different history from African-Americans, the refugees from Africa have a different identity and culture. One Uduk person said, "I do not want to be treated as an African-American. I have a different mindset from them" (U3).

9.4.10 Supporting families in the homeland

Refugees continue to have close relationships with family members left behind in their homeland or at a refugee camp. Despite struggling to make ends meet in the US, everyone interviewed was saving money to support family members back home. They felt that their families in their respective homelands had greater needs than they themselves, and that they could not survive without help. Because most of the refugees have low paying jobs, or two jobs, or work odd shifts, helping family members is a financial burden for them.

"Remittance" is the term for the financial transfers that refugees make to the people "back home" (Lindley 2009). According to Johnson and Stoll's (2011) research, sending remittances in certain cultures is an obligation and a very common practice. The motivations for sending remittances include economic disparities, filial piety, cultural norms of sharing, and the desire to maintain good relations should the refugee ever desire to return to the home country. Sending remittances invokes a feeling of pride on the part of the sender and keeps geographically distant family members connected. However, remittances have significant drawbacks. Refugees may give up opportunities to use their earnings to develop themselves through education, to meet other personal needs, to establish financial stability, or to engage with their refugee community in cultural events that teach their children cultural heritage. Furthermore, sending remittances has the potential to incite conflict among family members regarding who should receive money and how much should be sent.

9.5 Language and identity

This section describes how language impacts identity, and how the linguistic environment impacts the life of a refugee.

9.5.1 Mother tongue

Language is one of the identity markers that fosters tradition and culture. There have been documented cases of children being placed in a boarding school and taught to use a different language than their mother tongue in order to change their culture, language, and identity (Edwards 2009:122). "Language policies that effectively demand the eradication of a person's first language prevent people from freely expressing their identity" (Mooney et al. 2011:134). One's mother tongue or first language is tightly connected to one's emotions and associated with identity.

Because of this tight relationship between language and identity, language strengthens the ingroup connections among members of a language group, while weakening outgroup connections to nonusers of the language.

> … there are parallels between the sorts of social-psychological findings … and the approach taken by Le Page and Tabouret-Keller (1985), for whom 'acts of identity' involve attempts at strengthening in-group linguistic connections—via accent or dialect, for example; such efforts, of course, necessarily entail deemphasizing linkages with out-groups. The processes here are fluid and dynamic and may very well operate in 'automatic' or even unconscious ways. (Edwards 2009:27)

9.5.2 Instrumental language

In contrast to the integrative function of the first language and identity, an instrumental language is not so closely related to identity, but merely provides a way to communicate. Laponce (1987) reports differences between a mother tongue and a second language among bilinguals.

> Bilingualism by juxtaposition often dissociates a mother-tongue—the privileged language of the emotions—from the language of the school, an instrumental language which may very well develop privileged means of communication, but which rarely acquires the joyous or disturbing vibrations that permeate the language of childhood. … Instrumental language is the language of writing; the mother-tongue is also the language of song. (Laponce 1987:32)

9.5.3 Multilingualism

When people learn multiple languages in childhood, they oftentimes do not clearly distinguish between one as a mother tongue or first language and the other as a more instrumental or second language.

> I faced the first challenge as some of the operational concepts such as "ethnicity," "mother tongue," "language maintenance" and "identity," to

name a few, were not an easy fit to this complex sociolinguistic context. For example, the assumption that "mother tongue" referred to African local languages quickly proved wrong, as some participants spoke Arabic as their first language. Others learnt two or three languages from birth; therefore, these seemingly "neat" concepts had to be contested. (Hatoss 2013:xvii)

Zomis and Zotung Chins learned Burmese at school in Myanmar. By eighth or ninth grade, they were fluent in both Burmese and their mother tongues. However, they did not necessarily have an easy time learning English when they moved to the US. Out of twenty-five people interviewed, three were gifted in languages and managed to master several languages including English. Five spoke English without much trouble in daily living. But the rest of them struggled with English even though some of them were bilingual in their mother tongue and the national language of their home country. Being exposed to multiple languages did not guarantee that they would be able to learn other languages easily. In general, men spoke English better than women, people who had lived in the US less than three years needed translation for the interviews, and people who had left their homeland at the age of thirty-five and over needed translation as well.

9.5.4 Speech community

Linguistic ability enabled people to function in multiple speech communities.

Speaking a particular language means belonging to a particular speech community; speaking more than one may (or may not) suggest variations in identity and allegiances. Much of interest here rests upon arguments about the degree to which bilinguals possess either two (theoretically) separately identifiable systems of language, from each of which they can draw as circumstances warrant, or some more intertwined cognitive-linguistic duality. (Edwards 2009:248)

The ability to speak the languages of a speech community allows one to be identified with and belong to that speech community. Most of the interviewees who encountered other languages were only able to speak them at a minimal level. Three people were exceptions, however. They were very gifted in languages, and were able to join different speech communities during their journey.

9.5.5 Religion and language

It was possible to observe how Christian churches have helped their members to use their mother tongue, because the initial contacts with the interview participants for this research were made through churches where the first language of the participants was being spoken. The church has become a facilitator for learning and using the mother tongue. Gathering with others in the same language group has helped to preserve the language within the community. There are different degrees of how the mother tongue is promoted in the various churches. The Uduk interviewees in the Dallas area attend an American church and the service is in English. Because of the small size of the Uduk community in the Dallas area, they do not have a service in the Uduk language. However, during the fellowship time, they speak the Uduk language with one another, and they have a weekly gathering at a home on Friday nights to pray, worship, and study the Bible in Uduk. The Bembe interviewees attend a service in Swahili. Bembe member B1 reads the Bible at home in Swahili, English,

French, and Kibembe,[4] in that order. Family worship is in English; his children were born in Zimbabwe and have never been to Congo, nor learned Kibembe. Another Bembe speaker, B2, reads the Bible in Shona, English, Swahili, and French, in that order. Thus, their times of Bible reading and worship do not promote use of the Kibembe language. The Jarai church has a service in Jarai, but an English service for the children. The Zotung Chin church has a service in the Zotung language and has Zotung language classes for the children on Sunday. However, they read the Burmese Bible because the Zotung Bible was translated only recently, and they are not used to the Zotung Bible. Out of the five language communities examined, the Zomi church promotes the mother tongue the most. The pastor emphasizes the importance of speaking the Zomi language, and children memorize one Bible verse in the Zomi language every Sunday and one Bible chapter during vacation Bible school.

9.5.6 Refugees and language

Multilingualism is part of daily life in a refugee camp. Refugees must learn the common language in order to obtain food and other resources, get important updates and other information, and even escape life-threatening situations. Learning the common language that is used in the refugee camp is as necessary for survival as physical endurance and emotional fortitude. However, people interviewed for this paper were not proactive in socializing with other people groups. They stayed within their own group when coping with difficulties and only learned the minimal amount of the common language to get by. People with language skills became bridge-builders between the different ethnic groups in the refugee camp, and even to the wider community around them. Sometimes for the refugees "it was an advantage to be able to speak the language of his 'enemies'" (Hatoss 2013:119). Such people often had leadership roles or received favors from their own people group.

There are three different responses refugees have when they encounter a new language in a place where they have settled. One response is to hold tightly to their linguistic identity when they feel that it is being threatened. "For migrants and exiles, foreign languages are more a matter of necessity than choice; holding on to their native language becomes a matter of protecting and preserving their innermost identity" (Battisti and Portelli 1995:43).

Another response is to learn the dominant language as a second language. They choose that language as the instrumental language but keep their mother tongue as the language of identity, emotion, and communication with the ingroup.

The third response is to learn the dominant language and choose that language as a new primary language.

> Lambert, Gardner, Olton, and Tunstall (1968) showed, from an analysis of attitude and behavior in francophone students at McGill University, that it is appropriate to distinguish subjects whose learning of English is purely instrumental from those who learn it for the purpose of integration into a socially and economically superior group. (Laponce 1987:49)

In the US, English is the language used in everyday conversations, in schools, and in the workplace. It is expected that every American, including immigrants and refugees, will learn English in order to function in the US. English fluency is a determinant of how successful the refugee will be in assimilating into mainstream

---

[4] Kibembe is the language of the Bembe people.

society and gaining social mobility. The languages spoken by the refugees are not recognized outside of their minority language group. When a language is recognized only within a marginalized portion of the population, that language is not empowered. In the US, disparities in power exist between English and ethnic minority languages.

Refugees may choose to master English and make it their primary language in order to get the most benefit out of life in the US. In some cases, the motivation to learn English arises because there are not enough people who can speak the mother tongue.

> Language shift often reflects pragmatic desires for social mobility and an improved standard of living, and these are ignored by revivalists at their peril. ... There is no doubt, overall, that the most obvious and usual cause of language decline and death is an inadequate concentration of speakers faced with economically powerful and technically sophisticated neighbors. (Edwards 1985:50)

Children of refugees who grow up in the US may not be fluent in their parents' mother tongue in spite of the parents' wishes. Parents may speak to their children in the mother tongue, but not teach the children how to read or write it. The Zotung Chin church brought teaching materials from the homeland in order to teach their children the Zotung language. Once a year, about three hundred Zotung youths gather from all over the US to learn Zotung culture and language for one weekend.

There are several reasons why refugees do not institute formal or semiformal language education for their children. First, they themselves are oral learners and are not focused on literacy. Second, they do not have time to teach their children because many of them have two jobs or work odd shifts. Third, no educational resources are available for their languages. Their situation is very different from immigrants from majority people groups like Chinese or Koreans, who organize language schools for their children. Therefore, language shift occurs by the second or third generations; "language shift or death is a symptom of ... uneven power relations in the social fields where immigrants and indigenous members of the society see the dominant language ... as a route to success in the wider society" (Hatoss 2013:73).

In addition to lack of time and resources, having too many languages can be a barrier to preserving the mother tongue in the second generation. One couple interviewed shared about the language situation in their family. The husband's mother tongue is Kibembe, but he learned Shona, Ndebele, Swahili, Lingala, and French in Congo and went to Burundi and also learned Asax, Kirundi, and English. His wife is from the Bembe language group. She was born in Congo but moved to Burundi at the age of three, and she moved back to Congo for two years. She then lived in Zambia for three years, and then lived in Zimbabwe for seventeen years until she moved to the US in 2017. She speaks Swahili, French, English, Kibembe, and Kirundi, in order of fluency. The couple is talented in languages. They speak Swahili with each other, but they speak English to their children. The wife has thirty-two siblings from four different mothers and her siblings are scattered across Australia, Canada, Switzerland, Zimbabwe, Mozambique, Burundi, and South Africa, and they communicate through the smartphone app called WhatsApp. They use French, English, and Swahili to communicate among the siblings, but there is no single language everyone can understand.

9.6 Rebuilding identity

This paper has covered many aspects of life that refugees need to accommodate to when they are resettled in the US (or other host country), such as culture, language, technology, and literacy. Some accommodate by leaving their culture and language and religious affiliations behind. Others change by taking on the dominant language for instrumental roles but maintain their vernacular language for elements of their culture that they can retain in the home and within their ethnic community. Some do not change at all.

9.6.1 Assimilation

Refugees who settle in a new country may adjust by assimilating to the dominant culture in order to settle in and make their living. Ferraro (2006) described assimilation in three stages:

> Assimilation occurs when a racial or ethnic minority is absorbed into the wider society. … Assimilation involves several different forms, which usually progress in sequential states. The first stage of assimilation is cultural, whereby minority group members gradually surrender their own cultural features (such as language, values, and behaviors) while accepting those of the dominant group. The second form is social assimilation, in which minority group members join into secondary and eventually primary group relationships (such as churches, unions, and neighborhood associations) with members of the mainstream. The final stage of assimilation involves physical integration through intermarriage, whereby the biological distinctions between the minority and the majority groups gradually decline and disappear. (Ferraro 2006:339)

During the assimilation process, there will be varying degrees of loss of their ethnic culture and language—from nearly complete abandonment, retaining only token representations, to maintenance of both cultural practices and language use in certain protected domains. They strive to win approval and become part of mainstream society through the different stages of assimilation.

9.6.2 Counter-assimilation

Some refugees may resist assimilation into the US culture. They hold onto their ethnic heritage, culture, and language, and remain alienated from mainstream society. They want to keep the language and culture they had when they left their home countries. Even as the culture back home changes, the refugees continue to keep the culture as it was at the time they left, maintaining an archaic form of their culture and language, especially when there is little or no contact with their ethnic home. They desire approval from their people group, and they keep allegiance to their traditional way of life. Because women had fewer opportunities to work outside of their homes and fewer opportunities for exposure to the US culture, women were more likely to counter-assimilate than men.

9.6.3 Transnational culture

When refugees leave their homeland and move to a transitional country like a refugee camp, they may encounter many different ethnic groups as they strive to adjust to their new circumstances. There is another adjustment when they are finally resettled in a host country with a dominant culture, such as the US. They attempt to learn and to adapt to the new environment in a way that is most beneficial to themselves.

Even if people assimilate into mainstream US culture, they may keep the practices of their own ethnic culture for dealing with family issues and socializing within the ethnic group. In this case, they are operating within more than one culture and as a result, may develop multiple identities. "As migrants often need to reconcile sharply different cultural practices, identity development most often leads to multiple identities" (Hatoss 2013:156).

Refugees may embrace paradoxical cultural practices as they adjust to a new culture. Some can learn language and culture easily and are able to navigate different worlds and be flexible. As a result, they have created for themselves a transnational culture and are not tied to one particular culture.

9.7 Conclusion

Refugees are deprived of the fundamental right to live in the land of their cultural identity and personhood. Once resettled in a host country, refugees from a minority ethnic group may find that their original identity, which they may consider their true identity or at least the most important of their identities, becomes lost or hidden because their ethnic groups and languages are not recognized in the host society. Refugees from the majority culture and language of a homeland are more likely to be recognized by people in the host country and result in fewer identity issues for these refugees. There are disparities in power between English and ethnic minority languages, and they are expected to speak English. In response, refugees face three options—they may cling to their language and cultural traditions, assimilate into the US culture, or maintain both languages and cultures. Whichever path they choose, their identity is greatly impacted.

Multilingualism is a given, rather than a choice, for a minority language group living in the homeland. Living in a transitional place introduces them to additional languages that must be learned in order to survive. Placement in a host country forces the refugees to again learn yet another language. People who are gifted in languages can learn the new languages without much trouble, but many others struggle. In some families, there is no common language spoken by all the members—the members may be scattered across different countries. With the second generation and beyond, language shift occurs, as well as cultural loss. As refugees deal with changes in language and culture, their identities are also impacted and changed. Identity issues of refugees from a minority language group are very complex because of the nature of their uprootedness, accompanied by suffering and marginalization.

This study has described identity issues of refugees from minority language groups as exemplified by five minority groups settled in the area around Dallas-Fort Worth, Texas. It would be beneficial to have a similar study on how identity issues compare for refugees who settle in a host country that is closely similar to their own. Key questions to investigate would be the nature of multilingualism in the refugee context in terms of language choice and language shift, and how the identities of refugees change in relation to the length of time since the departure from the homeland, transitional country, and host country.

Appendix A: Data Summary

The following table summarizes data collected in the twenty-five interviews conducted for this study (where, *Years of being a refugee* is the elapsed time between departure from homeland and arrival in the host country, and *Years in refugee camp* is the duration of the interviewee's stay in a refugee camp).

Name	People group	Gender	Age	Age leaving homeland	Yrs of being refugee	Yrs in refugee camp	Yrs in US	Reason to leave homeland	Education level	Need for translation
Z1	Zomi	F	35	16	10	0	9	political	Bible school	no
Z2	Zomi	M	37	28	5	0	3	religion	Bible school	no
Z3	Zomi	F	31	21	4	0	6	political	no	yes
B1	Bembe	M	43	22	20	3	0.25	war	MA	no
B2	Bembe	F	45	3	42	2	0.25	war	college	no
B3	Bembe	M	72	49	20	20	1	war	no	yes
B4	Bembe	F	58	37	20	0	1	war	no	yes
B5	Bembe	M	65	43	18	18	5	war	no	yes
B6	Bembe	F	42	19	18	18	5	war	no	yes
B7	Bembe	M	37	15	17	17	1.5	war	university	yes
J1	Jarai	M	34	34	19	0	12	religion	Bible school	no
J2	Jarai	M	65	28	5	0	32	political	no	no
J3	Jarai	M	40	23	0.75	0	16	religion	no	no
U1	Uduk	M	34?	11	8-9	8-9	14	war	no	no
U2	Uduk	M	40	7	14	5	19	war	no	no
U3	Uduk	F	39	7	13	5	19	war	no	no
U4	Uduk	M	41	19	3	3	19	war	no	no
C1	Zutong	M	40	22	8	0	10	political	primary	no
C2	Zutong	M	36	25	2	0	10	political	9th	no
C3	Zutong	F	28	14	7	0	7	political	9th	yes
C4	Zutong	M	48	36	9	0	2	political	no	yes
C5	Zutong	F	47	44	1	0	2	political	no	yes
C6	Zutong	M	22	20	1	0	2	political	primary	no
C7	Zutong	M	31	27	1	0	3	political	no	yes
C8	Zutong	M	40	25	8	0	7	political	teacher training	no

Appendix B: Interview Questions

Experience in the homeland
1. What made you become a refugee?
2. Who among your family members left the homeland with you?

Experience in the transitional country
1. Where did you go between your homeland and the host country?
2. How was your life at a refugee camp or in a transitional country?
3. How many languages were spoken in the refugee camp?
4. How did you survive without understanding a common language in a refugee camp or in a transitional country? How did you provide for yourself financially?
5. When your child was born in a transitional country, what languages did the child learn first?
6. What was the greatest difficulty that you experienced in transitional places?

Experience in the host country
1. How do you answer to the question of "where are you from?"
2. How are your children adapting to the host country?
3. Which language do you speak to your children? How well do your children understand your mother tongue? What difficulties do you have in communicating with your children? Have you taught your mother tongue to your children?
4. Can you recall any incident when you had trouble with your children because of the cultural differences?
5. What is your dream about visiting your homeland?
6. What has caused the most difficulty in living in the host country?
7. What has been your most rewarding experience while living in the host country?
8. How often do you contact your family members around the world and what do you use to communicate with them?

References

Appadurai, Arjun. 1996. *Modernity at large: Cultural dimensions of globalization.* Public Worlds 1. Minneapolis: University of Minnesota Press.

Battisti, Francesca, and Alessandro Portelli. 1995. The apple and the olive tree: Exiles, sojourners, and tourists in the university. In Rina Benmayor and Andor Skotnes (eds.), *Migration and identity*, 35–51. Oxford: Oxford University Press.

Benmayor, Rina, and Andor Skotnes, eds. 1994. *Migration and identity*. International Yearbook of Oral History and Life Stories 3. Oxford: Oxford University Press.

Bernal, Victoria. 2006. Diaspora, cyberspace and political imagination: The Eritrean diaspora online. *Global Networks* 6(2):161–179.

Bida, Aleksandra. 2009. Cultural deterritorialisation: Communications technology, provenance and place. *Platform: Journal of Media and Communication* 1(July): 33–46.

Camino, Linda A., and Ruth M. Krulfeld, eds. 1994. *Reconstructing lives, recapturing meaning: refugee identity, gender, and culture change.* Basel, Switzerland: Gordon and Breach.

Chen, Sylvia Xiaohua. 2014. Toward a social psychology of bilingualism and biculturalism. *Asian Journal of Social Psychology* 18:1–11. DOI: 10.1111/ajsp.12088.

Coker, Elizabeth M. 2004. Dislocated identity and the fragmented body: Discourses of resistance among Southern Sudanese refugees in Cairo. *Journal of Refugee Studies* 17(4):401–419.

Edwards, John. 1985. *Language, society and identity*. The Language Library. New York: Blackwell.

Edwards, John. 2009. *Language and identity: An introduction*. Key Topics in Sociolinguistics. Cambridge: Cambridge University Press.

Ferraro, Gary. 2006. *Cultural Anthropology: An applied perspective*. Belmont, CA: Thomson Higher Education.

Fishman, Joshua A., and Ofelia García, eds. 2010. *Handbook of language and ethnic identity: Disciplinary and regional perspectives*. Vol. 1. Second edition. Oxford: Oxford University Press.

Giddens, Anthony. 1991. *Modernity and self-identity: Self and society in the late modern age*. Cambridge: Polity Press.

Hatoss, Anikó. 2013. *Displacement, language maintenance and identity: Sudanese refugees in Australia*. IMPACT: Studies in Language, Culture and Society 34. Amsterdam: John Benjamins.

Johnson, Phyllis J., and Kathrin Stoll. 2011. The impact of remittances on refugees' lives in Canada: Views of Sudanese and Vietnamese leaders and settlement counsellors. *Refuge* 29(1):53–64.

Lambert, W. E., R. C. Gardner, R. Olton, and K. Tunstall. 1968. Study of the roles of attitudes and motivation in second language learning. In Joshua A. Fishman (ed.), *Readings in the sociology of language*, 473–491. The Hague: Mouton.

Langberg, Diane, and Philip G. Monroe. 2016. Trauma as mission: A case study response to the scourge of sex trafficking. In Sadiri Joy Tira and Tetsunao Yamamori (eds.), *Scattered and gathered: A global compendium of diaspora missiology*, 470–477. Eugene, OR: Regnum.

Laponce, J. A. 1987. *Languages and their territories*. Toronto: University of Toronto Press.

Le Page, Robert B., and Andrée Tabouret-Keller. 1985. *Acts of identity: Creole-based approaches to language and ethnicity*. Cambridge: Cambridge University Press.

Lindley, Anna. 2009. The early morning phone call: Remittances from a refugee diaspora perspective. *Journal of Ethnic and Migration Studies* 35(8):1315–1334.

Makihara, Miki. 2010. Anthropology. In Joshua A. Fishman and Ofelia García (eds.), *Handbook of language and ethnic identity: Disciplinary and regional perspectives*, 32–48. Oxford: Oxford University Press.

Mooney, Annabelle, Jean Stilwell Peccei, Suzanne LaBelle, Berit Engøy Henriksen, Eva Eppler, Anthea Irwin, Pia Pichler, Siân Preece, and Satori Soden. 2011. *Language, society and power: An introduction*. Third edition. Abingdon, UK: Routledge.

Nicholson, Frances, and Patrick Twomey, eds. 1999. *Refugee rights and realities: Evolving international concepts and regimes*. Cambridge: Cambridge University Press.

Osborn, Donald Z. 2004. African languages and information and communication technology (ICT): Key elements for the future. Paper presented at the *Fourth Conference on Preserving African Languages*, University of Maryland—Eastern Shore, Salisbury, MD, November 4–7, 2004.

Tuitt, Patricia. 1999. Rethinking the refugee concept. In Frances Nicholson and Patrick Twomey (eds.), *Refugee rights and realities: Evolving international concepts and regimes*, 106–118. Cambridge: Cambridge University Press.

Turner, Victor W. 1969. *The ritual process: Structure and anti-structure*. Chicago, IL: Aldine.

UNHCR. 2010. *Convention and protocol relating to the status of refugees*. United Nations High Commission on Refugees. Accessed February 10, 2018. unhcr.org/protect/protection/3b66c2aa10.pdf/.

10
African Cross-Border Languages: Might or Plight?

Scott Smith

Abstract. Language development practitioners have tended to focus on individual languages-in-country, often without taking into account the needs of cross-border speech communities of the same language, or of significant diaspora speech communities in other countries. Twenty years of working with the realities of cross-border languages have shown this author the critical importance of including those realities in our considerations of language planning and development. This paper documents the 420 cross-border languages of Africa, and divides them into two main categories for analysis: the vehicular languages of wider communication between ethnic groups, and the limited languages used by a single ethnic group. In each case, we examine vitality levels in terms of speaker numbers and disruption factors such as levels of intergenerational transmission. Statistical analysis of limited cross-border languages (according to relative vitality levels) yields some unexpected and surprising conclusions about the plight (or is it the might?) of African cross-border languages. Practical approaches are suggested, which could be helpful in meeting particular needs of cross-border language communities.

10.1 Context and rationale for researching cross-border languages

What merit or interest could there be in a study of African cross-border languages? This author has been submerged for twenty years in the issue of cross-border languages, working with a Cameroonian language development organization from neighboring Equatorial Guinea.

In many ways, Equatorial Guinea could be perceived of as a linguistic microcosm of Africa, with Spanish, French, and Portuguese as official languages, as well as significant English influence and Arabic migrations. Equatorial Guinea has a Portuguese creole that is cross-border with lusophone São Tomé, an English creole that is cross-border with anglophone Cameroon and Nigeria, and a number of Bantu languages that are cross-border with francophone Cameroon and Gabon. Equatorial Guinea is predominantly hispanophone at the institutional level, which means Equatorial Guinea's languages also have significant diaspora communities many borders away, in faraway Spain (independence from Spain came in 1968). Experience shows us that development organizations and government institutions can tend to focus on languages-in-country, without taking into consideration their cross-border counterparts. Cross-border languages constitute distinct realities, and their unique challenges *and* potential advantages need to be taken into greater consideration for the purposes of language development in a multilingual and migrating world.

The nature and status of cross-border languages make it unreasonable to try to consider them as one coherent category. The situation of the Ge'ez language of Ethiopia and Eritrea, for example (dormant for a thousand years, yet still a language of identity for five religious communities), is significantly different from any of the large dialects that make up the Arabic macrolanguage.[1]

In section 10.2 of this paper, we identify groups of cross-border languages, breaking them down into smaller categories to allow for relevant comparison and analysis. Section 10.3 focuses on one major category, "vehicular" cross-border languages used for wider communication between ethnic groups. How does cross-border status impact language vitality at that level? Is it a help or a hindrance for a language to be divided between two or more countries? Are there specific advantages of cross-border status that can be used to further language development? In this section, we discuss the work of the African Academy of Languages, in promoting and developing vehicular cross-border languages.

In section 10.4, we focus on the second major category, "limited" cross-border languages (used by one ethnic language community), which have been divided into two or more speech communities in different countries. How does cross-border status impact language vitality at that level? What are the implications for development organizations serving these language communities? Are there specific challenges caused by cross-border status which need to be considered? In this section, we also discuss some helpful approaches that have been taken in central Africa to meet particular needs of limited cross-border language communities. Finally, section 10.5 discusses implications for development of cross-border languages, including some initiatives that have proven successful, and the value of inter-entity partnerships.

10.2 Describing the cross-border language situation of Africa

10.2.1 How many cross-border languages are there, and where in Africa are they?

It is difficult to calculate the precise number of cross-border languages in Africa. They are significant in number, cover an immense territory, and there is insufficient data to identify all of them since cross-border languages will often be given different names on different sides of the border. For example, the Bisio speech community of Equatorial Guinea is a subgroup of the Kwasio language community centered in Cameroon.[2] The only way for the *Ethnologue* to have recognized that both groups are members of the same language community was through the research of on-site personnel familiar with the languages in both countries.

---

[1] A macrolanguage is made up of several non-mutually-intelligible dialects, which are considered by some to be one united language.

[2] Simons and Fennig 2018. ethnologue.com/language/nmg/. Accessed 19 April 2018.

Professor Kwesi Prah believes that the vast majority of African languages are cross-border: "... we need to work in cooperation across borders because practically all African languages are cross-border speech forms, which defy the colonially inherited borders" (Prah 2003).

Sometimes the colonial-era division has been so influential that nationalists will resist the idea that two speech communities could be using the same language. Prah continues: "For the sake of flag and so-called national identity, Kamuzu Banda of Malawi refused to accept the reality of the fact that Cinyanja and Cicewa [sic] are the same language" (Prah 2003).

We can arrive at a close approximation of the overall number of cross-border languages from the 347 languages listed in the *Ethnologue* as being indigenous in two or more African nations.[3] This would represent a purist definition of "cross-border," in which an indigenous language community has been divided by one or more political boundaries. The *Ethnologue* lists an additional 73 languages that have significant speech communities in two or more countries. They would represent a broader definition of "cross-border," which also takes into consideration major migratory phenomena, such as economic migrants or war refugees. As an example, one-third of Cape Verde's Kabuverdianu speakers are out of the country,[4] making Lisbon, Portugal the third largest Kabuverdianu speech community in the world, after the Cape Verdean cities of Praia and Mondelo (Märzhäuser 2010).

For the purposes of this paper, we will work with the broader definition of cross-border languages (which includes significant diaspora communities) and the sum total of 420. This count of 420 would mean that cross-border languages make up roughly one-fifth of Africa's 2,143 known languages. The more purist classification of 347 indigenous languages whose territory was split by a modern political border would represent about one-sixth of Africa's languages.

Either way, cross-border languages represent a significant part of the complex linguistic picture of Africa. Fifty-three nations have one or more cross-border languages (every nation of Africa except six islands—Reunion, Seychelles, Mayotte, St. Helena, Ascension, and Tristan da Cunha). Cameroon, the most linguistically dense and diverse country per capita in Africa (with 277 languages and about 25 million people), is host to 42 different cross-border languages. Second to that is Nigeria, the most linguistically diverse and demographically numerous country in Africa (with 526 languages and about 190 million people). Nigeria hosts 25 cross-border languages. Nineteen different African nations (in order, Cameroon, Nigeria, Central African Republic, Democratic Republic of the Congo, Chad, Benin, Zambia, Ghana, Burkina Faso, Togo, Mali, Liberia, Guinea, Ethiopia, Sudan, Côte d'Ivoire, Senegal, Namibia, and Congo) have at least 10 cross-border languages each.

10.2.2 Africa: The maze of Berlin Walls that never went away

How did Africa come to have so many cross-border languages? Most of Africa's current national borders were established in 1884–1885 at the Conference of Berlin. Those making the decisions to carve and divide peoples' homelands were mostly European politicians, with very few Africans present or consulted in the process. Rivers and

---

[3] I am indebted to the *Ethnologue* database, without which this research would have been impossible, and to its Executive Editor, Gary Simons, who assisted by supplying for me a custom dataset on African cross-border languages.

[4] Simons and Fennig 2018. ethnologue.com/language/kea. Accessed 19 April 2018.

lines of longitude or latitude were more the order of the day than any consideration of the traditional territories of ethnic groups. Rivers were given special attention since rivers make a natural preexisting boundary that is identifiable, easily definable and enforceable, and relatively permanent. The problem with treating rivers as boundaries is that they inevitably split language communities, because almost never would a people settle on only one side of a river. Rivers were the major highways of the rainforests and the savannah. A comparison could be made to taking Europe's major autoroutes and autobahns, or America's interstate freeways, and turning them overnight into international boundaries, at times complete with penalties for daring to cross them in an attempt to visit one's mother or cousin.

These complexities are increased in the case of a country like Cameroon, where many of its language groups cross over into anglophone Nigeria, hispanophone Equatorial Guinea, or francophone Chad or Central African Republic or Gabon. This is not to mention the internal complexity of "the Cameroons" itself, which was Portuguese, then Spanish, then German, until it was divided into French Cameroon and English Cameroon.

10.2.3 Categorization of languages in Africa by the African Academy of Languages

The number and scope of cross-border languages is so significant in Africa that the African Academy of Languages (ACALAN) classifies all languages of Africa into six types, with two of those six being characterized in part by their cross-border status. The six types are:

- Widely spoken ("vehicular") cross-border languages
- Limited ("single ethnic") cross-border languages
- Widely spoken non-cross-border languages
- Limited non-cross-border languages
- Endangered languages
- Imported (or partner) languages[5]

ACALAN has made a very useful distinction in dividing the cross-border languages between those that are vehicular (wider communication) and those that are limited (single-ethnic), a distinction we will make use of in the remainder of this paper.

10.2.4 Further categorization of cross-border languages according to the EGIDS scale

We further categorize each of those two major categories of cross-border languages, according to multiple levels of language vitality. We classify vitality according to the Expanded Graded Intergenerational Disruption Scale or EGIDS (Lewis and Simons 2010), which expands on the original scale developed by Fishman (1991). Because EGIDS is a measure of vitality *disruption*, lower numbers indicate less disruption, and therefore greater vitality. Higher numbers indicate more disruption and more endangerment, and thus lesser vitality. We begin in section 10.3 with the vitality levels of vehicular cross-border languages, which have the lower EGIDS values from 0 (International) to 3 (Wider communication). Then in section 10.4, we classify the

---

[5] ACALAN, founding document: *Background*, in ACALAN.org/index.php/en/about-ACALAN/background/. Accessed 8 April 2018.

vitality status of limited cross-border languages, which have the higher EGIDS values from 4 (Educational) to 9 (Dormant).

10.3 The vitality of Africa's vehicular cross-border languages, and their impact on identity and language shift

10.3.1 EGIDS vitality levels of vehicular cross-border languages

EGIDS 0 (International)—Six world languages have been declared official at the international level by the United Nations. Chinese and Russian are the only two of those that are not vehicular languages of Africa. English (an official national language in twenty-two countries of Africa), French (which is similarly official in twenty-two countries), and Spanish (official in Equatorial Guinea) are classified separately in the above-mentioned ACALAN taxonomy as imported (or partner) languages. Therefore, the only international language to be classified as a vehicular cross-border African language is Arabic (which is an official national language in thirteen countries of Africa).

EGIDS 1 (National)—Another official national language across many countries in Africa is Portuguese, spoken in six countries including Equatorial Guinea, but Portuguese is also classified as an imported language, since it is not indigenous to Africa. Kiswahili is official in Kenya and Tanzania; Berber is official in Morocco and Algeria. There are twelve nations with a national language that is indigenous and official only in that country; the *Ethnologue* identifies nine of those as also being cross-border.[6] South Africa recognizes eleven official national languages, and the *Ethnologue* identifies seven of those as also being cross-border.[7]

Interestingly, Equatorial Guinea recognizes the most official national languages that are imported. It is the only nation in the world that recognizes Spanish, French, and Portuguese each as official languages, not to mention that it is the only nation in the world that recognizes a combination of any two of these three. Equatorial Guinea was first colonized by England, and also has the distinction of having a Methodist church in the capital city of Malabo that has used English as a church language for 191 years.

EGIDS 2 (Provincial)—Africa has a large number of languages with official status at the provincial level, and the *Ethnologue* identifies fifteen of those in seven countries as also being cross-border.[8] Two examples are Lingala (2.3 million speakers in Congo and Democratic Republic of the Congo, and official in northwestern regions of DRC) and Hausa (44 million speakers in seven countries, and official in nine provinces of Nigeria).

EGIDS 3 (Wider Communication)—According to EGIDS definitions, *all* vehicular cross-border languages have a strength of at least EGIDS 3 (Wider communication). EGIDS 3 languages, although not official, are widely used between multiple ethnic

---

[6] From nationsonline.org/oneworld/african_languages.htm. Accessed 8 April 2018. The nine countries are: Botswana, Central African Republic, Ethiopia, Lesotho, Madagascar, Tanzania, Rwanda, Somalia, and Swaziland.

[7] Those seven are: Sotho, Swazi, Afrikaans, Tsonga, Venda, Xhosa, and Zulu.

[8] These numbers and all the numbers relating to cross-border languages (including those reported in the figures below) are based on an extract from the *Ethnologue Global Dataset* sent in personal communication by Gary Simons, 12 April 2018.

communities for interchange and commerce. The *Ethnologue* identifies thirty-six EGIDS 3 languages as being cross-border. Two examples are Fang (1.1 million speakers in Equatorial Guinea, Cameroon, Congo, and Gabon) and Hassaniyya (8.8 million speakers in seven countries of Africa).

10.3.2 Speaker-number vitality of vehicular cross-border languages

Other measures of language vitality could be in terms of the number of users (speakers) and the number of uses (functions). In order to grasp the significance of vehicular cross-border languages, it is helpful to have a picture of their size, in relation to other African and world languages.

Table 1 gives a synchronic statistical snapshot of the median sizes of African vehicular cross-border languages (row 1b), as compared to other language groupings of Africa and the world. The number of speakers of African cross-border languages overall (row 1) is quite large. They make up one fifth of Africa's languages, and six of every ten Africans speak at least one cross-border language.[9] Rows 1a and 1b break those down into the limited (nonvehicular) cross-border languages, to be discussed further in section 10.4,[10] and the vehicular cross-border languages. The speaker populations for the latter are truly impressive. Making up only 3% of Africa's languages (row 3), they are spoken by more than half of all Africans. Their median speaker population is 587 times that of the world median language size (row 4). More impressive yet is the coverage of the subset of twelve vehicular cross-border languages for which ACALAN is developing language commissions (row 2). This is the topic of the next section.

Table 1. Vehicular cross-border language sizes compared with other African and world languages

Language groupings	Count	L1 users	L2 users	Total users	L1 median
1. Africa: all cross-border lgs	420	562,531,650	221,113,310	783,644,960	145,355
(a) Limited cross-border	355	136,510,070	1,144,910	135,654,980	86,000
(b) Vehicular cross-border	*65*	*426,021,580*	*219,968,400*	*645,989,980*	*4,110,000*
2. ACALAN Commission lgs	12	236,089,170	208,902,970	444,992,140	12,340,760
3. Africa: all Indigenous lgs	2,143	980,437,811	-	-	30,000
4. World: all languages	7,097	6,777,788,053	-	-	7,000

---

[9] Based on current Africa population of 1.28 billion. worldometers.info/world-population/africa-population/. Accessed 21 April 2018.
[10] Simons and Fennig 2018. ethnologue.com/statistics/. Accessed 14 April 2018. Data in the top six lines comes from this page. Remaining data sent by the *Ethnologue* editor, personal correspondence.

10.3.3 The African Academy of Languages and vehicular cross-border language commissions

In a 2001 speech to the African Academy of Languages, Professor Ayo Bamgbose stressed:

> Widely spoken cross-border languages have the potential of serving as a model for empowerment, for they have a large population to back them and materials prepared in one country can be circulated and used in another. Hence to extend their use to a wider range of domains should not be problematic once the necessary language development work has been done. (Bamgbose 2002)

The unique challenges and potentials of cross-border language groups have been recognized by ACALAN, and they are establishing twelve Vehicular Cross-border Language Commissions. The Statutes of ACALAN recognize two kinds of working structures: National Language Structures and Vehicular Cross-border Language Commissions (ACALAN 2001).

The twelve Commissions being established within the five zones of Africa are:
- North Africa: Modern Standard Arabic, Berber
- West Africa: Hausa, Mandinka, Fulfulde
- East Africa: Kiswahili, Somali, Malagasy
- Southern Africa: Cinyanja/Chichewa, Setswana
- Central Africa: Lingala, Beti-fang[11]

These twelve Commission languages chosen by ACALAN are shown in table 1, number 2. They include two of the sixteen largest world languages that are used as a second language by more than a hundred million people: Kiswahili and Arabic (taking into consideration only the Arabic spoken in Africa). They include four additional macrolanguages, all with potential for written standardization (Berber, Fulfulde, Malagasy, Beti-fang). These twelve languages are a first language to 24% of Africa's people and used as a second language by another 21%. Seven of the twelve are official national languages.[12] Three are official provincial languages (EGIDS 2), and the other two are EGIDS 3 (Wider communication).[13] It is clear that ACALAN has chosen significant languages across Africa as their primary focus for language development. These are languages that, in terms of both number of first language speakers and vehicular status, could be developed to perform alongside other major languages on the world stage.

---

[11] ACALAN.org/index.php/en/about-ACALAN/working-structures/the-vehicular-cross-border-language-commissions. Accessed 8 April 2018.

[12] Those seven are: Kiswahili, Hausa, Berber, Setswana, Malagasy, Chichewa, and Somali. An eighth, Beti-fang, was an official national language during the regime of Equatorial Guinea's first president, Francisco Macías Nguema (1968-1979).

[13] Lingala is official in the northwestern regions of the Democratic Republic of the Congo, and Fulfulde/Pulaar in the Senegambia region and the Senegal River valley of Senegal. Hausa is official in nine states of northern Nigeria. Mandinka and Fang are EGIDS 3.

10.3.4 The impact of vehicular cross-border languages on identity and language shift

In order to understand how vehicular languages are impacting identity and language shift in Africa, we need to see the distinction between first language (L1) and second language (L2) users of these languages. Although all speakers could be speaking the language for vehicular (inter-ethnic) purposes, only the use by L2 speakers would have implications for identity-shift or language-shift. Table 1 above gives us the breakdown between L1 and L2 speakers of cross-border African languages.

It is significant that more than one in every six Africans (220 million out of 1.2 billion total) are speaking at least one of these vehicular cross-border languages as a second language. The impact of vehicular languages overall is actually much greater than that, when we add in the significant number of L2 speakers of imported (European) languages and of the vehicular non-cross-border languages (though the numbers of these last two categories are beyond the scope of this paper).

For decades, English and other European languages were vilified as "killer languages" that would eventually wipe out African languages (Price 1984; Nettle and Romaine 2000). But research since 2000 has been demonstrating that the fastest growing languages in Africa are these African vehicular languages, which are being adopted as languages of urban or national identity. Language is a prominent marker of identity, and Africans (unless they migrate to Europe or America) would have no reason to adopt European or American identities. African national and continental languages have become markers of African identity and pride.

Salikoko Mufwene, in his 2005 article on "The Myth of Killer Languages," articulates this observation well:

> English is not really the "killer language" that non-global approaches to language endangerment have painted it to be, certainly not in relation to the indigenous languages of former exploitation colonies. Moreover, it does not have the kind of agency that would have made it a killer, because it is (would-be) speakers who kill their languages by opting to speak another language, which amounts to what is known as language shift. In the case of sub-Saharan Africa, for instance, it is important to take account of the expansion of the indigenous lingua francas that also function as urban vernaculars and are spreading at the expense of traditional ethnic languages and apparently also of the colonial European languages which continue to function as official languages. (Mufwene 2005:45)

This author recently heard a vivid illustration of a vehicular language replacing a traditional ethnic language. An elderly African colleague said, in reference to an old friend: "I've known him all his life, but I never knew he was Balengue, until his wife died, and he cried in Balengue." In this case, the Balengue identity was probably one of the man's most deep-rooted identities, the only way he could express his most profound anguish. But it was a limited ethnic identity, which had very few fellow users and few perceived functional uses outside of his tiny homeland. So he had chosen not to display this identity to others for most of his life, and instead to function within a broader national identity, which involved using the vehicular language.

In other cases, the identity shift and accompanying change in language repertoire is more toward an urban identity and sometimes an urban language. Eighty percent of Equatorial Guineans live in continental Africa and never use the Equatorial Guinean Pidgin language. But in the island capital of Malabo, Pidgin is a growing and thriving language of urban identity, especially among the youth. Only 5,000 Fernandino people (descendants of freed slaves who began the colony) speak the mesolect as a mother tongue creole, but more than 60,000 young L2 speakers use the basilect as an urban pidgin. If one learns to speak Pidgin well, without a continental Fang accent, he is an insider, and will often be greeted as *Dîman* (etymology, "the man"). Anyone who does not speak Pidgin, or speaks it poorly, can be pejoratively classified as *Batamán* (a person from Bata, the continental port city). West African Pidgin has been growing so rapidly, from Sierra Leone to Cameroon, that in 2017 the BBC decided to begin continuous radio broadcasting in Pidgin. In November 2011, the author donated to Equatorial Guinea National Television a full-length video in Pidgin, *Di Poblik laif fo Jesús* [The Public Life of Jesus]. On a return trip to the island the following May, we were informed that public demand had led to almost weekly showings since the November debut.

Out of 1.2 billion (18%), 220 million Africans have adopted the second-language use of cross-border languages. At the same time, increasing numbers of Africa's children are not learning their ethnic mother tongues. The *Ethnologue* also cites 18% (389 out of 2,143) of Africa's languages as being in trouble or dying (EGIDS 6b to 9).[14] While these two 18% figures are measuring different things, they ironically symbolize how vehicular cross-border languages are having a powerful impact on identity and language shift, as some language communities begin to shift away from their ethnic minority languages, and shift toward these languages of urban, national, and continental identity.

In the context of the African Union and continental politics seeking to unite Africa behind common goals (such as the United Nations Sustainable Development Goals or the strategic framework of the New Partnership for Africa's Development), the status of vehicular languages being cross-border is much more of a help than a hindrance in overcoming tribal or regional barriers to unity.

10.4 The vitality of Africa's limited cross-border languages, and their impact on language shift and development

We now turn to the remaining African cross-border languages, which ACALAN classifies as "limited" to one ethnic community and not generally used by other groups for wider communication.

10.4.1 EGIDS vitality levels of limited cross-border languages

For each EGIDS level, we give an illustrative example of a limited cross border language with that vitality level, followed by the total number of languages and countries listed by the *Ethnologue* in that category.

EGIDS 4 (Educational)—Ngbaka, a Ubangian language of Congo and the Democratic Republic of the Congo, has 1,016,650 speakers in 850 villages. For more than twenty years there has been an active adult literacy and education program, and Ngbaka is taught at all school levels. The *Ethnologue* lists 30 such Educational cross-border languages, centered in 17 African nations.

---

[14] Simons and Fennig 2018. ethnologue.com/region/Africa/. Accessed 14 April 2018.

EGIDS 5 (Developing)—Kwasio has 22,000 speakers across Cameroon, Gabon, and Equatorial Guinea. They have incipient literacy and are developing a corpus of literature, but are not yet using Kwasio as language of instruction in schools. There are 166 such Developing cross-border languages, listed for 32 countries of Africa.

EGIDS 6a (Vigorous)—Baka has 43,200 speakers across Cameroon and Gabon. Fifteen thousand are monolinguals (mostly women). There are current efforts to raise the literacy rate (5%). There are 144 Vigorous cross-border languages in 38 African countries.

EGIDS 6b (Threatened)—Gyele has 4,300 speakers across Cameroon and Equatorial Guinea. Not only is their language threatened, but also their culture and survival as an ethnic group. They occupy and need a large area of forest to survive as hunter-gatherers. The Chad-Cameroon Pipeline has recently devastated a large area of their territory, as has the new deep-water port south of Kribi. The Cameroon government has set aside a protected buffer area of almost 700,000 hectares in and around the Campo Ma'an National Park to compensate for these losses. There are fourteen threatened cross-border languages of Africa in eight nations.

EGIDS 7 (Shifting)—Tshuwau is a Khoisan language spoken by 5,540 bushmen of Botswana and Zimbabwe. There are six Shifting cross-border languages of Africa in five countries.

EGIDS 8a (Moribund)—Hya, a Chadic language, has 2,940 speakers across Nigeria and Cameroon, the only African language currently listed as Moribund and cross-border.

In discussing cross-border realities, it is important to realize that speech communities identified with the same language may have different EGIDS levels on each side of the border. For example, the Ndoola speech community of Nigeria has vigorous orality (EGIDS 6a), while the Ndoola speech community of Cameroon is moribund (EGIDS 8a). The Ndoola village of Dodeo in Cameroon has shifted to Fulfulde, and had only three elderly speakers of Ndoola as of 2014.

EGIDS 8b (Nearly extinct)—Boguru of South Sudan and Democratic Republic of the Congo (those in DRC are refugees from troubled South Sudan) has an ethnic population of 500, but few L1 speakers. Boguru is the only African cross-border language currently listed in the Nearly Extinct category.

EGIDS 9 (Second language only)—Ethiopic, also called Ge'ez, of Ethiopia, Eritrea, and communities in Israel, is used only as a second language by an unknown number of people. Christian Scriptures translated into Ge'ez seventy-six years before the birth of Mohammed were foundational to developing the Christian identity which maintained Ethiopia as the only African state to remain a Christian nation from the early church period and through 1,400 years of Islamic expansion across north Africa. Although Ge'ez evolved into modern speech forms like today's Amharic, this language—dormant now for almost a thousand years—continues to serve as a language of history and identity for five major Christian and Jewish communities in three nations. The *Ethnologue* lists four Second-language-only cross-border languages in four countries of Africa.

10.4.2 Statistical analysis of limited cross-border language vitality

Our initial hypotheses concerning cross-border status was that limited cross-border languages would suffer greater disruption and weaker vitality rates as a result of the "disturbances" caused by the border divisions in these language communities. The data suggest that the opposite is true.

Table 2 presents a table summarizing the relative vitality of cross-border versus non-cross-border languages in Africa. For each EGIDS level, it reports the number of languages at each level, with a break down by cross-border versus non-cross-border.

Table 2. Comparing cross-border versus non-cross-border languages by EGIDS levels

EGIDS levels	Cross-border languages	Non-cross-border languages	Total across Africa
EGIDS 4 Educational	30	48	78
EGIDS 5 Developing	166	372	538
EGIDS 6a Oral Vigorous	133	885	1,018
EGIDS 6b-7 In Trouble	20	235	255
EGIDS 8a-9 Dying	6	128	134
Totals	355	1,668	2,023

Based on the above data, there are three significant observations that can be made about the vitality of limited cross-border languages in Africa as compared to non-cross-border languages. For each of these, we created a 2x2 table of observed versus expected values, and then used a chi-square analysis to test if the observed differences in cross-border versus non-cross-border languages are significant. The result in all three cases is that the difference is significant at the 99.9% confidence level ($p < 0.001$).

(1) Significantly more limited cross-border languages have become languages of education (EGIDS 4) than their non-cross-border counterparts (8.5% versus 2.9%).

Table 3. Observed values, cross-border versus non-cross-border languages of education

EGIDS levels	Cross-border languages	Non-cross-border languages	Total across Africa
4 Language of education	30 (8.5%)	48 (2.9%)	78 (3.9%)
5-9 Not language of education	325 (91.5%)	1,620 (97.1%)	1,945 (96.1%)
Totals	355 (100%)	1,668 (100%)	2,023 (100%)

(2) Significantly more limited cross-border languages are developed with orthographies and literacy (EGIDS 4 + 5) than their non-cross-border counterparts (55% versus 25%).

Table 4. Observed values, cross-border versus non-cross-border languages of orthography and literacy

EGIDS levels	Cross-border languages	Non-cross-border languages	Total across Africa
4-5 Literacy development	196 (55.2%)	420 (25.2%)	616 (30.4%)
6-9 Not literacy development	159 (44.8%)	1,248 (74.8%)	1,407 (69.6%)
Totals	355 (100%)	1,668 (100%)	2,023 (100%)

(3) Significantly more limited cross-border languages are transmitted intergenerationally (EGIDS 4 + 5 + 6a) than their non-cross-border counterparts (93% versus 78%).

Table 5. Observed values, cross-border versus non-cross-border, intergenerational transmission

EGIDS levels	Cross-border languages	Non-cross-border languages	Total across Africa
4-6a Transmitted to all children	329 (92.7%)	1,305 (78.2%)	1,634 (80.8%)
6b-9 Not transmitted to all children	26 (7.3%)	363 (21.8%)	389 (19.2%)
Totals	*355 (100%)*	*1,668 (100%)*	*2,023 (100%)*

While these three statements can be statistically validated, that does not begin to explain *why* these statements would be true. Several hypotheses which might explain the strong vitality performance of cross-border languages over non-cross-border languages:

- It is possible that since cross-border languages tend to be larger than the non-cross-border languages, they are chosen for development sooner than their smaller counterparts.
- Border cities will often have greater economic resources and job possibilities (due to advantages in both trade and transportation). This can result in more financial resources being available for education and language development in general.[15]
- Border wealth could also mean lower levels of urbanization draining these areas of young people (i.e., no need to go to the capital for a job, if there is work here at the border).
- Border wealth could also mean more resources for local education, also keeping young people in the home area and leading to more stable communities with more stable language vitality.
- A stronger EGIDS level for a cross-border language may reflect realities on only one side of the border. The EGIDS level listed in the *Ethnologue* for a language will be the highest EGIDS estimate in all of the countries which report "in country" speech communities of that language.
- Cross-border languages may be twice as likely to enjoy favorable language development policies, given that two governments are involved, rather than just one.

10.4.3 The impact of limited cross-border languages on identity and language shift

It was anticipated that this research would reveal data that emphasizes the "might" of vehicular cross-border languages (which are better-served in their vehicular roles by being cross-border), as well as the "plight" of limited cross-border languages (presumably more hurt than helped by their cross-border status, which seemingly diminishes their access to both users and uses of the language). Instead, we have seen that many limited cross-border languages show evidence of vitality, at least

---

[15] Although center-periphery theories assert that border cities tend to be the furthest distances from the economic advantages of a central capital area, Chang (2010) points out that border cities have distinct advantages in both trade and transportation, which leads to enhanced economic resources and opportunities in these border cities, especially in the manufacturing sector (which depends highly on both trade and transportation).

with vigorous oral use and often with orthography and literacy development, or even being used as languages of instruction. More research would be needed to establish the causal factors for limited languages that show greater vitality as a correlation with being cross-border.

But there is another side to the real plight of many limited cross-border languages. Cross-border speech communities rarely have symmetrical territories, or speaker numbers, or even the same EGIDS vitality levels. In many cases, a tiny sliver group will have been cut off from their lifeline to the remainder of their ethnic community. Numerous limited cross-border languages are also suffering the devastation of identity-shift and language-shift away from their ethnic language and toward an urban or national language.

It is possible that these statistical analyses could be affected somewhat, if the reported EGIDS levels apply to only one side of the border, and if the EGIDS level is lower on the other side. Perhaps the side with stronger vitality represents the "might," and the weaker side represents the "plight."

Based on twenty years of cross-border language work, this author continues to be convinced that cross-border languages tend to have a more difficult challenge in language development, and have to overcome real obstacles in developing and promoting a unified language. More study is needed before accepting these statistical correlations as adequately capturing reality.

If differing EGIDS levels are discovered between two adjacent communities of speech which form part of the same cross-border language community, then it would be interesting to investigate whether one of the two countries has a language policy that is more conducive to language development. There are many complex factors that can play a part in divergent cross-border vitalities. As ACALAN points out on its official web page:[16]

> Apart from marginalization, the partition of Africa, with the resulting division of populations speaking the same language, has had a number of consequences. First, divergent policies pursued by different colonial administrations have led to different treatments for the same language group. For example, while one African language is used in primary education in one territory, the same language is completely ignored in another. Second, the entrenchment of different official languages has created a barrier in communication and collaboration. Third, the fact that the same African language is subjected to contact with two different official languages has resulted in divergent influences, in orthography, loanwords and code-mixing.

10.5 Understanding the implications for development of cross-border languages

10.5.1 Some initiatives that can benefit cross-border language development programs

Following are some strategies and methods that have been employed by language development programs involving cross-border languages and with which the author is familiar.

---

[16] ACALAN.org/index.php/en/about-ACALAN/background. Accessed 10 April 2018.

Mother tongue radio programs do not need a passport to cross national borders. In one language development project, the chief and his council asked us to work with two young men who had weekly radio programs in the vernacular language. Over the next couple years, they kept listeners informed about the ongoing efforts to research the language and develop an orthography. Listeners on both sides of the border were excited and motivated.

Android phone apps can also spread easily across borders. Several health apps (AIDS and infant dysentery) and other translated text apps have been developed in cross-border languages. Google Play Store makes them freely available, even for remote diaspora. Targeted Google ads can be purchased to promote free downloads on both sides of the border.

Vernacular Facebook pages or other web pages can be easily accessed in multiple countries. Gaining Facebook "likes" on such pages can promote the apps and other mother tongue materials referenced above.

Cross-border workshops can be helpful in uniting the cross-border community in their development initiatives. These were used when two Equatorial Guinean men attended six workshops in Cameroon over a three-year period. The prestige reference dialect was developed in Cameroon, but those two represented the majority dialect with the "most pure" form of the language, so their input was highly valued.

An international congress for a language community also builds unity and partnerships. Such a congress was held in Cameroon, inviting cross-border cousins from both Equatorial Guinea and Gabon. At that congress, participants established a language development committee and a translation committee.

Language work completed in one country can speed up parallel work in another country. In many cross-border situations, two dialects that are linguistically the same language will have to be treated as two distinct languages due to sociolinguistic reasons (differing histories, worldviews, loan words, and orthography preferences if involving two national official languages). Our team was able to obtain funding for a Cameroonian linguist to complete a two-year BASAL (Basic Standardization of African Languages) project in Cameroon Bakoko, then adapt his materials for Basek in Equatorial Guinea, with the result that the cross-border development went much faster than it otherwise would have.

Many recent software programs are available that can be useful for rapid adaptation of materials between related cross-border dialects. For example, the RENDER translation software facilitates using audio texts in one language as a model for translating them orally into a cross-border dialect or related-language, without having the confusing distraction of two competing orthographies (RENDER uses oral drafting, rather than written).[17]

Sharing of technology, knowledge, and skills is helpful. The Fa d'Ambu language spoken in Equatorial Guinea had ten years of development and translation experience by the time a related dialect in São Tomé began their language development. The experienced mother-tongue translator has offered his texts as reference texts, and may eventually become available to this new development project as a consultant.

Dividing responsibilities can benefit both sides. Three cross-border language projects are being developed predominantly in Cameroon, but participants on the Equatorial Guinea side have been able to assist by developing additional promotional and literacy materials.

---

[17] lingtransoft.info/apps/render/. Accessed 28 April 2018.

10.5.2 Localization of development efforts, by increasing partnerships with existing community groups and organizations

Too often, language development efforts have not taken into consideration the cross-border varieties, simply because the organization involved does not have active work in the neighboring country. Partnerships between development organizations and local communities and other organizations can alleviate that.

The African Academy of Languages has publicized goals, not only to develop the twelve Vehicular Cross-border Language Commissions, but also to develop and promote "the use of African languages in all domains of life in Africa." Their objectives include:

- To empower African languages in general and vehicular cross-border languages in particular, in partnership with the languages inherited from colonization;
- To ensure the development and promotion of African languages as factors of African integration and development.[18]

ACALAN also promotes six major projects to develop African languages:

1. Building a corpus of children's stories in African languages;
2. Promoting African languages in computing and cyberspace;
3. Training translators and interpreters;
4. MA and PhD programs in applied linguistics;
5. Making word lists and dictionaries, updating and developing key terminology in African languages;
6. Building an atlas of languages in Africa.[19]

Some or all of these could be shared goals for any other language development organization working in African languages.

10.6 Summary and conclusion

We have presented evidence that Africa's cross-border languages are strong, and perhaps even stronger on the whole than other African languages. There is ample evidence that vehicular languages are beginning to replace some of the limited single-ethnic languages. But even within the limited single-ethnic languages, we discovered surprising new evidence that the cross-border languages appear to fare better than their non-cross-border counterparts.

But it would be unfair to give the impression that the picture is all positive and good for the future of cross-border languages. There are numerous instances of smaller fragmented speech communities where border divisions have hurt their overall vitality. Many of these language groups are also experiencing identity shift and language shift toward more predominant languages. It is critical that development organizations not overlook these marginalized cross-border speech communities.

As nongovernmental organizations partner in the development of African languages, it is important to recognize the vitality and prominence of cross-border languages, and the value of partnering with governmental organizations at national

---

[18] acalan-au.org/viewcontent3.php?tab=2/. Accessed 23 April 2018.
[19] acalan.org/index.php/en/major-projects/african-linguistic-atlas-project/. Accessed 23 April 2018.

levels, and with official continent-wide efforts, in the development of cross-border languages and of all African languages.

References

ACALAN. 2001. Statutes of ACALAN, Chapter III, Article 22. Accessed 28 April 2018. acalan.org/index.php/en/about-acalan/main-decisions/statutes-of-acalan#SectionIII.

Bamgbose, Ayo. 2002. Mission and vision of the African Academy of Languages. *Special Bulletin of ACALAN*, January 2002, 24–27. Reproduced in Neville Alexander (ed.) 2004, *The intellectualization of African languages*, 60–66. Cape Town: PRAESA.

Chang, Bo Won. 2010. The power of geographical boundaries: Cultural, political, and economic border effects in a unitary nation. MA thesis. Iowa State University, Ames, IA. Accessed 4 September 2018. lib.dr.iastate.edu/cgi/viewcontent.cgi?article=2328&context=etd/.

Fishman, Joshua A. 1991. *Reversing language shift: Theoretical and empirical foundations of assistance to threatened languages*. Clevedon, UK: Multilingual Matters.

Lewis, M. Paul, and Gary F. Simons. 2010. Assessing endangerment: Expanding Fishman's GIDS. *Revue Roumaine de Linguistique* 55(2):103–120. Accessed 11 April 2018. lingv.ro/RRL 2 2010 art01Lewis.pdf/.

Märzhäuser, Christina. 2010. Cape Verdean Creole in Lisbon – young generation's perspective. *TRANS: Internet-Zeitschrift für Kulturwissenschaften* 17. Accessed 19 April 2018. inst.at/trans/17Nr/1-3/1-3_maerzhaeuser17.htm/.

Mufwene, Salikoko. 2005. Globalization and the myth of killer languages: What's really going on? In Graham Huggan and Stephen Klasen (eds.), *Perspectives on endangerment*, 19–48. Hildesheim, Germany: Georg Olms Verlag.

Nettle, Daniel, and Suzanne Romaine. 2000. *Vanishing voices: The extinction of the world's languages*. Oxford: Oxford University Press.

Prah, Kwesi Kwaa. 2003. Going native: Language of instruction for education, development and African emancipation. In Birgit Brock-Utne, Zubeida Desai, and Martha Qorro (eds.), *Language of instruction in Tanzania and South Africa (LOITASA)*. Dar-es-Salaam: E and D Publishers. Preprint: msu.ac.zw/elearning/material/1179313328Going native Prah.doc/.

Price, Glanville. 1984. *The language of Britain*. London: Edward Arnold.

Simons, Gary F., and Charles D. Fennig, eds. 2018. *Ethnologue: Languages of the world*. Twenty-first edition. Dallas, TX: SIL International. Online version: ethnologue.com/.

Part Three
Heart Matters

11
"Heart Language" as a Technical Term: A Critical Review

Gary F. Simons

Abstract. The phrase "heart language" has come to be used like a technical term among practitioners and promoters of Bible translation in minority languages. However, it has never been a technical term among scholars of language. We show that, in fact, it has fairly recently emerged in the literature of organizations that promote the Bible translation cause to a religious audience. But the use of the term within the Bible translation community has two fundamental problems: (1) it serves to perpetuate a conceptual bias that idealizes the world in monolingual terms, and (2) it hinders the Bible translation community's participation in the academic discourse about the functions of language in a multilingual world. The paper ends with a call for scholars in the Bible translation community to avoid using "heart language" as a technical term and rather to articulate the essential concepts that underlie the notion using terminology that aligns with the broader academic literature.

11.1 SIL's historical language ideology

Writing on the topic of language ideologies for the collection of papers in the journal *Language* on "SIL International and the disciplinary culture of linguistics" (Dobrin 2009), linguistic anthropologist Courtney Handman writes:

> SIL and other translation organizations' materials specifically focus on the mother tongue, or 'heart language' as it was once called (see Cowan 1979). A speaker's first, native language holds a special place in Christian translation literature, as the language in which the Scriptures and other materials can best be understood by receptor communities. (Handman 2009:637)

Her characterization of SIL as focusing on mother tongue is accurate, as is the citation of Cowan 1979 as an authoritative source for the underlying ideology. However, one aspect of the statement is not accurate. The wording implies that Cowan used the term "heart language" and that the term is now falling out of vogue. In fact, the exact opposite is the case. Cowan did not use the term; rather, as we show below, it has come into vogue since he wrote his book.

George Cowan was a long-time early president of Wycliffe Bible Translators (1957-1981). His book contains a section on terminology within the chapter on "Which language?" (1979:55–68), where he defines his term of choice in this way:

> By *mother tongue* (or *native language,* without any pejorative sense) we mean the language spoken from infancy. This language is the first, and perhaps the only one spoken. It seems natural to a person and is adequate to talk about all of life's situations.

Neither the term "heart language," nor even the word "heart," appears in the chapter.[1]

Kenneth L. Pike, the earliest and longest serving president of SIL (1942–1979), was the most prominent figure in the making of SIL (Aldridge and Simons 2018). He addresses the same question in an essay entitled, "We will tell them, but in what language?" (Pike 1962:104–109). He never speaks of "mother tongue," but uses the term "local language" in the opening paragraph—perhaps a sign of being attuned to the terminology more likely to be used in academic circles. He does, however, appeal to the metaphor of the language of one's birth:

> To me, however, this program [of trying to reach the ethnic groups of the world through a trade language] appears very difficult. The preacher says in Ecclesiastes 10:10: "If the ax is dull and its edge unsharpened, more strength is needed." The Sword of the Spirit, though it still cuts deeply, seems to have a dull edge unless it is wielded in the language in which a man was born.[2] (Pike 1962:105)

I have been unable to find any evidence that Pike ever spoke of "heart language." There is a passage in which he uses "language of the heart," but with a completely different meaning. He concludes the lead essay in *Language and Faith,* a book published by Wycliffe Bible Translators to promote the work of SIL, with these words:

> Let's see if you and we can serve our neighbor, giving to him the documents which have let us become one community, citizens of heaven, talking the common language of the heart. (Pike 1972:30)

Here he is using the phrase to refer not to any particular human language, but to a transcendent capacity to communicate across languages.

Pushing the timeline back further to William Cameron Townsend, who co-founded SIL in 1934, we similarly find no evidence of "heart language" as a term. The two volumes of the digitally released *Quotable "Uncle Cam"* (Hibbard 2007, 2009) provide a 130,000-word corpus of selected excerpts from talks and letters that is easy to search. The word "heart" occurs 92 times in the corpus, but never in association

---

[1] Note that Cowan's definition makes no appeal to an emotional function; rather, his characterization of the mother tongue as "seem[ing] natural to a person" resonates with John Watters' contribution, chapter 14 in this part of this volume, which speaks of it as an "acquired reflex language."

[2] This sentence contains two biblical allusions: to Hebrews 4:12, "For the word of God is … sharper than any two-edged sword, piercing even to the dividing asunder of soul and spirit," and to the testimony of the witnesses to the Pentecost event in Acts 2:8, "How hear we every man in our own tongue, wherein we were born?" (both quoted from the King James Version). The latter also served as the title for an article that Pike published describing the work of SIL (Pike 1959).

with language.[3] The term "mother tongue" occurs only three times, so neither was that his preferred way of talking about the languages that were the focus of SIL's attention. The following phrases never occur: native language, vernacular language, local language, first language. The most common modifiers of "language" in the corpus are: "Indian" (14 times), "their" (17 times), "every" (27 times), and "own" (32 times). One might surmise that bilingualism was so rare in his early experience that he did not find it necessary to develop terms for distinguishing languages by function—the mental model was that everybody had their own language.

11.2 Searching for the origins of "heart language"

If the terminology of "heart language" did not come from these early leaders of the movement, where did it come from? I began the search by consulting with SIL's Corporation Secretary[4] to try to discover when the term first surfaced in the official records of the organization. The earliest occurrence he found was in 1997, in a letter written by a Board member. Another significant milestone in the history of the term came in 2001, in an informational report to the SIL Board about the work of Seed Company, in which it was reported that their mission is "to translate the Scriptures into the heart language of people groups still without God's Word."

The longer phrase "language of the heart" was first proposed in 1998 as the label for one of SIL's core values; the shortened form "heart language" did occur in the text discussing the rationale. The longer phrase became part of Board policy in 2001 when the core values were adopted.[5]

To search for evidence of when "heart language" first started to be used in SIL literature, I was able to use the corpus of *LinguaLinks Library*—a CD-ROM published in 2003 containing the full text of every issue of *Notes on Anthropology, Notes on Linguistics, Notes on Literacy, Notes on Scripture Use, Notes on Sociolinguistics, Ethno-Info,* and *READ,* plus the full text of about sixty books. Figure 1 shows a plot of the number of occurrences per half decade over the last twenty-five years of the previous century. The earliest occurrence in that collection of literature is in an article by Margaret Wendell (1975). The next occurrence was not until 1980. It climbs to a rate of four occurrences per year in the early 1990s, but given the total volume of

---

[3] A quote has sprung up all over the Web, which is attributed to Townsend, but never with the citation of a source: "Understanding Scripture in a language other than the heart language in which we think and experience emotion is like trying to eat soup with a fork. You can get a little taste, but you cannot get nourished." Given that Townsend never uses the term "heart language" in the corpus compiled by Hibbard (2007, 2009), this quote sounds dubious. I therefore put the question to Hibbard, who was Townsend's personal secretary for decades and now curates the archive of his papers. His response: "I never heard Townsend speak about the 'soup with a fork' idea" (personal communication, 4 April 2018).

[4] I am indebted to George Shultz, the current Corporation Secretary for SIL International, and to his predecessor, Gene Burnham, who collaborated to answer my query in a personal communication dated 30 January 2018.

[5] One must hasten to add, however, that this involved only the adoption of "language of the heart" as a label. The text of the core value only affirms "the effectiveness of [all] languages for communication and access to knowledge." The statement makes no appeal to the metaphorical basis of the label, nor does it imply in any way that only one language is effective for any given individual.

all books and articles published per year, that means it was still occurring rather infrequently.

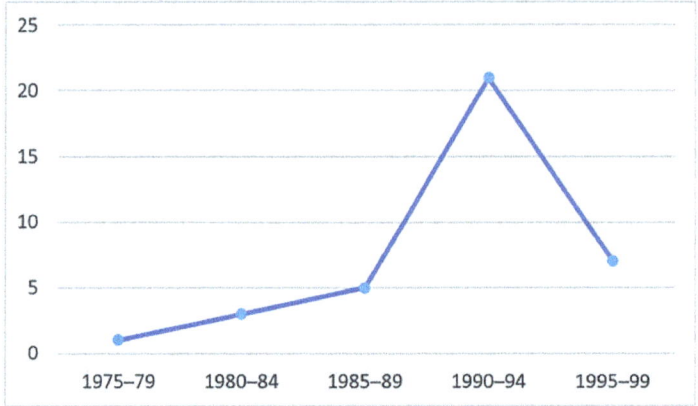

Figure 1. Occurrences of "heart language" in *LinguaLinks Library* per half decade.

Could we push the search for the first occurrence in the literature of SIL's movement back even further? For help with this I turned to SIL's Corporate Historian[6] who examined an archive of all the issues of *Translation*—the magazine published from 1943 to 1975 by Wycliffe Bible Translators to promote the cause to its constituency. He found the following progression of passages, beginning with words from the organization's founder in 1956, which speak of the "heart" in describing the spiritual impact of Bible translation:

- "... translating the Scriptures, planting them in the hearts of the people, ..." (W. C. Townsend, "In this generation," *Translation*, Winter 1956–1957, p. 2)
- "I want His Word to be written in my heart and remain there. ... May I not receive His Word in my hands alone but also in my heart." (Juan Lopez Mucha, translated from *La Biblia in Mexico, Translation*, Fall 1958, p. 16)
- "God's Word pierced our hearts." (Testimony of Chol believers as reported by staff writer, "The new word: Chols read own New Testament," *Translation*, Spring 1961, p. 4)
- "... in a language that reaches their heart." (Bernie May, "Report on JAARS," *Translation*, Summer 1961, p. 7)
- "... receiving the Word of God, which has been translated into his language, into his heart." (Advertisement for *White Condor* film,*Translation*, Winter 1961 –1962, p. 16)
- "An Apache woman—who also spoke English—said recently upon hearing the Gospel in her own tongue, 'It goes into my head in English, but it goes down into my heart in my own language." (Staff writer, "Why Bible translation?" *Translation*, Summer 1962, p. 16)

---

[6] I am indebted to Boone Aldridge who eagerly joined in the search for the roots of "heart language" and helped immensely by his investigations in the archive and his encouraging correspondence. The quotes reported here were compiled by him in a personal correspondence dated 6 April 2018.

- "… the flame of God's Word is kindling fires in the hearts of those who hear, …" (Betty Stevens, "Amuesha victory," *Translation*, Summer 1963, p. 6)
- "What better can we leave the people than God's Word in the language of their hearts?," (Kenneth Weathers, quoted in John Beekman, "Translation treasures," *Translation*, Summer 1963, p. 11)

This leads up to the earliest known use of "heart language" in the Wycliffe literature, which occurs in 1968.[7] It is in an article by a Wycliffe staff writer that introduces the newly formed Wycliffe Associates (described as a "layman's auxiliary organization") and invites readers to join the new organization:

> Wycliffe Bible Translators chose the illustrious name of the great English translator to identify their linguistic organization, since their primary purpose is "to preach the gospel, not where Christ was named," through the translated Word into the "heart" language of the primitive peoples, the "tongue wherein 'they' were born."[8] (Betty Stevens, "Are you on the home team," *Translation* March–April 1968, p. 16)

The use of "heart" in all of the above examples is metaphorical. And many of the examples occur in a context that is rich with other metaphors. Metaphorical language is known to have a persuasive edge over literal language (Sopory and Dillard 2002; Charteris-Black 2011) and one can easily surmise that this helps to explain the rise of the term within a genre of literature that is inherently promotional.

11.3 Fitting terminology to audience

The investigations of the preceding section find that the term "heart language" appears to have been coined by a Wycliffe staff writer when announcing the birth of Wycliffe Associates and to have come to maturity when it was incorporated into the official mission statement of Seed Company. These three organizations have something in common, namely, that their primary function has been to promote the cause of Bible translation among Christians in the United States and to raise resources for such work. That leads to the hypothesis that the explanation for the rise of "heart language" as a term lies in its effectiveness in communicating the need for Bible translation to that constituency.[9]

This hypothesis could be tested by looking into the extent to which the term is used by different kinds of organizations. The site-search and exact-search features of

---

[7] I am indebted to my colleague Ken Olson for pointing out that earlier uses of "heart language" can be found by searching Google Books Ngrams (books.google.com/ngrams/). For instance, he discovered Miller (1917) which uses both "mother tongue" and "heart language" in a discussion of whether American children of Swedish immigrants should get their religious instruction in English or Swedish. While the term can be found in older literature, its appearance within the Wycliffe literature appears to have arisen independently of any prior use.

[8] The use of single and double quotes in this extended quotation is copied exactly from the source. The use of scare quotes around "heart" suggests that the author was aware that a new phrase was being coined. The other double quotes indicate quotations from the King James Bible (Romans 15:20 and Acts 2:8, respectively). The single quotes within the second quotation would be rendered as square brackets by a modern editor; they indicate the substitution of "they" in place of the "we" that is in the original text.

[9] One could observe that "heart language" has taken on the flavor of a marketing term.

Google make it possible to do something like this.[10] Table 1 shows a comparison of the usage of "mother tongue" versus "heart language" on the websites of the four organizations that have been mentioned so far. They are listed in increasing order of the number of webpages containing the phrase "heart language." Note that while both terms are used on all four sites, "mother tongue" is used over five hundred times more often than the counterpart on the SIL website, whereas "heart language" is used twenty-six times more often on the Wycliffe Associates website.

Table 1. Comparison of terminology usage on four organizational websites

Organizational website	Number of pages containing "mother tongue"	Number of pages containing "heart language"
SIL International (sil.org)	26,800	50
Wycliffe USA (wycliffe.org)	342	389
Seed Company (theseedcompany.org)	1,760	927
Wycliffe Associates (wycliffeassociates.org)	134	3,540

A good baseline for comparison is the English Wikipedia. It reflects a consensus of what are widely considered to be proper technical terms. Using the search box on any page at en.wikipedia.org and using double quotes around the search term to match the exact phrase, reveals that "heart language" occurs in only 3 pages[11] of the entire Wikipedia (for instance, one occurrence is in words quoted from a Bible organization communique concerning the death of SIL's John Bendor-Samuel[12]. By contrast, "mother tongue" occurs in 5,641 pages.[13] The alternative term, "native language," occurs on 4,730 pages. But both of those terms are described as having known problems, so the consensus of Wikipedia editors is that "first language" (occurring on 5,569 pages) is the preferred term. The two former terms are thus redirected to the latter term. "First language" (with its abbreviation, L1) is also the preferred term in the *Ethnologue* (ethnologue.com).

Another technical term that is favored for some academic purposes is "local language." (It occurs on 2,263 pages of the Wikipedia.) After discussing the pros and cons of the various alternatives, this is the term that Grenoble and Whaley

---

[10] The data displayed in table 1 and figure 2 are based on Google site searches performed on 28 April 2018. A site search is performed by including the keyword "site:" prepended to a domain name as a search term. For instance, *site:sil.org* limits the search just to pages occurring on the sil.org website. The terms were further matched using an exact search, that is, by placing "mother tongue" or "heart language" within double quotes in the search box. Thus a search for *site:sil.org "mother tongue"* counts and lists all the pages at sil.org containing that exact phrase. See documentation on Google advanced search: google.com/advanced_search/.

[11] The search, in fact, yields 13 hits (on 31 April 2018), but reading down the list of context snippets we see that 10 of them are cases in which the two words collocate (sometimes even with intervening punctuation) without forming the phrase "heart language."

[12] en.wikipedia.org/wiki/John_Bendor-Samuel/.

[13] Since "mother tongue" is a recognized term that redirects to a particular article, it is necessary to use the Advanced Search option in Wikipedia to get the count and list of pages containing the term.

(2006:13-16) choose to use in their book on *Saving Languages*. It is also the term that Lewis and Simons (2016) use in *Sustaining Language Use*. Figure 2[14] shows the relative frequency of the terms mentioned thus far within the English language literature that has been scanned by the Google Books project (Michel et al. 2011). We see that "mother tongue" has been the most popular, but peaked in 1980 and is now on par with "native language." "First language" and "local language" were hardly used before 1940, but have been rising ever since with "first language" beginning to approach the popularity of the first two. By comparison, "heart language" is barely in evidence.

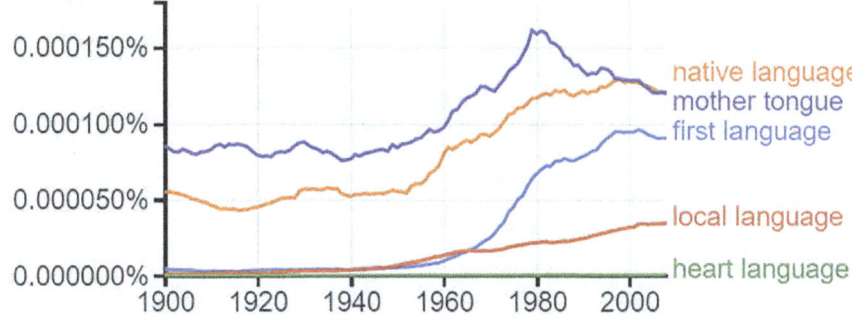

Figure 2. Relative frequency of language terminology since 1900.

A website selects its terminology to fit its target audience. Figure 3 provides an analysis of terminology on the websites of twenty-four organizations that are related to the Bible translation movement (with Wikipedia and UNESCO also included for comparison). The green bar represents the use of "first language" and "local language" which are grouped into the same category as representing the use of technical terms for a more academic audience. The blue bar represents the use of "mother tongue" as a popular term for a general audience. The yellow bar represents the use of "heart language" as a more emotive term for a religious audience. The number of occurrences of each term was found using exact site search with Google; the graph in figure 3 charts the relative proportions of the three terminology types. The top group of three websites are those in which the technical terms predominate; the second group of fourteen are those in which the popular terminology predominates; and the final group of seven are those in which the religious terminology predominates.

---

[14] Go to books.google.com/ngrams/ to generate similar graphs.

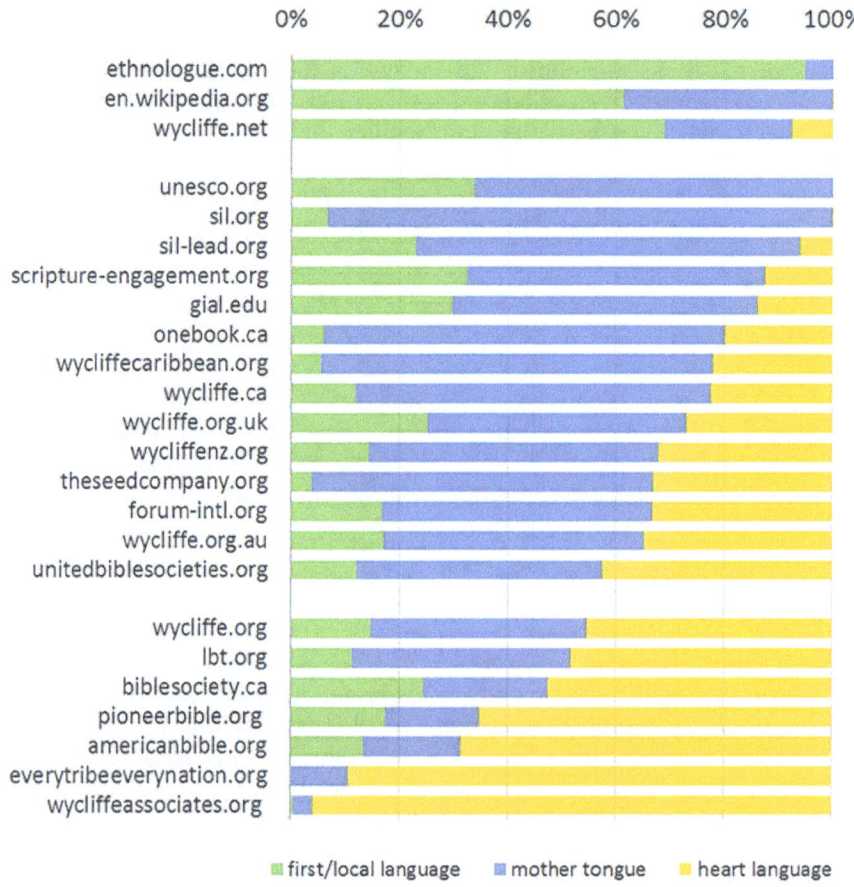

Figure 3. Organizational websites by dominant style of terminology (technical versus popular versus religious).

Perhaps the most surprising result in figure 3 is that the Wycliffe Global Alliance (wycliffe.net) appears at the top of the chart as having predominantly technical terminology. A possible factor here is that the terms preferred for a technical audience are also more modern—"mother tongue" is somewhat dated at present. The Wycliffe Global Alliance is only ten years old, and thus was able to begin developing its website using modern terminology without having a large backlog of older material. Another factor, though, is that they do have a truly global audience. While metaphors of the heart as the seat of emotions abound across Romance and Germanic languages (Gutiérrez Pérez 2008), they are far from universal. Thus the "language of the heart" fails to resonate with many Africans, Asians, and Pacific Islanders. With respect to the hypothesis that "heart language" is prevalent where it has proven effective for fundraising, it is relevant to note that Wycliffe Global Alliance (unlike all the other Wycliffe organizations in the lower part of the chart) is not directly involved in fundraising.

Having explored the history of the term "heart language" and the extent of its use, we now turn to a discussion of problems that are inherent in using the term.

Particularly in focus are problems with trying to use "heart language" as a technical term when writing about language.

11.4 Perpetuating a monolingual bias

While the term "heart language" may have the positive result of moving a particular kind of audience to action, the way the term is being used is also having the negative result of perpetuating a conceptual bias that idealizes the world in monolingual terms. We have shown that Townsend's original rhetoric simply spoke of "their own language"—no further description was needed in the case in which a people did not use other languages to any appreciable extent. For monolinguals, it is safe to assume that their one language performs all the functions of language in their daily life.

As recognition grew that multiple languages were typically relevant in the life of a people, it became necessary to use terms that would distinguish their "own" language from outside languages. "Mother tongue" emerged as the term favored in the SIL literature to identify the language learned from infancy in the home, as opposed to other languages learned later in life. That first language could no longer be assumed to perform all the functions of language in the life of the people, but it was typically the language of deep and intimate communication within the group and thus appropriate for Bible translation. Therefore, it worked to substitute "the mother tongue" in place of "their own language" in the rhetoric of the founding era.

However, in the process of rebranding "mother tongue" as "heart language" for a newer audience, things seriously break down if we continue this pattern and simply substitute the new term in statements that previously used the former term. This is because "mother tongue" evokes the manner in which the language was acquired,[15] but "heart language" is about how the language functions in daily life. There is often a one-to-one correlation, but this is by no means a given. For instance, an oft-repeated definition is, "Your heart language is the language you dream in." The wording of that definition assumes that a person has only one such language. But what if you can dream in two languages, as many bilinguals report doing?

Another kind of breakdown can occur in the rhetoric of "translating the Bible into the heart language of a people group." Again, the definite article in this wording encodes the presumption of a single language, but it also implies another inherent assumption, namely, that the one language is the traditional local language. But in a situation where a people group has undergone significant shift toward an outside language, the traditional language may no longer be understood well enough to "speak to the heart." This can even be the case for some who learned the traditional language as a mother tongue, but began the shift to another language at an early age. (This explains the title of the paper by Daniel Paul, chapter 13 this volume, "When none of my heart languages is my mother tongue.")

The rhetoric of "heart language," at least when indiscriminately used as a substitute for "mother tongue," serves to perpetuate a conceptual bias that seems to idealize a situation in which people have just one language that matters.[16] If the term

---

[15] This is not as true today as it once was, since in the context of language shift, "mother tongue" is also taking on a purely identificational meaning in the sense of "the traditional language of my mother, which I am not able to speak."

[16] It should be noted that on 25 September 2018, four months after this paper was presented at the Pike Center symposium on "Language and Identity in a Multilingual,

is to be used at all, it should be as the label for a way that a language functions in life and not as a synonym for "mother tongue" or "first language." So what function is it? Seeking the answer to that question should drive us into the academic literature to see what experts are saying about the functions of language.

11.5 Hindering academic discourse

Another negative result of using the term "heart language" is that, when used in its written literature, it serves to isolate the Bible translation community from the wider academic discourse about the functions of language in a multilingual world. While such isolation might be expected for the promotional literature, it poses a serious problem for scholarship. Terminological isolation has two undesirable consequences: the wider academic world will not benefit from scholarship couched in terminology that it finds off-putting, and the ears of the Bible translation community will not be attuned to hear what the wider academy is saying.

In his contribution to a symposium on the topic of "What is Christian scholarship," Nicholas Wolterstorff, a leading Christian philosopher and a professor emeritus at Yale University, concludes with this summary statement:

> It is the calling of the Christian scholar to think and act with a Christian mind, and to speak with an appropriate Christian voice, as she engages in her discipline. (Wolterstorff 2014:17)

A key aspect of speaking with an appropriate Christian voice is that it "be a voice that can genuinely be heard by one's fellow scholars in the discipline—a voice such that it contributes to the dialogue of the discipline" (Wolterstorff 2014:9). It is necessary for the Christian scholar to know the vocabulary and the ways of thinking and speaking of the mainstream practitioners of the discipline; otherwise, she cannot speak into the discipline in a way that the mainstream can hear and accept. To the mainstream, talk of "heart language" is likely to sound amusing or quaint at best, or because of the religious overtones, seriously off-putting at worst. But the concept behind "heart language" encompasses far more than religion—it is wonderfully holistic, as the contribution by John Watters in this part of the volume so eloquently presents. Is there a label for the concept that would allow the Bible translation community to speak more effectively into the wider scholarly dialogue about these issues? Watters offers a proposal: "acquired reflex language."

The flip side of the scholarly dialog is listening. In order to listen for how the wider academic literature could inform understanding of the holistic concept that lies behind "heart language," it is necessary to know the vocabulary of the discipline and to recognize when relevant things are being said. To what extent is "heart language" the same as the language of intimate insider communication—what sociolinguists simply call the language of the home domain, or as it is sometimes more poetically rendered, "the language of hearth and home"? To what extent is "heart language" a matter of deep comprehension versus deep emotional impact versus deep self-identification or intentionality? The contributions which follow (chapter 12 Kyle Harris, chapter 13 Daniel Paul, and chapter 14 John Watters) are good examples of delving into the academic literature to learn how it might inform our understanding.

Migrating World" (Penang, Malaysia, May 10–15), Wycliffe USA issued revised messaging guidelines on "Heart language and multilingualism." The new guidelines instruct against using wording which implies that people have just one "heart language."

11.6 Conclusion

Though the phrase "heart language" has come to be used as something of a technical term within the Bible translation community, it appears to be a term that developed primarily as a way of promoting the cause of Bible translation to a religious audience. It is not defined well enough, nor accepted broadly enough, to be used as a technical term. Rather than doing so and creating a literature that is isolated from the academic mainstream, scholars in the Bible translation community are encouraged to articulate the essential concepts that underlie the notion using terminology that aligns with the broader academic literature. In so doing we will be better able to contribute to and learn from the wider scholarly dialog about the functions of language in our multilingual world.

References

Aldridge, Boone, and Gary Simons. 2018. Kenneth Pike and the making of Wycliffe Bible Translators and SIL International. *Christianity Today: Christian History*, posted 2 February 2018. christianitytoday.com/history/2018/february/kenneth-pike-sil-wycliffe.html/.

Charteris-Black, Jonathan. 2011. *Politicians and rhetoric: The persuasive power of metaphor.* Second edition. New York: Palgrave Macmillan.

Cowan, George. 1979. *The word that kindles.* Chappaqua, NY: Christian Herald Books.

Dobrin, Lise. 2009. SIL International and the disciplinary culture of linguistics: Introduction. *Language* 85(3):618–619.

Grenoble, Lenore A., and Lindsay J. Whaley. 2006. *Saving languages: An introduction to language revitalization.* New York: Cambridge University Press.

Gutiérrez Pérez, Regina. 2008. A cross-cultural analysis of heart metaphors. *Revista Alicantina de Estudios Ingleses* 21:25–56.

Handman, Courtney. 2009. Language ideologies, endangered-language linguistics, and Christianization. *Language* 85(3):635–639.

Hibbard, Cal, ed. 2007. *Quotable "Uncle Cam": Selected observations from one of God's servants, W. Cameron Townsend.* Waxhaw, NC: SIL International, Townsend Archives.

Hibbard, Cal, ed. 2009. *Quotable "Uncle Cam": Selected observations from one of God's servants, W. Cameron Townsend.* Vol. 2. Waxhaw, NC: SIL International, Townsend Archives.

Lewis, M. Paul, and Gary F. Simons. 2016. *Sustaining language use: Perspectives on community-based language development.* Publications in Ethnography 42. Dallas, TX: SIL International.

Michel, Jean-Baptiste, Yuan Kui Shen, Aviva Presser Aiden, Adrian Veres, Matthew K. Gray, The Google Books Team, Joseph P. Pickett, Dale Hoiberg, Dan Clancy, Peter Norvig, Jon Orwant, Steven Pinker, Martin A. Nowak, and Erez Lieberman Aiden. 2011. Quantitative analysis of culture using millions of digitized books. *Science* 331(6014):176–182. doi.org/10.1126/science.1199644/.

Miller, Samuel M. 1917. The language problem. *The Lutheran Companion* 25(1):639–640. books.google.com/books?id=PWY0AQAAMAAJ/.

Pike, Kenneth L. 1959. Our own tongue wherein we were born (The work of the Wycliffe Bible Translators and Summer Institute of Linguistics). *The Bible Translator* 10(2):70–82.

Pike, Kenneth L. 1962. *With heart and mind: A personal synthesis of scholarship and devotion.* Grand Rapids, MI: Eerdmans.

Pike, Kenneth L. 1972. Language and faith. In Cornell Capa and Dale Kietzman (eds.), *Language and faith*, 18–30. Santa Ana, CA: Wycliffe Bible Translators.

Sopory, Pradeep, and James P. Dillard. 2002. The persuasive effects of metaphor: A meta-analysis. *Human Communication Research* 28(3):382–419.

Wendell, Margaret M. 1975. An experimental project for production of reading material in a preliterate society. *Notes on Literacy* 18:1–9.

Wolterstorff, Nicholas. 2014. "Fides quaerens intellectum" [Faith seeking understanding].[17] In Thomas M. Crisp, Steve L. Porter, and Gregg A. Ten Elshof (eds.), *Christian scholarship in the twenty-first century: Prospects and perils*, 1–17. Grand Rapids, MI: Eerdmans.

---

[17] Wolterstorff presented this paper in a 2012 symposium at Biola University on the topic of "What is Christian scholarship?" A video recording is available at: cct.biola.edu/resources/fides-quaerens-intellectum/.

12
L1 and L2 Comprehension and Emotional Impact among Early Proficient Bilinguals

Kyle Harris

Abstract. Voices from inside the Bible translation movement commonly express the notion that the language learned first and in the home and which uniquely expresses one's identity—a people's so-called "heart language"—is uniquely suited to deep level communication of and impactful engagement with Scriptures. This concept is largely true in speech communities where people primarily use their first language (L1) and are only marginally proficient in languages of wider communication (LWCs). In other speech communities where people develop native speaker competency in multiple languages from an early age, the idea that the local vernacular uniquely facilitates comprehension and impact is not supported by research. This paper discusses research suggesting that for early proficient bilinguals and multilinguals, comprehension and impact can be equally experienced in multiple languages. This implies that in contexts in which people achieve high levels of fluency in multiple languages from an early age, Bible translation agencies may decide that a vernacular translation is not needed or if a vernacular translation is needed, it may be for reasons other than improved comprehension and impact.

The following are key terms used throughout the chapter:

- *Age of onset* or *age of acquisition:* The age at which a person begins learning a specific language.
- *Critical period:* A period early in life during which humans possess a heightened sensitivity and ability to learn languages.
- *Early acquisition:* Starting to learn a language during the critical period.
- *Late acquisition:* Starting to learn a language after the critical period.
- *Simultaneous bilinguals:* People who began learning L1 and L2 at the same time.
- *Sequential bilinguals:* People who began learning L2 after they began learning L1.
- *Balanced bilinguals:* People who have equal proficiency across L1 and L2.

- *Proficient bilinguals:* People who have native speaker proficiency in L1 and L2.
- *Dominant language:* Describes a situation where a person is more fluent in one language of his or her repertoire and uses that language more frequently and over a wider range of domains.

12.1 Introduction

Those in the Bible translation movement are very familiar with the notion of "heart language," which has come to be used in the promotional literature as a synonym for "mother tongue" (see the paper by Gary Simons, chapter 11 this volume). It is typically conceptualized as the language which is uniquely connected with a person's ethnic identity and culture. Because of these connections and because it is learned at an early age and to a level of fluency not normally achieved with languages of wider communication, it is thought that the mother tongue (as the "heart language") is uniquely suited for deep-level communication and for fostering transformational engagement with the Scriptures. Monson (2015), for example, gives a good example of this thinking:[1]

> The ordinary person doesn't know LWC (language of wider communication) well because it is not their heart language. It is not the language their mothers spoke to sooth them as infants. It's not how they tell their spouse and kids they love them. It smacks of business and politics. Not love. … Though much good still has come from the Bible's influence in a second language, the word of God in the heart language has far more power to change hearts and lives. … The roots of a second language grow only as deep as the intellect. They do not reach the heart. … Care for the least of these, without the soul-saving and soul-consoling message of Jesus in the heart language, is not much different than the physical help a secular organization could provide.

This understanding of the mother tongue as "heart language" is built on several assumptions. First, it assumes that the mother tongue is always one's ethnic or traditional language. Second, that people understand their mother tongue better than they do the language(s) of wider communication. Third, that because the mother tongue is learned and used in intimate domains, it engages the emotions more fully. And fourth, that because the mother tongue functions in the intimate domains of family and friends, it speaks to more important areas of people's lives.

This conception of the importance of the mother tongue for clear communication of and impactful engagement with the Scriptures may be valid in contexts where people grow up monolingual and only learn a second language (typically a LWC) much later in life, if at all. In many language groups, for example, only the elite and the highly educated are fluent in the language(s) of wider communication. Others have a much lower level of fluency. In these kinds of contexts, the local vernacular will typically hold a primary place in people's lives, thought, and social interactions. Therefore, a quality vernacular translation should be both more comprehensible

---

[1] Other examples are: Australia Bible Society 2011; Bible Society of Singapore 2015; Wycliffe Bible Translators UK 2017.

and more able to engage the emotions than a translation in a language of wider communication.

But what about contexts in which people grow up as proficient bilinguals from a very early age, developing native-speaker fluency in two or more languages? In Indonesia, for example, where I currently live, many children learn their local language and Indonesian either simultaneously or sequentially at an early age. Those who learn sequentially usually begin learning Indonesian when they start elementary school between the ages of five and seven, even though they probably will have had at least some previous exposure to the language. The 2010 Indonesian census revealed that 84% of those aged five to nine were already able to speak Indonesian [ind] in addition to their local language.[2] The result of early age of onset of both L1 and L2 learning is a high level of proficient bilingualism. Multilingualism is, therefore, the norm in Indonesia, with the majority of people in the country having some capability in the national language in addition to fluency in one (or more) local languages. In these multilingual contexts, language use is determined by a multitude of factors including, among others, language domain, social norms, and shifting identities.

The question that this paper seeks to answer is whether or not the assumption of communicative and affective advantages commonly associated with mother tongues are valid in a context like Indonesia where proficient early bilingualism is the norm. Put another way, is the local vernacular more comprehensible and more impactful than the national language in contexts where both languages are learned early in life to native-speaker fluency?

In an effort to answer this question I will first examine recent research on the relationship between the age of onset of second language (L2) learning and ultimate fluency attained. Second, I will discuss recent research related to the comparative emotive power of first (L1) and second languages as a function of age of L2 acquisition. If it is found that first languages demonstrate no advantage in comprehension and emotive impact over languages of wider communication when those languages are learned very early in life, it would be necessary for those of us in the Bible translation movement to rethink the foundation upon which we have so often built our case for producing translations in these deeply multilingual contexts.

12.2 Comprehension

The first assumption upon which the importance of mother tongue translations is based is that those translations are more comprehensible than equivalent translations in a language of wider communication. In this section I will look specifically at the correlation between the age of onset of L2 acquisition, that is, the age at which people begin to learn the second language, and their ultimate ability to achieve native-speaker fluency. I expect that if a person is able to achieve native-speaker fluency in a second language, they will be able to comprehend the Scriptures in that language at least as well, and perhaps even better than in their vernacular. This is especially the case if L2 has traditionally been the primary language used in the church or other religious domains.

---

[2] From the official website of the 2010 census, see "Population 5 years of age and over by age group and ability to speak Indonesian." Accessed April 30, 2018. sp2010.bps.go.id/index.php/site/tabel?tid=283&wid=0/.

12.2.1 Critical Period Hypothesis

The white-crowned sparrow is able to perfectly reproduce its species' song only if exposed to the song between ten and fifty days of age. Exposure to the song either before or after that critical period will result in abnormal song development (Marler 1970). Other birds and animals exhibit similar kinds of critical periods during which they exhibit heightened ability for specific types of learning (Mayberry and Kluender 2018).

Much of the recent research into the relationship between the age of acquisition and the ultimate fluency attained in a second language has focused on the question of whether or not a critical period exists during which humans exhibit a heightened ability to learn languages. The idea of a critical period for language learning was introduced by Penfield and Roberts (1959) and further developed by Lenneberg (1967). The Critical Period Hypothesis (CPH), as it is commonly understood today, states that humans possess a heightened sensitivity and ability to learn languages during a bounded period early in life. This period of heightened sensitivity includes onset, peak, and offset periods. For language learning, the onset period is thought to coincide with birth or to begin shortly thereafter. Language sensitivity rises rapidly to a peak and remains at that level for several years. Finally, the language sensitivity begins to gradually decline until the heightened sensitivity disappears altogether (De Groot 2011; Birdsong 2005). The end of the offset period is usually thought to coincide with puberty. After the end of the offset period, people retain the ability to learn languages but will not be able to achieve native speaker fluency across all components of language. Figure 1 illustrates how the CPH conceptualizes language sensitivity over time.

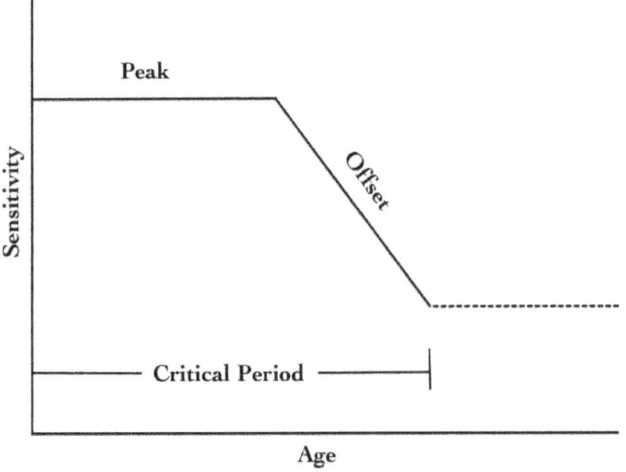

Figure 1. A graphical representation of the Critical Period Hypothesis. Note that for this representation, the onset is assumed to occur at birth.

The CPH leads to two important predictions. First, only those L2 learners who begin the learning process during the critical period will be capable of achieving native-speaker fluency. Second, after the end of the offset period there should be no further degradation in language learning capabilities. From the end of the offset onward, people's ability to learn languages should remain relatively stable as they age (Birdsong 2005; DeKeyser 2012). The first prediction is most salient to the purposes of this paper.

12.2.2 Critical Period Hypothesis in the light of research

The first prediction of the CPH, that only L2 learners who begin the learning process during the critical period have the potential to achieve native speaker fluency in the language, has been validated by recent research. While some studies have discovered people who claimed to have achieved native speaker competence even though they began their L2 learning after the offset period, typically those studies have focused on the knowledge or performance of only certain aspects of the language such as pronunciation, morphosyntax, or the lexicon. When competency is evaluated across the entire range of pronunciation, morphosyntax, and lexicon, it is found that only those who begin learning during the critical period are able to achieve native speaker fluency in all aspects of the language (Abrahamsson 2012:192).

If the ability to achieve native speaker fluency ends at the end of the offset period, then for the purposes of evaluating the potential for early learners of L2 to achieve native speaker levels of fluency, it is important to understand when the offset begins and ends. Various studies have identified the start of the offset period to be between 5 and 7 years of age (Johnson and Newport 1989; Pinker 1994; Granena and Long 2013, DeKeyser 2000; Birdsong 2005; Abrahamsson 2012). The end of the offset period varies according to the component of language. Granena and Long (2013), for example, in a study of Chinese learners of Spanish [spa], found that the offset period for phonology ended at about age twelve. The offset period for lexis and collocation ends between the ages of nine and twelve, while for learning morphosyntax the offset period ended in the mid-teens. They found, however, that although the offset period ended at different points for different language components, the beginning of the offset period for all three components of language started at about age six.

It is interesting that this age corresponds to the age at which almost all children in Indonesia begin elementary school where Indonesian is taught and used (Barakat and Bengtsson 2017). Therefore, even those children who have grown up to that point in largely monolingual contexts are introduced to Indonesian at an age when achieving eventual native speaker fluency across phonology, lexis, and morphosyntax is still possible.

Of course, not everyone who begins learning a second language during the critical period will ultimately achieve native speaker fluency in that language. Much depends on the quality of instruction, the length of instruction and exposure, and the degree to which the second language is learned and used in natural social contexts outside of the formal instruction. Those who leave school after only a few years and who live in a context where the local language is the primary means of communication, for example, may never achieve a high level of fluency in the national language even though they may have started learning the L2 before the start of the offset period.

In Indonesia, all instruction is conducted in Indonesian after the third year of school. In addition, the school environment often brings students into relationship with teachers and other students from outside the local language community. For these relationships, Indonesian serves as a lingua franca. In this environment, students are able to achieve a high level of competence in the national language because it is learned and used extensively in a variety of formal and informal contexts. The result is that those who stay in the educational system long enough are able to achieve native speaker fluency in the national language in both production and comprehension.

12.2.3 Implications for L2 comprehension

The most important implication of the current research on age effects on L2 learning is that in contexts like Indonesia we can't simply assume that the vernacular translation always offers advantages in comprehension over equivalent national translations. Depending on the duration, quality, and social contexts in which L2 learning occurs, early (before puberty) simultaneous or sequential bilinguals are quite capable of achieving native speaker levels of comprehension in both the local and the national language. For those who have achieved native speaker competence in the LWC, a vernacular translation will not be more understandable than an equivalent in the LWC.

Proficient bilinguals, may, in fact, consider a national language translation to be more comprehensible than an equivalent vernacular translation, especially if they attend churches that primarily use the national language translation. Those having that kind of church background will already have learned the religious vocabulary and key terms in the national language. Therefore, the national language translation will have a comprehension advantage over a vernacular translation in cases where the religious vocabulary and key terms have yet to be learned in that language.

In addition, where the national language and national language translation(s) are primarily used instead of the vernacular translations in the religious or church domain, people may sense that the national language is more appropriate for religious expression. This use of the national language in the religious or church domain may cause people to feel more familiar and comfortable with the national language translation than they do with their vernacular Scriptures. This feeling of familiarity can cause them to perceive that the Indonesian translation is easier to understand than the vernacular.

12.3 Impact

A second assumption upon which the importance of mother tongue translations is based is that the mother tongue is more impactful or more able to engage the emotions than an equivalent translation in the L2. In this section I will present an overview of ways by which researchers attempt to compare the emotiveness of L1 and L2 and then will discuss the findings of recent research. Finally, I will discuss the implications of this research on the comparative emotional impact of L1 and L2.

12.3.1 Two theories of emotion

Pavlenko (2014) discussed the two main paradigms for understanding emotions, deterministic and emergent, and how those paradigms result in different understandings of the relationship between language and emotion. The deterministic paradigm proposes the existence of a set of emotions that are shared across all of humanity. This basic set of emotions includes, for example, "anger, fear, sadness, joy/happiness, disgust, and surprise. These emotions represent innate affect programs that are triggered by external stimuli to produce the same patterns of response across cultures ..." (Pavlenko 2014:250).

From the deterministic point of view, emotions are language independent. The basic set of emotions is the same across all cultures. Therefore, when learning how to describe or express emotions in a new language, it is only necessary to learn the new ways in which the basic set of emotions is encoded in that language and to link those words to the preexisting categories.

The emergent paradigm, on the other hand,

> views emotions as emergent phenomena that (a) arise in the process of subjective appraisal of incoming stimuli in terms of individual needs and goals, (b) integrate cognitive appraisals, physiological states, behavioral consequences, and discursive resources, and (c) lead to culturally appropriate reactions and courses of action, as well as internalization of new emotion categories that do not have a counterpart in the L1. (Pavlenko 2014:251)

There are several problems with the deterministic paradigm. First, there is no general agreement among researchers about what emotions compose the basic set of emotions common to all people and cultures (Pavlenko 2014). A second problem is the extensive differences that are found in emotion terminology between different languages and cultures. If all humans share the same basic set of emotions, it would be expected that the lexicons of different languages would reflect that similarity. What is found, however, is significant dissimilarity in the ways that different languages and cultures conceptualize and categorize emotions. Some cultures, for example, conceptualize emotions together with physiological states—hunger, thirst, and anger belonging to the same category. Other cultures conceptualize emotions as "relational phenomena that arise between, and not inside, people" (Pavlenko 2014:254). A third problem with the deterministic paradigm is that terms used in different languages to describe the spectrum of emotions divide the emotional world very differently. For example, "Russian [rus] and Samoan [smo] have two terms that roughly connote anger, German [deu] and Yankunytjatjara [kdd] three, Mandarin Chinese [cmn] five, and Biblical Hebrew [hbo] seven such terms" (Pavlenko 2014:256).

Because of these problems, the emergent paradigm aligns better with the significant differences in the ways that various languages and cultures conceptualize, categorize, and refer to different emotions. These differences, however, produce difficulties in comparing emotiveness across different languages.

12.3.2 Measuring impact

Researchers have adopted various approaches to measure the relative emotiveness of L1 and L2. These approaches can be roughly categorized as subjective or objective. Subjective approaches are based on the expressed perceptions of bilinguals of the relative emotional impact of words and phrases in the first and second languages. Objective approaches include measuring skin conductance responses (SCRs) and early posterior negativity (EPN) effects as well as word recall tests.

Subjective responses rely on bilinguals' self-reporting of the relative emotiveness of various categories of words and phrases. These categories include endearments, childhood reprimands, insults, swear or taboo words, and emotion inducing words like "cancer" or "puppy." Subjects are exposed to words from different categories in their first language and the equivalents for those words in their L2. They are then asked to rate the relative emotional impact of those words.

Objective approaches attempt to measure physiological responses to emotive words in L1 and compare those responses to equivalent words in L2. SCR tests are based on the same physiological phenomena which underlie polygraph tests.

Increased sweating of the fingertips accompanying perceived danger or threats results in an increase of skin conductivity within 1 to 1.5 seconds of experiencing the stimulus and lasting from 2 to 6 seconds (Caldwell-Harris and Ayçiçeği-Dinn 2014:3). While threats result in high levels of SCR increase, it has been found that hearing positive or negative emotive words can produce similar effects. Exposing subjects to emotive words and measuring the resulting changes in skin conductance can provide physiologically based evidence about the emotiveness of words and phrases across different languages (Harris 2004).

EPN tests are based on the phenomenon in which the time it takes for the brain to respond to positive and negative emotion words differs from the response timing for neutral words. This response timing is measured by electrodes and is used as an indicator of emotiveness (Opitz and Degner 2012).

Word recall tests are based on findings that people remember highly emotive words better than they do emotionally neutral words (Rubin and Friendly 1986). Several studies have been conducted in which people rate the emotional impact of words in L1 and L2 and afterwards are given a recall test to test their memory of the words. Unfortunately, taken together these studies are inconclusive because of their disparate results (Ferré et al. 2010).

12.3.3 Issues with measuring techniques

There are two main problems associated with attempting to measure emotional responses across different languages. These problems revolve around cultural and language differences (Pavlenko 2008; Dewaele 2008).

Cultural differences may create a misalignment between the emotiveness of similar words across different languages. For example, in many collectivist cultures there are strong social constraints on showing or expressing anger. In individualistic cultures, like the United States, those constraints are much weaker. Caldwell-Harris et al. (2011), for example, studied a group of Chinese-English bilinguals, most of whom were late bilinguals, having learned English [eng] after the age of twelve. These Chinese L1 speakers reported higher levels of emotive response in Mandarin but they actually preferred using English to express emotions because English was not associated with the same social constraints as Mandarin. Therefore, it would be expected that the results of a comparison of the relative impact of emotion terms would depend in part on the cultural background of the person being tested. The validity of research studies that do not carefully control for the cultural background of the sample may be compromised by these cultural differences.

A more widespread problem is created by the misalignment between how different languages divide up the emotional spectrum. As already noted, an emotion which is expressed by a single word in one language might be divided into three or four different words in another, each covering a different facet of the emotion. When measuring emotiveness of different words and phrases across languages, it can be difficult to ensure that the words and phrases being tested convey the same range of meanings in each language. Lack of attention to this detail can skew the results of the study.

12.3.4 Studies of L1 and L2 emotiveness

A number of studies have revealed that emotionally laden words, phrases, and expressions are more impactful in L1 than in L2. Dewaele and Nakano (2013), for example, using a five-point Likert scale, asked 106 participants to rate each of the languages in their repertoire on how logical, serious, emotive, fake, and different they feel when using that language. The researchers found that the participants "reported feeling significantly more authentic, more logical, more emotional and more serious in their L1, with gradually lower values for languages which they had acquired later in life, and in which they felt significantly less proficient" (p. 117). Although Dewaele and Nakano mention a relationship between the age of acquisition and feelings, they did not actually ask the participants at what age they began learning the various languages in their repertoires.

Harris, Ayçiçegi, and Gleason (2003) studied Turkish [tur] speakers who had come to the Boston area for graduate studies or for professional employment. Because of the language requirements of their studies or employment, these participants were classified as proficient bilinguals. Their initial exposure to English was, however, either in high-school or university foreign language programs. For that reason they would be considered late proficient bilinguals. Using skin conductance Harris, Ayçiçegi, and Gleason (2003) measured the participants' reactions to taboo words and reprimands. They found that taboo words in Turkish elicited a slightly more emotional response than in English while childhood reprimands elicited much higher emotional responses in Turkish than in English. This later finding suggests a correlation between emotiveness and the emotional contexts in which language is learned.

Using an online questionnaire, Dewaele (2004b) surveyed 1,039 multilinguals about the perceived emotive impact of swear words and taboo words in the various languages in their repertoires. They found that generally swear words and taboo words were perceived to be more emotive in L1 than in L2, L3, etc. Several factors, however, were found to mitigate those perceived differences. When a language other than L1 was the dominant language, for example, the emotiveness of L1 was weaker relative to the dominant language. Other factors which influence the relative emotive impact of the various languages include whether the language(s) were learned in a formal or informal context, language proficiency, frequency of language use, and the age of onset of language learning.

Not all studies have indicated that the emotiveness of L1 is always greater than that of other languages in a multilingual's repertoire. When studies have controlled for one or more of the factors mentioned by Dewaele (2004b) as affecting emotive impact, a more nuanced picture of the relative emotiveness of language emerges. Caldwell-Harris et al. (2011), for example, analyzed the relationship of emotiveness to age of acquisition in a pilot study of late and early Mandarin-English bilinguals. They found that 53% of Mandarin speakers who began learning English after the age of twelve felt that Mandarin was more emotive than English while only 6% felt that English was more emotive. Two-thirds of those who began learning English before the age of five, on the other hand, felt that English and Mandarin were equally emotive.

In a study of proficient Spanish/Catalan [cat] and Spanish/English bilinguals, Ferré et al. (2010) tested the recall of emotive words in the different languages. Using this memory test, they determined that for these proficient bilinguals there was no difference in the ability to recall emotive words in L1 compared to L2. They controlled for language dominance, learning context, and age of L2 acquisition and found that none of these factors affected the relative emotiveness of L1 and L2.

Harris used skin conductance tests to study emotional responses among late and early Spanish-English bilinguals to four categories of emotional expressions, including "taboo words, reprimands, endearments, and insults" (2004:231). She found that those who began learning English in mid to late childhood demonstrated a higher level of emotional response to Spanish emotive expressions than to English. On the other hand, those who began learning English in early childhood demonstrated similar emotional responses in Spanish and English. In this study, those who began learning English early in life reported a higher level of proficiency in English than those who started learning English later in life. This suggests that age of onset may be a factor in relative emotiveness of languages only insofar as it correlates to other factors such as proficiency and the context of learning.

12.3.5 Factors related to relative emotiveness of L1 and L2

As indicated above, studies have identified several factors that are salient to the relative emotiveness of L1 and L2. These include the age at which people begin learning L2, language proficiency, the contexts within which that learning takes place, and language dominance. Note that these factors are not discrete; rather, there is some interdependence between the factors. For example, learning L2 at an early age may correlate with the context in which the learning took place and may also relate to ultimate language dominance and proficiency. Harris, Gleason, and Ayçiçegi (2006) suggested that although the age of acquisition correlates with emotiveness of L2, that correlation does not indicate causation. Rather, the age of acquisition correlates with other factors, like context of learning, which do have a causal relationship with emotiveness.

Probably the most important factor that relates to the ultimate emotiveness of L2 is the context within which L2 is learned. Bloom and Beckwith (1989) noted that two important developments relating emotions and language occur in the early childhood years. First, these are the years in which language is first learned and second, it is the period of life during which the emotional regulation system develops. The natural, relational context within which early language learning occurs creates an environment in which emotionally laden events are connected to language. Scoldings and reprimands, warnings of danger, displays of affection, and so on typically connect emotions, actions, and language. This connection of language and emotion in particular kinds of events helps explain why emotional impact is often described as being more intense in L1 than in L2. When L2 language learning begins after the period in which the emotional regulation system develops and occurs through formal classroom instruction rather than natural social interaction, the L2 probably will not develop the same connections to autobiographical emotionally laden events as does L1.

This connection between emotiveness and the context within which a language is learned implies that L2 may develop increased emotiveness as the language is used over time in natural social interactions where emotionally laden events are experienced. The more connections there are in the memory between L2 and emotional events, the more likely L2 is to trigger equivalent levels of emotional impact as L1. Harris, Gleason, and Ayçiçegi stated that "language comes to have a distinctive emotional feel by virtue of being learned, or habitually used, in a distinctive emotional context" (2006:272).

Language dominance refers to "which language is generally most accessible in day to day life. It is the language that is most highly activated, and can be the default language for speaking and thinking" (Harris, Gleason, and Ayçiçegi 2006:264). Note that dominance is not to be equated with proficiency. Also, it is not necessarily the same as L1. We have several friends who attend university in Bandung (a Sundanese speaking area of Indonesia). All of these students are highly fluent in both their vernacular language and Indonesian. Because, however, they live outside their home area, they seldom have opportunities to speak their vernacular language. Over time, because they are in a context where they only use the national language, it is highly likely that Indonesian will become their dominant language, even though it is their second language and even though they are equally proficient in both L1 and L2.

Dominance relates to emotiveness because if L2 is the dominant language, it is almost certainly being used in emotional contexts. Through that process of use, the emotiveness of L2 will increase with time as more connections are made between emotional events and language. It is highly likely, therefore, that in situations where L2 has come to be the dominant language, it will develop similar levels of emotiveness as L1.

12.3.6 Implications for the emotional impact of L2

Because L1 is learned early in life in emotional contexts and because in those early years L1 is the dominant language, typically L1 is experienced as more emotive than L2. If, however, L2 is learned to native speaker fluency starting early in life in natural emotion-laden contexts it is likely to achieve parity with L1 in emotiveness. Even if the onset of acquisition of L2 is later in life, if L2 is learned largely in naturally emotional contexts where connections can be established in the memory between emotions and language, it is to be expected that differences between the emotiveness of L1 and L2 will disappear. This is especially true if L2 becomes the dominant language (Pavlenko 2004; Dewaele 2004a; Dewaele 2008).

For these reasons, in contexts like that which is found in many areas of Indonesia where young people grow up as early simultaneous or sequential bilinguals with their local vernacular and Indonesian, vernacular translations will not necessarily be more emotionally impactful than equivalent translations in Indonesian. In areas, however, where for various reasons people are not able to achieve high levels of L2 fluency and where L2 is not used regularly or in emotional contexts, engagement with a quality translation in the local language could still have a more emotional impact than what would be experienced through a national language translation.

12.4 Conclusion

In light of this recent research, Bible translation agencies may want to consider their frequent appeal to the special place of the mother tongue as "heart language" in producing greater comprehension and impact. In many areas of the world, bilingualism or multilingualism is the norm. People are learning and using their local language as well as LWCs starting early in life and are achieving high levels of fluency in multiple languages. In contexts like these, an appeal to higher levels of first language comprehension and emotional impact as a justification for vernacular Bible translation does not appear to be valid.

This is not a call to abandon Bible translation in these kinds of contexts. For one thing, larger language groups are seldom homogenous. What may be true of people living in larger cities may not be true for others living in more rural areas. To understand a situation more fully, it will be important to conduct thorough surveys of the language group across a representative sample of different speech communities to determine the degree of bilingualism or multilingualism, in terms of repertoire, patterns of use, and in levels of fluency.

In some cases, it may be found that one of the available national language translations will be equally comprehensible and impactful as an equivalent vernacular translation would be. Even in those cases, however, we should not be too quick to abandon the idea of vernacular translation. There may be other reasons for producing a vernacular translation that do not relate to comprehension or impact. For example, in areas where there is a strong connection between the local language and the people's ethnic identity, they may prefer to use a vernacular translation even if it offers no particular advantages in comprehension or impact. This is illustrated by certain church groups in Indonesia having strong connections with specific ethnic groups. These churches use the vernacular translation because of its ethnic connection. Another possible reason exists where there is a desire to contextualize Christianity, which may otherwise be primarily seen as a foreign import.

A limited test of several different Scripture products could reveal which, if any, vernacular Scripture products would likely have the most impact in a particular multilingual context. Such an approach would allow testing of products in various media and formats, including oral, written, visual, and artistic expressions of Scripture. This article is a call for Bible translation organizations, in particular, to reexamine basic assumptions about the benefits of vernacular translations that may not be true in in a growing number of multilingual contexts.

References

Abrahamsson, Niclas. 2012. The age of onset and nativelike L2 ultimate attainment of morphosyntactic and phonetic intuition. *Studies in Second Language Acquisition* 34:187–214. DOI:10.1017/S0272263112000022/.

Australia Bible Society. 2011. Bible translation support. Accessed April 30, 2018. www-archive.biblesociety.org.au/projects/indigenous/bible-translation-support/.

Barakat, Bilal, and Stephanie Bengtsson. 2017. What do we mean by 'school entry age'? Conceptual ambiguity and its implications: the example of Indonesia. *Comparative Education* 54(2):203–224. DOI:10.1080/03050068.2017.1360564/.

Bible Society of Singapore. 2015. Translation. bible.org.sg/about-us/translation/.

Birdsong, David. 2005. Interpreting age effects in second language acquisition. In Judith F. Kroll and Annette M. B. De Groot (eds.), *Handbook of bilingualism: Psycholinguistic approaches*, 109–127. Oxford: Oxford University Press.

Bloom, Lois, and Richard Beckwith. 1989. Talking with feeling: Integrating affective and linguistic expression in early language development. *Cognition and Emotion* 3:313–342.

Caldwell-Harris, Catherine L., and Ayşe Ayçiçeği-Dinn. 2014. Emotional phrases don't feel as strong in a foreign language: Physiological studies. *Impuls—The Psychology Journal of the University of Oslo*. Preprint: academia.edu/download/33328895/Caldwell-Harris_EmotionsBilingualism.docx/.

Caldwell-Harris, Catherine L., Jimmy Tong, Winvy Lung, and Sinlan Poo. 2011. Physiological reactivity to emotional phrases in Mandarin-English bilinguals. *International Journal of Bilingualism* 15(3):329–352. DOI:10.1177/1367006910379262/.

De Groot, Annette M. B. 2011. *Language and cognition in bilinguals and multilinguals: An introduction*. New York: Psychology Press.

DeKeyser, Robert M. 2000. The robustness of critical period effects in second language acquisition. *Studies in Second Language Acquisition* 22:499–533.

DeKeyser, Robert M. 2012. Age effects in second language learning. In Susan M. Gass and Alison Mackey (eds.), *The Routledge handbook of second language acquisition*, 442–460. New York: Routledge.

Dewaele, Jean-Marc. 2004a. Blistering barnacles! What language do multilinguals swear in?! *Sociolinguistic Studies* 5:83–105. DOI:10.1558/sols.v5i1.83/.

Dewaele, Jean-Marc. 2004b. The emotional force of swearwords and taboo words in the speech of multilinguals. *Journal of Multilingual and Multicultural Development* 25:204–222. DOI:10.1080/01434630408666529/.

Dewaele, Jean-Marc. 2008. The emotional weight of *I love you* in multilinguals' languages. *Journal of Pragmatics* 40:1753–1780. DOI:10.1016/j.pragma.2008.03.002/.

Dewaele, Jean-Marc, and Seiji Nakano. 2013. Multilinguals' perceptions of feeling different when switching languages. *Journal of Multilingual and Multicultural Development* 34:107–120. DOI:10.1080/01434632.2012.712133/.

Ferré, Pilar, Teofilo García, Isabel Fraga, Rosa Sánchez-Casas, and Margarita Molero. 2010. Memory for emotional words in bilinguals: Do words have the same emotional intensity in the first and in the second language? *Cognition and Emotion* 24:760–785. DOI:10.1080/02699930902985779/.

Granena, Gisela, and Michael H. Long. 2013. Age of onset, length of residence, language aptitude, and ultimate L2 attainment in three linguistic domains. *Second Language Research* 29:311–343. DOI:10.1177/0267658312461497/.

Harris, Catherine L. 2004. Bilingual speakers in the lab: Psychophysiological measures of emotional reactivity. *Journal of Multilingual and Multicultural Development* 25:223–247. DOI:10.1080/01434630408666530/.

Harris, Catherine L., Ayse Ayçiçegi, and Jean Berko Gleason. 2003. Taboo words and reprimands elicit greater autonomic reactivity in a first language than in a second language. *Applied Psycholinguistics* 24:561–579. DOI:10.1017/S0142716403000286/.

Harris, Catherine L., Jean Berko Gleason, and Ayse Ayçiçegi. 2006. When is a first language more emotional? Psychophysiological evidence from bilingual speakers. In Aneta Pavlenko (ed.), *Bilingual minds: Emotional experience, expression and representation*, 257–283. Clevedon, UK: Multilingual Matters.

Johnson, Jacqueline S., and Elissa Newport. 1989. Critical period effects in second language learning: The influence of maturational state on acquisition of English as a second language. *Cognitive Psychology* 21:60–99. DOI:10.1016/0010-0285(89)90003-0/.

Lenneberg, Eric H. 1967. The biological foundations of language. *Hospital Practice* 2(12):59–67. DOI:10.1080/21548331.1967.11707799/.

Marler, Peter. 1970. A comparative approach to vocal learning: Song development in white-crowned sparrows. *Journal of Comparative and Physiological Psychology* 71:1–25. DOI:10.1037/h0029144/.

Mayberry, Rachel I., and Robert Kluender. 2018. Rethinking the critical period for language: New insights into an old question from American Sign Language. *Bilingualism: Language and Cognition* 21(5):886–905. DOI:10.1017/S1366728917000724/.

Monson, Jordan. 2015. There is no good Bible for over a billion people. *Desiring God*, 5 February 2015. www.desiringgod.org/articles/there-is-no-good-bible-for-over-a-billion-people/. Accessed April 30, 2018.

Opitz, Bertram, and Juliane Degner. 2012. Emotionality in a second language: It's a matter of time. *Neuropsychologia* 50:1961–1967. DOI:10.1016/j.neuropsychologia.2012.04.021/.

Pavlenko, Aneta. 2004. Language choice and emotions in parent–child communication. *Journal of Multilingual and Multicultural Development* 25:179–203. DOI:10.1080/01434630408666528/.

Pavlenko, Aneta. 2008. Emotion and emotion-laden words in the bilingual lexicon. *Bilingualism* 11:147–164. DOI:10.1017/S1366728908003283/.

Pavlenko, Aneta. 2014. *The bilingual mind: And what it tells us about language and thought*. New York: Cambridge University Press.

Penfield, Wilder, and Lamar Roberts. 1959. *Speech and brain mechanisms*. Princeton, NJ: Princeton University Press.

Pinker, Steven. 1994. *The language instinct: How the mind creates language*. New York: William Morrow.

Rubin, David C., and Michael Friendly. 1986. Predicting which words get recalled: Measures of free recall, availability, goodness, emotionality, and pronunciability for 925 nouns. *Memory & Cognition* 14:79–94. DOI:10.3758/BF03209231/.

Wycliffe Bible Translators UK. 2017. Our impact. wycliffe.org.uk/about/our-impact/.

13
When None of My Heart Languages Is My Mother Tongue

Daniel Paul

Abstract. This paper explores whether recasting the phrase "heart language" as potentially plural and/or nonlocal could redeem it for the crucial function of identifying which speech varieties will serve a community best. Elucidating essential concepts such as comprehension, development, emotional impact and transformative impact enables a more precise understanding of the roles subconscious and conscious information-processing play in how we respond to messages. It also helps us to see that both a degree of comprehension and, crucially, high potential for an intuitive response are necessary factors for any given speech variety to communicate with impact. The paper goes on to explore how such speech varieties may be identified within the language inventory of any given community, building on the concept of social capital (Coleman 1988). Using two case studies from Tajikistan for illustration, it concludes that the most impactful speech varieties—and hence those best suited to language development—are those which a community's members are using to promote social capital amongst the groups in which they desire to be insiders.[1]

13.1 Introduction

13.1.1 "Heart language": A not-so-simple concept

Nelson Mandela is widely quoted to have said that "If you talk to a man in a language he understands—that goes to his head. If you talk to him in his [own] language—that goes to his heart."[2]

We intuitively recognize some kind of truth behind this statement, and the idea of "speaking to people's hearts" is compelling. Hence the popularity of "heart

---

[1] I am grateful to all those who made comments on drafts of this paper, including in particular Richard Brown, Mike Frechette, John Clifton, Phil King, Hannu Sorsamo, and the volume editors.

[2] For instance, Laka (2014). One thinks also of the quote attributed to Willy Brandt: "If I am selling to you, I speak your language. If I am buying, dann müssen Sie Deutsch sprechen [you must speak German]" (Ratcliffe 2012:225).

language" as a cover term for a community's local language or mother tongue,[3] and as an implicit justification for projects in such languages on the basis that they will lead to the greatest impact. To the question "In which speech variety will language development, language documentation, or Bible translation serve this community best?" the answer is given: "In the community's heart language."

Simons (2021, chapter 11 this volume) shows that while the term "heart language" may be motivational, it also perpetuates "a conceptual bias that idealizes the world in monolingual terms." The realities of today's multilingual world simply do not allow us to say that the best way to communicate a message to a community is always in its heritage language or mother tongue. While this may commonly be true, there are many other cases where the community has chosen, for example, to drop its heritage identity altogether and adopt an outgroup identity along with its associated language (Lewis 2021, chapter 3 this volume); or to use different languages for different functions. Our task here is to consider whether recasting the term "heart language" as potentially plural and/or nonlocal could redeem it for the crucial function of identifying which language(s) will serve a community best. That is, despite its inadequacies as a term, can the constellation of essential concepts which underlie the phrase nonetheless point the way forward for speech communities evaluating which languages to use, develop, and translate material into when they have more than one in their inventory.

Since the impact of language operates at two different levels, this will involve unpacking two questions:

1. *How* do "heart languages" achieve their greater power, in terms of cognitive categories such as comprehension (section 13.2) and affective impact (section 13.3)? What are the psychological mechanisms involved, and what light do these shed on the question of which languages and media it would be most valuable to work in?
2. *Why* do messages impact a community more powerfully if they are expressed in a "heart language"? We will answer this by exploring the contribution that different speech varieties can make to a community's social capital (section 13.4). This explains what motivates a community to grasp and be transformed by messages to a greater or lesser extent, depending on the language in which they are delivered.

13.1.2 Some useful core concepts

Like the term "heart language," several other terms in this field are intuitively appealing but hard to define, such as development, comprehension, and emotional impact. Some terms in academic literature will be helpful as we build on these concepts during our discussion below.

Owen Barder, Director for Europe at the Center for Global Development, appeals to complexity science to show that definitions of development which focus on human well-being will always be inadequate unless they include reference to the capacity of the community's underlying social systems to sustain and improve that well-being (Barder 2012). He proposes that development should be conceived of in terms of how fit for purpose these systems are to enable **self-organising complexity**. This concept neatly incorporates ideas of agency, capacity, and sustainability, and sits well with SIL's definition of community-based language development as "a series of

---

[3] See Brown (2009:85) and Chiang (2010:5), respectively.

ongoing planned actions that a language community takes to ensure that its language continues to serve its changing social, cultural, political, economic, and spiritual needs and goals."[4]

Comprehension is a slippery notion on several fronts. We will explore in section 13.2 how it relates to understanding an utterance, using Relevance Theory (Wilson and Sperber 2004) to show how a hearer recovers a speaker's intended meaning and then goes on to infer its significance for their own situation. More broadly, we must bear in mind that comprehension is a subdomain of **language proficiency**. The ability to speak, write, read, and listen in a regional language may well vary across a community depending on factors such as how well educated someone is and how widely they travel. They may be able to understand something when they hear it, but have trouble passing the message on in that same language. And their level of understanding may vary quite widely depending on the topic, be it kitchen implements, mechanical engineering, or religious philosophy. Assorted *domains of knowledge* are commonly talked about by particular people using particular languages. These realities mean that any language development or literature production in a community must consider how widely and well the language in question is understood, and whether that language is the most appropriate one for the topic.[5]

A related issue is the fact that people have varying **language ideologies**, resulting in a potential opposition between the importance of comprehension and of agency. Deloach (2016) builds on Keane's (2007) work to show that language is not universally conceived of primarily as a vehicle for conveying one's sincere thoughts, and certainly not when it comes to considering the role of Scripture. Many communities view the purpose of language more in terms of agency than comprehension, and will place much more value on how the delivery of a message is performed than on how well they understand the message's content.

Finally, "emotional impact" is another term which sounds reasonable, but risks circumscribing the debate. Rather than forcing a dichotomy between emotion and cognition, we suggest it is more helpful to differentiate between **subconscious intuition** and **conscious rational thought**—or "seeing-that" and "reasoning-why" in Margolis's (1987) terms. (Note that although emotion can play a salient role in Type 1 thinking, most intuitions do not rise to the level of emotions.) Haidt (2001) endorses this approach: we make most of our decisions and judgements on the basis of quick, automatic intuitions, influenced by society and culture; whereas reasoning is usually a post hoc construction generated later, not least to justify our conclusions to others. Haidt memorably describes this with analogies of an emotional tail wagging the rational dog (Haidt 2001),[6] and a reasoning rider leaning

---

[4] sil.org/language-development/. For the Christian, these spiritual needs and goals would include, both individually and in community, what the Westminster Shorter Catechism (Kelly 1994) defines as the chief end of human beings: "to glorify God, and to enjoy him forever."

[5] We note too the importance of genre and media. The L1 may well be appropriate for oral, as opposed to written, material; and it may be preferred for subjects of artistic expression such as stories, songs, proverbs, poetry, or drama. In the context of language development, this may mean promoting the use of the L1 in such domains, acknowledging it as one community "heart language"; while providing written religious material in an LX, which may or may not be a second "heart language" for the community. After all, the community may well have learned from childhood to use LX in the religious domain, especially if they have received religious instruction in that language.

into the direction in which the intuitive elephant is already turning (Haidt 2012). The thinking underlying this distinction is perhaps best known in terms of Stanovich and West's (2000) Type 1 (subconscious, intuitive) versus Type 2 (rational thought) theory.[7]

As for the concept of impact itself, we turn to Experiential Learning Theory for the idea that knowledge results from a combination of grasping and transforming experience (Kolb 1984:41). Responding to a message involves a holistic process of adaptation, including grasping (experiencing concretely and conceptualising abstractly) and then allowing transformation to occur through both reflection and active experimentation. Robbins (2001) observed that in Melanesian linguistic ideology, a person must wait to see how others respond to their speech to know if it is true or not. There is much to learn from this perspective. For our purposes here, it is worth bearing in mind that impactful communication is communication that is not just understood, but that transforms the hearer accordingly.

13.2 Comprehension

We turn now to the *how* of "heart language" impact. In this section we will argue that in at least one sense, comprehension is a necessary condition for impact, but not a sufficient one.

"Heart language" terminology in the public domain often makes reference to "the language I understand best." What exactly is "better comprehension," and how does this correlate with a message's impact? Wilson and Sperber's (2004) Relevance Theory approach is useful for its attempt at a comprehensive account of the interpretive processes a hearer may employ in order to understand an utterance. While not all of these processes are always equally salient, they do help to illustrate the challenge it can be to grasp a speaker's meaning, even within one's own language and culture. Brown (2012:381) sets out five of these processes:

1. Decoding the utterance into possible semantic representations.
2. Using contextual assumptions to ground each semantic representation in a context accessible to the addressee, and then resolving ambiguities and implicit roles and references in order to hypothesize the proposition intended by the speaker—an **explicature**.
3. Hypothesizing the speaker's **propositional attitude** toward that proposition, and the nature of their **speech act**.[8]
4. Testing contextual assumptions and implications for optimal relevance, in order to arrive at manifestly intended **implicatures**.
   Beyond this process of recovering the speaker's intended meaning (the cognitive effects stimulated in the hearer's mind by these explicatures and implicatures), the hearer may then go on to infer its **significance** for their own cognitive environment. Brown (2012:356) describes this significance as the additional interaction between the authorial meaning as inferred by a hearer and the hearer's own concepts and assumptions:

---

[6] Popularized in Heath and Heath (2010).
[7] Popularized in Kahneman's (2011) *Thinking, Fast and Slow*.
[8] Sometimes referred to as "illocutionary force" (e.g., asserting, questioning, demanding, warning, etc.).

5. Realizing "**additional cognitive effects** that result from the implications of that meaning, ones which the author did not manifestly intend."

We can illustrate these steps with an example. A schoolchild who enters a British classroom and fails to close the door may be asked by the teacher, "Were you born in a barn?" The hearer will first need to decode this grammatically and semantically. For example, they will need to understand that "you" refers to "me" but that "barn" is generic. They will need to know that a barn is a large, agricultural building in which animals or animal feed are usually stored, and so on. Beyond identifying this basic proposition, the **explicature**, they will then also to ascertain the **speech act**—superficially a question, but in fact a directive (see below)—and realize that the teacher is adopting an ironical stance (**propositional attitude**) towards that proposition: in Britain it is not normal to be born in a barn, after all.

The schoolchild will also need to combine an understanding of this ironical stance with the physical context (a door has been left open), and the cultural knowledge that both (a) British barn doors are rarely closed, if the barn has one at all, and (b) this is a common thing to say when someone wants a door to be closed (in the Netherlands, one equivalent is *Ben je in de kerk geboren?* "Were you born in a church?"). The manifestly intended **implicature** then becomes clear: the teacher is telling the student to close the door. Beyond this, **additional cognitive effects** may include a determination on the part of the student to avoid leaving the door open in the future, at least in this teacher's classroom.

Ultimately, then, the message is fully grasped at the cognitive level when all of the speaker's implicatures have been successfully recovered. And this is in itself a prerequisite for maximum impact: the creation of significance, when the hearer applies the message of an utterance to new situations or in new ways and allows it to transform them. Note that a hearer may be able to recover some or all of the implicatures, and even to infer significance, without fully parsing all of the utterance's grammatical and lexical details. This means that although comprehension in this sense is clearly a necessary condition for impact to take place, it does not require full proficiency in the language. And it is not a sufficient condition, for reasons we shall explore in the next section.

13.3 Intuitive impact

In the introduction (section 13.1.2) we noted the importance of not just grasping a message but also allowing it to transform us. A message's impact beyond the rational level will be conditioned by the range and depth of intuitive response that the speech variety used can arouse in the hearer. We also saw that emotion is just one part of a wider set of fast, subconscious responses to stimuli which may be termed Type 1 thinking. It is this kind of thinking on which most of our decisions and judgements are based, which is why it plays such a crucial role—alongside comprehension—in the impact a message can have.

Both Type 1 and Type 2 are kinds of information processing, which includes higher cognition (including conscious reasoning) as well as lower cognition: visual perception, memory retrieval, and intuition. It turns out, however, that intuition is by far the most influential on our decision making.

We can identify four crucial implications of multilingualism for the role of intuitive (Type 1) thinking:

1. Even if such thinking is subconsciously controlled, it is still partly linguistic. And multilingual speakers will prefer to receive messages in the speech variety that maximizes the ease of an intuitive response, because conscious reasoning takes more effort.
2. Many psychologists have observed that our decisions are less biased when we approach a problem using a language learned later than early childhood (e.g., Keysar et al. 2012, Costa et al. 2014). Reviewing the literature, Pavlenko (2012) observed that both L1 and LX[9] have their advantages. "First language advantage" refers to the increased automaticity of affective (i.e., emotional) processing in the L1: "emotionality of the interactions increases implicit relevance of particular verbal stimuli and enhances formation of long-term memory traces. Stronger traces, in turn, facilitate activation and lead to perceptual prioritization of these stimuli" (Pavlenko 2012:425).
3. Although emotions may dominate proportionately few of our many daily fast and unconscious responses to stimuli, they deserve further exploration here because of the evidence that emotion concepts themselves are linguistically relative: "Findings from cognitive science suggest that language dynamically constitutes emotion because it activates representations of categories and then increases processing of sensory information that is consistent with conceptual representations" (Lindquist et al. 2015:106). This negates the value of differentiating areas of the brain involved with emotion versus reason, or of differentiating between emotion and cognition more generally, since "when a body state or action counts as an instance of emotion, the brain regions that orchestrate additional information are the same ones that are engaged to create meaning during semantic processing" (Pavlenko 2012:423). If we experience emotion in terms defined partly by the language(s) we used during our childhood period of emotional development, this offers an explanation for the increased automaticity of affective processing in that language (or those languages): there will be an alignment, with less risk of mismatch, between any emotional categorization assumed in the message and by the hearer respectively.
4. This leads to a wider cultural point. Barrett (2012:419) argues that an emotion "is an intention that is enacted when embodied conceptual knowledge is brought on line to shape the perception of a physical state, binding that physical state to an event in the world (so that it becomes something more than a mere physical sensation)." From this perspective, "If emotion categories are ontologically subjective categories, then they can be thought of as collective cognitive tools that allow members of the same culture … to represent and shape the social meaning of physical events. Emotion categories may be considered scripts about what emotions are and how they work, or

---

[9] L1, L2, and LX terminology is helpfully summarized in Pavlenko (2012:407). In this paper, L1 refers to the language an individual first acquired as a child (typically from birth), and LX to any other languages they know. We prefer "LX" over "L2" in order to mitigate the risk of privileging bilingualism over multilingualism. There are also cases where an L2 or L3 can attrite, giving way to an L4 as a speaker's most proficient variety. "LX" allows for these cases.

complex narrative schemes that give meaning to changes in the body." Scripts and narrative schemes will prove relevant when we consider the cognitive dimension of social capital in the following section (13.4).

Writing early in the last century, Smith (1930:8) suggested that:

> Men need two kinds of language, in fact; a language of the home, of emotion, of unexpressed associations; and a language of knowledge, exact argument, scientific truth, one in which words are world-current and steadfast in their meanings. Where the mother tongue does not answer both needs, the people must inevitably become bilingual; but however fluent they may succeed in being in the foreign speech, its words can never feel to them as their native words. To express the dear and intimate things which are the very breath and substance of life a man will fall back on the tongue he learnt not at school, but in the house—how, he remembers not. He may bargain in the other, or pass examinations in it, but he will pray in his home speech. If you wish to reach his heart you will address him in that language.[10]

The word "intimate" is significant here, suggestive as it is of a relationship between the emotional and identity components of language. We will turn to the question of identity shortly. But we conclude this section with the observation that intuitive response is a second, necessary condition for impact. This must be qualified with the caveat that it is hard to identify just one intuitively powerful language when many in multilingual communities learned not just their L1 but also one or more LXs in childhood (Harris 2018, chapter 12 this volume). An individual or community may experience roughly equivalent intuitive responses to the same message in two or more speech varieties.

In such cases, which variety is the "heart language"? Feenstra (2018, chapter 5 this volume) cites two anecdotal examples where an L1 Frisian [fry] speaker used an LX to express their emotions: English [eng], for a brief love note; and Dutch [nld], for a eulogy at a funeral. In the first case it would seem that the teenage Dutch speaker who used English was doing so in a context tightly controlled by a specific genre, and probably did not have any commitment to the social capital of English-speaking social networks at that time. In the second case, the eulogist's commitment to the social capital Dutch offered him is clear, to the point that he had shifted to Dutch as his language of choice in daily communication. Dutch had become a "heart language" for him.

13.4 Social capital

So far we have seen that both some degree of comprehension and a high potential for intuitive response are necessary factors for any given speech variety to communicate with impact. This is reflected in the common practice of language surveyors investigating language development needs, who have traditionally focused their assessment on two key areas: proficiency in regional languages (or intelligibility of regional dialects, as the case may be) and language attitudes. Alongside this, both surveyors and language documentation specialists are interested in ethnolinguistic

---

[10] Note that Smith uses not "heart language" but "language of the home," which accurately describes the language used for home domains of use.

vitality, which plays into questions of group identity and language maintenance and shift.

This section will outline the explanatory power of social capital as a concept for pulling these and related ideas together. We will argue that "heart languages" are best conceived of as those speech varieties in which language development work is most likely to be effective, and that they may be identified as **those patterns of communicative behaviour which their users believe will best promote social capital amongst the communities of which they desire to be insiders**. Those patterns of communicative behaviour may take the shape of multiple languages, resulting potentially in multiple "heart languages," and their users may belong to multiple communities. Such communities could constitute, for example, a heritage ingroup, two groups (amongst whom knowledge is compartmentalized or hybridized), or an outgroup (to which others have assimilated). Lewis (2018, chapter 3 this volume) explores such categories further.

The concept of social capital entered mainstream thinking with Putnam's (2000) book *Bowling Alone*. Putnam moves away from the essentially economic perspective on social capital popularized by Coleman (1988) and others to define the notion as "social networks and the norms of reciprocity and trustworthiness that arise from them" (Putnam 2000:19) and "features of social life—networks, norms and trust—that enable participants to act together more effectively to pursue shared objectives" (Putnam 1996:56). Recall Barder's framing of development in terms of self-organising complexity.

Put simply, social capital is key in motivating a community to cohere in groups larger than their own kinship systems. Language both catalyzes social capital, and is a part of its substance (Clark 2006): the first as a means of communication, the second as an intrinsic part of a community's cultural makeup. It is the first function that we are particularly interested in here, as we consider which languages people use to invest in communities as diagnostic of where they perceive their interests to lie and what they are open to.

Nahapiet and Ghoshal (1998) suggest three dimensions of social capital: the structural, the relational, and the cognitive. The structural dimension concerns the configuration of linkages between individuals which sociolinguistic theory conceptualizes in terms of social networks. Dense, multiplex social networks help to promote intra-community interdependence, facilitating vernacular language maintenance (Landweer 2000) and increasing the community's capacity for self-organising complexity (see section 13.1.2 above), which is key to helping them achieve their wider goals.

The relational dimension concerns facets which are crucial to social collaboration such as trust and trustworthiness, norms and sanctions, obligations and expectations, and identity and identification. Coleman (1998:S98) cites the Jewish social structures underlying the wholesale diamond market in New York City, showing how high degrees of trust are key to successful transactions. He also gives the example of a mother describing how she felt safe allowing her young children to play unsupervised in a city park in Jerusalem, something she would not have felt safe to do when her family had earlier lived in suburban Detroit. Coleman suggests that this difference can be described as a difference in social capital available in the two places: "In Jerusalem, the normative structure ensures that unattended children will be 'looked after' by adults in the vicinity, while no such normative structure exists in most metropolitan areas of the United States. One can say that families have available to them in Jerusalem social capital that does not exist in metropolitan areas of the United States."

The importance of these two dimensions suggests that those evaluating the likely success of language development projects would do well to conduct some social network analysis, and to investigate the levels of trust and reciprocity which the different parts of the networks bear. For example, to whom do community members turn for help with their financial, legal, and medical needs? What favours can family heads call in when they need them, and from whom?

The cognitive dimension refers to those resources providing shared representations, interpretations, and systems of meaning among parties. They include shared languages and shared narratives. The latter play a significant role in levels of group allegiance (Eberhard 2021, chapter 2 this volume).

Putnam (2000) divides social capital into two kinds: bonding and bridging.[11] The three dimensions of capital—structural, relational, and cognitive—can apply to both kinds, impacting intragroup and intergroup relations respectively. *Bonding social capital* relates to the more exclusive social networks which are characterized by the presence of specific reciprocity. It is typical of close-knit groups that are primarily inward looking. The L1 often has a role maintaining solidarity between group members. *Bridging social capital*, in contrast, relates to social networks which are inclusive and outward looking; they stimulate a broader kind of reciprocity, and evoke the concepts of mobility and modernization discussed above. An LX can be more effective as a lever of power.[12] As we shall see below, this contrast is helpful in explaining the difference between communities which choose to preserve their heritage identity and those which shift to adopt an outgroup identity.

13.5 Case studies and application

Lewis (2021, chapter 3 this volume) observes that "One way to understand ethnicity is in terms of real or imagined shared ancestry and bloodlines, a history of colocation, and a shared lore regarding origins and cosmology." Inevitably there are parallels here to the relational, structural, and cognitive dimensions of social capital outlined above, because group identity is grounded in who we are, where we are, and what we know together. Perhaps the root of the problems with the way "heart language" terminology has been used is an assumption that language and identity always map onto each other in a one-to-one relationship.

---

[11] A third category sometimes proposed is "linking capital": social networks with access to institutional power (e.g., Clark 2006).

[12] Individuals may consider social capital to accrue to them even from languages which they do not speak well. For this reason, identifying their "heart languages" is a somewhat different exercise from assessing ethnolinguistic vitality: which languages communities will choose to use in particular speech environments or domains. For the latter, Karan (2011) is a useful guide. For an example of language as bonding social capital, see Vaish et al. (2010); for one bridging social capital example among many, see Stanton-Salazar and Dornbusch (1995). Roche (2017:212) comments: "Berliner et al. (2012) discuss how issues of bonding social capital work out at the community level in practical terms through such social practices as gossiping, envy, and sharing. The practice and theory of language maintenance and revitalization has much to gain from a discussion of how various forms of capital contribute to community resilience."

Recall our understanding of group identity as "the perception of group belonging constructed by members of a particular community through the experience of a shared narrative, together with the internally accepted markers of that belonging" (Eberhard 2021, chapter 2 this volume). This definition is helpful in reminding us that group belonging is constructed, and that markers of belonging must be internally accepted and are not universal or absolute. This should caution us against "heart language" definitions which necessarily tie a language and a group together on the basis of single factors such as kinship (e.g., "mother tongue") or geography ("language of the homeland"). The following two case studies help illustrate how the role of such factors may not be so straightforward, and how using the concept of social capital could help communities and practitioners focus their language development activities.

13.5.1 Kinship and the Ishkashimi

Joseph (2004:74) notes that the dispositions (Bourdieu's [1977] "habitus") which socially determine our speaking in particular ways are inculcated into us from early childhood. This is a period when the environment for language acquisition is generally dominated by close family members, which is a strong force for homogeneity in traditional, village communities which consist of a network of extended families. The Expanded Graded Intergenerational Disruption Scale (EGIDS) and Sustainable Use Model (SUM) are tools for identifying the current state of vitality of a language, and enabling the community to identify a sustainable level of use to aim for (Lewis and Simons 2010, 2016). These tools range from international and national languages through languages which are at least used for face-to-face communication by all generations in a community, and onto languages which are threatened, shifting, moribund, or extinct. The importance of kinship helps to explain why the EGIDS scale assigns such significance to the question of whether or not a community's child-bearing generation adults are transmitting their L1 to children in the home. If they are not, the potential of the language for sustainable use has reached a tipping point.

The Ishkashimi [isk] language is spoken in two villages in Tajikistan—Ryn and Sumjin (Müller et al. 2005). In Ryn, Ishkashimi men place a high value on using only Ishkashimi within the village; it is the language of the home and the first language for all children. Significantly, while the majority of wives (59%) are Wakhi [wbl] or Tajik [tgk], they are expected to learn Ishkashimi and use it with their children in all domains. As a result, Ishkashimi is vital in this village, and is being passed on to the younger generation. As the "father tongue," men take a special responsibility for teaching the language to wives from other ethnic groups and to children. In the village of Sumjin, on the other hand, there are higher levels of contact with Tajik, including 87% of wives who are ethnically non-Ishkashimi, and Tajik-speaking women do not learn Ishkashimi but use Tajik with both neighbours and family members. Since many men now accept Tajik as the language of the home, Ishkashimi is in danger of being replaced gradually by Tajik as the language of the family and daily life.

The story of these two villages raises some important issues. One obvious one is that what is normally termed "mother tongue" may in this case best be described as a "father tongue." Another is that some children in Sumjin acquire different languages from their respective parents, resulting in two L1s acquired from birth. Third, although the two villages are only twenty kilometers apart, the vitality of the

L1 is very different. In Ryn, Ishkashimi is alive and well. In Sumjin, intergenerational transmission has mostly ceased, and only men value Ishkashimi as an important language. It is likely that this village's vernacular will be Tajik in one generation's time.

While Lewis and Simons (2016:40) legitimately highlight the value of a community resisting the loss of their language and cultural identity, it is also the case that communities are often strongly motivated to shift to a language of wider communication across all domains as part of constructing an identity for themselves that is bound up with "a conception of modernity as communication extending beyond their village and their country to the world at large" (Joseph 2004:23). This is summed up by Edwards (1997:35) as the overriding need for "mobility and modernization."

We may imagine a typical Ishkashimi speaker who has three speech varieties in her repertoire. Ishkashimi, her L1, might be one of her "heart languages." She does not speak it well across all domains, but enough to recover implicatures and infer significance in some. It does carry some emotive impact for her and she values it as an expression of identity and of bonding social capital. Tajik, her second speech variety, is the language she understands best, and also carries high intuitive impact —she learned it as a young child. It is an expression of her national identity, and a form of bridging social capital. It is a second "heart language," because she is also invested in the Tajik-speaking community as an insider. She has learned Russian [rus] too, and uses it proficiently in some instrumental domains. But although she has good comprehension, material in Russian has little intuitive impact for her; and she has no significant commitment to the promotion of social capital amongst Russian-speaking social networks. Russian, despite her proficiency in it, is not one of her "heart languages."

The import of these conclusions is that language development activity is likely to have significantly more impact in Ishkashimi and Tajik than in Russian for a community of such speakers. Production of literature in both languages may have value, but probably in different genres and media of communication respectively; while language maintenance or documentation efforts in Ishkashimi may well be appreciated despite the community's greater proficiency in Tajik.

13.5.2 Geography and the Yaghnobi

It is often easy to make a one-to-one link between a language and the territory in which it is spoken. Lewis and Simons (2016:53) state that "a community not only shares physical objects but cultural objects as well. The meaning of physical items in the world comes from this shared cultural understanding. … The mountain, river valley, plain, or jungle in which they live is not just any mountain, river, plain, or jungle. There is a history, a lore that invests the geographic location with meaning." This is illustrated by the Yaghnobi-speaking [yai] communities of Tajikistan (Paul et al. 2005). Their traditional homeland is the Yaghnob River Valley in the northwest of the country. Individuals from this valley went on to found all the other Yaghnob communities, which include three other significant locations of interest to us here. In the early 1970s, the entire valley population was forcibly relocated to work on the cotton plantations of Zafarabad, on the northwest border with Uzbekistan. Some have since returned to the valley, while others had voluntarily migrated before that date to the mountain village of Zumand and to the village of Dughoba, a short bus ride from the national capital, Dushanbe. In three of these four settlements there has been very little language shift, and a situation of stable orality (Lewis and Simons 2016:151) prevails.

For the villages of Zumand and the Yaghnob Valley, this sustainability derives not least from their geographical isolation, highly elevated and two hours' walk from the nearest public transport.[13] In Zafarabad, on the other hand, the ethnolinguistic vitality of the language remains strong despite extremely high contact with Tajik. Why is this the case when in Dughoba, another settlement where Yaghnobi speakers interact daily with Tajik speakers, language shift is taking place? There appear to be two key factors. One is a high degree of solidarity in Zafarabad, illustrated by dense, multiplex social networks[14] and strong attachment to their single heritage; whereas the migration to Dughoba, which was voluntary, has led to lower solidarity and a much greater degree of social interaction and hence integration with Tajiks. The other factor is strong diglossic patterns in Zafarabad, whereby the domains in which it is appropriate to use Tajik or Yaghnobi are clearly differentiated, while high Tajik proficiency is only required of those certain individuals in society who have roles which regularly situate them in Tajik domains.

In this scenario we see a cluster of groups who share an ethnicity but differ regarding the communities in whose social capital they are invested. Alongside the villages of Zumand and the Yaghnob Valley, whose relative isolation leads to the continued use of the L1, we find two contrasting diaspora communities. In Zafarabad, a commitment to promote bonding social capital means that language development activities there will likely be most fruitful in Yaghnobi; whereas in Dughoba, the commitment to promote bridging capital has led to language shift. Language development efforts in Yaghnobi there hold much less promise.

13.6 Conclusion

We have seen that some degree of comprehension and a high potential for intuitive response are necessary factors for any given speech variety to communicate to a community with impact. We explained comprehension in terms of a grasping of the implicatures in the message, and an inference and acceptance of significance leading to some kind of action or other change. Meanwhile, a language with the potential for high intuitive response will produce numerous cognitive effects, including increased automaticity of processing and perceptual prioritization.

John Watters (2021, chapter 14 this volume) identifies one's "heart language" as

> the center of convergence between emotion, intentionality, authenticity, veracity, well-being, security, and existential presence, … [It is] where one is just there, sensing veracity, authenticity, and depth of feeling. … For many people, there is one language, and for others, a set of languages, that connect deeply with the core of their being, their consciousness, and self-awareness within the larger, external world.[15]

---

[13] Laponce (1987) observes that communities using less widely spoken languages are often geographically more peripheral than are racial or religious minorities.

[14] Milroy (1980) found in Ireland that where close-knit localized network structures existed, there was a strong tendency to maintain nonstandard vernacular forms of speech.

[15] These factors are hallmarks of Type 1 (subconscious, intuitive, fast) thinking, which we have seen is substantially more important in determining one's "heart language" than Type 2 (conscious, rational) thinking. Meanwhile, the highlighting of veracity and

This allowance that "heart languages" may constitute a set reminds us of the danger of understanding "heart language" as necessarily a single heritage language or dialect of a community. Since languages are in any case parts of constructed, multiple identities,[16] there is often no simple one-to-one relationship between a language and a people group. It is for the community to decide which languages, dialects, and media will serve it best.

Returning to the core concepts from our introduction (section 13.1.2), we may now construct an integrated conclusion:

> Speech communities will be most beneficially transformed, in terms of progress towards self-organising complexity and its attendant benefits, by information couched in speech varieties which have a high potential for intuitive response and are sufficiently comprehensible. The best way to identify these speech varieties is to look at those which a community's members are using to promote social capital amongst the groups in which they desire to be insiders.

This may lead to an acknowledgement that language shift is beyond the point of reversal. On the other hand, it may lead to a deeper valuing of their heritage language(s). Engaging with communities through language development work helps to create bridges, as artists are empowered to publish and distribute their work, literacy primers help older generations to share the heritage language with their grandchildren, and younger generations reconnect with modes of expression they had once thought lost to them. Even where a "heart language" is only sustainable at the level of identity, it can be an instrument that members of dynamic speech communities use to build social capital for internal cohesion and connections to the outside world; and it can underlie a distinctive set of literary genres, spoken or sung, which carry tremendous affective value.

References

Barder, Owen. 2012. *What is development?* Accessed May 5, 2018. cgdev.org/blog/what-development/.

Barrett, Lisa Feldman. 2012. Emotions are Real. *Emotion* 12(3):413–429.

Berliner, Peter, Line Natascha Larsen, and Elena de Casas Soberón. 2012. Case study: Promoting community resilience with local values–Greenland's Paamiut Asasara. In Michael Ungar (ed.), *The social ecology of resilience: A handbook of theory and practice*, 387–297. New York: Springer.

Bourdieu, Pierre. 1977. *Outline of a theory of practice.* Translated by Richard Nice. Cambridge Studies in Social and Cultural Anthropology 16. Cambridge: Cambridge University Press.

---

authenticity chimes with and casts light on Putnam's (2000) emphasis on reciprocity and trust in his definition of social capital. Rafael (2015:90) summarizes: "In the heart language, there ceases to be a gap between the speaker and his or her speech."

[16] Joseph (2004:42) notes a trend in academic discussions of linguistic identity away from essentialism, analyzing linguistic identity as a given and fixed aspect of who an individual or group is, to constructionism, where linguistic identity is something changing and variable as it is constructed and performed. Meanwhile, Yip (2016) notes the danger of essentializing culture for those engaged in missionary work.

Brown, Richard. 2009. Language matters like bright sunlight: The benefit of communicating in heart language. *International Journal of Frontier Mission* 26(2):85–88. Accessed September 19, 2018. ijfm.org/PDFs_IJFM/26_2_PDFs/85-88_Brown_et_al.pdf/.

Brown, Richard. 2012. *Cognitive hermeneutics: A linguistic framework for biblical interpretation*. Ms.

Chiang, Samuel E. 2010. The passion for orality. In Samuel E. Chiang (ed.), *Orality breakouts: Using heart language to transform hearts*, 3–8. Hong Kong: International Orality Network.

Clark, Tom. 2006. Language as social capital. *Applied Semiotics / Semiotique Appliquee* 8(18):29–41.

Coleman, James S. 1988. Social capital in the creation of human capital. *The American Journal of Sociology* 94, Supplement: Organizations and Institutions: Sociological and Economic Approaches to the Analysis of Social Structure, S95–S120.

Costa, Albert, Alice Foucart, Inbal Arnon, Melina Aparici, Jose Apesteguia. 2014. "Piensa" twice: On the foreign language effect in decision making. *Cognition* 130(2):236–254.

Deloach, Daniel A. 2016. *Knowing God in Melanesia: Schemas relevant to vernacular Scripture engagement*. PhD dissertation. Fuller Theological Seminary, Pasadena, CA.

Eberhard, David. 2021. Identity choices of minoritized communities: Testing the identity construction factors. In J. Stephen Quakenbush and Gary F. Simons (eds), *Language and identity in a multilingual, migrating world*. Publications in Sociolinguistics 9. Dallas, TX: SIL International.

Edwards, John. 1997. Language minorities and language maintenance. *Annual Review of Applied Linguistics* 17:30–42.

Feenstra, Jaap. 2021. Identity and melting pots: Negotiating identity by resisting or pursuing accommodation. In J. Stephen Quakenbush and Gary F. Simons (eds), *Language and identity in a multilingual, migrating world*. Publications in Sociolinguistics 9. Dallas, TX: SIL International.

Haidt, Jonathan. 2001. The emotional dog and its rational tail: A social intuitionist approach to moral judgment. *Psychological Review* 108(4):814–834.

Haidt, Jonathan. 2012. *The righteous mind: Why good people are divided by politics and religion*. New York: Pantheon.

Harris, Kyle. 2021. L1 and L2 comprehension and emotional impact among early proficient bilinguals. In J. Stephen Quakenbush and Gary F. Simons (eds), *Language and identity in a multilingual, migrating world*. Publications in Sociolinguistics 9. Dallas, TX: SIL International.

Heath, Chip, and Dan Heath. 2010. *Switch: How to change things when change is hard*. New York: Broadway.

Joseph, John E. 2004. *Language and identity: National, ethnic, religious*. Basingstoke, UK: Palgrave Macmillan.

Kahneman, Daniel. 2011. *Thinking, fast and slow*. New York: Farrar, Straus and Giroux.

Karan, Mark E. 2011. Understanding and forecasting ethnolinguistic vitality. *Journal of Multilingual and Multicultural Development* 32(2):137–149.

Keane, Webb. 2007. *Christian moderns: Freedom and fetish in the mission encounter*. The Anthropology of Christianity 1. Berkeley, CA: University of California Press.

Kelly, Douglas F. 1994. The Westminster shorter catechism. In John L. Carlson and David W. Hall (eds.), *To glorify and enjoy God: A commemoration of the 350th anniversary of the Westminster Assembly*. Edinburgh, UK: Banner of Truth Trust.

Keysar, Boaz, Sayuri L. Hayakawa, and Sun Gyu An. 2012. The foreign-language effect: Thinking in a foreign tongue reduces decision biases. *Psychological Science* 23:661–668.

Kolb, David A. 1984. *Experiential learning: Experience as the source of learning and development*. Upper Saddle River, NJ: Prentice Hall.

Laka, Itziar. 2014. Mandela was right: The foreign language effect. Accessed April 6, 2018. mappingignorance.org/2014/02/03/mandela-was-right-the-foreign-language-effect/.

Landweer, M. Lynn. 2000. Indicators of ethnolinguistic vitality. *Notes on Sociolinguistics* 5(1):5–22. Accessed May 18, 2018. sil.org/sociolx/ndg-lg-indicators.html/.

Laponce, J.A. 1987. *Languages and their territories*. Toronto: University of Toronto Press.

Lewis, M. Paul. 2021. Remembering ethnicity: The role of language in the construction of identity. In J. Stephen Quakenbush and Gary F. Simons (eds), *Language and identity in a multilingual, migrating world*. Publications in Sociolinguistics 9. Dallas, TX: SIL International.

Lewis, M. Paul, and Gary. F. Simons. 2010. Assessing endangerment: Expanding Fishman's GIDS. *Romanian Review of Linguistics* 55(2):103–120.

Lewis, M. Paul, and Gary F. Simons. 2016. *Sustaining language use: Perspectives on community-based language development*. Publications in Ethnography 42. Dallas, TX: SIL International.

Lindquist, Kristen A., Ajay B. Satpute, and Maria Gendron. 2015. Does language do more than communicate emotion? *Current Directions in Psychological Science* 24(2):99–108.

Margolis, Howard. 1987. *Patterns, thinking, and cognition: A theory of judgment*. Chicago, IL: University of Chicago Press.

Milroy, Lesley. 1980. *Language and social networks*. Language in Society 2. Oxford: Blackwell.

Müller, Katja, Elisabeth Abbess, Daniel Paul, Calvin Tiessen, and Gabriela Tiessen. 2005. Ishkashimi: A father's language. How a very small language survives. In John M. Clifton (ed.), *Studies in Languages of Tajikistan*, 223–250. St. Petersburg, Russia: SIL International.

Nahapiet, Janine, and Sumantra Ghoshal. 1998. Social capital, intellectual capital, and the organizational advantage. *The Academy of Management Review* 23(2): 242–266.

Paul, Daniel, Elisabeth Abbess, Katja Müller, Calvin Tiessen, and Gabriela Tiessen. 2005. The ethnolinguistic vitality of Yaghnobi. In John M. Clifton (ed.), *Studies in Languages of Tajikistan*, 65–105. St. Petersburg, Russia: SIL International.

Pavlenko, Aneta. 2012. Affective processing in bilingual speakers: Disembodied cognition? *International Journal of Psychology* 47(6):405–428.

Putnam, Robert D. 1996. Who killed civic America? *Prospect Magazine*, March 1996.

Putnam, Robert D. 2000. *Bowling alone: The collapse and revival of American community*. New York: Simon and Schuster.

Rafael, Vicente L. 2015. Betraying empire: Translation and the ideology of conquest. *Translation Studies* 8(1):82–93.

Ratcliffe, Susan (ed.). 2012. *Little Oxford dictionary of quotations*. Fifth edition. Oxford: Oxford University Press.

Robbins, Joel. 2001. God is nothing but talk: Modernity, language, and prayer in a Papua New Guinea society. *American Anthropologist* 103(4):901–912.

Roche, David. 2017. Linguistic vitality, endangerment, and resilience. *Language Documentation and Conservation* 11:190–223.

Simons, Gary F. 2021. "Heart language" as a technical term: A critical review. In J. Stephen Quakenbush and Gary F. Simons (eds), *Language and identity in a multilingual, migrating world*. Publications in Sociolinguistics 9. Dallas, TX: SIL International.

Smith, Edwin. 1930. *In the mother tongue*. London: British and Foreign Bible Society.

Stanovich, Keith E., and Richard F. West. 2000. Individual differences in reasoning: Implications for the rationality debate. *Behavioral and Brain Sciences* 23:645–665.

Stanton-Salazar, Ricardo D., and Sanford M. Dornbusch. 1995. Social capital and the reproduction of inequality: Information networks among Mexican-origin high school students. *Sociology of Education* 68(2):116–135.

Vaish, Viniti, Teck Kiang Tan, Wendy Bokhorst-Heng, David Hogan, and Trivina Kang. 2010. Language and social capital in Singapore. In Lisa Lim, Anne Pakir, and Lionel Wee (eds), *English in Singapore: Modernity and management*, 159–180. Hong Kong University Press.

Watters, John R. 2021. Reflections on "Language of the Heart" or "Acquired Reflex Language." In J. Stephen Quakenbush and Gary F. Simons (eds), *Language and identity in a multilingual, migrating world*. Publications in Sociolinguistics 9. Dallas, TX: SIL International.

Wilson, Deirdre, and Dan Sperber. 2004. Relevance theory. In Lawrence R. Horn and Gregory Ward (eds.), *The handbook of pragmatics*, 607–632. Oxford: Blackwell.

Yip, George. 2016. Introducing post-postmodern missiology. *Evangelical Missions Quarterly* 52(3):262–270. Accessed February 28, 2018. missionexus.org/introducing-post-postmodern-missiology/.

14
Reflections on "Language of the Heart" or "Acquired Reflex Language"

John R. Watters

The heart can wander and lose its home.

Abstract. This paper provides a set of personal reflections exploring the metaphoric expression "heart language." A series of vignettes leads to questions about the experiential or philosophical role that various languages play in individual lives in noticeably different circumstances. These vignettes support the notion of "heart language" as a reality at the core of our being and which could be referred to more descriptively as an "acquired reflex language." After the vignettes, I close by asking what this acquired reflex has to do with language. I propose a few perspectives based on both biological and social theories with implications for the place of language in our lives. These might offer some possible directions for further research and deeper understanding.

14.1 Reflections

The notion of "heart language" is a contested one. However, I think it is a worthy metaphor in capturing the point of convergence between emotion, intentionality, authenticity, veracity, well-being, security, and existential presence.[1]

In June 1973 my wife, Kathie, and I arrived at Victoria Station in London. We had just arrived from France where we had spent ten months learning as much French [fra] as we could in that time. We needed to find a taxi to Marylebone Station to catch a train to High Wycombe. We found a queue outside along the road, something common in the UK but not so in France, so I asked Kathie to wait in the queue while I went to the head of the queue to see if it was for taxis. It was. When I returned I found Kathie in tears. They were flowing down her face. I asked her what was wrong.

---

[1] *Emotion* concerns mental affections or feelings, e.g., love, horror, or pity, as opposed to cognition. *Intentionality* concerns commitment to pursue action in the future. *Authenticity* concerns what is genuine and valid relative to what is real. *Veracity* concerns what is true and consistent relative to what is real. *Well-being* concerns being contented and healthy, a sense that things are the way they should be in body and in mind. *Security* concerns feeling safe from danger, both physical and emotional. *Existential presence* concerns a sense of being present in the given environment, both in body and in spirit.

She said nothing. She said something like, "It is just that I can look at all these signs on buildings and along the street and I don't have to think to know what they mean. It's just there." What is it about one's own language that is "just there"?

I think of the woman in the Mbeya region in Tanzania. She participated in an educational course about HIV and AIDS. At the end she said something like, "I heard all of this before in Swahili [swa], but I did not believe what I heard. Now that I heard it in my language I know it is true." What is it about one's language that it has the voice of veracity as opposed to the language of the outsider, or the oppressor?

I think of Oga in Ikom, Nigeria. He works in the local government, but is also an entrepreneur and provides a number of different services to clients. He is an elder in his church and preaches periodically. He grew up in an Ejagham [etu] village and speaks the language well. His wife, a school teacher, also speaks Ejagham but prefers to speak to us in English [eng]. Their young children, growing up in the town of Ikom, do not speak Ejagham but (Pidgin [pcm]) English. One evening as I was sitting alone with Oga, we got onto the topic of the Ejagham New Testament. I asked him if he read it, because I knew he had to preach in English in town, not in Ejagham. He said he did read it. He explained. When things are not going well, or there are difficulties I sit down with my Ejagham New Testament and read. Gradually my heart is stilled, and I am aware that God (*Obhasi*) is still God and he cares for us. I can relax and rest in him." What is it about the Scriptures in one's childhood language that allows it to calm the emotions and return one to confidence in God?

I think of Catholic Archbishop Verdzikov, now deceased, in Cameroon. Back in October 1976, he shared an experience he had in his own language. His name may sound like a Slavic name (*Verdzikov*), but he is a speaker of the Nso' language in Cameroon, and he said his name means "born in the bush." One Sunday he visited his home area and spoke in one church in Pidgin English and in the other in his home language, Nso'. Both churches were country churches with only Nso' [lns] speakers in them. He told the same jokes and gave the same message in both. He noticed that few people laughed at his Pidgin English jokes, but when he told them in Nso' there was much laughter and response. When he taught the lesson in Pidgin English, he received few audience responses to various phrases or important points, but in the Nso' service he received many responses and affirmations. The next week he went back to the same two churches to continue his experiment. This time he did the same as the week before, but there was a difference. In the first church it was the same group of people, but in the second, the attendance had doubled. What is it about jokes and spiritual teaching in their own language that captures the physical and emotional response of a people?

I think of Liz who grew up as a child of missionaries in Algeria. She went to school in French, played on the streets with her friends speaking Arabic [arb], and lived with her parents and siblings where they used American English in the home. I met her in 1972–73. She was one of the French teachers at the French school we attended. I thought of her as American, but one day I saw her in animated conversation with some north Africans, all speaking Arabic together. That led me to ask her what language she thought in and what language she dreamed in. She went to university in the USA and spoke fluent American English. Now she was serving as a professor of French. And she could speak fluent Arabic. In response, she did not know the answer to the question. She asked me to give her a week to figure it out. She came back after a week and said she had figured it out. She said that she continues to think and dream most often in the language she last spoke in. What is it about knowing a language fluently like a home language that allows us to think and dream in it? What allows the heart to wander and expand its boundaries to permit more than one language to speak deeply to us?

I think of educated Ejagham speakers with PhDs in economics, science, engineering, and military degrees (from the Royal Military Academy Sandhurst in the UK or the École de guerre in France), doctors, lawyers, professors, and so on. These are the educated elite, constituting less than 1% of the Ejagham population. They are the bright and successful. These are often the ones who spent the first twelve years of their lives as infants and in primary school living in the home area and speaking their home language. However, their secondary and tertiary education took them outside their home area and for years into their adulthood. They speak Ejagham well enough to function back home, but now feel more comfortable in English or French or both. If I am to have a deep conversation with them about life and worldview issues, it will not be in Ejagham. It will take place in English in most cases. These are the brightest, but most of them would not make the best translators because they never gained the art of Ejagham. Their linguistic aptitude and art is stronger in English. They know the basic grammar of Ejagham but not the multitude of idioms and metaphors or the poetic turns of phrase that are used back at home. What is it that allows the heart to give space to another language to flourish as part of an expanded identity? What is it about their role in society and the people they spend all day with that allows them to become at home in a European language?

Certainly the woman in the home village fixing the evening sauce and fufu, the school teacher in the local elementary school, the entrepreneur-government worker, the church leader, the fluent multilingual, and the highly educated leader, all have different identities, composed of a complex mix of ascribed and achieved markers, but one marker that is part of each of their complexes is the reality that they speak the home language or a set of home languages, whether elegantly or instrumentally. For many people, there is one language, and for others, a set of languages, that connect deeply with the core of their being, their consciousness, and self-awareness within the larger, external world.

These experiences with language are existential and instantaneous, not delayed by rational reflection or repetition, not intentional. These experiences are not at the surface level but reach down into the deeper levels of our being, our well of subconsciously archived experience. We could metaphorically say they are experiences of a "heart language" or "language of the heart" in which one is just there, present, sensing veracity, authenticity, and depth of feeling. It is not reflective cognition.

The association of language with the heart is an ancient conjunction. The Psalmist in speaking to his God brings "word" and "heart" together in Psalm 119, verse 11: "I have hidden your word in my heart that I might not sin against you." The Psalmist speaks of the "word" and placing it in a metaphorical "hidden" space of the metaphorical "heart." One could choose another body part such as the liver, the stomach, or another part that a given culture associates with the center of deep emotions and intentions to serve as the metaphor. If the desire is for a reference that is less of a metaphor and something more descriptive, they could be called "acquired reflex languages." They are languages that reach the deepest part of our being.

Paul (chapter 13 this volume, see section 13.1.2) suggests the important distinction here is that between subconscious intuition and conscious rational thought. He references Stanovich and West's (2000) typology of modes of thinking, popularized by Kahneman (2011:19–105 in particular). Type 1 mode of thinking involves the subconscious, intuition, and is automatic, while Type 2 mode of thinking involves rational thought, conscious deliberation, and calculation.

So, a "language of the heart" or "acquired reflex language" can be attributed to what is automatic in our thinking, to our intuitions. The reaction of "That really speaks to my heart," which someone may have in response to what they just heard, does not flow from rational thought and conscious deliberation. Instead, it flows from the subconscious—from our deeper, more hidden life.

14.2 Notes relative to theoretical models

It is claimed above that an "acquired reflex language" is one that reaches the deepest part of our being. It was suggested that it is a Type 1 mode of thinking, something automatic, dependent on the subconscious and intuition. However, in terms of language, to what can "reaching the deepest part of our being" possibly refer? Perhaps it would be helpful to consider various theoretical perspectives that might shed some light on the topic. Among the possibilities are those that treat language as a biological phenomenon and those that treat it as a social phenomenon. In answer to the question, each of the following paragraphs will end in the interrogative mood because it is not clear how the notion of an acquired reflex language would relate unambiguously to the given theoretical model.

Consider Berwick and Chomsky's (2018) biological model, the Strong Minimalist Thesis, which they also refer to as the "biolinguistic program" that has in view "the theory of the genetic component of the faculty of language" (2018:89). They propose that language involves three components, a base component, a sensorimotor component, and a conceptual-intentional component. The base component involves the notion of Merge that builds or composes "a digitally infinite array of hierarchically structured expressions" (2018:89). It is the "CPU" of language (2018:111). The sensorimotor component or "externalization" system related to the base "includes morphophonology, phonetics, prosody," and other matters involved in the production and analysis of spoken language or of sign language (2018:111). The conceptual or "internalization" systems involve reasoning, "inference, interpretation, planning … and other elements of what is informally called 'thought'" (2018:89). The base component relates to the need to answer the question of how children learn a language when they do not have access to exhaustive input about the language and yet they can produce what would be potentially an infinite number of sentences in that language. Does an acquired reflex language relate to all three components? If so, in what ways does it relate to each component? Is one component more central to an acquired reflex language? How are the systems that relate the base component to the internalization and externalization components involved? Would there be a distinction between those hierarchically structured expressions connected to the conceptual systems that require processing time and those that are automatic or immediate, the latter being the acquired reflex or deepest parts of language?

Consider the EvLab at MIT[2] where language is being researched as a biological phenomenon and where the goal is to identify specific domains of the brain to which language could be correlated. In other words, the goal "is to understand the computations we perform and the representations we build during language processing and to provide a detailed characterization of the brain regions underlying

---

[2] Ev Fedorenko's Language Lab; see evlab.mit.edu/.

these computations and representations" (Fedorenko 2018). The lab uses new techniques adapted from functional magnetic resonance imaging (fMRI) methods to identify which brain regions are involved in linguistic processing. Three questions motivate the research:

1. What is the structure of "the language network"?
2. How does the language network interact with other networks in the brain?
3. What are the differences between individuals in language processing and how do those differences relate to behavior and genetics?

They have arrived at a set of key discoveries:

1. There are regions in the brain that are "functionally specialized" for "high-level language-processing."
2. There is a sensitivity throughout the language network to lexical, syntactic, and semantic processing.
3. A number of regions in the brain are domain-general in that they can handle a variety of similar tasks across the regions.
4. Neural activity increases as the brain analyzes the complex meaning of a sentence as it is being uttered but it does not increase in processing a reading of a word list or a series of grammatical structures on their own.

In an interview by *The New Yorker* (Thurman 2018), Fedorenko reports that all her subjects that are administered an fMRI "show less brain activity when working in their mother tongue" than when working in another language. Everyone also shows greater effort when working in a language they do not know well. However, in this case, polyglots—speakers of multiple languages—do not appear to work as hard as those who are not polyglots. It apparently is an issue of efficiency. In processing language, they use a smaller area of their brain. So, if the brain has regions that are specialized for language, and generally all people spend less energy in understanding their mother tongue than a language they know less well, could an acquired reflex language be identified as relating to a smaller area of the brain than is otherwise needed, indicating a more efficient use of the part of the brain specialized for language?

Consider Bucholtz and Hall (2004), who consider language to be a social phenomenon. They refer to their model as "tactics of intersubjectivity." It recognizes the social (i.e., status) and political (i.e., power) relations that contribute to the construction of identity through a variety of symbolic resources that include language as a major one. They argue that "the interconnections between language and identity are multiple, complex, and contextually specific" (2004:375). For them, language practices reflect social identities. They do not constitute them. Furthermore, social identities are not an attribute of an individual or a group, but of social situations. As such, language has social meaning (pragmatic or contextual) and referential (semantic) meaning. In developing the model of tactics of intersubjectivity their goal is to accommodate markedness, essentialism, and institutional power, all three being central components of identity. So, how is an acquired reflex language situated socially? In what ways might its realization require a relevant social situation to motivate it? What is involved in relating the individual to the social situation that calls on an acquired reflex language? Relative to which component or components—markedness, essentialism, institutional power—is such an acquired reflex language most relevant?

Finally, consider Bourdieu (1977:73–95, 1980:52–79), who has developed the anthropological concept of *habitus*. Barclay (2015) quotes from Bourdieu (1977:82-83, the italics being in the original), that at a deeper level than can be articulated as a culture's norms and rules, a culture operates by what Bourdieu calls a habitus:

> a system of lasting, transposable dispositions which, integrating past experiences, functions at every moment as a *matrix of perceptions, appreciations, and actions* and makes possible the achievement of infinitely diversified tasks.

As Barclay notes, for Bourdieu the habitus is not something a person comes to possess or have, but is something a person is, indistinguishable from the physical person. So, in what sense is an acquired reflex language not something a person possesses but something that over time has become an integral part of who that person is, a part of the matrix of perceptions, appreciations, and actions—a part of the person's membership in the habitus that characterizes the person's culture?

Applying the interrogative mood in the above paragraphs is intended to open doorways to further research. An acquired reflex language likely has biological underpinnings and operations, but it also has social and cultural dimensions and ramifications, participating in the developing matrix of the given culture.

References

Barclay, John M. G. 2015. *Paul and the gift*. Grand Rapids, MI: William B. Eerdmans.
Berwick, Robert C., and Noam Chomsky. 2018. *Why only us: Language and evolution*. Cambridge, MA: MIT Press.
Bourdieu, Pierre. 1977. *Outline of a theory of practice*. Translated by Richard Nice. Cambridge Studies in Social and Cultural Anthropology 16. Cambridge: Cambridge University Press.
Bourdieu, Pierre. 1980. *The logic of practice*. Translated by Richard Nice. Stanford, CA: Stanford University Press.
Bucholtz, Mary, and Kira Hall. 2004. Language and identity. In Alessandro Duranti (ed.), *A companion to linguistic anthropology*, 369–394. Oxford: Blackwell.
Fedorenko, Eveline. 2018. EvLab research. Online at: evlab.mit.edu/research/.
Kahneman, Daniel. 2011. *Thinking, fast and slow*. New York: Farrar, Straus, and Giroux.
Paul, Daniel. 2021. When none of my heart languages is my mother tongue. In J. Stephen Quakenbush and Gary F. Simons (eds), *Language and identity in a multilingual, migrating world*. Publications in Sociolinguistics 9. Dallas, TX: SIL International.
Stanovich, Keith E., and Richard F. West. 2000. Individual differences in reasoning: Implications for the rationality debate. *Behavioral and Brain Sciences* 23:645–665.
Thurman, Judith. 2018. The mystery of people who speak dozens of languages: What can hyperpolyglots teach the rest of us? *The New Yorker*, September 3, 2018. Online at: newyorker.com/magazine/2018/09/03/the-mystery-of-people-who-speak-dozens-of-languages/.

Part Four
Descriptive Studies

15
Linguistic Identity and Dialect Diversity: A Conundrum with Regard to Magar Kham

Stephen Watters

Abstract. The northern Magar of Rolpo and Rukum districts of central Nepal speak a linguistically diverse set of Tibeto-Burman speech varieties collectively known as "Magar Kham." This paper focuses on several related issues surrounding their ethnic identity as it relates to linguistic diversity. Specifically, I describe the local controversy of whether or not their speech varieties should be considered as a family of languages or a family of dialects. The reference to language or dialect is of particular importance in Nepal because language has come to be a proxy for ethnic identity, and in so doing brings hope of representation in the political system. Magar Kham activists are willing to listen to differing perspectives, accepting that there are several major speech varieties in Magar Kham-speaking areas. This acceptance, more than anything, gives cause for hope in addressing concerns for the loss of linguistic diversity.[1]

15.1 Introduction

In the discipline of linguistics, globalization is considered to be one of the primary causes of the loss of small (and sometimes not so small) minority languages and cultures (Crystal 2000; Krauss 1992). However, it has also been pointed out that the factors which contribute to language and culture endangerment, and the eventual shift to other languages, is a complex phenomenon involving many local factors. The interrelationship between global and local factors that contribute to language endangerment has been referred to as "glocalisation" (Fishman 2002:272).

---

[1] In writing this article, I am indebted to Karna Bahadur Budha for openly dialoguing with me about his views on language and ethnicity among the Magar Kham, and to DanRaj Regmi for providing me with current information about LINSUN (the Linguistic Survey of Nepal) and its ongoing research of language diversity in Nepal. An earlier version of this paper was written during my time as a graduate student in the linguistics program at Rice University. I am indebted to Dr. Christina Willis Oko and Dr. Nancy Niedzielski for the many comments which helped improve that version of the paper.

It is not surprising that since the phenomenon is a complex interplay of many competing factors, the response from within the discipline of linguistics varies a great deal, evolving from when the study of endangered languages first became a prominent feature within the discipline in the 1980s and 1990s. It is not the purpose of this paper to trace the development of these views, or to provide a full treatment of current views, except to note that many of them draw on models from the biological sciences. In Dixon's (1997) adaptation of the punctuated equilibrium hypothesis, for example, periods of human history go through stages of stability during which groups of people with roughly equal prestige live next to one another, speaking their own language or dialect. At various points, the equilibrium is "punctuated" and drastic changes occur during these by-comparison brief periods of time, and these trigger significant changes within language. While language change has always existed, the punctuated equilibrium hypothesis sees the modern phenomenon of loss of linguistic diversity as unprecedented, and the pace of change as dramatic and alarming.

The endangerment of language communities has had a profound and galvanizing effect on linguistics as a discipline with a renewed focus on studying language in human social context, and a focus on the documentation of language in its natural and cultural environment (not only its description in grammars and dictionaries). Concern for endangered language communities has brought renewed interest in language variation (both between languages and within a single language). The study of language and its patterned use in society, however, is no longer of interest only to academics. A heightened sense of awareness of the imbalances between peoples has grown among many language communities around the world. This is no less true for the language communities of Nepal who, in the wake of the People's Movement of 1990, began to advocate for the recognition of their ethnic and linguistic identities (Raeper and Hoftun 1992). While academic motivation is guided by improving our understanding of the science of language, the interest of language communities in Nepal is to acquire equal representation alongside other language communities, and to express their own distinct identities as they push back against the perceived hegemony of mainstream Nepali [nep] linguistic and cultural norms. In the wake of these efforts, language and ethnicity have become strongly politicized in Nepal.

The confluence of global, national, and local factors is at the center of the issue of language revitalization in Nepal. The enumeration of languages in *Ethnologue* gives international voice to linguistic identities, and provides sanction for lobby of those identities at a national level. For some language communities, revitalization means reversing the erosion of language use (Hinton 2001:5,7). Language revitalization is used in this paper, however, in its broadest sense, referring to the research that goes into and subsequent development of programs that result in establishing (or reestablishing), maintaining, and expanding the use of a language in as many social and cultural domains as possible (Tsunoda 2006).[2] As such, revitalization in Nepal constitutes primarily a practical activity, such as the production of educational materials and written materials for use in local government, or in producing media programs for the local radio.

In this paper, I focus on several related issues surrounding language identity of the northern Magars of Rolpo and Rukum districts of central Nepal, who speak a diverse set of Tibeto-Burman speech varieties collectively known as Magar Kham.[3]

---

[2]The expansion of language use into these more formal domains is based on the eight steps toward reversing language shift (Fishman 1991).

Specifically, I describe the local controversy of whether or not the Magar Kham speech varieties should be considered as a family of languages or a family of dialects. The reference to language or dialect is of particular importance in Nepal because language has come to be a proxy for ethnic identity, and in so doing brings hope of representation in the political system (even if the political system, as of yet, only allows for limited ethnic representation).

A related controversy is whether or not a single written standard language for the northern Magar can achieve the goals of education and adequate communicability for all northern Magars. It is too early to say what effect, if any, the expansion of one written variety will have on spoken varieties of the same language, but at the very least, it punctuates a change in the equilibrium of which Dixon speaks that will affect the domains of language use. Creating a standard from one variety (or an amalgamation of varieties) perpetuates the politicized nature of language, and ironically has the potential of contributing to the very thing it sets out to reverse— a reduction of speech domains for the speech varieties not chosen for a written standard.

In spite of disagreeing with the development of a single standard written language for all Magar Kham varieties, I have taken an approach which Bradley (2011:46) refers to as a sojourner, who as an outsider "maintains a long-term cooperative relationship with a language community." In walking the language development journey with the northern Magar, I engage in a process of give-and-take. While our views are sometimes in conflict, Magar Kham activists are willing to listen to differing perspectives, and to accept that there are several major speech varieties in Magar Kham-speaking areas. This acceptance, more than anything, gives cause for hope in addressing concerns for the loss of linguistic diversity, whatever form language development might take among them.

Given the politicization of language and identity, I argue that care must be taken in interpreting works like *Ethnologue* or the languages listed in the national census of Nepal. They are used as standards, but they may not reflect issues of linguistic identity or true linguistic diversity. In writing this paper, then, I wish to highlight both identity and diversity in the hope that language development efforts will better achieve the goals of language conservation and empowerment of the community. Language development has a higher chance of success when it takes into account the linguistic ecosystem in which it belongs, and this entails a clearer understanding of the heterogeneous nature of language and the linguistic identities associated with them.

In this paper I will explore several related topics: linguistic diversity among the Magar Kham based on my own earlier sociolinguistic work and D. Watters' grammatical studies in section 15.2; the emergence of modern ethnic and linguistic identities in Nepal, specifically among the Magar Kham, in section 15.3; language policy regarding minority languages in Nepal and how language policy is imbued with a standard language ideology in section 15.4; recent expressions of linguistic identity by Magar Kham language activists, and, in particular, that they have taken on a standard language ideology in sections 15.5 and 15.6; and, finally, I respond to the expression of standard language ideology in section 15.7.

---

[3] Linguists and anthropologists familiar with earlier academic literature will notice the change in nomenclature from "Kham Magar" to "Magar Kham." This change comes at the request of the Nepal Magar Association, which is explained in section 15.5.

The basic flow of the paper, then, is organized around explaining how it is that, in spite of a fair degree of linguistic diversity among the northern Magar, the rise of identity politics has contributed to the politicization of language, and that this in turn contributes to the obfuscation of linguistic diversity. I will draw on my experience of being associated with the northern Magar for much of my life. I lived in Kathmandu, Nepal, during the 1990s and 2000s where I had a dual role as a visiting scholar at Tribhuvan University and as a researcher with SIL International. During these years, I had daily or weekly contact with Magar Kham speakers in an urban setting. My formative years in the 1970s, however, were spent coming and going from the village of Taka Shera, a large traditional community in the northern Parbate dialect area of the northern Magar homeland, and where my father, David Watters, was involved in linguistic research and translation under the auspices of SIL International. My perspective of the northern Magar is unique, as both an insider and outsider, giving me a long-term, intergenerational view of life among the northern Magar people.

15.2 Linguistic diversity among the Magar Kham

The Himalayan region, stretching some 2,000 miles (about 3,200 kilometers) from Afghanistan in the west to Myanmar in the east, is regarded as one of the ten biodiversity mega-centers of the world (Turin 2007). In addition to a wealth of ecological zones rich in animal and plant species, this stretch of land is home to some 1,000 languages, accounting for nearly one-sixth of the world's languages (Simons and Fennig 2018). Some 123 of these languages from four different language families are spoken in Nepal (Eppele et al. 2012), demonstrating a remarkable diversity for a country which is about a 100 miles (160 kilometers) wide and 500 (800 kilometers) long. Magar Kham, the focus of this paper, is a Tibeto-Burman language, and Nepali, the national language of Nepal, is Indo-Aryan (in the Indic branch of Indo-European languages).

The northern Magar live off the western end of Dhaulagiri massif in central Nepal (see map 1). The northern reaches of their territory are bounded by permanent glaciers and peaks in excess of 20,000 feet (6,000 meters), and is a prime habitat for the blue sheep and the endangered snow leopard (D. Watters 2002:4). Traditionally, the Magar Kham ran large herds of sheep and goats through these alpine areas in the summer months.

Map 1. Northern Magar homeland

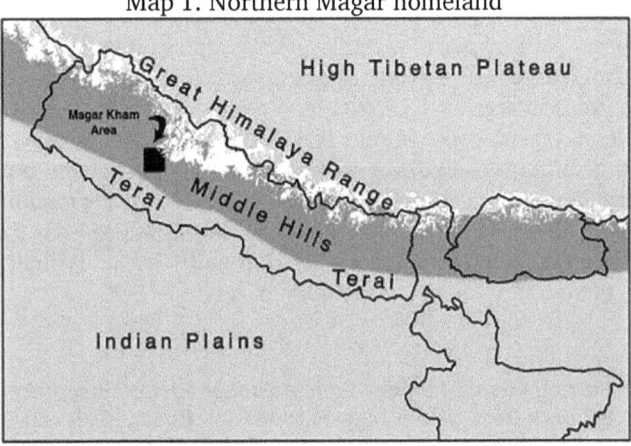

The Magar Kham maintain permanent villages in the upper valleys of the rivers that flow off of the Dhaulagiri massif westward toward the Sani Bheri, as well as the upper tributaries of the Lungri and Bhuji Khola. The lay of the land for much of this region is characterized by ridges which run in an east-west direction at an altitude in excess of 10,000 feet (3,000 meters), and valley floors between 5,000 and 10,000 feet (1,500 and 3,000 meters). Motorable roads are only beginning to reach the edges of this region. Most Magar Kham-speaking villages remain several day's walk from the end of the nearest road. Only 2% of the land is under cultivation, and to cultivate even this, agricultural plots are maintained on slopes with as much as a 45 degree slope (D. Watters 2011:153). Given the ranges in altitude, the ruggedness of the terrain, and difficulty of travel between Magar Kham-speaking regions, it is not surprising that this area is marked by forms rich in ecological and linguistic diversity.

My own sociolinguistic work among the northern Magar stems from research I conducted in the late 1980s. It remains in unpublished form, but D. Watters makes mention of it when writing about Magar Kham dialects, synthesizing my work in sociolinguistics with his own work in vocabulary and verb paradigm comparison and historical reconstruction of proto-Magar-Kham (D. Watters 1998:26). My research suggests that lexical similarity[4] between speech varieties ranges between 50–70%, a range that makes it difficult to predict how well speakers from the different communities might understand one another. Additional recorded text studies between three Magar Kham-speaking areas indicate that intelligibility is quite low: around 30% between the Gamale [kgj] and Takale [kjl] dialects (a dialect within Western Parbate), and about 60% between the Takale and Nishel [kif] dialects (a dialect of Eastern Parbate). Whatever these percentages may mean, perhaps, the more telling evidence for difficulty of communication is the fact that when doing the research for this study, my Takale traveling companions had to resort to Nepali for communication, particularly in the Gamale and Sheshi [kip] speaking areas (S. Watters 1988).

One of the things that contributes to low intelligibility between speech communities is the polysynthetic agglutinating nature of Magar Kham morphology. D. Watters explains that "[e]ach of the dialects exhibits a complex morphology with multiple affixes attached to stems of every class. Though the categories marked are much the same from one dialect to another, their surface representations and syntactic arrangements are often different. What may be suffixing in one dialect may be prefixing in another, and the morphemes themselves may have derived from entirely different etyma" (2002:13–14). This rearrangement in surface representations can be illustrated with the words 'see' and 'hit' in four major dialects, as in table 1 (adapted from D. Watters 1998:28).

---

[4]Lexical similarity is here measured as the phonological similarity required for presumed ease of communication, rather than the shared diachronic history of cognate counts (see Blair 1990 for the methodology of determining lexical similarity). According to D. Watters (2002), Gamale [kgj] and Takale [kjl] dialects are 90–95% similar.

Table 1. Magar Kham verb morphology in four speech varieties

Speech varieties	we see them	we hit them
Takale	ge-ra-rĩːh-zya 1P-3P-see-CONT	ge-ra-poh-zya 1P-3P-hit-CONT
Nishel	ba-ge-rə̃ːh-rə CONT-1P-see-3P	ba-ge-thəta-rə CONT-1P-hit-3P
Gamale	ye-rəhŋ-jə-ẽ-rə PRE-see-CONT-1P-3P	ye-coh-jə-ẽ-rə PRE-hit-CONT-1P-3P
Sheshi	rəhŋ-jya-ya-waŋ see-CONT-1P-3P	tup-jya-ya-waŋ hit-CONT-1P-3P

The verb phrases under each column for each speech variety mean the same thing, and can be translated as 'we see them' and 'we hit them'. The verb root 'see' has a similar phonological form in each of the dialects. If one was doing a word list comparison, these would be regarded as "the same". A careful comparison of the affixes in each column reveals that each dialect marks "the same" grammatical categories. That is, each dialect has an affix for first-person plural (1P), third-person plural (3P), and progressive aspect (CONT). In addition, many of the affixes have a similar phonological form: the third-person plural agreement marker is some variation of *ra*, with the exception of the Sheshi *wang*. However, taken in the context of the verb phrase, the position of each affix changes relative to the position of the verb. Continuing with a description of *ra*, in Takale it occurs in the slot immediately prior to the verb, in Nishel immediately after the verb, and in Gamale and Sheshi in the last slot of the verb phrase.

In the phrase 'we hit them', not only are the affixes in different positions, but the verb root itself is different. Even if on linguistic analysis the morphology can be demonstrated to be part of a similar system, it is not difficult to understand why intelligibility between language communities is low.

The composite view of earlier intelligibility studies, observation of language use when traveling through Magar Kham-speaking areas, and morphosyntactic comparison demonstrates that Magar Kham comprises at least four distinct speech varieties, with numerous sub-varieties. One might even go so far as to say that on paper the major groupings "look" like different languages, and for communicative purposes are like different languages. This is not surprising, in fact, even expected, given our understanding of the Himalayan region as a "mega-center" for ecological and linguistic diversity. It is on the basis of this research that editions of *Ethnologue* have enumerated four distinct Magar Kham languages.

15.3 Ethnic identity as a foil of linguistic diversity

In this section, I briefly summarize the emergence of linguistic and ethnic identity in Nepal as it is described in the anthropological literature. This is followed by the view of ethnic identity among the northern Magar that emerges in the work of de Sales (2000) and D. Watters (1998, 2002, 2011). This will serve as a backdrop for explaining why linguistic and ethnic identity might ignore, or downplay, linguistic diversity.

The emergence of ethnic identity in Nepal is something of an intellectual curiosity given that anthropologists and ethnographers note that when they first began their field research in the 1970s and 1980s, many minority communities had a significantly different sense of identity than they do now (Gellner et al. 2008). De Sales (2000:68) observes that identity politics was unheard of among the northern Magar as late as the early 1980s (when she first began research among them), but notes that by end of the 1990s they had "... resorted to an intensified sense of identity in relation to their 'country'."

Gellner et al. observe that "ethnic feelings develop in very specific contexts of opposition and competition" (1998:9). In Nepal, these feelings developed in the context of the *Jana Andolan I* (People's Movement of 1990), when the late king Birendra stepped down, and the democratic party system was instituted. Gellner takes a "modest version" of modernism for Nepal, suggesting that nationalism and ethnicity are a relatively new phenomenon in response to the newly emerging political system in Nepal, but that ethnic identity is ancient. Moreover, it is possible to see each of these threads at work, mutually informing the other in response to newly emerging situations. Gellner illustrates this fluidity when quoting from Brass (1991:75):

> Whether or not the culture of the group is ancient or is newly-fashioned, the study of ethnicity and nationality is in large part the study of politically induced cultural change. More precisely, it is the study of the process by which elites and counterelites within ethnic groups select aspects of the group's culture, attach new value and meaning to them, and use them as symbols to mobilize the group, to defend its interests, and to compete with other groups. In this process, those elites have an advantage whose leaders can operate most skillfully in relations both to the deeply felt primordial attachments of group members and the shifting relationships of politics.

Gellner points out that emerging ethnic identities cannot be explained solely through the notions of resistance and opposition. Numerous studies suggest that much of Nepal has undergone a profound process of Hinduization (Allen 2008). Hinduism spread through much of Nepal, not because of a government plan, but because local leaders had to learn the language of the nation, and take on Hindu practice in order to fit in with the Hindu elite (Pfaff-Czarnecka 1991). The spread of Hinduism is explained, then, as a process of adoption and adaptation. As they adopted the language and practices of the elite, bilingualism in Nepali grew, and is no doubt related to the "ambient" bilingualism in Nepali in the middle hill communities studied by Webster (1997).

This explains the often conflicted and ironic nature of ethnic and linguistic activism in Nepal. On the one hand, it is an effort in resistance against the perceived hegemony of Hindu elites (and their language). On the other, it exhibits features of adoption and adaptation as language communities acquire skill in Nepali and English in order to better navigate the vagaries of political affairs in Nepal.

It is well documented that for most of Nepal's modern history (beginning in the mid 1700s), the building of a single unified Hindu nation has come at the cost of suppressing the many ethnic, linguistic, and religious identities of communities within its borders. Until the promulgation of a new constitution establishing parliamentary democracy in 1990, the nation has had an official policy of one language, one culture, and one religion. This policy has had different implications for different periods; the banning of all languages and cultures under the Rana regime prior to 1950s, or the insistence of Nepali as the language of education during the Panchayat era (1962–1990).

Political and economic power have been vested in a ruling class which was Hindu in religion and culture, and which spoke Nepali. Peoples without this identity had little access to economic or political power beyond their local situations. When the one language, one culture, one religion policy was lifted in 1990, it opened the door to the possibility of participation on the national scene; repressed identity could be expressed. This is not to say, however, that prior to 1990 the lower castes and ethnicities of Nepal were powerless, or that they did not use the political system for their gain. As de Sales (2000:45) notes, "Ethnic identities in this period seem to have been labels that one could change, labels that had political, economic, and legal reference, rather than a social or cultural one." This use of identity was only reinforced in the People's Movement of 1990, and explains in part the proliferation of ethnic and linguistic identities enumerated in the 2001 and 2011 census reports (see section 15.3.1).

15.3.1 National language ideologies in the census reports

In this section, I describe the linguistic and ethnic reporting that have gone into the national census reports. These reports illustrate how caste, ethnic, and language names belie the national agenda of the time, and that only in the recent 2011 census has self-identification of language and ethnicity been possible. It is only in this census, for example, that Magar Kham is first enumerated as a distinct language.

The census reports before the 1990 People's Movement were based on the Hindu *varna* system, which in Nepal divides traditional Hindu society into clean and untouchable castes. The clean castes are further divided between the *tagadhari* "twice-born' castes who wear the sacred thread of Hinduism, and the groups collectively known as *matwali* or "drinking' castes. The former category includes such castes as Brahmins, Thakuris, and Chhetris. It is to the "drinking' level of the hierarchy to which most of the ethnic groups have been absorbed into the Hindu caste system (Caplan 1973:43). Thus, even in the 1991 census report (after the People's Movement of 1990), many of the groupings were based on this categorization, but with additional ethnic categories: 30 caste groups, 26 ethnic groups, and 4 in an "other" category. This tradition of conflating caste and ethnicity as a way of categorizing peoples continues; in the 2011 census there was an interesting mix of 58 castes, 64 ethnic groups, and 3 "other" groups (for a total of 125 distinct "groups").

One of the notable aspects of the decadal Nepalese census is the regular addition and subtraction of castes, ethnicities, and languages. The recent additions to the number of castes and ethnicities in the 2011 census is explained by Sharma (2014) as instrumentalism: an attempt at representation in the modern political system of Nepal.

In addition to caste/ethnic distinctions, the changes in the number of languages listed in each decade of the census reports since 1951, given in table 2, reflect changes in the official stance on linguistic diversity in Nepal, as well as a rising awareness of cultural and linguistic identity. Sharma explains that in the 1952/1954 census the 58 languages were grouped as dialects; the decline in languages in the 1961, 1971, and 1981 census are attributable to the promotion of the Nepali language to the exclusion of other languages; and a rising number of languages following the 1991 census are a result of emerging linguistic and ethnic identities (Sharma 2014:29).

Table 2. Variability in languages reported in census reports in Nepal

Number of Languages	Year of Census Report
58	1952/1954
36	1961
17	1971
18	1981
32	1991
92	2001
123	2011

There is a good deal of overlap in the 2011 census between the names of the languages and the categorization of people based on ethnicity. Some of this overlap stems from the fact that certain ethnicities and the languages they speak have been officially acknowledged since the beginning of the census reports. For example, many people familiar with Nepal will know the designations Chepang [cdm], Gurung [gvr], Lepcha [lep], Limbu [lif], Magar, Newar [new], Rai [dwz], Sherpa [xsr], Tamang, and Tharu, and have the understanding that there is a one-to-one mapping between ethnicity and language for these peoples. However, there is little overlap between the enumerations of caste and language: in Nepal it is implicit, for example, that the hill castes Bahun, Chhetri, Sanyasi Dasnami, and Thakuri all speak Nepali (that is, a many-castes-to-one-language mapping).

It is not clear from looking at Sharma's report whether some of the newly acknowledged languages also represent newly self-identified ethnicities, or whether the speakers of these languages are considered, or consider themselves to be, part of an ethnic designation separate from language. Many of the newly acknowledged languages were designated formerly as belonging to the Rai group, but now self-designate as distinct according to linguistic affiliation. On the other hand, speakers of Magar Kham, whose language is also newly acknowledged in the 2011 census report, continue to self-designate as belonging to the Magar ethnicity.

Sharma (2014) is insightful in many ways, but perhaps more than anything, underlines the fact that an accurate picture of linguistic diversity is only just beginning to emerge (in large part, due to the efforts of the Central Department of Linguistics, Tribhuvan University; see also Eppele et al. 2012). The primary criteria for differentiation in the census have been based on ethnicity and caste until recently. Thus, in the past, the Magar ethnicity was absorbed into the *varna* system as a "drinking' caste, and they were regarded as speaking a single Magar language. It is only recently that Magar has been recognized as an ethnicity apart from the caste system, and in the 2000s that the Magar ethnicity speak more than a single language. The official three languages (as listed in the official census) of the Magar ethnicity are now Magar, Kham, and Kaike [kzq][5], although the Nepal Magar Association prefers the designations Magar Dhut, Magar Kham, and Magar Kaike.

The recognition of several distinct languages spoken by the Magar represents significant progress in the recognition of linguistic diversity at the national level. Thus, it is now more readily accepted that there is not a one-to-one correspondence between ethnicity and language. However, there is still room for improvement. At some level, it should also be recognized that there is not a one-to-one correspondence between officially recognized languages and intelligible speech varieties. This is

---

[5] D. Watters (2006) demonstrates that Kaike is actually a Tamangic language, further illustrating that ethnicity can be a poor proxy for linguistic affinity.

already beginning to happen in the Rai group of languages which were formally classified as a single language, but are now separated on the basis of self-identification and linguistic differences. Given the heightened awareness of linguistic identity in Nepal, one wonders whether Magar Kham speakers will also self-identify as separate languages in future decades.

Which peoples will merge or separate ethnic and linguistic identities in the future remains to be seen. The fact that this is a constantly evolving situation, however, must be taken into account in documentation and revitalization efforts. While ethnic names and linguistic labels help to enumerate linguistic diversity, they also obfuscate it, and may not be a good proxy for measurement of diversity. As illustrated here in the census reports, the addition and subtraction of ethnicities and languages has as much to do with government policies and the rise of identity politics as it does with actual cultural and linguistic diversity.

15.3.2 Northern Magar identity

In this section, I write specifically on the development of the northern Magar identity. I refer primarily to the work of de Sales, but draw also on the writing of D. Watters. A synthesis of their research points to the fact that while a northern Magar identity has always been present, it has become more salient and conscious as a result of contrast with the broader Magar ethnic identity and resistance toward mainstream Nepali language and culture, as well as participation in and resistance to the Maoist People's War.

In the 1950s, reports of the broader Magar identity "were less concerned with making demands and rather more concerned with self-criticism," and were aimed at "root[ing] out the evils that existed in Magar society" (de Sales 2000). That is, they viewed themselves in the way that they were undoubtedly viewed by the Hindu elite —wallowing in the abomination of the *matwali* "drinking' castes—which according to de Sales emphasized the vices of "overspending and overdrinking" (see section 15.3.1 for a description of the Hindu caste system in Nepal).

However, religious and ethnic repression was much more than a sense of religious inferiority or lack of virtue with regard to the standards of Hinduism. Hinduism was the state religion, and other religions were illegal. Northern Magar shamans— even though an indigenous religious system—were, among other things, forbidden from beating their drums. Many of the northern Magars who became Christian met with police brutality and were punished with prison. On either count, the northern Magars were not able to practice their religious traditions, and by any human rights standards, it was oppressive.

Hasta Ram Budha Magar, a close Magar Kham-speaking family friend, described his people as "lost and forgotten at the foot of the snows." This is not unlike how de Sales reports that the Magar describe their homeland as dead ends, forgotten by the rest of the world. It is partly this sense of being forgotten which has made the northern Magar more disposed to joining in projects that would make their homeland more respectable (de Sales 2000:48).

However, D. Watters describes opportunities for education in Nepali as met with skepticism and suspicion. Children who were sent away for education in Nepal returned to their villages without employment, but with an understanding that they were no longer part of the work force, and that they were part of the privileged class. The newly educated forged alliances with the outside administration, and the average uneducated villager was no match for the web of self-serving policies and stratagems of these alliances. Villagers had to "pay timber tax, house tax, trail tax, pig tax, and even dog tax. Shamans had to pay drum tax" (D. Watters 2011:162). If this is what education brought, then most northern Magars wanted nothing to do with it. One of the first orders of business for the Maoists when they began their uprising in 1996 was to settle these grudges. The educated who participated in these oppressive schemes were tortured and executed.

When the People's Movement ushered in parliamentary democracy, the northern Magar welcomed the overthrow of the king and the Hindu establishment. For many, the oppression of the past had been lifted. Furthermore, de Sales (2000:49–50) insightfully notes that "when the United Nations declared 1993 'International Year of Indigenous Peoples' it provided world backing for local problems."

In spite of the 1990 People's Movement, no one from the newly constituted ethnic organizations was elected to parliament in the 1991 or 1994 elections; political and economic power essentially continued in the hands of the Hindu elite. Born partly out of frustration with this, the Maoist political party turned to armed resistance in 1996, ending in 2006 with the signing of the Comprehensive Peace Accord. The Maoist uprising and subsequent decade-long war has been documented elsewhere (Thapa 2003, 2004), but for our purposes, illustrates that another important aspect of the rise of ethnic and linguistic identities in Nepal has been the appropriation of ethnic identities as a means of grassroots resistance. Whereas in the past, ethnic and linguistic identity was something to be suppressed, with the Maoists it became an important means of fighting against the established Hindu elite.

There is an explicit linkage between land and identity for the northern Magar that has been noted for communities around the world. De Sales describes them as belonging to their *des* "land', which is a term ironically borrowed from Nepali. This sense of belonging to land can be found in D. Watters' (2011:146–147) description of an interchange between Satal Singh (a northern, Parbate dialect Magar Kham speaker) and a southern Magar who no longer spoke Magar. In this interchange, Satal Singh implies that when one loses one's own language, one also loses the ability to be distinctive, and this is not far off from being overrun by the power of the Hindu elite. Maintaining one's own language is the first step in maintaining one's identity, and the land which gives you that identity.

> As we sat in the shade of the veranda waiting for our meal to be cooked, Satal Singh began telling me a humorous story of his late uncle's encounter with a bear. ... Suddenly, we were interrupted by a stranger who had been eyeing us from the other side of the veranda. "Tell your story in Nepali so we can all enjoy it," he said, rather pompously. Satal Singh whirled around with an invective that surprised both me and the stranger. "Why should I stop speaking Kham?" he answered with hostility, obviously interpreting the man's request as a challenge. Now it was the stranger's turn to be offended. "It's all a bunch of gibberish; what good is it?" There was contempt in his voice. Satal Singh was on his feet in an instant. "You poor devils," he said with feigned pity, "you've let the Brahmins talk you into giving up your language, and now you want me to give up mine. I'll never do it. When you lost your language, you lost your land and everything else worth having. We'll never do that. We still have our language."

The Magar have documented that they come from a land known as *Magarant*, and that it was present before the time of Prithvi Narayan Shah's unification of Nepal in the mid 1700s. An interesting part of this history is the fact that there were two Magarant kingdoms: the *Athara Magarant* and the *Barha Magarant* which are roughly co-extensive with the current Magar Kham-speaking areas and the Magar Dhut-speaking areas. Magar Kham speakers continue to self-identify as belonging to the Magar ethnicity, but are now careful to identify as originating from the land of the Athara Magarant.

In tracing identity among the northern Magar, it is clear that it has evolved from what it was as late as three decades ago. Perhaps one of the biggest differences is the fact that, for most northern Magar, linguistic and ethnic identity is more salient, pronounced, and conscious.

15.4 Responses to linguistic diversity

In this section, I report on national language policy recommendations, made largely in the hope and possibility of redress for the linguistic wrongs of the Hindu elite, and the possibility of the use of other languages in the formal political structures of modern Nepalese society.

In 1994 His Majesty's Government (the government of Nepal until it became a Republic in 2006) asked for a series of recommendations for a national language policy. What followed was *The Report of National Languages Policy Recommendation Commission,* which was based on significant research and interviews with over sixty linguists and educators. This resulted in a fourfold classification of Nepalese languages based on practicalities such as how much is already known about the language, whether or not the language was used in written domains, and how much development might be required to use it in primary education. This fourfold classification is as follows:

1. languages with a written tradition
2. languages in the process of developing a written tradition
3. languages without a written tradition (the primary bulk of languages in Nepal)
4. dying languages

The Commission specified a phased approach whereby primary language instruction begins in languages with a written tradition, pedagogical materials begin to be developed in languages with a developing written tradition, and research begins in languages without a tradition. Phase two and three continued down the ladder of languages, such that each subsequent category moves through phases of research, development of pedagogical materials, and use as a language of instruction in primary education.

As part of this process, the Commission recognized the difficulty in developing the languages of the country for pedagogical purposes without understanding the heterogeneity of its speech communities. They recommended an "authentic linguistic survey" be conducted in order to identify and delimit the speech communities of the country. They envisioned a process of identifying dialects, and then selecting one of these as the "norm," based on such things as "the linguistic capability of the dialect speakers, number of speakers, literate tradition, attitudes of the speakers towards the dialects, etc." (Yadava and Grove 2008:15). It was suggested that the process in selecting the norm is "painless" when the differences between dialects is "marginal."

Inherent in the Commission report is a standard language ideology (SLI) which, as defined by Lippi-Green, is "a bias toward an abstracted, idealized, homogeneous spoken language which is imposed and maintained by dominant bloc institutions and which names as its model the written language" (2007:64). In this case, the implicit goal of the recommendations seems to be to work toward a variety which would function as a standard language, even if no such standard now exists.

The Commission is optimistic in its tone with aspirations of a well-functioning multilingual society, and the hope of education in each of the minority languages of Nepal.[6] However, as time has gone on, it has become clear that "the process through which languages are now being recognized for potential use in education is a lesson in state-society accommodation and in the fluidity of group boundaries" (Sonntag 2001:162). The criteria for determining the languages of education (along with the delineation of a distinct ethnic identity) is a political process of give-and-take (2001:164). It is as much about, if not primarily about, the negotiation of power relations, rather than linguistic distinctiveness or the ability to communicate, as illustrated by the change in the number of languages in the decadal census (see section 15.3.1).

Nepalese linguists have been somewhat conflicted about the political nature of this process, trying to steer a course of "academic objectivity," promoting the development of written language, while at the same time trying to determine the distinctiveness of the many undocumented languages and dialects of the country. When living in the country, I joined with them, trying to lend expertise in technical aspects such as identifying the number of contrastive tones in the Tibetic languages with the "objectivity" of acoustic software (cf. S. Watters 1999, 2002, 2003). However, as it turns out, these kinds of things were largely irrelevant in developing an orthography, and the primary debates were about historicity (tying to a primordial past in Tibet) and modernity (integrating with the nation state of Nepal), rather than the synchronic contrastiveness of sounds.

One of the assumptions made by the linguistic community in Nepal (including myself) has been that language conservation entails both documentation and revitalization. While documentation seeks to extract a view of language as it is actually spoken and used in society at a particular point in time, revitalization is a process of reversing language shift, and ultimately developing it so that it can be used in written and more formal domains (Fishman 1991; Hinton 2001). It is also assumed that the development from a spoken to written language entails a process of standardization and normalization. Almost all multilingual education and nonformal education projects in Nepal are based on this idea, and the content of materials is driven by the national curriculum of the nation-state.

However, in 2007, the Ministry of Foreign Affairs of Finland and the Ministry of Education and Sports (MOES) of Nepal sponsored a two-year "bottom-up community-based" approach to multilingual education (MLE) under the directorship of David Hough. Indigenous knowledge systems, beliefs, values, and practices informed content and methodology, and additionally, no effort was made to normalize or standardize the language used to document these (Hough et al. 2009). While educational projects which privilege indigenous knowledge systems are not uncommon in many parts of the world, this particular project was unique in Nepal. I am unaware of

---

[6] In Nepal, minority languages are referred to as national languages (*rashtriya bhasa*). These are defined by the Constitution of Nepal 1991 as any language spoken as a mother-tongue in any part of Nepal (Part 1, Article 6). They are contrasted with Nepali, which has status as the "language of the nation" (*rashtra bhasa*) and which is the official language (Part 1, Article 6).

whether or not MOES was able to extend this pilot study and incorporate its vision in long-term sustainable educational programs (but third-party reports suggest that, unfortunately, it ended when the funding ended).

It is apparent that the original approach espoused in the 1994 Commission report, and the more recent project undertaken under the leadership of Hough, are significantly different in their ideology. The former is characterized by a standard language ideology which seeks to develop and promote a normalized form of the language; the latter by a preservationist ideology which promotes indigenous knowledge systems. The language communities themselves, which as I will describe for the northern Magar in section 15.5, have tended toward a standard language ideology, and to appropriate this standardized form as a means of establishing a unique political identity. Each of these approaches and the ideologies which drive them have differing implications for the language.

15.5 Magar Kham: A family of languages or dialects

In this section, I report on a recent development which took place in January 2013, which illustrates the way in which the northern Magar have taken on the standard language ideology inherent in the policies of the country, and used the modern political process to express this unified view of their linguistic identity.

Mr. Karna Bahadur Budha, vice-chairman of the Nepal Magar Association (NMA), Central Committee, and some members of NMA visited the Central Department of Linguistics (CDL), Tribhuvan University, and submitted a letter expressing concern with the results of the linguistic survey of southern Magar Kham-speaking areas, as was conducted in 2011 under the auspices of LINSUN (the Linguistic Survey of Nepal), and which provided information to *Ethnologue*. The main complaints of the request letter as reported to me by DanRaj Regmi, director of LINSUN, include the following (and I quote):

1. "Without the consent and consultation of Nepal Magar Association, Central Committee, the dialects of Magar language are identified as independent languages in *Ethnologue*."
2. "The Magar community is against the misleading research findings as appeared in David Watters' grammar page No. 9" [2002, *A Grammar of Kham*].

The concern of the NMA over the representation of "dialects" as "independent languages" is certainly understandable, given the politicized nature of linguistic identity, and standard language ideology inherent in the overall fabric of language policy in the country. The expression of group identity at a national political level, and its corollary in linguistic identity, requires homogeneity as its underpinning. The first complaint, however, strikes me as unfair to the communities studied for the survey report. The linguistic survey employed the participatory method, a method which follows a group interview methodology and bases its results on community opinion and views. The survey did not base its findings on community-independent research such as comparison of vocabulary, intelligibility studies, or grammatical studies (as I had done in my 1987 survey). That is, it was members of the Magar Kham-speaking communities themselves who put forward the idea that there are distinct varieties spoken by them. No doubt, the concern on the part of the NMA is the treatment of these varieties as "languages" rather than dialects.

Not all northern Magar share Budha's views on ethnic and linguistic identity as evidenced, for example, in the long-standing debate over whether the language should be referred to as "Pang" or "Kham." As far as I understand, that debate is over, but other Magar Kham-speaking regions have expressed interest in their own speech varieties. Christopher Wilde reports that community leaders in the Gamale area met recently to discuss modifying the current Magar Kham orthography to more closely reflect their own dialect pronunciation (personal communication: email, 2014).

In regard to the second concern, the issue has to do ostensibly with nomenclature, and how the northern Magar wish to refer to themselves in modern Nepal. The D. Watters passage being referred to is:

> *Kham* is the name of a language, or group of languages, spoken by the four northern clans of the Magar tribe: the Budhas, Puns, Ghartis, and Rokhas. The long recognized Magar language is spoken by the southern clans: the Ranas, Thapas, and Ales, i.e. the 'Magars proper.' Several days' walking separates the two groups, and it has been suggested by some that the Northern Magars, the speakers of Kham, are not really Magars at all, but "originally came of a different stock" (Northey and Morris 1928:189). How both groups came to be called by the same tribal name may never be known. To avoid ambiguity with the Magars who speak Magar, however, I began in 1973 (Watters and Watters) to refer to the people as "Kham Magars." (D. Watters 2002:9)

The NMA desires that the language of the northern Magars be referred to as "Magar Kham," and their ethnicity as "Magar" (and, therefore, why this article now uses this nomenclature). At the time that D. Watters was writing in 1973, the northern Magars did not yet have an established national linguistic identity, and even in the early 2000s, at the time of the writing of *A Grammar of Kham*, their linguistic identity was still in flux, with nomenclature vacillating between "Pang" and "Kham." However, I am sure that most linguists, including the late D. Watters (if I, as his son, may speak posthumously on his behalf) would be happy to oblige in employing this revision, providing it represents a true consensus of the community, and not just the political elite.

In responding to the disagreement over nomenclature, and the dialect/language distinction, the CDL expressed the view that misinformation can be corrected, and that they are "committed to the preservation, promotion and development of the languages with the active participation of the concerned communities." CDL reports that one of the lessons learned in this interchange is that linguistic research should not be carried out without the prior consent of a central organization of the language community, and that the results of the research should not be published without "convincing" the community. Presumably, what is meant by this is to garner approval for the results of the research, and where this does not meet community expectations, to attempt to explain the validity of the results to the community. It is not clear what happens if there is lack of agreement between research results and community opinion.

15.6 Magar Kham aspirations

In this section, I discuss the dynamic nature of language communities adapting to modern Nepal, and demonstrate evidence of the conflicting nature of this process among Magar Kham speakers.

Wesson (2013), writing specifically of heritage languages in the North American context, but generalizing broadly, is critical of intervention efforts, as though it is required that we in the West protect and save others from our own cultural hegemony. He criticizes such efforts of not understanding the "plural, conflictual, hybrid, and dynamic" nature of culture (and language), suggesting that languages evolve and adapt to meet the communicative needs of the community, even if language changes drastically. Wesson says that intervention also fails to recognize the agentivity of the language community, as though they were "primitive ecologists," or blameless victims of the inexorable march of Western hegemony. Rather, "Our goals should not be cultural stasis and isolation, but rather dynamic cultural revivals that benefit from the past—and its unique historical cultural precedents—in creative assertions of identities in the present" (Wesson 2013:117).

Shneiderman (2009) illustrates another view of agentivity in writing about the formation of political consciousness among the Thangmi, who are a small community of north central Nepal. Shneiderman borrows the idea of a "capacity to aspire" from Appadurai (2004) in explaining Thangmi responses to the People's War—that the Thangmi envision "alternative and national orders" and their own agentive role in building them. This contrasts with "pre-political" actors, who can only "resist" and who are unable to express aspiration.

The northern Magar demonstrate many of the hallmarks of the things of which Wesson and Shneiderman speak, namely, resistance, aspiration, and the assertion of modern identities. They have demonstrated subtle forms of resistance, evidenced by levels of bilingualism in some of their traditional communities. In unpublished bilingualism studies using recorded text tests in 1987, I tested speakers from the Taka community with two Nepali texts—one a short colloquial narrative, and the other a personal narrative of a young educated Nepali Brahmin, but told in a more formal style. The latter was thought to represent the variety of Nepalese found in higher education, media, and political discourse. Takale Magar Kham speakers scored an average of 78% on the colloquial text, and I discontinued the more formal text, as the early set of respondents were not able to score any points. Most respondents reported that Nepali Brahmins might as well be speaking another language (recall that in this methodology both texts are hometown tested, which means that mother-tongue Nepali speakers were able to score 100% on both tests).

These low levels of bilingualism are curious in light of the "adoption and adaption" evidenced in earlier times. In publishing a dictionary of Magar Kham as it is spoken in the village of Taka (with generous reference to other dialect areas), D. Watters reports that as much as 25% of the vocabulary can be traced to Indo-Aryan sources. One of the domains in which this vocabulary is used is in traditional material culture, such as Magar Kham *arə̃i* "forge' [Nepali *arə̃*], or Magar Kham *cimta* "tongs' [Nepali *cimṭa*]. With the advance of the Aryan immigrants into Western Nepal (pre-1700s), the Magar Kham speakers would have been some of the first Tibeto-Burman speakers to be encountered there. However, D. Watters speculates that the early Nepali linguistic influence on their language came not from the high priestly and warrior castes, but from the settlement of the *kamis* and *damais*, the artisan castes that brought with them superior tools for agriculture. More modern influences from Nepali are found in borrowing from domains such as finance and government (D. Watters 2004).

That the northern Magars incorporated so much vocabulary from Aryan immigrants in the pre-1700s is early evidence that the northern Magar were "adapting" and "adopting" to the changing human systems in which they lived. Their language was not supplanted by the influx of Aryan immigrants, and neither did they remain isolated or uninfluenced by these changes in demography. In fact, today, as in much of Western Nepal, *kamis* and *damais* can be found in all Magar Kham-speaking villages, whose function is now less in artisanship, and more in the "untouchable" functions of religious rituals. However, linguistic "adapting" and "adopting" have gone the other way also, so that many *kamis* and *damais* speak a pidginized Magar Kham with an admixture of Nepali.

I have interpreted the lower levels of bilingualism found in my 1987 study to be an indication that "adoption and adaption" had not taken place in later periods like it had with the first influx of Aryan immigrants, or like it seems to have in other parts of the country. It would be interesting to learn how this has changed since my earlier studies. It goes without saying that based on my interactions with them through the 1990s and 2000s, bilingualism levels among the northern Magar living in the urban setting of Kathmandu have dramatically increased.

Perhaps one of the more remarkable achievements of the northern Magar community has been the successful lobbying for recognition of their language at the national level. Until the late 2000s, it was officially recognized that there was only one language spoken by the Magar. However, in 2008 and the years following, the political establishment considered developing a federalist system of government with the country divided into numerous autonomous regions; these regions were to be formed on the basis of a major ethnicity in that region. The Magar autonomous region was one such region proposed under this scenario. There were a number of Magar Kham speakers who were a part of this political process, and they were able to successfully lobby for national recognition of several distinct Magar languages. These are Magar Kham (for Magars living in Athara Magarat), Magar Dhut (for Magars living in Barha Magarat), and Magar Kaike (for those living in Sahartara of Dolpa). As noted in section 15.3.2, Athara and Barha Magarat are the historical lands of the Magar nation. Although a federalist system with autonomous regions is no longer a likely political structure to be adopted in Nepal, one of the positive outcomes of this process is an increased awareness of linguistic diversity and its acceptance at a national level. In this sense, then, the northern Magar demonstrate that they are a "fully modern people" able to negotiate and create modern identities.

15.7 Lack of fit

Having demonstrated the "modernity" of Magar Kham speakers, I turn now to discuss my own response to these expressions of identity. I argue that the desire of the community to view Magar Kham speech varieties as dialects should be honored, partly as a way of diffusing the political tensions surrounding this issue. However, this is not without giving up on linguistic diversity, but to refocus the research effort on the documentation and conservation of linguistic diversity.

It is implicit in modern anthropological and linguistic scholarship that ethnic and linguistic identity involves a process of reinterpretation and creation. Sometimes this involves more agentive expressions such as in acts of resistance and creative attempts at aspiration, but at other times involves more subtle "barely conscious" processes such as the on-going Hinduization of the middle hills. The role of an outside researcher in this creative process is not without controversy. Many linguists take a positive view of the ethnic-language activist (Woodbury 2003), and some go so far as to say that the autonomy of group sustainability trumps the preservation of non-renewable cultural resources—their need to adjust to a changing world supersedes "preservation" (Wesson 2013). In the context of ethnicity in Nepal, Gellner takes a more somber view:

"I would say rather that anthropologists, with their tradition of studying the everyday lives of ordinary people, have a particular duty to document the lack of fit between what activists say and the feelings and perceptions of those on whose behalf the activists claim to speak." (2008:22–23)

Linguists, undoubtedly, follow in this same tradition, paying particular attention to the everyday language of ordinary people. Bradley refers to the importance of the role of a sojourner, who as an outsider "maintains a long-term cooperative relationship with a language community" (2011:46). I have espoused this approach, engaging in the language revitalization effort even when I do not fully agree with the ideology or efficacy of the approach being espoused by northern Magars. Thus, as illustrated in this paper, I do not agree with the standard language ideology inherent in the attempts to develop a single written language for all Magar Kham varieties, but as a sojourner with them, I walk the language revitalization journey with them. At different points along the way, I am given opportunity to speak my views. In this process of give and take, there is much that can be learned from each other, even if we have conflicting views. Karna Bahadur Budha, for example, is far from dogmatic and rigid in his beliefs about language. In private email conversations (Feb–May, 2014 in a mix of English, Nepali, and Magar Kham), Budha proved helpful, engaged, and interested in collaboration in lexicography and documentation projects. Moreover, he was aware that there are many varieties of Magar Kham. Neither Budha nor I understand best how to respond to the diversity of Magar Kham speech varieties; it poses a conundrum for both of us. As such, language revitalization may better be formulated as a journey with many unknowns, and the pathway as entailing discovery, negotiation, and education about the nature of the linguistic ecosystem in which the community lives.

However, given the politicization of language and identity, I argue that care must be taken in interpreting the enumeration of languages in *Ethnologue* and the Central Bureau of Statistics (Nepal). The nature of lists forces a unitary, one-dimensional view of language. A speech variety may or may not actually be distinct enough to be a separate language, but if it makes the list, it gets recognition and resources. I am aware of some of the difficulty of maintaining good lists, but the fact that language varieties fit within a linguistic ecosystem must be better represented, especially when the representation serves as the basis for language policy decisions or the procurement of funds for documentation projects. I propose that one place to start is to have short encyclopedic entries with simple prose descriptions. For the northern Magar, such a description, in short form, might be formulated as:

> Magar Kham comprises a family of several mutually unintelligible speech varieties each of which is separated from the other by high mountain barriers. These are Parbate, Gamale, and Sheshi. Within each of these areas, every village speaks its own variety and is distinguishable by at least minor changes in vocabulary, phonology, and morphology. There are also speech varieties that do not obviously relate to any of the other major groups, such as the varieties spoken in the single villages of Ghusbang and Miruli.

This kind of encyclopedic entry can give a more accurate view of linguistic diversity than the unitary categorization of lists, although I am aware that even an encyclopedic style entry must categorize speech varieties at some level of abstraction. However that may be, prose entries may help in diffusing the politicized nature of language and identity, giving opportunity for the recognition of linguistic diversity within a common linguistic and ethnic identity. It may help in language documentation and conservation, as well, where these activities can more realistically and honestly be about the documentation of a language variety, with the recognition that there may be other distinct language varieties with the same cultural and political identity that also require documentation. The focus of language documentation and conservation, then, can be more about discovering human diversity, and understanding the dynamic nature of the linguistic ecosystem in which language varieties belong.

15.8 Summary

In this paper, I have described the controversy over whether or not Magar Kham is composed of a family of languages or dialects. The controversy, not surprisingly, entails much more than linguistic similarity and mutual intelligibility. At its core, the controversy involves issues of linguistic identity and aspirations of what can be achieved through that identity. New linguistic aspirations can be attributed, in part, to the rise of linguistic and ethnic identity in the modern political context in Nepal, and this in turn to glocalisation—a complex interplay of both global, national, and local factors.

The rise of ethnic identities is a curiosity among anthropologists and ethnographers who study Nepal in that communities have a markedly different sense of identity now than they did several decades ago. This is described as both a process of resistance and adoption and adaptation, as ethnicities have both pushed back against the normative values of mainstream Hindu Nepali culture while at the same time adopting certain practices so as to fit within the national system (Gellner et al. 2008). Shneiderman (2009) describes one of the features of this as an ability to aspire.

The northern Magar demonstrate all of these aspects in response to the human systems of modern Nepal. At some point in the not so distant past, they had significant contact with Nepali migration, enough to affect one quarter of their vocabulary, and yet were able to adapt and retain most aspects of their linguistic heritage. They resisted Nepalese cultural hegemony as evidenced in low levels of bilingualism, in maintaining traditional religious practices, and in a certain level of participation in the Maoist People's Uprising. Within this backdrop, they have demonstrated the capacity to aspire and carve out a nationally recognized linguistic identity within the overall Magar ethnicity.

While all of this bodes well for the survival of the northern Magar ethnicity, the rise of a linguistic identity will potentially have an adverse effect on the diverse varieties known collectively as Magar Kham. The national language policy recommendations of the country are imbued with standard language ideology, and this ideology has been adopted by the northern Magar. A single linguistic identity has been appropriated and asserted at a national level with the assumption that all speech varieties identified as Magar Kham can be served through a single standardized form.

Recent discussions between the Central Department of Linguistics, Tribhuvan University and the Nepal Magar Association over whether to delimit these speech varieties as dialects or languages in *Ethnologue* further illustrates the political, negotiated nature of linguistic identities in Nepal. Considering these diverse speech varieties as languages is perceived as a threat to a cohesive ethnic identity. Ignoring the diversity in the name of a single common linguistic identity, ironically, relegates the varieties to the same marginal status which the Magar Kham have resisted.

I noted that care must be taken in interpreting the list of languages in reference works like *Ethnologue*, since lists by their very nature can only offer a unitary, one dimensional view of language. I proposed that short encyclopedic entries with prose descriptions offer a helpful alternative in representing both linguistic diversity and linguistic identity. I do this partly as an attempt to diffuse the debate over language and dialect among the Magar Kham, and partly to advocate on behalf of the diversity of which I am aware. I do this with the desire that the aspirations of the northern Magar be honored, and with the hope that they will see linguistic diversity not as a threat, but as a part of their linguistic heritage, even a heritage that has value and efficacy in modern Nepal.

References

Allen, Nicholas J. 2008. Hinduization: The experience of the Thulung Rai. In David Gellner, Joanna Pfaff-Czarnecka, and John Whelpton (eds.), *Nationalism and ethnicity in Nepal*, 20:303–324. Kathmandu, Nepal: Vajra Publications.

Appadurai, Arjun. 2004. The capacity to aspire: Culture and the terms of recognition. In Vijayendra Rao and Michael Walton (eds.), *Culture and public action*, 59–84. CA: Stanford University Press.

Blair, Frank. 1990. *Survey on a shoestring: A manual for small-scale language surveys*. SIL International Publications in Linguistics 96. Dallas, TX: SIL International and the University of Texas at Arlington.

Bradley, David. 2011. Resilience thinking and language endangerment. In Bai Bibo and David Bradley (eds.), *Extinction and retention of mother tongues in China*, 23–47. Beijing, China: Nationalities Press.

Brass, Paul R. 1991. *Ethnicity and nationalism: Theory and comparison*. Delhi: Sage.

Caplan, Lionel. 1973. Inter-caste marriages in a Nepalese town. In Christoph von Fürer-Haimendorf (ed.), *Contributions to the anthropology of Nepal*, 40–61. Warminster, UK: Aris and Phillips.

Crystal, David. 2000. *Language death*. Cambridge: Cambridge University Press.

Constitution. 1991. Constitution of the Kingdom of Nepal VS 2047 (1990). *Himalaya, the Journal of the Association for Nepal and Himalayan Studies* 11(1), Article 6. digitalcommons.macalester.edu/himalaya/vol11/iss1/6/.

De Sales, Anne. 2000. The Kham Magar country, Nepal: Between ethnic claims and Maoism. *European Bulletin of Himalayan Research* 19:41–71.

Dixon, R. M. W. 1997. *The rise and fall of languages*. Cambridge: Cambridge University Press.

Eppele, John W., M. Paul Lewis, Dan Raj Regmi, and Yogendra P. Yadava, eds. 2012. *Ethnologue: Languages of Nepal*. Kathmandu, Nepal: SIL International and Central Department of Linguistics, Tribhuvan University.

Fishman, Joshua A. 1991. *Reversing language shift: Theoretical and empirical foundations of assistance to threatened languages*. Clevedon, UK: Multilingual Matters.

Fishman, Joshua A. 2002. Endangered minority languages: Prospects for sociolinguistic research. *International Journal on Multicultural Societies* 4(2): 270–275.

Gellner, David N., Joanna Pfaff-Czarnecka, and John Whelpton, eds. 2008. *Nationalism and ethnicity in Nepal*. Kathmandu, Nepal: Vajra Publications.

Hinton, Leanne. 2001. Language revitalization: An overview. In Leanne Hinton and Ken Hale (eds.), *The green book of language revitalization in practice*, 3–18. San Diego, CA: Academic Press.

Hough, David, Ram Bahadur Thapa, and Amrit Yonjun-Tamang. 2009. Privileging indigenous knowledges: Empowering MLE in Nepal. In Ajit K. Mohanty, Minati Panda, Robert Phillipson, Tove Skutnabb-Kangas (eds.), *Multilingual education for social justice: Globalising the local*, 146–161. New Delhi: Orient Blackswan.

Krauss, Michael. 1992. The world's languages in crisis. *Language* 68:4–10.

Lippi-Green, Rosina. 2007. *English with an accent: Language, ideology, and discrimination in the United States*. Abingdon, UK: Routledge.

Pfaff-Czarnecka, Joanna. 1991. State and community: Changing relations of production after the unification of Nepal. In Henri J. M. Claessen and Pieter van de Velde (eds.), *Early state economics*, 229–262. New Brunswick, NJ: Transaction Publishers.

Raeper, William, and Martin Hoftun. 1992. *Spring awakening: An account of the 1990 revolution in Nepal*. New Delhi: Viking.

Sharma, Pitamber. 2014. *Some aspects of Nepal's social demography: Census 2011 update*. Kathmandu, Nepal: Himal Books.

Shneiderman, Sara Beth. 2009. The formation of political consciousness in rural Nepal. *Dialectical Anthropology* 33:287–308.

Simons, Gary F., and Charles D. Fennig, eds. 2018. *Ethnologue: Languages of the world*. Twenty-first edition. Dallas, TX: SIL International. Online version: ethnologue.com/.

Sonntag, Selma K. 2001. The politics of determining criteria for the languages of education in Nepal. In Thomas Fleiner, Peter H. Nelde, and Joseph-G. Turi (eds.), *Law and language(s) of education*, 161–174. Basel, Switzerland: Helbing and Lichtenhahn.

Thapa, Deepak, ed. 2003. *Understanding the Maoist movement of Nepal*. Chautari Books Series 10. Kathmandu, Nepal: Martin Chautari.

Thapa, Deepak. 2004. *A kingdom under siege: Nepal's Maoist insurgency, 1996 to 2003*. With Bandita Sijapati. Kathmandu, Nepal: Zed Books.

Tsunoda, Tasaku. 2006. *Language endangerment and language revitalization: An introduction*. Berlin: De Gruyter.

Turin, Mark. 2007. *Linguistic diversity and the preservation of endangered languages: A case study from Nepal*. Talking Points 4/07. Kathmandu, Nepal: International Centre for Integrated Mountain Development.

Watters, David E. 1998. The Kham language of west-central Nepal (Takale dialect). PhD dissertation. University of Oregon, Eugene.

Watters, David E. 2002. *A grammar of Kham*. Cambridge Grammatical Descriptions. Cambridge: Cambridge University Press.

Watters, David E. 2004. *A dictionary of Kham: Taka dialect (a Tibeto-Burman language of Nepal)*. Kathmandu, Nepal: Central Department of Linguistics.

Watters, David E. 2006. The conjunct-disjunct distinction in Kaike. *Nepalese Linguistics* 22:300–319.

Watters, David E. 2011. *At the foot of the snows: A journey of faith and words among the Kham-speaking people of Nepal*. With Steve and Daniel Watters. Poulsbo, WA: Engage Faith Press.

Watters, Stephen. 1988. A sociolinguistic profile of Kham Magar dialects. Ms.

Watters, Stephen. 1999. Tonal contrasts in Sherpa. In Yogendra P. Yadava and Warren W. Glover (eds.), *Topics in Nepalese linguistics*, 54–77. Kathmandu, Nepal: Royal Nepal Academy.

Watters, Stephen. 2002. The sounds and tones of five Tibetan languages of the Himalayan region. *Linguistics of the Tibeto-Burman Area* 25(1):1–66.

Watters, Stephen. 2003. An acoustic look at pitch in Lhomi. In Tej Ratna Kansakar and Mark Turin (eds.), *Themes in Himalayan languages and linguistics*, 247–264. Kathmandu, Nepal: South Asia Institute and Tribhuvan University.

Webster, Jeff. 1997. Indicators of bilingual proficiency in Nepali among Tibeto-Burman peoples of Nepal. *CNAS Journal* 24(2):233–262.

Wesson, Cameron. 2013. Rumors of our demise have been greatly exaggerated: Archaeological perspectives on culture and sustainability. *Sustainability* 5: 100–122.

Woodbury, Tony. 2003. Defining documentary linguistics. *Language Documentation and Description* 1:35–51.

Yadava, Yogendra P., and Carl Grove, eds. 2008. *The report of National Languages Policy Recommendation Commission 1994 (2050VS)*. Kathmandu, Nepal: Central Department of Linguistics, Tribhuvan University.

16
Hiding Your Identity: The Case of Talysh

John M. Clifton and Calvin Tiessen

Abstract. In this paper we investigate the claim that members of the Talysh community of Azerbaijan identify as Talysh within their own communities, but outside their community they self-identify as Azerbaijani, and that this identification as Azerbaijani is an attempt to hide their Talysh identity. In an effort to explain why they self-identify as Azerbaijani in the broader community, we examine the commonly held belief that this is an attempt to distance themselves from a failed bid for increased autonomy shortly after the independence of Azerbaijan. However, a comparison with the Lezgi in Azerbaijan and the Pamiri in Tajikistan shows this is too simplistic. We suggest that the attempt to hide their identity as Talysh is due to a combination of factors including a history of derision within Azerbaijan, and recent attempts by outside powers to use the failed bid for increased autonomy for propaganda purposes.[1]

16.1 Introduction

The concept of *identity* (or *ethnic identity* or *ethnolinguistic identity*) plays a central role in many areas of sociolinguistics, as well as in related fields such as literacy and orthography. For example, Karan (2011) argues that social identity is one of the factors that affects ethnolinguistic vitality which, in turn, is a predictor of language shift. In the area of literacy, Schwab (1994) discusses ways in which identity based on a nonprestigious Caribbean English dialect or creole can be threatened by literacy in Standard English, and avenues to approach literacy without destroying that identity. In the area of orthography, Saxena (1994) discusses the use of multiple scripts for Panjabi, especially linking the use of Gurmukhi versus Devanagari with the religious identity of the user. More recently, Sebba (2007) discusses multiple cases of orthographic practices tied to issues of identity.

---

[1] This is a revised version of a paper that was presented at ConCALL-3 (Conference on Central Asian Languages and Linguistics) at Indiana University, Bloomington, Indiana, March 2–4, 2018; SECOL 2018 (Southeastern Conference on Linguistics) at Virginia Tech University, Blacksburg, Virginia, April 19–21, 2018; and the Pike Center symposium on "Language and Identity in a Multilingual, Migrating World," at Penang, Malaysia, May 10–15, 2018. We are grateful for comments made by participants at all three conferences, as well as comments from Daniel Paul and the editors of this volume.

It is often convenient to assume that a given group has single, common identity. For example, in discussing ethnolinguistic vitality, Ehala (2010:208) refers to "language and identity shift" as a single process—a shift of one implies a shift of the other. Assumptions of common identities also allow us to talk about borders between groups with different identities. Borders may be difficult to determine with exactitude, given that identity is often complicated due to the interaction of nationality, ethnicity, and language. But the assumption in this model is that we are dealing with indeterminacy, as opposed to multiple identities for a given speaker or community (Omoniyi 2010:127).

Opposed to this model in which a given group has a single, common identity that can change over time, Lewis (chapter 3 this volume) argues that both individuals and groups can have multiple identities, each of which is exploited as appropriate. Furthermore, language is often a major component in establishing each of these identities. For example, while Lewis can self-identify as Welsh, in large part through association with Welsh [cym] as the language of his ancestors, he has an even stronger identity as an American, tied in part to his use of American English [eng].

In this paper we investigate the claim that members of the Talysh community of Azerbaijan exhibit both Talysh and Azerbaijani identities in different contexts. Within their own communities, they identify as Talysh. But outside their own communities, they self-identify as Azerbaijani. For example, while a significant percentage of taxi drivers in the capital, Baku, identify as Talysh within their own community, most of their non-Talysh passengers would claim they are not acquainted with any Talysh people. Similarly, we know of pastors who wanted to get to know members of the Talysh community, not realizing that prominent members of their congregation were Talysh.

To account for these differences in perception, we propose that many members of the Talysh community in Azerbaijan have a dual identity: as Talysh and as Azerbaijani. This is especially true for Talysh [tly] speakers living in urban areas close to Baku. Moreover, members of the Talysh community actively use this dual identity to hide their Talysh identity when they function in the broader community. In section 16.2, we examine the Talysh situation, particularly in light of the commonly held belief that Talysh speakers project an identity as Azerbaijani to distance themselves from a failed bid for increased autonomy shortly after the independence of Azerbaijan. However, a comparison of the Talysh with the Lezgi of Azerbaijan and the Pamiri groups of Tajikistan in section 16.3 shows that this is too simplistic. These groups, while they were involved in similar movements, do not show the same level of hidden identity. In section 16.4 we suggest that the differences are rooted in a combination of broader international factors as well as in the perceptions of the outside community. In the final section, we outline implications of the situation for conducting research among groups like the Talysh. Especially in urban areas, we suggest that research needs to be conducted using qualitative methodology, identifying potential respondents through the use of social networks.

16.2 The Talysh community

The Talysh people live on both sides of the border between Azerbaijan and Iran. According to the Azerbaijani census figures, there were almost 77,000 Talysh in Azerbaijan in 1999 and almost 112,000 in 2009. Actual figures, however, could be considerably higher. Matveeva (2002:17) refers to claims that there could be as many as 250,000 Talysh. Our research,[2] based on interviews with local officials, indicated there could be 500,000, of whom 400,000 live in the core Talysh districts (Tiessen 2003:11).

The Talysh [tly] language is a Northwestern Iranian language, related to Farsi [pes], Dari [prs], and Kurdish (Stilo 2015). There are three dialect areas of Talysh (Bazin 1980)[3] as shown in map 1. The Central and Southern dialects are contained entirely within Iran, while most of the Northern dialect is in Azerbaijan. Due to tensions between the two countries, the border between Azerbaijan and Iran is closely monitored, as is research within the Talysh community.

Map 1. Dialects of Talysh

© 2012. Arnold Platon. Wikimedia Commons, used under CC BY-SA 3.0 license. commons.wikimedia.org/wiki/File:Talysh_language_dialects.svg/.

While Miller (1953) reported that proficiency in the Azerbaijani language was low among the Talysh community, more recent research indicated a high level of

---

[2] From 1999 to 2002, we were part of a research team made up of members of the North Eurasia Group of SIL International, which was tasked with investigating language use and attitudes among most of the communities in Azerbaijan using less widely spoken languages. The team operated under the auspices of the Academy of Sciences of Azerbaijan.

[3] According to Stilo (2015), the Southern and Northern/Central dialects are so divergent that they have low mutual intelligibility. Paul (2011) provides objective support for this claim: Wordlists from Northern and Southern Talysh show only 76% lexical similarity, and comprehension testing indicates that the three dialects are not immediately intelligible, although intelligibility rises to 90% with sufficient exposure.

proficiency in Azerbaijani (Pirejko 1976; Isaev 1979; Rastorgueva 1979). Our research results supported the claim that most Talysh are highly proficient in Azerbaijani (Clifton et al. 2005e). Even in the most isolated village, 60% of the individuals taking an Azerbaijani Sentence Repetition Test[4] scored at a "full professional" level of 4/4+ as described by the Interagency Language Roundtable (ILR n.d.), while another 28% scored at a "professional working" level of 3/3+. In less isolated villages, 75% of respondents scored at a 4/4+ level, while an additional 21% scored at a 3/3+ level. In the less isolated villages, then, only 4% scored at less than a "professional working" level.

This is not surprising given that all formal education has been in Azerbaijani for at least a century,[5] as have television, radio, and the vast majority of the print media. It is this high level of proficiency in Azerbaijani that allows members of the Talysh community to pass as ethnic Azerbaijani as indicated in the introduction. The postindependence levels of proficiency in Azerbaijani documented by Clifton et al. (2005e) are especially unremarkable given the claim by Clifton (2013) that Azerbaijani has taken the role traditionally played by colonial languages in situations of settlement colonization. This has led to an even increased level of proficiency in Azerbaijani.

While high levels of proficiency in the national language are expected, they do not necessarily lead to a community taking on a completely new identity—just as high levels of proficiency in a colonial language do not necessarily lead to identity and language shift (Mufwene 2008). In the case of Talysh, respondents reported a pattern of language use similar to that seen in many communities, in which Azerbaijani is used in formal domains like school and government, while Talysh is generally used in informal domains including on the street and in the teahouse. There was also a noticeable difference between residents of mountain (more isolated) and lowland (less isolated) villages: along with lower levels of proficiency in Azerbaijani, residents of mountain villages used Talysh in a wider range of contexts.

The one situation in which our predictions were not met was the home. We expected a high use of Talysh in the home both within and between all age groups, since it is a prime example of an informal domain. What we actually found was that parents frequently indicated that they used Azerbaijani with school-aged and, in some cases, preschool-aged, children. These parents uniformly indicated that their children needed to have a good command of Azerbaijani so they would do well in school. Upon further questioning, parents told us they believed this would not affect the long-term vitality of Talysh, since children would pick up Talysh on the street. In spite of the fact that they used Azerbaijani with the children, they were confident that Talysh would be spoken for the foreseeable future.

The high use of Talysh in spite of the high levels of proficiency in Azerbaijani supports our general perception that the Talysh are proud of their language and culture. They expect that their children and grandchildren will be speaking the language even if Azerbaijani is used in the home with school-aged children. In fact,

---

[4] In a sentence repetition test (SRT), individuals are asked to repeat a series of increasingly complex sentences in the target language. For more information, see Radloff (1991).

[5] Isaev (1970) reports that while Talysh school materials were developed in the 1930s, they were viewed by the government as an experiment that was socially unhelpful. The decision was made that all education should be in Azerbaijani to promote interaction throughout the country.

the use of Azerbaijani with school-aged children supports our analysis in which the Talysh have two separate identities. On the one hand, parents expect that their children will identify in the village as Talysh, while at the same time they expect a better command of Azerbaijani will allow them to function as Azerbaijani outside the village.

In a related study, Tiessen (2003) examined language use among the Talysh living in Sumqayıt,[6] an urban center located approximately 50 kilometers (31 miles) northeast of Baku on the north side of the Absheron peninsula. With a population of nearly 300,000, Sumqayıt is the third largest city in Azerbaijan. Tiessen (2003:17) estimates that up to 80,000 residents of Sumqayıt are ethnic Talysh, thus making it an excellent focus for research on urban Talysh.

Tiessen (2003) found patterns of language use which parallel the patterns found among many immigrant families. Talysh who moved to Sumqayıt more recently use Talysh less than those who moved there as part of earlier migrations. An even more pronounced decline in the use of Talysh was observed among the second and third generations, regardless of when their parents or grandparents migrated to Sumqayıt. While the use of Talysh is declining in Sumqayıt, Tiessen (2003:102) notes that this decline is generally tied to positive attitudes towards Azerbaijani or Russian, not negative attitudes towards Talysh. The shift towards Azerbaijani is a pragmatic one based on the usefulness of Azerbaijani vis-à-vis Talysh.

In light of the positive attitudes towards Talysh, the question that arises is why people want to identify as Azerbaijani in situations outside the village. In discussions with members of both the Talysh community and the larger Azerbaijani community, the conventional wisdom was that most Talysh self-identify as Azerbaijani outside the region to distance themselves from charges of separatism that can be traced back to the short-lived Talysh-Mughan Autonomous Republic.

The Talysh-Mughan Autonomous Republic (TMAR) was proclaimed in the midst of full-scale hostilities between Azerbaijan and Armenia over the status of Nagorno-Karabakh. These hostilities occurred between 1992 and 1994, while the establishment of the TMAR was declared in 1993. Although some have claimed that the goal of the instigators was an independent country (Socor 2005), there is no clear evidence that this is the case. In the Soviet political system, the term "autonomous republic" is used for a region with a greater degree of autonomy within a republic, not an independent entity. While most autonomous republics are within the Russian Federation, there is already one autonomous republic in Azerbaijan, the Nakhchivan Autonomous Republic. The use of the term "autonomous republic" in the name of the proclaimed entity is an indication that the instigators did not intend to secede from Azerbaijan. There certainly was no indication that the establishment of the Talysh-Mughan Autonomous Republic was meant to encompass the Talysh regions of Iran.

In spite of the fact that the goals of the Talysh-Mughan Autonomous Republic were apparently limited to increased autonomy, there is no evidence that there was ever any significant local support for the concept (Cornell 2011). In fact, it was reported that the downfall of the republic was directly preceded by a demonstration of 10,000 people against it (New York Times 1993). The republic existed for only a few months before it was suppressed by the central government.

---

[6] Also appears as Sumgayit. Sumqayıt is the spelling using the current Latin-based orthography. Sumgayit is a transliteration from the older Cyrillic orthography.

Most Talysh are reticent about discussing this part of their history, and do not want to do anything that could be seen by the national government as separatist in nature. Hence, the conventional wisdom that the Talysh desire to self-identify as Azerbaijani so as not to appear to be supportive of separatism in any form seems reasonable.[7] In section 16.3, however, we question this claim by examining two communities in which members feel free to acknowledge their heritage identity and language in spite of past conflict.

16.3 The Lezgi and Pamiri communities

Both the Lezgi community in Azerbaijan and the Pamiri community in Tajikistan were embroiled in conflict shortly after the collapse of the Soviet Union. Unlike the Talysh, however, these events have not resulted in attempts to hide their heritage identities and languages. We will examine the Lezgi in section 16.3.1 and the Pamiri in section 16.3.2.

16.3.1 The Lezgi community

The Lezgi community is divided between Azerbaijan and the Russian Republic of Dagestan, as shown in map 2.

Map 2. The Lezgi homeland

© 2011. Yerevanci. From Wikimedia Commons, used under CC BY-SA 3.0 license. commons.wikimedia.org/wiki/File:Lezgin_map.png/.

---

[7] The question arises as to whether the Talysh wish to distance themselves from separatism in general, or from the TMAR. We believe that while separatism in general is seen as negative, the formation of the TMAR is the focus of the claims of separatism. Since the only overt manifestation of separatism among the Talysh was the establishment of the TMAR, there is no other basis for leveling charges of separatism against the Talysh. If it were not for the short-lived TMAR, the issue of separatism would likely not have taken on such a prominent role.

The Lezgi [lez] language is a member of the Nakh-Daghestanian family (Haspelmath 1993; Schulze 2015).[8] According to the 2009 census, there are 180,300 Lezgi in Azerbaijan, although there are credible claims that census figures are considerably understated (Matveeva and McCartney 1998:217; Matveeva 2002:17; Cornell 2005:259).

Azerbaijan became independent in late 1991. Shortly before that, in June 1990, the Lezgin political group Sadval was organized in Dagestan. Its primary purpose was to unite the Lezgi communities on both sides of the border into one entity, either independent, or as part of Azerbaijan or Russia. Matveeva and McCartney (1998:232–238) provide an overview of the response of the Azerbaijani government to Sadval that we summarize here. They note that Sadval includes both moderate and more radical elements, and is also interwoven with other Lezgi movements. That makes it difficult to determine exactly what policies are being advocated by Sadval. For example, Mukhuddin Kakhrimanov, a retired general, referred to forces that would be available to forcibly change the border. But while he was a Sadval activist, he was also the head of the Lezgin National Council, and so it is difficult to determine in what role he made the statement.

The Dagestani government was generally more tolerant of Sadval activities than was the Azerbaijani government. Sadval was registered as a Russian organization off-and-on since 1992, but it has never been registered in Azerbaijan. While there were meetings between the Azerbaijani government and Sadval in 1992–1993, the official position of Azerbaijan was that Sadval is a terrorist organization. In 1996, eleven members of Sadval were convicted of instigating the 1994 explosion in the Baku subway. Sadval renounced the goal of Lezgi statehood in 1996, but the Azerbaijani government expressed skepticism as to their sincerity. In December of 1996 seven Sadval members were put on trial for attacking a Russian border post in 1993; they were convicted in March 1997. The following year, 1998, one Lezgin was convicted and another was charged with terrorism on behalf of Armenia, with whom Azerbaijan is still officially at war over the situation in Nagorno-Karabakh. Also in 1998, a Lezgin was sentenced to thirteen years in prison for attacking a border post in 1993 and attempting to establish an independent Lezgi state.

There appears to be little support for Sadval among the general Lezgi population (Matveeva and McCartney 1998:234); in fact, Lezgi people we talked to tried to distance themselves from Sadval. In addition, our research showed that in most locations self-reported proficiency in Azerbaijani was high (Clifton et al. 2005c).[9] Given this state of affairs, it would not be surprising to find the Lezgi attempting to project their identity as Azerbaijani rather than Lezgi. But this is not the case. Our experience is that even in urban settings, Lezgi are eager to project their identity as Lezgi, not Azerbaijani.

16.3.2 The Pamiri community

The Pamiri people live in the Gorno-Badakhshan Autonomous Region[10] of Tajikistan as well as in neighboring regions in Afghanistan and China. The name Pamiri comes

---

[8] The Nakh-Daghestanian family is also known as the Northeast Caucasian family (Smeets 1994).

[9] The one exception was in the border town of Nabran, where respondents indicated a higher level of proficiency in Russian. Reported proficiency in Lezgi was also lower in Nabran than elsewhere.

from the Pamir Mountains, which dominate the region. The Pamiri speak a number of Iranian languages: Shughni [sgh],[11] Yazgulyami [yah], Wakhi [wbl], and Ishkashimi [isk], as shown in map 3. Further subclassification uniting all these languages is speculative (Wendtland 2009, Korn 2016);[12] the term "Pamiri" is a geographic, not genetic, designation (Wendtland 2009:173). While the national language, Tajik [tgk] is also Iranian, it is a member of the much larger Southwestern Iranian subgroup, not closely related to any of the Pamiri languages.

Map 3. Languages of Tajikistan (and Kyrgyzstan)

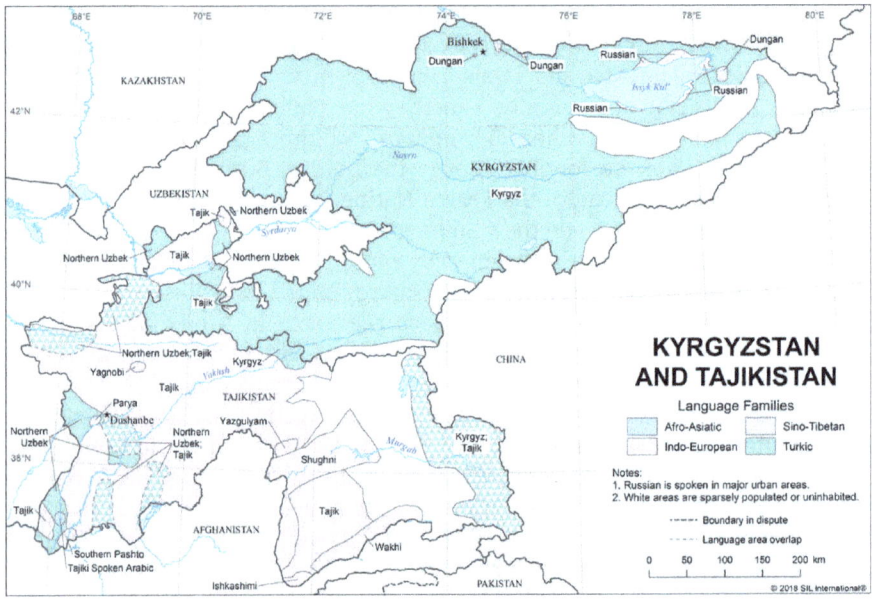

Tajikistan descended into civil war shortly after declaring independence in late 1991. The civil war had numerous causes. Unique among the Central Asian republics, Tajikistan lacked a clear national identity (Rubin 1993). The entity that was established first as an autonomous region within Uzbekistan in 1924 and then as a separate republic in 1929 united disparate highlands and lowlands regions that had no historical unity, excluded the historic Tajik cities of Samarqand and Bukhara,[13] and established the Pamirs as an autonomous republic reporting directly to Moscow

---

[10] Here and elsewhere in this paper we are using the term "region" to translate the Russian term *oblast'*.

[11] Shughni has a number of relatively divergent varieties. While most Western scholars consider them to be a single language, and they share a single ISO 639-3 code, many Russian scholars consider them to be closely related separate languages (Mirzabdinova 1991). For the purposes of this discussion, we treat all the varieties as a single language.

[12] The Pamiri languages have traditionally been categorized as Northeast Iranian (Sims-Williams 2011/1996), although Wendtland (2009) and Korn (2016) call this classification into question.

[13] These cities remained part of Uzbekistan because they were surrounded by Uzbek-speaking rural areas (Rubin 1993). The fact that it was reasonable for them to remain part of Uzbekistan did nothing to lessen the resentment of the way the border was drawn.

(Heathershaw and Herzig 2011). Much of the actual governing happened at the level of the extended clan, based on familial ties both real and fictional (Akbarzadeh 1996; Collins 2004), further weakening the central government. The Pamiri people functioned as one of these extended clans. As already noted, their languages are quite different from the national language, Tajik. In addition, they practice the Ismaili form of Shi'a Islam rather then the Sunni Islam practiced elsewhere in Tajikistan (Rubin 1993).

Further weakening the Tajik state was the fact that it was the poorest of all the Central Asian republics. During the Soviet period, the economy had been kept afloat by large-scale subsidies from Moscow. These subsidies declined in the period immediately preceding the break-up of the Soviet Union and, of course, were entirely discontinued after independence. This led to discontent among significant parts of the population (Rubin 1993).

The pre- and postindependence government of Tajikistan was controlled by the Communist Party, which was dominated by groups from the city and district of Khujand in the northwest of the country (see map 4). In return for economic support, the ruling elite from Khujand were joined by militias from the impoverished Kulob region in the southwest (see map 4). The opposition, composed of democratic, nationalist, and Islamic forces, began seriously challenging the ruling elite in 1990 (Rubin 1993). In 1992, less than a year after independence had been proclaimed, the conflict turned into a full-scale civil war. It is estimated that between 60,000 and 100,000 people were killed and up to 700,000 people were displaced during the conflict (Tunçer-Kilavuz 2011).

The opposition drew much of its support from groups from Garm (central Tajikistan, see map 4) and the Pamirs, as well as from Islamists.

Map 4. Cities of Tajikistan

Perry-Castañeda Library Map Collection. Courtesy of the University of Texas Libraries, The University of Texas at Austin. https://maps.lib.utexas.edu/maps/commonwealth/tajikistan_trans-2007.jpg. Public domain.

Most of the Pamiri who joined the opposition were part of movements calling for either revival of Tajik identity or democratization. Initially, the opposition prevailed in the conflict, even participating in a coalition government for a short time. Soon thereafter, both Russia and Uzbekistan provided support for the Communists (by now renamed the Popular Front), which was thereby able to re-exert its control. However, the civil war dragged on for years, with a peace agreement not being signed until June 1997, when the opposition surrendered to the central government. As part of the peace process, a Commission on National Reconciliation was established to integrate members of the opposition into government structures (Smith 1999).

While the overall civil war did not end until 1997, fighting in the Pamirs ended significantly earlier, largely due to the involvement of the Aga Khan Foundation (AKF). As spiritual leader of Ismaili Islam, the Aga Khan plays a major role in the life of Pamiri people. The AKF provided massive amounts of humanitarian aid to the Pamiri region beginning in 1993. As a precondition for this aid, the AKF brokered a deal between the Pamiri and the central government in which the Pamiri agreed not to push for independence while the central government agreed not to send troops to the Pamirs (Kevlihan 2016).

Even though the Pamiri involvement in the civil war ended early, their involvement in an uprising against the central government was of a considerably greater magnitude than that of the Talysh. The fact that the end of the uprising was negotiated in Tajikistan, but suppressed in the case of the Talysh, might suggest that the aftereffects should be less for the Pamiri than for the Talysh. However, the tensions that existed between the warring groups in Tajikistan made it questionable for a considerable period of time whether the settlement would hold (Smith 1999). While conducting sociolinguistic research among the Pamiri in 2003 and 2004, it was not unusual to hear comments similar to those we heard in the Talysh region, comments that recognized the fact that ethnic Tajiks viewed Pamiri with a certain level of suspicion, and a desire to establish themselves as model citizens of the country of Tajikistan. During our research, we found uniformly positive attitudes towards Tajik (Abbess et al. 2010; Müller et al. 2008; Müller et al. 2010a; Müller et al. 2010b; Tiessen et al. 2010). Tajik was perceived as especially valuable in earning money and gaining respect.

In spite of these positive attitudes, we found pronounced variation in reported levels of proficiency in Tajik.[14] Some of the variability was tied to gender (men generally are more proficient than women), isolation (members of more isolated villages are less proficient than are members of villages with ready access to Tajik-speaking towns), and travel (proficiency and travel outside the region are positively correlated). But there was also variation between language communities. For example, in Yazghulami villages all the men over 30 and the women over 50 are reported to have at least professional proficiency in Tajik (Tiessen et al. 2010). In Wakhi villages, most community members between the ages of 31 and 55 are reported to have professional or full proficiency in Tajik, but this proficiency is not shared by younger people— a situation the local community attributes to limited access to Tajik-speaking areas as a result of the civil war (Müller et al. 2008). Reported proficiency is lower in Shughni, but this may well be tied to the fact that Shughni is the language of wider communication for many of the Pamiri communities and therefore Shughni speakers have less need to use Tajik (Abbess et al. 2010; Müller et al. 2010b).

The variability is especially pronounced in the two Ishkashimi villages located in Tajikistan.[15] Residents of Sumjin village seem to be shifting to Tajik, while the use of Ishkashimi remains strong in Ryn village. This variation, however, is tied to marriage patterns, not any attempt on the part of the residents of Sumjin hide their Ishkashimi roots. Approximately 85% of the wives in Sumjin are native Tajik speakers, mostly from the surrounding Tajik villages. In Ryn on the other hand, only 10% of the wives

---

[14] It could be argued that lower levels of proficiency in Tajik are tied to higher levels of proficiency in Russian. Proficiency in Russian is definitely higher in the Pamirs than among the Talysh. Our research, however, suggests that proficiency in Russian is generally lower than proficiency in Tajik in rural areas. Furthermore, the factors correlating with lower levels of proficiency in Tajik also correlate with lower levels of proficiency in Russian. That is, there is generally positive, not negative, correlation between proficiency in Russian and Tajik.

[15] A majority of Ishkashimi communities and speakers live in neighboring regions in Afghanistan.

are native Tajik speakers (Müller et al. 2010a). Thus, even in villages undergoing shift, the reason seems to be local, not tied to identity as a result of the civil war.

The use of language with children is another indication that the Pamiri people are not trying to hide their traditional identities. Unlike the situation in Talysh, where parents are using Azerbaijani with their preschool-aged children, teachers we interviewed in all the Pamiri villages report that most children have rudimentary to no command of Tajik upon entering school. While parents value Tajik, we did not find patterns of language use in the Pamirs that corresponded to those we found among the Talysh. In summary, Pamiri people value the Tajik language, and want to be seen as loyal subjects of the Tajik nation, but are not trying to hide their identities as Pamiri.

16.4 Talysh revisited

At the end of section 16.2 we presented the commonly held view that the Talysh desire to self-identify as Azerbaijani was tied to the wish to distance themselves from the short-lived attempt to establish the Talysh-Mughan Autonomous Republic. In section 16.3, however, we question this view since neither the Lezgi nor the Pamiri communities desire to self-identify as Azerbaijani or Tajiki, respectively, in spite of similar histories of conflict with the newly emerging national identities after the breakup of the Soviet Union. In this section we suggest that the reason the Talysh self-identify as Azerbaijani is actually tied to a complex set of factors, including but not limited to the history of conflict.

A major factor in the current self-identification as Azerbaijani is that the Talysh people have traditionally been more widely derided than other groups. A common quip among ethnic Azerbaijanis is, "A Talysh man is crazy after twelve midnight." The quip, used when a Talysh person does something the ethnic Azerbaijani considers different or strange, ranges in intent from humorous to derogatory. This is said even in the presence of Talysh in spite of the fact that the speakers know the Talysh consider it to be offensive.

Ethnic Azerbaijanis often make comments about Lezgis as well, even when Lezgis are present. Comments about the Lezgi often hint at the tendency for Lezgis not to waver in their opinions or pursuit of their objectives. If a Lezgi takes a strong stance in the course of conversation, an Azerbaijani may openly comment, "He's a Lezgi," which elicits laughter about Lezgi stubbornness.

The intent of humor directed at the Lezgi and the Talysh is quite different. Ethnic Azerbaijani have a respectful attitude towards Lezgi culture, especially toward Lezgi men, who are considered admirably masculine.[16] Humor regarding Lezgis is considered to be laughing with the Lezgi person. Use of comments like, "He's a Lezgi," are not limited to situations which could be considered negative. It could, for example, be made if a Lezgi is working hard in a group setting while others are not taking the activity so seriously. This draws attention to the stereotypic Lezgi commitment to their objectives. Lezgi speakers recognize comments like these as a form of compliment, and will typically laugh in response. In fact, Lezgi speakers may even initiate the interaction: a Lezgi who realizes that their persistence has been noticed may say, "Hey, I'm Lezgi!" Again, this will elicit laughter.

---

[16] As Daniel Paul (personal communication) notes, the stereotypic Lezgi man carries knives and is a fighter. Masculinity is a highly valued trait throughout the Caucasus.

In contrast, humor regarding the Talysh is considered to be derogatory. The intention of this humor is to laugh at the Talysh person, and the Talysh person who is so targeted does not join in. Talysh speakers have lamented to Tiessen about the derogatory joking at their expense.

This derision of the Talysh may be rooted in the fact that they have traditionally been more isolated than most other ethnicities in Azerbaijan. Overall, Talysh communities are more isolated than are communities that use other less widely spoken languages in Azerbaijan. While, as noted above, the Talysh have high levels of proficiency in Azerbaijani, it still is not as high as the levels observed in Tat or Lezgi (Clifton 2009; Clifton et al. 2005c). While there are groups that have lower levels of proficiency, for example, the Khinalug (Clifton et al. 2005d) and Kryz (Clifton et al. 2005b), these other groups do not have the same level of prominence since they have far fewer speakers and far fewer settlements over a much smaller area. In addition, the Talysh communities are physically separated from communities speaking other less widely spoken languages, as shown in map 5. While most of the less widely spoken languages in Azerbaijan are spoken in the north of the country, Talysh is isolated in the south.

Map 5. The languages of Azerbaijan

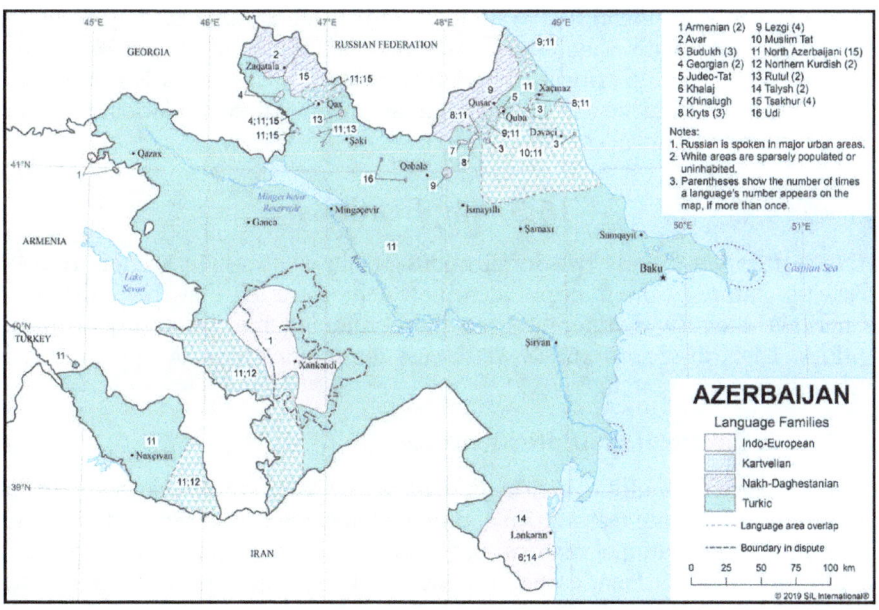

Finally, while the Talysh-Mughan Autonomous Republic never had widespread local support and was quickly suppressed, the governments of Armenia, Iran, and Russia have been accused of using the Talysh situation to foment unrest in the region. Coene (2009:161–162) traces Russian involvement back to the establishment in 1919 of the pro-Bolshevik Talysh Mughan Socialist Republic to counter the newly independent state of Azerbaijan, although it was folded into the Azerbaijani Soviet Socialist Republic in 1920, and suggests that Russia supported the establishment of the Talysh-Mughan Autonomous Republic in 1993.

More recently, in May 2005, the Iranian Studies Department of Yerevan State University in Armenia hosted the First International Conference on Talysh

Studies. The conference, which included Armenian and Iranian scholars, along with representatives from the Talysh National Movement and the Talysh diaspora in Russia, "appeared designed at least in part to resurrect the issue of autonomy for the Talysh group in Azerbaijan" (Socor 2005).

In 2013, Armenia started a Talysh-language radio station (Goble 2013), and a Talysh-language television station was established apparently backed by Russia (Goble 2014). Both these media outlets seek to encourage Talysh feelings of resentment towards the central government in Baku. Later, in 2015, the Russian news agency IAREX published an article claiming that historically the Talysh region was never a part of Azerbaijan (Goble 2015).

The result of these and similar actions by Russia, Armenia, and Iran is that the question of Talysh identity vis-à-vis Azerbaijan has remained a sensitive topic. The majority of Talysh speakers continue to emphasize their "Azerbaijani-ness" when interacting with the larger society.

Clifton (2013) argues that national languages have played the role in an ecology of language that Mufwene (2001) claims for colonial languages in settlement colonization. Speakers of less widely spoken languages need to function well in the national language if they are to fully participate in the modern state. In the case of the Talysh, however, we claim that a more immediate result is that community members have developed dual identities.[17] Within their own communities, they want to be seen as Talysh. But within the broader community the identity they want to project is that of Azerbaijani. A critical part of this new set of identities is proficiency in both the heritage language and the national language, and the intentional avoidance of Talysh outside the local community.

16.5 Implications

In this section we discuss two implications of our analysis. In section 16.5.1 we discuss the nature of the multiple identities, demonstrating that the desire to hide the heritage identity is different from more common manifestations of multiple identities. Then, in section 16.5.2 we discuss the implications for hidden identities for sociolinguistic research.

16.5.1 The nature of multiple identities

For some speakers, multilingualism is seen as the addition of languages to one's repertoire for pragmatic reasons. An additional language could be useful for political or economic or educational reasons. But learning, for example, the language of the colonizer or a multinational corporation does not necessarily change one's identity. The Dean of the Faculty of Education at the ADA University in Baku shared with Tiessen that her son uses Russian social media. Because he is well-educated, it is impossible to tell that he is not Russian; he "looks" and "sounds" Russian online. But this does not mean that he is trying to hide his Azerbaijani identity or to project a Russian identity. It is simply that his identity as a Russian or Azerbaijani is irrelevant

---

[17] It is not clear whether the Lezgi and Pamiri also have dual identities, or whether they see themselves as integrated Lezgi-Azerbaijani and Pamiri-Tajik. But whether they have dual identities or integrated identities, their situations are different from that of the Talysh, in that they do not attempt to hide their Lezgi or Pamiri identity when functioning in the broader community.

at the beginning of an interaction. When a deeper interaction develops, he is quick to clarify that he is not Russian, he just speaks Russian. His identity, then, is an Azerbaijani who can also function in a Russian-language context. In a situation like this, it is unclear that the speaker actually has multiple identities. In this situation, language appears to be simply a tool to use for interaction; the Dean's son is not trying to take on or project the identity of a Russian.

For other speakers, the use of another language can serve as a symbol of identification with the addressee. When we began making plans to conduct sociolinguistic research in Azerbaijan, we were told that we could use Russian as a language of wider communication. So all our team members were bilingual in English and Russian. We were also careful to ensure we had a mixed-gender team since we knew that in many situations it would be awkward for a male researcher to work with women in the local communities. On our first trip to the Talysh region, however, we found that there were no women in many of the villages who could understand Russian. So a top priority was gaining proficiency in Azerbaijani, especially for the women on our team. While we were able to gain adequate proficiency to conduct basic research in Azerbaijani, however, our Azerbaijani proficiency was quite limited. So when we met with local government officials, we always began the conversation in Azerbaijani, but the officials would switch to Russian as soon as they discovered we could speak Russian. We could have short circuited the process by beginning in Russian, as all government officials knew Russian well. However, we discovered that when we began a conversation in Azerbaijani, most local officials were much more accommodating and happy to work with us. Our use of Azerbaijani showed solidarity with the local officials; we identified with the country in which we were working. While the Dean's son used Russian for ease of communication, he did not want to be identified as a Russian. Our team, on the other hand, used Azerbaijani as a symbol of identification, even though communication was much easier in Russian.

Still another aspect of language and identity is highlighted in the following observation from the Mexican-American journalist Jorge Ramos (Werman 2018):[18]

> Sandra Cisneros, the wonderful writer, [...] told me that I am an amphibian. And I think she's right. [...] I think I live in two worlds. Right now we're having a conversation in English. But just in a few hours I'll be doing a newscast in Spanish, and then I'll be talking to my kids in Spanglish. And I go back and forth. [...] I'm also a translator, I'm trying to translate the Latino and the Latin American reality to a ... English-speaking community, and then what's happening in the US to an audience that feels more comfortable in Spanish, so I go back and forth and sometimes I'm Mexican and sometimes I'm American, sometimes I'm Chilango,[19] sometimes I'm Chicano [... .]

Ramos' characterization is probably accurate for many multilinguals. They can function in each language, operating with a somewhat different identity in each. Each language and each identity is public: Ramos does not try to hide his Mexican roots when speaking English, or hide his American identity when speaking Spanish.

The situation of Talysh speakers is quite different from that of Ramos. Their situation is in many ways more similar to that described by W. E. B. Du Bois (1903/

---

[18] The transcription is by Clifton.

[19] Chilango is a Mexican slang term for someone from Mexico City.

2015:5) when he says that African Americans have a double identity: "an American, a Negro; two souls, two thoughts, two unreconciled strivings; two warring ideals in one dark body, whose dogged strength alone keeps it from being torn asunder." He describes a desire to merge the two identities

> [...] into a better and truer self. In this merging he wishes neither of the older selves to be lost. [...] He simply wishes to make it possible for a man to be both a Negro and an American, without being cursed and spit upon by his fellows, without having the door of Opportunity closed roughly in his face.

The point of Du Bois' analysis is that while African Americans may want to merge the two identities, they have not been allowed to. It appears to us that Talysh speakers live with the same struggle. They would like to function like the Lezgi, being both a Lezgi and an Azerbaijani, or like the Wakhi, being both a Wakhi and a Tajik. But they feel that if they are both a Talysh and an Azerbaijani they will not be accepted. And since (unlike most African Americans) it is difficult to tell the difference between an ethnic Talysh and an ethnic Azerbaijani, it is possible for them to hide their Talysh identity when they interact with the broader Azerbaijani culture.

Of course, it is not just African Americans and Talysh who face this situation. When we were looking for an apartment in Baku, we worked with a real estate agent who introduced himself as Turkish. After several weeks of talking with us about the interactions we had in villages spread throughout Azerbaijan, he suddenly told us that while he was a Turkish citizen, he was actually ethnically Kurdish. Like the Talysh, he felt he would be accepted more readily if he hid his heritage identity. Along the same lines, after presentations of this paper at conferences, we have been approached by members of less widely used languages with similar stories. In most cases, however, the situations paralleled that of African Americans rather than the Talysh, since the members of these communities are generally physically different from members of the majority communities.

A practical outcome of situations like that of the Talysh is that groups like the Talysh are likely to be greatly underrepresented in census figures, even if the census takers make a concerted effort to obtain an accurate count. Since a census is related to the national government, not the heritage community, respondents are likely to self identify with the national ethnicity.

16.5.2 Methodology for studying hidden identities

While there were challenges conducting research on language use, proficiency, and attitudes among the Talysh who live in traditional Talysh villages, these challenges were tied to political sensitivities due to the proximity of the Talysh communities to the Iranian border. Once in the villages, we found people were very open about their Talysh identity, and willingly helped us in our research. The fact that we were accompanied on the first trip by Novruzali Mammedov, an ethnic Talysh researcher from the Azerbaijani Academy of Sciences, greatly facilitated our acceptance by the local communities, but we saw no reticence on the part of village residents even when Dr. Mammedov was not able to accompany us. This is not unexpected given that the desire to hide their Talysh identity is generally limited to their interaction within the context of the larger Azerbaijani society.

Conducting research with Talysh in urban areas is considerably more difficult. Some of these difficulties are due to the nature of the urban environment. During our research among the Juwri[20] [jdt] in the town of Qırmızı Qəsəbə (Clifton et al. 2005a), we attempted to interview residents in 51 randomly selected homes. Families in six homes were not ethnically Juwri, a situation which was not surprising since there are very few urban areas that are ethnically homogeneous. In 28 of the remaining 45 homes, either no one was at home or no one was willing to work with us. In general, we found people in an urban area to be leery of working with researchers with whom they do not have a relationship outside the research context.

These difficulties are exacerbated when working in urban areas with the Talysh, since Talysh in this environment self-identify as Azerbaijani, not Talysh. This makes it difficult to even identify members of the Talysh community in urban areas. As noted in section 16.2, Tiessen (2003) conducted sociolinguistic research among the Talysh living in Sumqayıt, an urban center with up to 80,000 Talysh residents (Tiessen 2003:17).

In spite of the large numbers of Talysh living in Sumqayıt, it is impossible to compile either a random sample or representative sample. First, there is no list of all the residents of Sumqayıt;[21] and second, there has never been an attempt to record the ethnicity of the residents of Sumqayıt. An additional, and possibly even greater problem, is political and social sensitivity. A large percentage of Sumqayıt's population consists of refugees from the occupied territories of Azerbaijan, making research in Sumqayıt a sensitive subject. These problems compound the difficulties presented by the fact that Talysh in urban areas actively identify as Azerbaijani, not Talysh.

Tiessen (2003) found that it was only possible to connect with urban-based Talysh by working through personal introductions within a Talysh social network. Beginning with members of the Talysh community we met in Baku, Tiessen asked to be introduced to other Talysh members of those individuals' social networks. This is a form of "snowball sampling" (Johnstone 2000:92) in which interviewees, rather than situations, are identified. As the process progressed, special attention was paid to asking for contacts who exhibited similar or dissimilar behavior from that of the person being interviewed. In this way, Tiessen was able to gain a broad understanding regarding the range of behaviors being investigated (Becker 1998:83–88; Wood and Christy 1999:185–186), along with a good sense of how common each alternative was.

The research itself, while based on a series of questionnaires, was framed in more of a conversational model. That is, while the researcher attempted to obtain the information included in a series of questionnaires, the actual process took the form of a conversation. Most of the interviews took place in private homes, with other members of the (extended) family present. This was much more culturally appropriate than interviewing individuals one-on-one. While the interviewer needed to be aware of situations in which the interviewee was being unduly influenced by others in the room, the format had the advantage of gaining multiple perspectives with regard to any given question.

---

[20] This language is also know as Judeo-Tat, Jewish Tat, Juhuri, and Mountain Jewish. Juwri is given as the autonym in *Ethnologue,* ethnologue.com/language/jdt/.

[21] While there are government records of housing registrations, many residents are not officially registered. These unregistered individuals include refugees, individuals living with family members but not personally registered, and individuals who are living in residences registered to someone else.

It can be argued that a qualitative study such as that conducted by Tiessen is inherently less rigorous than a more traditional quantitative study conducted with a representative sample of community members. Guba and Lincoln (1981:103–104), however, propose that the four criteria used to evaluate the rigor of quantitative studies (internal validity, external validity, reliability, and objectivity) have parallels within the field of qualitative research (credibility, fittingness, auditability, and confirmability). As long as researchers ensure these criteria are being met, there is no reason that qualitative research should be any less rigorous than quantitative research.

In fact, Becker (1998) argues that in many situations qualitative research is more likely to yield valid results than is quantitative research. The underlying goal of quantitative research is to determine what the norms of behavior are, that is, the behavioral patterns that are most common. If one of our goals, on the other hand, is to determine the breadth of behavioral patterns, a quantitative study could accidentally fail to include community members who exhibit less common behaviors. If, however, we use snowball sampling, we can explicitly ask to be led to community members who exhibit patterns different from those of the community members with whom we begin. In this way, we can gain a fuller picture of the variation inherent in any community.

In conclusion, conducting research among communities like the Talysh in which certain behaviors are intentionally hidden, can give rise to research programs that are of wider use. This is especially true as we look ahead to further research in urban settings or in settings in which we want to gain insights into the full range of variation that is present in all language communities.

References

Abbess, Elizabeth, Katja Müller, Daniel Paul, Calvin Tiessen, and Gabriela Tiessen. 2010. Literacy and the vernacular in Tajik Badakhshan: Research in Rushani, Khufi, Bartangi and Roshorvi. *SIL Electronic Survey Reports* 2010-015. Accessed 18 May 2018. sil.org/resources/publications/entry/9004/.

Akbarzadeh, Shahram. 1996. Why did nationalism fail in Tajikistan? *Europe-Asia Studies* 48:1105–1129.

Bazin, Marcel. 1980. *Le Tâlech, une région ethnique au nord de l'Iran* [The Talysh, an ethnic region in northern Iran]. Paris: Editions ADPF.

Becker, Howard S. 1998. *Tricks of the trade: How to think about your research while you're doing it.* Chicago Guides to Writing, Editing, and Publishing. Chicago, IL: University of Chicago Press.

Clifton, John M. 2009. Do the Talysh and Tat languages have a future in Azerbaijan? *Work Papers of the Summer Institute of Linguistics, University of North Dakota Session* 49. Accessed 9 Mar 2018. arts-sciences.und.edu/summer-institute-of-linguistics/work-papers/_files/docs/2009-clifton.pdf/.

Clifton, John M. 2013. Colonialism, nationalism and language vitality in Azerbaijan. In Elena Mihas, Bernard Perley, Gabriel Rei-Doval, and Kathleen Wheatley (eds.), *Responses to language endangerment: In honor of Mickey Noonan: New directions in language documentation and language revitalization,* 197–219. Amsterdam: John Benjamins.

Clifton, John M., Gabriela Deckinga, Laura Lucht, and Calvin Tiessen. 2005a. Sociolinguistic situation of the Tat and Mountain Jews in Azerbaijan. *SIL*

Electronic Survey Reports 2005-017. Accessed 4 Jun 2018. sil.org/resources/publications/entry/9077/.

Clifton, John M., Laura Lucht, Gabriela Deckinga, Janfer Mak, and Calvin Tiessen. 2005b. The sociolinguistic situation of the Khinalug in Azerbaijan. *SIL Electronic Survey Reports* 2005-007. Accessed 4 Jun 2018. sil.org/resources/publications/entry/9007/.

Clifton, John M., Laura Lucht, Gabriela Deckinga, Janfer Mak, and Calvin Tiessen. 2005c. The sociolinguistic situation of the Lezgi in Azerbaijan. *SIL Electronic Survey Reports* 2005-012. Accessed 20 Sep 2013. sil.org/resources/publications/entry/9090/.

Clifton, John M., Janfer Mak, Gabriela Deckinga, Laura Lucht, and Calvin Tiessen. 2005d. The sociolinguistic situation of the Kryz in Azerbaijan. *SIL Electronic Survey Reports* 2005-006. Accessed 4 Jun 2018. sil.org/resources/publications/entry/9143/.

Clifton, John M., Calvin Tiessen, Gabriela Deckinga, and Laura Lucht. 2005e. Sociolinguistic situation of the Talysh in Azerbaijan. *SIL Electronic Survey Reports* 2005-009. Accessed 20 Sep 2013. sil.org/resources/publications/entry/9135/.

Coene, Frederik. 2009. *The Caucasus: An introduction*. Routledge Contemporary Russia and Eastern Europe Series 17. Abingdon, UK: Routledge.

Collins, Kathleen. 2004. The logic of clan politics: Evidence from the Central Asian trajectories. *World Politics* 56:224–261.

Cornell, Svante E. 2005. *Small nations and great powers: A study of ethnopolitical conflict in the Caucasus*. Caucasus World. London: RoutledgeCurzon.

Cornell, Svante E. 2011. *Azerbaijan since independence*. Studies of Central Asia and the Caucasus. Armonk, NY: M. E. Sharpe.

Du Bois, W. E. B. 2015. *The souls of black folk*. With an introduction and chronology by Jonathan Scott Holloway. Originally published 1903. New Haven, CT: Yale University Press.

Ehala, Martin. 2010. Ethnolinguistic vitality and intergroup processes. *Multilingua—Journal of Cross-Cultural and Interlanguage Communication* 29:203–221.

Goble, Paul. 2013. Re-opening the Talysh question in Azerbaijan: Armenian, Iranian and Russian 'traces'. *Eurasia Daily Monitor* 10(76). Accessed 4 Jun 2018. jamestown.org/program/re-opening-the-talysh-question-in-azerbaijan-armenian-iranian-and-russian-traces/.

Goble, Paul. 2014. Who is behind the new Talysh-language TV broadcasts in Azerbaijan? *Eurasia Daily Monitor* 11(219). Accessed 9 Dec 2014. jamestown.org/program/who-is-behind-the-new-talysh-language-tv-broadcasts-in-azerbaijan/.

Goble, Paul. 2015. Is Moscow putting the Talysh in play against Azerbaijan? *Eurasian Daily Monitor* 12(21). Accessed 4 Jun 2018. jamestown.org/program/is-moscow-putting-the-talysh-in-play-against-azerbaijan/.

Guba, Egon G., and Yvonna S. Lincoln. 1981. *Effective evaluation: Improving the usefulness of evaluation results through responsive and naturalistic approaches*. Jossey Bass Higher & Adult Education Series. San Francisco, CA: Jossey-Bass Publishers.

Haspelmath, Martin. 1993. *A grammar of Lezgian*. Mouton Grammar Library 9. Berlin: De Gruyter.

Heathershaw, John, and Edmund Herzig. 2011. Introduction: The sources of statehood in Tajikistan. *Central Asian Survey* 30:5–19.

Interagency Language Roundtable (ILR). n.d. ILR skill level descriptions. Interagency Language Roundtable. Accessed 27 Sep 2012. govtilr.org/.

Isaev, M. I. 1970. *Sto tridtsat' ravnopravnyx (o jazykax narodov SSSR)* [Сто тридцать равноправных (о языках народов СССР) / About the 130 equal languages of the peoples of the USSR]. Moscow: Akademija Nauk SSSR.

Isaev, M. I. 1979. *Jazykovoe stroitel'stvo v SSSR* [Языковое строительство в СССР / Language development in the USSR]. Moscow: Akademija Nauk SSSR.

Johnstone, Barbara. 2000. *Qualitative methods in sociolinguistics.* Oxford: Oxford University Press.

Karan, Mark E. 2011. Understanding and forecasting ethnolinguistic vitality. *Journal of Multilingual and Multicultural Development* 32:137–149.

Kevlihan, Rob. 2016. Insurgency in Central Asia: A case study of Tajikistan. *Small wars and insurgencies* 27:417–439.

Korn, Agnes. 2016. A partial tree of Central Iranian: A new look at Iranian subphyla. *Indogermanische Forschungen* 121:401–434. Accessed 15 May 2018. halshs.archives-ouvertes.fr/halshs-01333448v4/.

Matveeva, Anna. 2002. *The South Caucasus: Nationalism, conflict and minorities.* London: Minority Rights Group International.

Matveeva, Anna, and Clem McCartney. 1998. Policy responses to an ethnic community division: Lezgins in Azerbaijan. *International Journal on Minority and Group Rights* 5:213–252.

Miller, B. V. 1953. *Talyshskij jazyk* [Талышский язык / The Talysh language]. Moscow: Akademija Nauk SSSR.

Mirzabdinova, S. 1991. *Khufskij dialekt rushanskogo jazyka* [Хуфский диалект рушанского языка / The Khufi dialect of the Rushani language]. Dushanbe, Tajikistan: Donish.

Mufwene, Salikoko S. 2001. *The ecology of language evolution.* Cambridge: Cambridge University Press.

Mufwene, Salikoko S. 2008. *Language evolution: Contact, competition and change.* Cambridge Approaches to Language Contact. New York: Continuum.

Müller, Katja, Elizabeth Abbess, Calvin Tiessen, and Gabriela Tiessen. 2008. Language vitality and development among the Wakhi people of Tajikistan. *SIL Electronic Survey Reports* 2008-011. Accessed 28 Aug 2013. sil.org/resources/publications/entry/9157/.

Müller, Katja, Elizabeth Abbess, Daniel Paul, Calvin Tiessen, and Gabriela Tiessen. 2010a. Ishkashimi: A father's language: How a very small language survives. *SIL Electronic Survey Reports* 2010-013. Accessed 18 May 2018. sil.org/resources/publications/entry/9082/.

Müller, Katja, Elizabeth Abbess, Daniel Paul, Calvin Tiessen, and Gabriela Tiessen. 2010b. Language in community-oriented and contact-oriented domains: The case of the Shughni of Tajikistan. *SIL Electronic Survey Reports* 2010-016. Accessed 18 May 2018. sil.org/resources/publications/entry/9232/.

New York Times. 1993. Caucasus city falls to Armenian forces. *New York Times International*, 24 Aug 1993. Accessed 13 May 2018. nytimes.com/1993/08/24/world/caucasus-city-falls-to-armenian-forces.html?pagewanted=al/.

Omoniyi, Tope. 2010. Borders. In Joshua Fishman and Ofelia García (eds), *Handbook of language and ethnic identity: Disciplinary and regional perspectives*, 1:123–134. Oxford: Oxford University Press.

Paul, Daniel. 2011. A comparative dialectal description of Iranian Taleshi. PhD dissertation. University of Manchester, UK.

Pirejko, Lija A. 1976. *Talyshsko-russkij slovar'* [Талышско-русский словарь' / Talysh-Russian dictionary]. Moscow: Izdatel'stvo Russkij Iazyk Russian Language Publisher.

Radloff, Carla F. 1991. *Sentence repetition testing for studies of community bilingualism.* SIL Publications in Linguistics 104. Dallas, TX: SIL International and the University of Texas at Arlington.

Rastorgueva, V. S. 1979. *Osnovy iranskogo jazykoznanija* [Основы иранского языкознания / Foundations of Iranian linguistics]. Moscow: Akademija Nauk SSSR.

Rubin, Barnett R. 1993. The fragmentation of Tajikistan. *Survival* 35:71–91.

Saxena, Mukul. 1994. Literacies among the Panjabis in Southall. In Mary Hamilton, David Barton, and Roz Ivanic (eds.), *Worlds of literacy*, 195–214. Clevedon, UK: Multilingual Matters.

Schulze, Wolfgang. 2015. From Caucasian Albanian to Udi. *Iran and the Caucasus* 19:149–177.

Schwab, Irene. 1994. Literacy, language variety and identity. In Mary Hamilton, David Barton, and Roz Ivanic (eds.), *Worlds of literacy*, 134–142. Clevedon, UK: Multilingual Matters.

Sebba, Mark. 2007. *Spelling and society: The culture and politics of orthography around the world.* Cambridge: Cambridge University Press.

Sims-Williams, Nicholas. 2011/1996. Eastern Iranian languages. In Ehsan Yarshater (ed.), *Encyclopædia Iranica*, VII, Fasc. 6:649–652. New York: Encyclopædia Iranica Foundation.

Smeets, Rieks. 1994. Introduction. In Rieks Smeets (ed.), *The North East Caucasian languages, part 2*, vii–xix. Delmar, NY: Caravan Books.

Smith, R. Grant. 1999. Tajikistan: The rocky road to peace. *Central Asian Survey* 1999:243–251.

Socor, Vladimir. 2005. Talysh issue, dormant in Azerbaijan, reopened in Armenia. *Eurasia Daily Monitor* 2(104). Accessed 13 May 2018. jamestown.org/program/talysh-issue-dormant-in-azerbaijan-reopened-in-armenia/.

Stilo, Donald L. 2015. The polygenetic origins of the Northern Talyshi language. In Uwe Bläsing, Victoria Arakelova, and Matthias Weinreich (eds.), *Studies on Iran and the Caucasus: In honour of Garnik Asatrian*, 411–454. Leiden: Brill.

Tiessen, Calvin. 2003. Positive orientation towards the vernacular among the Talysh of Sumgayit. MA thesis. University of North Dakota, Grand Forks.

Tiessen, Gabriela, Elisabeth Abbess, Katja Müller, and Calvin Tiessen. 2010. Language access and Tajik language proficiency among the Yazghulami of Tajikistan. *SIL Electronic Survey Reports* 2010-018. Accessed 18 May 2018. sil.org/resources/publications/entry/9099/.

Tunçer-Kilavuz, Idil. 2011. Understanding civil war: A comparison of Tajikistan and Uzbekistan. *Europe-Asia Studies* 63:263–290.

Wendtland, Antje. 2009. The position of the Pamir languages within East Iranian. *Orientalia Suecana* LVIII:172–188. Accessed 14 May 2018. diva-portal.org/smash/get/diva2:305485/fulltext01.pdf/.

Werman, Marco. 2018. Jorge Ramos feels like a stranger, more random acts of kindness, and a visit to the world's largest furniture show. *PRI's The World* 3 May 2018. Accessed 10 May 2018. pri.org/programs/pris-world/jorge-ramos-feels-stranger-more-random-acts-kindness-and-visit-worlds-largest/.

Wood, Michael, and Richard Christy. 1999. Sampling for possibilities. *Quality and Quantity* 33:185–202.

17
Language Choice and Language Attitudes in Identity Formation among the Roma of Sadova

Marlute van Dam

Abstract. This paper discusses the multilingual situation of the Roma from a village in Southern Romania, where all people speak at least Romani and Romanian. It discusses which languages people are most likely to speak in specific contexts, why these people speak a certain language in a specific context, what people's attitude is to the languages they speak, and what role these languages play in their identity formation. The Roma people from this research demonstrate that Romani plays an important role in their identity formation. However, people's behavior does not always correlate with their attitude to their language. Although Romanian is seen by many people as the language of the outsider, people still prefer this language in many domains. For language development work to be successful, it is important to answer the question why people prefer what language in what domain and what influences people's behavior.

17.1 Aims

The Romanian government and several other organizations are attempting to improve the situation of Roma, including through language development work and literacy and religious initiatives. Some of these programs, for instance in schools, use only Romanian [ron]. Other initiatives have tried to develop a single, standardized, version of Romani (the language of the Roma) and implement this in the school curriculum. Other organizations try to work with and promote several Romani dialects. In order for these programs to function optimally, it is important to get a better understanding of the linguistic situation of the Roma people. This case study aims to contribute to the understanding of this complex multilingual situation.

17.2 Background

This case study focuses on the language situation of the Roma people living in or originating from the village of Sadova in Southern Romania. The Roma, also known as gypsies, form a minority in every country where they live. The village of Sadova consists of both Roma and Romanians,[1] who live in separate areas of the village.

In Romania, there are an estimated 1.8 million Roma,[2] although the official figures state that there are only about 600,000 Roma (see Klimovitz 2015). In Sadova, an estimated 20% of the 6,500 citizens are Roma (according to the census of 2011),[3] which would be about 1,300 people, with the remainder being Romanians. The real number of Roma in Sadova and in Romania is difficult to estimate, as many Roma are registered as Romanians, and many people who officially live in Sadova actually live abroad.

Halwachs (2012:250) describes Romani as a "heterogeneous cluster of varieties with a homogeneous core—a common morphology and a common lexicon." The core Romani vocabulary contains many words from Sanskrit, Persian, and Greek. There are many varieties of Romani, some varieties being mutually intelligible, but many varieties have a low rate of mutual intelligibility. This is because in every region where they live, they have adopted words and structures from surrounding languages. The Romani dialect spoken in Sadova has been heavily influenced by Romanian, which is evident in all segments of the language, as for example the vocabulary and grammar. This dialect is labeled as South-Vlax Romani (ISO 639-3 code: rmy), while the people refer to themselves as Ursari, Caramidari (brick workers), or Romanian Roma.

Many Roma have a low position in society and live in poverty. Many, both from Sadova and other places, have told me that it is more difficult for them to find a job, and that if two people apply for a job, the non-Roma person is often preferred over the Roma person. Many negative stereotypes persist about Roma, and they are often accused of being thieves, unreliable, lazy, and not willing to integrate. On the other hand, special places are reserved at universities for Roma people and a number of non government organizations are trying to improve their living situation. Since the fall of communism, the borders have opened, enabling many people from Romania to move abroad. Many Roma from Sadova have moved to Italy, Germany, and other countries. Some have settled in these countries, but many travel back and forth between these countries and Romania. Very few Roma in Sadova have not spent a considerable time outside of Romania. Almost all the people who have settled abroad still have a house in Sadova. People also build houses in Sadova for their children, even though these children grew up outside of Romania. They use the money they earn abroad to improve their houses or to support their family members who are not able to travel. In this way, the Roma from Sadova have been able to create better living circumstances for themselves and their close relatives.

The fieldwork for this case study was conducted over a period of three years, during which time I lived with a Roma family in the village of Sadova and worked as a translation facilitator in a Bible translation project for the Roma[4] I consider

---

[1] The focus here is on ethnicity, both Roma and Romanians have the Romanian nationality.

[2] http://rm.coe.int/CoERMPublicCommonSearchServices/DisplayDCTMContent?documentId=0900001680088ea9/

[3] https://www.recensamantromania.ro/wp-content/uploads/2012/08/TS2.pdf/. Accessed April 2018.

[4] I would like to thank all the participants of this research for their willingness in sharing with me part of their lives. I am also thankful for all who have shown me such hospitality in the process, I am especially thankful for "my grandmother', who has made it possible to do my research and has taught me many things about her culture. I would like to thank Florian Tanasie for his help in carrying out this research, for his helpful comments, and

myself a participant observer, gradually learning the language and customs of the people with whom I live. Part of my work involves analysis of the Romani language and of the multilingual situation in this village. The people here have been very hospitable to me and have accepted me as part of their family; when they talk about me, they call me their "daughter." And as for me, many of the Roma of this research have become my "grandmothers," my "grandfathers," "aunts," "uncles," "brothers," "sisters," and friends.

17.3   Research questions

Before I came to Sadova, I had some assumptions about the multilingual situation of the Roma people there. I assumed, as a native Dutch [nld] speaker, that Romanian was for them what English [eng] is for me: we speak it, we understand it, but we do not consider it our language. I assumed that they all considered Romani to be their mother tongue, the language they speak best and the one with which they identify. While this assumption does not seem to be completely wrong, the situation does seem to be more complex, since Roma people here grow up with both Romanian and Romani and use these languages often interchangeably. This led me to think that the differences between these two languages are not very important to the people here, but also this assumption did not do justice to the complexity of the situation. Therefore, I decided to ask the people themselves. This paper describes the results of this research, which examines the multilingual situation of the Roma in Sadova by asking the following questions:

- What are the motivations for language choice of the Roma people in Sadova?
- What do these motivations say about people's language attitudes and personal identities?
- What implications do the answers to the above questions have for language development work?

17.4   Theoretical background

In this case study I discuss multilingualism from a societal perspective (see Edwards 2013 for a classification of multilingualism). While discussing multilingualism from a societal perspective, one should keep in mind that people usually belong to several different types of communities or social groupings (Romaine 2013). All the different communities people belong to influence the way they speak and identify themselves. For example, the community we discuss is the village of Sadova, but since people are able to travel abroad (during communism this was not possible), people from this community have settled in several places around the world, mostly in Italy and Germany. People thus identify with different societies—Romanian, Italian, or German. This ultimately influences the entire Roma community, including those who have never travelled, as aspects of German and Italian culture reach older people

---

because he has facilitated my stay in Sadova. I would also like to thank Carmen Tanasie for reading through this paper and giving me helpful comments. I would like to thank David and Sari Gardner for their helpful comments and the information they have given to me. Furthermore, I would like to thank Maggie Canvin, Wilco van den Heuvel, and Maik Gibson and all the other people who helped me by reading through my paper and giving me helpful comments.

who remained behind. Thus, although the Roma people from this study participate in different speech communities (Romani-Romanian, Romani-Italian-Romanian, and the Romani-Romanian-German speech communities), they belong to the same language community. Many people participate in several speech communities, since they travel between Germany, Italy, and Romania.

The most important languages in this Roma community are Romani and Romanian, and most of the members of this community are able to speak at least these two languages. As a result, the Romani variant that the Roma people speak is highly influenced by Romanian. Those who travel to and live in other countries also often speak the language of this other country. Very few non-Roma people can speak Romani. Some non-Roma people who are in close contact to the Roma can understand it and know some words, but they usually do not speak it.

Even the preceding brief description of the community in focus reveals a complex situation. The next section will discuss the theoretical tools used to analyze this situation. Four concepts are discussed in turn: multilingualism, language choice, language attitudes, and identity.

In the analysis of multilingualism, I have been influenced by Gumperz's notion of "verbal repertoire'. Every person, whether monolingual or multilingual, has several codes in his or her verbal repertoire (see, for example, Coronel-Molina 2009). According to Gumperz (1964:137), the verbal repertoire "contains all the accepted ways of formulating messages." In different situations, a different way of speaking is needed. The language or code that people speak at home with family or friends may be different from the language people speak in official situations. The difference between a multilingual situation and a monolingual situation is that in a multilingual situation, the different codes people use are distributed across different languages, such as Romani and Romanian. For example, the Roma people speak Romani at home, but Romanian in the shop, school, or church. But it is not the case that people simply use different languages strictly for functional purposes. Associated with the different languages are also notions of pride, shame, and social status. The use of different languages or codes can also be used to signal social belonging—as a way to mark or form one's identity (see Joseph 2010).

To study language choice, Sridhar (1996:51) follows Fishman (1965) in using the following question: "Who uses what language with whom and for what purposes?" According to Fishman, there are three main factors that explain language choice; these factors need to be considered together as none of them can explain the whole phenomenon of language choice on its own. The first factor is *group identity*. Speaking a certain language allows identification with a certain group. For example, people speak Romani at home to identify themselves with the home culture, and Romanian at work to identify with those at the workplace. But a person might chose to speak in Romanian with Roma people, or Romani with another Roma person at the workplace. Therefore Fishman concludes that group identity answers only part of this question, and one also needs to look also at a second major factor, that of *situation*. Multilingual people often consider their home language to be less official, informal, and therefore not appropriate for certain situations. The third important factor in language choice is *topic*. The reason to speak about a topic in a certain language may be that the other language lacks the words necessary to talk about this topic, or that this topic is usually discussed in this language. The notion that combines these three factors is that of "domains of use" (Fishman 1965:67) – "who speaks what language to whom and when", in what situation and about what topic.

In order to study language attitudes in a multilingual situation, the status of the different languages is an important factor. Not every language has the same status. Thompson (1991:5) points out, summarizing Bourdieu's thought, that languages are in fact "the product of a complex set of social, historical and political conditions of formation." Bourdieu himself describes status as the "relation between linguistic habitus and the markets on which [the language users] offer their products" (Bourdieu 1991:38). In order to understand the language situation, one should also understand the social situation in which these language operate. Bourdieu introduces the ideas of "language as symbolic power" and language as a "kind of wealth" (1991:43). Peirce (1997) gives an example of this when she describes immigrants learning English in Canada: they want to learn to speak the variety of the majority so they will have more chances of social success. Romanian and other national languages like German [deu], French [fra], and English [eng] can help people to enhance their social status. As a result, Roma who go to school are more interested in learning these languages than in studying Romani. Looking at the situation in Sadova, Romani is a low-status language. For example, when Romanians and Roma speak with each other, they almost always speak in Romanian. Romanian is the official national language; Romani is a recognized minority language. All official institutions use Romanian; school is in Romanian and in shops people will usually use Romanian. When people are able to speak and write Romanian well, they are recognized as having a higher status than people who do not speak and write this language so well. The prejudices against the Roma themselves are also visible in people's opinion about the language; Romanians often say that Romani is an ugly language or they make fun of how it sounds. This phenomenon that one language is more valued than the other is what Sridhar (1996:6) calls the "asymmetric principle of multilingualism." This principle does not, however, mean that Romani has no value. In certain contexts, Romani is valued more than Romanian. In a multilingual setting, the different languages play different roles in the shaping of the identity of a person (Fuller 2007). What this could mean in this situation is that Romanian will be used to give people a higher status in the majority society while Romani will be used to build social relationships within the Roma community. As a Romani speaker myself, I have found that it is easier to build relationships with Roma people when I speak Romani than when I speak to them in Romanian.

In studying language attitude, I use the mentalist view. Morgan defines the mentalist view as follows: "Attitudes are literally mental postures, guides for conduct to which each new experience is referred before a response is made" (Morgan 1934:47). According to Taufe'ulungaki (1994:87) "the mentalist regards attitude as a state of readiness, that is, it is a mediating factor between any stimulus affecting any individual and that individual's response." In other words, the attitudes we have guide us in making our choices. This "state of readiness" is "organized through experience" (Allport 1935:191). For example, a Roma can consider the use of Romani inappropriate to non-Roma strangers because the Roma are often told not to do this by Romanians. The mentalist view divides this concept into three subconcepts: feelings, beliefs, and behavior (see Coronel-Molina 2009:9). Although behavior is part of attitude, it is important to note that what a person feels and believes does not always coincide with behavior. A person may say that he or she thinks that something is a good thing, but his or her behavior does not necessarily match this. In fact, these three concepts may differ greatly; people's feelings do not always coincide with their beliefs and people do not always act on what they feel or believe. In order to understand what determines a person's behavior, many more factors need to be taken into consideration, such as pressure from outside, traditions, and so on.

For the study of identity, I use the sociocultural linguistic framework of Bucholtz and Hall (2005, 2010). They describe sociocultural linguistics as a "broad interdisciplinary field concerned with the intersection of language, culture, and society." They have developed a framework for the study of identity that works from the definition that "identity is the social positioning of self and other" (2005:586). They see identity as an "emergent" product (2010:19). Identity is thus not something stable, but it emerges in society through language, among other means. It is the way people speak about each other and themselves that helps to form their identity. As Tang (1997:577) puts it, "The identity of an individual is not fixed but is developed and accentuated by being compared with others" (see also Lewis, chapter 3 this volume). Defining identity this way helps to account for the identity formation of multilingual people who do a lot of travelling; all the languages and cultures they encounter influence how people identify themselves. An example of Roma people socially positioning themselves is when people talk about other groups. Often people will say that the negative stereotypes about Roma are because of another Roma group. In this way, they hope they can maintain their Roma identity, but gain more respect from outsiders.

Now that we have looked at the different concepts, we return to our question of what role language choice and language use play in the identity formation of the Roma in Sadova.

17.5 Methodology

I used several methods to answer the questions previously posed. The main method I used for data gathering is participant observation (DeWalt and DeWalt 2011). My fieldwork in Sadova started in January 2015 and continues today, consisting of living for extensive periods in this village, where I share a house with an older woman, participating in the daily life of the village people, visiting several families every day, and taking extensive notes of situations that seem interesting to me. I also joined a group when they went to sell watermelons in a city about five hours from where we live, and I joined several families when they went from Romania to Germany. Further, I have done semistructured interviews with people from a wide range of ages and from different families, asking them about language issues, the difference between Roma and non-Roma, and when people speak what language and why.

In addition to my observations and interviews, I collected responses to a questionnaire about people's attitudes to the different languages that they speak. This questionnaire consists of four questions. The reason for a short questionnaire is that I wanted it to be easy to remember, so that I could recruit others to help me carry out the interviews. However, during most of the interviews I asked additional questions about specific subjects that came up. The interviewees were thirteen women and twelve men, with ages ranging from 8 to 82. People over 50 were overrepresented: 10 under 50 versus 15 over 50. I interviewed three children, aged 8, 10, and 12. To motivate the children to answer my questions, I gave each of them 1 leu (about 0.20 Euro); the adult interviewees were not paid. All of the interviewees were from Sadova, but some of them live abroad nowadays and only come to Sadova for short visits. Three of the interviews were conducted in Germany with Roma from Sadova who live now in Germany. The other interviews took place in Sadova, but many of the interviewees have lived a considerable time outside of Romania, mostly in Italy.

Only two of the interviewees, two older women, had never left Romania. Some interviewees attended church services and some did not. Most of these interviews were conducted by me, and three interviews were conducted by Florian Tanasie (Roma colleague). Eleven interviews were conducted in one-on-one conversations. The information from the other fourteen interviewees was gathered in five small-group interviews; the groups ranged from two to five people. Some interviewees found it difficult to answer these open questions. In those cases I made the questions into closed questions, to make them easier to answer. The disadvantage of this approach was that these answers were shorter and less informative. The interviews were recorded and later transcribed and analyzed.

The four questions of the questionnaire are:

- What does the Romani language mean for you?
- What does the language of the *gajo* (non-Roma people) mean for you?
- What would a Bible in Romani mean for you?
- What do you want to change in the situation of the Roma people?

These questions served as the frame for the interviews. Based on what people said, I would ask them additional questions. The first two questions concern the language attitudes of the people, the third question is also concerned with language attitude, but along with this question I would also ask them questions about language behavior, such as, in what language they would prefer to read the Bible, in what language do they pray, in what language do they think, and why.

The last question is intended to elicit attitudes about society. The participants in the interview were invited to talk about society, how non-Roma people look at them, and what problems they face as Roma people. However, interviewees usually talked about other Roma, that the Roma people were in need of change. This probably has to do with how the question was formulated. When I became aware of this problem, I often rephrased the question or asked additional questions to invite people to also talk about what problems Roma people face in today's society.

After analyzing the results, I discussed my analysis with three Roma people, one from Sadova and two from elsewhere, to see if the findings resonated with their own understandings and to avoid making mistakes in representing the Roma people.

I am aware that these questions are very limited, and that one should be cautious to make big claims based on the results of this questionnaire. In my future research I hope to be able to expand this questionnaire and to also use more community-based approaches, in order that the voice of this community will be heard more clearly.

17.6 Questionnaire results

In this section I discuss the results from the questionnaire. In the next section I compare this with my own observations and attempt to provide answers to the research questions.

When people are asked about what the Romani language means for them, the answers primarily reveal positive attitudes towards this language and insight into how the language relates to identity. They mostly answer that it is their mother tongue, the language they grew up in, and that they speak this language because they are Roma. Many people stress the importance of growing up in this language and learning the basics of life in this language. It is the first language they learned. Several people said that they feel more liberty when they speak Romani. Some people were proud that the language is spoken all over the world and that wherever you go in the world, you can find Roma people to whom you can speak and who will help you. All the respondents reply that they have a positive view of their language and that they like their language.

When people are asked about what the non-Roma language (Romanian) means for them, it does not seem that people have a more positive attitude to Romanian than to Romani and it seems that most respondents do not link it directly to their identity. Only one woman said that she spoke Romanian because she did not only identify as Roma, but also Romanian. The other people gave mostly functional reasons for speaking Romanian. For example, many people said that it is necessary to speak this language because they live in Romania. One woman said that they need it for integration. Integration is a recurrent theme in discussions about Roma in society; it is mostly used in the sense of being able to participate in the society. This was also reflected in another response: a man said that young people need it to get along at school and to be able to find a job. The notion of pride also seems to be connected with speaking Romanian: one woman, who did not identify Romanian as "her" language, said that she was proud to be able to speak Romanian as well. The reason she gave was that it was not only the Roma people who speak this language. She does seem to have a more positive attitude towards Romanian than towards Romani.

People assess their ability to speak Romanian in different ways. One man said that it is a second language that he can speak perfectly. One woman said it did not matter too much; she speaks both languages, and sometimes she uses one, sometimes the other. Sometimes she prays in Romani, sometimes in Romanian, but mostly in Romanian. It did not seem significant for her. However, other people said that they spoke Romani better than Romanian. One young man said that Romanian is a strange language. This might well be because he lives in Germany and does not speak Romanian often any more. A seventy-year-old woman said that she found it difficult to speak Romanian, or that she did not speak Romanian as well as Romani, because in the village she only speaks Romani with people. A sixty-five-year-old woman and a woman in her early forties also said that this was the case for them. Most people preferred Romani over Romanian, but one boy (thirteen years old) said that he thought German and Italian [ita] were better than both Romani and Romanian. Also, the other children I interviewed separately were very positive about German and said that they really wanted to learn that language.

It appears to be the norm that Roma children learn Romani first in the home and acquire Romanian at a later age. They learn Romanian before the end of the critical period and encounter Romanian in many domains from an early age, so that they are able to acquire native fluency (see Harris, chapter 12 this volume). This was affirmed by several interviewees. During one of the interviews, a two-year-old boy was present. I asked whether he could speak Romanian and his grandmother replied not yet, but that they would teach him that later. He does however encounter Romanian, because sometimes his grandmother speaks to people in Romanian and everything on the television is in Romanian. Another interview was with a mother who has a three-year-old son. He did not speak Romanian yet; he would learn that when he went to kindergarten. I asked two boys how old they were when they learned Romanian, one answered at the age of four and the other answered at the age of six.

Based on the responses of the first two questions, one would expect that most people would prefer Romani in many contexts. And indeed, people are generally positive about a Bible in Romani and say that they would like to have a Bible in Romani. One man said that Romanians look down on the Roma people. One reason was that they do not even have a Bible in their language, so when they read the Bible they need to use the language of the non-Roma people. One man said that it is the right of every people to have the Bible in their own language. However, others said that a Bible in Romanian is better than in Romani, because Romani is difficult to read and they are just as fluent in Romanian as they are in Romani. Also, most people do not use the portions of the Romani Bible that have been translated and many people prefer to pray in Romanian. When asked why this is, they answered that they learned to do it this way and that this is what they are used to. One woman said that the reason why it is difficult to read Romani is because it does not have a fixed alphabet and they did not learn to read in Romani. She said that it is important to have an audio version of the Romani Bible, and that people would prefer an audio version of the Bible in Romani over a Romanian Bible. Another man said that he prays both in Romani and Romanian, but that he could feel the power of God more when he prayed in Romani.

Looking at other domains, two girls said that there were certain domains where they used only Romanian and not Romani, and where it would be difficult to use Romani. They gave the example of counting and doing business; they would find it very difficult to do that in Romani. People usually write in Romanian, unless they do not want non-Roma to understand what they have written.

So the positive view people have about their language does seem to have some influence on language choice: many people say, for example, that they would prefer to hear the Bible in Romani. However, other people who preferred Romani more generally, said that they preferred the Bible and other written material in Romanian.

In the responses to the last question, the respondents' struggle with the negative aspects of Roma identity came up. When asked about what needs to be changed in the situation of the Roma people, most people mentioned that they want to change the "character of the Roma." The answers include that Roma people need to "live better lives," be "more loving, steal less, lie less," they need to "be punished so that they will improve their lives," and they need to "be educated." Two girls said that they wanted to change the "Romani law", meaning customs that one is expected to follow. When I asked them to explain which customs they wanted to change, they said that as a woman you wear a skirt and a head covering and that you marry at a young age. A woman said that she did not want to change anything and that people who are knowledgeable, men, should change something if they wanted to. One person mentioned that Roma people are discriminated against and that other people look down on them. That respondent also indicated that the society of the majority population needs to change to improve the Roma situation. When asked about problems in the society, people say that poverty is a significant problem and that it is difficult especially for Roma people to find a job in Romania. Another problem people often mention is that their families are spread out over Europe now and that they are never together as a whole family any more.

One woman who now lives in Germany told me she was ashamed to tell people in other countries that she is Romanian because of the bad reputation Romanians have. I asked her whether she preferred to say that she is Roma and does not have anything to do with Romanians. She answered that that would be worse, it is better to say that you are Romanian. But in both cases, one has to work hard to prove oneself. This negative view of Roma ethnicity held by both Roma and non-Roma could also be an important factor in language choice and identity formation. However, contrary to what I would expect, it does not seem to influence people's language attitudes, as most respondents seem to be very positive about their language.

17.7 Discussion of interview results in combination with other observations

17.7.1 General observation: language use

Romani in Sadova is used by all generations. The Roma children in Sadova learn Romani as their first language. Roma only use Romani to speak to other Roma, even in the presence of Romanians. Romanians do not tend to speak Romani, so Roma always speak to them in Romanian. In church people will speak Romani to each other before and after the church service. There are three different churches Roma people in the village attend: two have their church services in Romanian, and one in Romani unless there is a Romanian visitor. There seems to be a difference between the older and the younger generation. Many from the older generation claim that they speak Romani better than Romanian. Many from the younger generation say that there is no difference in their Romani and Romanian; they speak both of these languages perfectly. Children under the age of fifteen claim they speak Romani better and that they do not speak Romanian well. Older men seem to have fewer problems with Romanian than older women (older women are also often not able to read). I have not noticed this difference in the younger generation; both men and women from this generation claim to speak Romani and Romanian equally fluently. However, some people from younger generations do say that they speak Romani better than Romanian; these are mostly people who have lived outside of Romania for extensive periods.

17.7.2 Motivations for language choice

The main motivation for language choice is the identity of the interlocutors. Many people give the following rule as a general rule for language choice: if Roma people speak to other Roma people (who speak the same or a similar dialect), they will speak in Romani; if they speak to Romanians, they will speak Romanian.

There are, however, exceptions and these are the cases I will focus on. Sometimes Roma people use or switch to Romanian in situations where everybody speaks Romani, so that strictly speaking they could speak Romani.

One context where people do not speak Romani even when only Roma people are present is in situations where there are Roma from different regions, speaking different dialects. People will often use the national language in this case, to make sure that what they are saying is understood. This happens if people meet other Roma during their travels, or if they are visited by other Roma speaking a different dialect.

But sometimes even if they all speak the same dialect, people will still use Romanian. The concept of domains is important to answer this question (Fishman 1972:437, as cited by Sridhar 1996:53). For example, Romani is almost never used in written texts. This is true even when Roma people text/app each other on mobile phones or comment on each other's posts on social media. Sometimes, however, if people do not want an outsider to understand, they will write in Romani.

Another example is the church service; even if there are only Roma people present at church, most church services are still in Romanian.

In talking to people about why they do not use Romani in church, at first people usually say that that is what they are used to. In church, people have learned how to pray, read the Bible, and preach in Romanian. As a result, it is difficult for people to do any religious practices in Romani, as illustrated by the following quotation:

> "I can't pray in Romani. Sometimes at home I start praying in Romani and then I say, God, please forgive me, I don't know what to say, and then I continue in Romanian." (Personal communication, Roma lady, sixty-three years old)

But when one looks more closely, the notions of shame and honor appear as important components of language attitude. Several people told me that some time ago some people used to preach and pray in Romani. They were told by their pastor to stop doing that, and to practice preaching and praying in Romanian instead. The reason they were given was that when a Romanian comes to church, everything needs to be in Romanian, and if they are not able to preach and pray well in Romanian they will make fools of themselves.

The following interaction shows the importance of shame in language choice: One day I was walking home from the market with a friend. My friend met someone she knew and they started talking. They started talking in Romani, but when the man noticed that I was listening in, he switched to Romanian. My friend asked another question in Romani, the man answered in Romani and then switched back again to Romanian, saying: *Mi-e rusine fața de doamna* [I am ashamed because of the lady], and he continued in Romanian. He thought I was Romanian and did not know that I speak Romani, so he was ashamed to speak Romani in front of me, even though I was not participating in the conversation. This could also be seen as a way to show respect—it is seen as not respectful to speak a language that is not understood by others. It often happens to me, that although people know I speak Romani and speak Romani most of the time when I am in the village, they still refuse to speak to me in Romani. I think this is because they do not know me well, and they want to show me respect by speaking Romanian to me. It could also be a way to relate to outsiders. If a person is not Roma, they do not feel comfortable speaking in Romani to them.

Another instance of somebody avoiding speaking Romani because of shame was during a watermelon-selling trip. When we were at the market selling watermelons, one man said to a woman that she should not speak Romani any more. Otherwise, the Romanians may not want to buy their watermelons. He was trying to avoid the stigma of an unreliable gypsy, by using the language of the majority.

Closely connected with the issue of shame is that of prestige. It is seen as something prestigious or honorable if you can speak Romanian well. A lady answered the question "what does *gayikanes* (the language of the *gajo*, non-Roma people, in this case Romanian) mean to you?' as follows:

> "We are proud that we can also speak Romanian, because also the *gajo* (non-Roma people) can speak it, not just us."

People who speak Romanian well are elevated to a higher social status. These people usually play an important function in bridging the gap between Roma and Romanians. For example, they will present the needs of the Roma to the local government, or may lead a group of people in the workplace. This shows the role of the different languages in shaping people's social identity (see Fuller 2007). Many Roma people are aware that if their children do not speak Romanian well, they might suffer at school. Many are aware that if a child is to do well at school and later in the majority society, knowledge of Romanian is important.

Another point that is often mentioned when I speak to people about their language is that they say they do not speak the original Romani. Romani has been in contact with Romanian for a long time. This is similar to what Pratt (1991:34) calls a "contact zone," where two languages meet "in contexts of highly asymmetrical relations of power." As a result, the Romani speakers from Sadova use many Romanian loanwords and Romanian structures. Also, people use a lot of code-switching. One reason why people use code-switching is to quote Romanian people or quote from books written in Romanian. Sometimes people first say something in Romani and then repeat it in Romanian; this could be for emphasis. When they speak with me, it could be that they are trying to make sure that I understand what they meant, but they also do it when they speak to each other. The use of loanwords and code-switching has led me to believe that people do not see a clear boundary between their two languages, but it seems from the questionnaire that most people do consider the difference between the two languages to be important.

One woman had said that she felt more freedom when she spoke in Romani, even though she can speak Romanian very well. Part of the reason may be that when she speaks Romani, she can also use the Romanian words, so she can say it in whatever language it comes to her first. However, when she speaks Romanian, she can only use the Romanian words, so she needs to filter all the Romani words from her speech.[5]

17.7.3 Language attitudes

The Romanian language is the official language and also the higher status language in Romania. Romani is seen as inferior, partly because the speakers of Romani are seen as inferior. This was also evident from the responses to the questionnaire concerning problems in the situation of the Roma people. These responses reflected the stereotypes held about Roma by the majority culture: Roma people steal, lie, and are not honest.

However, all the respondents of the questionnaire stated that Romani is important for them and that part of being Roma is to speak Romani. People also said that they like their language and they consider their language important enough to pass on to their children. It seems that those who were interviewed and observed had a deeper connection with Romani than with Romanian, saying that they only learned Romanian out of necessity, because as a citizen of Romania it is important to speak the national language. Only one woman identified herself as also being Romanian. Judging from this, people have a positive view of their language, and one would think that people would prefer all communication to be in Romani, because that is the language with which they most strongly identify. However, in a conversation from a year ago with a young woman who grew up in Italy, she told me that she thought her language was not beautiful and that the Italian language was better. Another man told me that he did not like Romani, and preferred to speak Romanian. He said that the reason for this was that his mother was Romanian. As Romaine (2013:317) noted: "It is very important not to confuse attitude with behavior." The woman and the man who had a negative view of their language seemed to use Romani on just as many occasions as the people who had a positive view of their language.

---

[5] See Son, chapter 7 this volume, for another interpretation of this kind of language behavior as trans-languaging—the use of all of one's linguistic resources without regard to the boundaries of "named languages"—also connected with the notion of freedom.

Considering the three concepts that are related to attitude: feelings, beliefs and behavior (see Coronel-Molina 2009:9), many people show a positive feeling toward their language, considering it their mother tongue, the language that they speak best, and have the strongest relationship with. Feelings of both pride and shame are connected with this language. As for beliefs, they relate this language to their ethnicity, and that a Roma person should speak Romani. Because people of their ethnicity usually have a lower social status, the language is also often considered as having a lower status than the national language. This makes people consider the language inappropriate in certain situations—it is seen as inappropriate, shameful, or strange in some domains.

17.7.4 Identity

In the last question of the questionnaire, I expected that people would say that they wanted to be less discriminated against, that they would like to have more possibilities to find a job, or that they wanted to be more affluent. Instead, almost all of the respondents talked about the negative character of the Roma people that needed to change. This could also have been caused by the way the question was phrased. The points they mentioned were all similar to the stereotypes that are assigned to them by non-Roma people, like stealing, credibility, and education level. This point is connected with the shame that some Roma feel in using their language in front of non-Roma people, which points toward a feeling of inferiority. The feeling of inferiority that many Roma people have towards their ethnicity and their language is also reflected in the pride that some people have in being able to speak a non-Roma language. People can enhance their social position by speaking Romanian very well.

However, people do show pride in their language. The Romani language seems more influential for people's identity than the non-Roma language. There was one man who told me that he did not consider Romani or Romanian important for his identity. He said that he speaks both of these languages just as well and that he did not have a preference for either language. However, it seems that most of the respondents to the questionnaire do see a clear difference between the two languages, and see Romani as their own language, while Romanian is the language they speak out of necessity.

One can see that language choice is a tool to influence one's position in society: prestige, showing respect, and doing better in school are reasons for people to use Romanian. Signaling social belonging to the Roma ethnicity is an important reason to speak Romani. Although people say that they have a positive attitude toward their language, it is visible in the way they talk about themselves that people actually have a combination of pride and shame when it comes to their ethnicity and the use of their language. Language choice is a tool for influencing identity, and at the same time, one's identity is an important reason for language choice.

17.8 Implications for language development work

Many Roma people see Romanian as the language of outsiders, and some even claim that they have been forced to learn it. However, most of them see the benefit of using Romanian and respect the language because it helps them to get along in society. Because of the prestige Romanian has, it is the preferred language in many domains.

So in some domains, like the written domain, Roma people will prefer Romanian over Romani. Attempts to implement Romani at schools have not been successful in Sadova, because there is no teacher available who wants to teach Romani. The fact that nobody is willing to become a teacher in Romani, and that no efforts are made to make this possible, points to a disinclination on the part of Roma people.

People can feel insecure and limited if they are in a situation where they are allowed to speak only one language, because in their home situation people make extensive use of code-switching or trans-languaging. It would be helpful to allow people to use trans-languaging in a learning situation (like schools and churches) so that they can use their whole repertoire while learning new things (see Son chapter 7 this volume). The fact that these Roma people use many loanwords and often switch to Romanian while speaking Romani, does not mean that they disrespect their language. They still clearly identify with their language and see a clear boundary between the situations where you can use both Romani and Romanian and the situations where you can use only Romanian.

The results from this research do show that Romani is important for the identity formation of people; however, it also shows that people's language behavior does not always mirror their language attitudes. This mismatch is influenced by social factors that determine which language is appropriate in which situations. To understand these social factors better, more research needs to be done on how the notions of honor and shame influence people's choices.

For language development work to be successful, the focus of the language development work should not be on one language only, but on the whole linguistic repertoire of the people in focus. Future research feeding into language development work should include more participation from the community, so that their needs can be met in a more adequate way.

References

Allport, Gordon W. 1935. *Handbook of social psychology*. Worcester, MA: Clark University Press.
Bourdieu, Pierre. 1991. *Language and symbolic power*. Cambridge, MA: Harvard University Press.
Bucholtz, Mary, and Kira Hall. 2005. Identity and interaction: A sociocultural linguistic approach. *Discourse Studies* 7(4–5):585–614.
Bucholtz, Mary, and Kira Hall. 2010. Locating identity in language. In Carmen Llamas and Dominic Watt (eds.), *Language and identities*, 18–28. Edinburgh: Edinburgh University Press.
Coronel-Molina, Serafin M. 2009. *Definitions and critical literature review of language attitude, language choice and language shift: Samples of language attitude surveys*. Monograph (2009). Bloomington: Indiana University. scholarworks.iu.edu/dspace/bitstream/handle/2022/3785/Definitions-Critical-Review-of-Topics-in-Sociolinguistics.pdf/.
DeWalt, Kathleen M., and Billie R. DeWalt. 2011. *Participant observation: A guide for fieldworkers*. Second edition. Lanham, MD: AltaMira.
Edwards, John. 2013. Bilingualism and multilingualism: Some central concepts. In Tej K. Bhatia and William C. Ritchie (eds.), *The handbook of bilingualism*, 5–25. Malden, MA: Blackwell.
Fishman, Joshua A. 1965. Who speaks what language to whom and when? *La Linguistique* 1(2):67–88.

Fishman, Joshua A. 1972. Domains and the relationship between micro- and macrosociolinguistics. In John J. Gumperz and Dell Hymes (eds.), *Directions in sociolinguistics: The ethnography of communication*, 435–453. New York: Holt, Rinehart and Winston.

Fuller, Janet M. 2007. Language choice as a means of shaping identity. *Journal of Linguistic Anthropology* 17(1):105–129.

Gumperz, John J. 1964. Linguistic and social interaction in two communities. *American Anthropologist* 66.6(2):137–153.

Halwachs, Dieter W. 2012. Romani teaching: Some general considerations based on model cases. *European Yearbook of Minority Issues* 9:249–269.

Joseph, John E. 2010. Identity. In Carmen Llamas and Dominic Watt (eds.), *Language and identities*, 9–17. Edinburgh: Edinburgh University Press.

Klimovitz, Christopher. 2015. *The Roma of Romania: What's in a name? A stakeholder assessment on constitutional identity*. Glenside, PA: Center for Global Studies, Arcadia University.

Morgan, John J. B. 1934. *Keeping a sound mind*. New York: Macmillan.

Peirce, Bonny Norton. 1997. Language, identity, and the ownership of English. *TESOL Quarterly* 31(3):409–429.

Pratt, Mary L. 1991. The art of the contact zone. *Profession* 33–40.

Romaine, Suzanne. 2013. The bilingual and multilingual community. In Tej K. Bhatia and William C. Ritchie (eds.), *The handbook of bilingualism*, 489–512. Malden, MA: Blackwell.

Sridhar, Kamal K. 1996. Societal multilingualism. In Sandra Lee McKay and Nancy H. Hornberger (eds.), *Sociolinguistics and language teaching*, 47–70. Cambridge: Cambridge University Press.

Tang, Cecilia. 1997. The identity of the nonnative ESL teacher on the power and status of nonnative ESL teachers. *TESOL Quarterly* 31(3):577–580.

Taufe'ulungaki, 'Ana Maui. 1994. Language community attitudes and their implications for the maintenance and promotion of the Tongan language. *Directions* 16:84–108.

Thompson, John B. 1991. Editor's introduction. In Pierre Bourdieu, *Language and symbolic power*, 1–31. Cambridge, MA: Harvard University Press.

18
Ethnolinguistic Landscapes of Madagascar: Surviving a Century of Erosive Language Policies

Leoni Bouwer

Abstract. The aim of this paper is to sketch some views of the multilingual language ecology of Madagascar. It stresses the importance of understanding the ethnolinguistic and language choice realities from the reported perspective of insiders, in the hope that it may contribute credible perspective for decision makers, developers, and investors on the role of language—many of them facing significant failure in the sectors of education, church, legislation and environmental matters. It proposes an analysis of the language use situation in terms of Ethnolinguistic Identity Theory (ELIT) and suggests that any innovation and development effort which bypasses the insider view and the language identity of the individuals affected is likely to be less successful than it could be.

18.1 Imagine the scene

Island. Lush. Green. Efficiently supporting an amazing diversity of life. Where elephant birds graze, dwarf hippopotami dream in the waters, and reptiles abound—from crocodiles in mighty rivers to the tiniest chameleon and a stunning miniature frog on a branch. Primates (lemurs), birds and BIRDS, and rainforest and spiny forest, venerable giants holding court, sounds and smells, spices, textures, color, and space. Ready to receive humans into her heart under the sun.

Elsewhere, in Southeast Asia, population growth, demographic pressure and ancient seafaring-trader lifestyles push successive migrations of Austronesian peoples to Madagascar, starting around the time of the birth of Christ. People to whom the ocean had never been a barrier. Who settled and were nurtured by the island where they multiplied and established themselves as the *tompon-tany* 'lords/owners of the land'.

Semitic seafarers passed by, in pre-Islamic times, and some of these stayed. Subsequent Arabic migrants brought Islam, and are particularly remembered for bringing a way to write, called *Sorabe*, used to record important information about origins, astrology, and medicine in Arabic script; some seventeenth century manuscripts have been preserved to this day. Arabs brought African slaves (the Makoa and others) who were later liberated and became integrated with the

Malagasy. Other Asians came. European seafarers passed by—Portuguese, Dutch, Scandinavian, English, French. Slave traders came—European, Swahili, Arabic. They took away unknown numbers of Malagasy into slavery. The ethnic landscape today consists of eighteen officially recognized ethnic groups (see map 1).

A few Catholic missionaries came sporadically pre- and post-Reformation. Among these were Lazarists, who translated a Catechism into the Tanôsy [txy] language on the east coast in 1657. Then Protestant English missionaries arrived in the nineteenth century, riding on the colonial efforts of Great Britain. These missionaries successfully produced a Bible translation and school materials, facilitating great empowerment for one particular people group of Madagascar, the Merina of the central plateau (see map 1).

Map 1. Ethnic groups of Madagascar

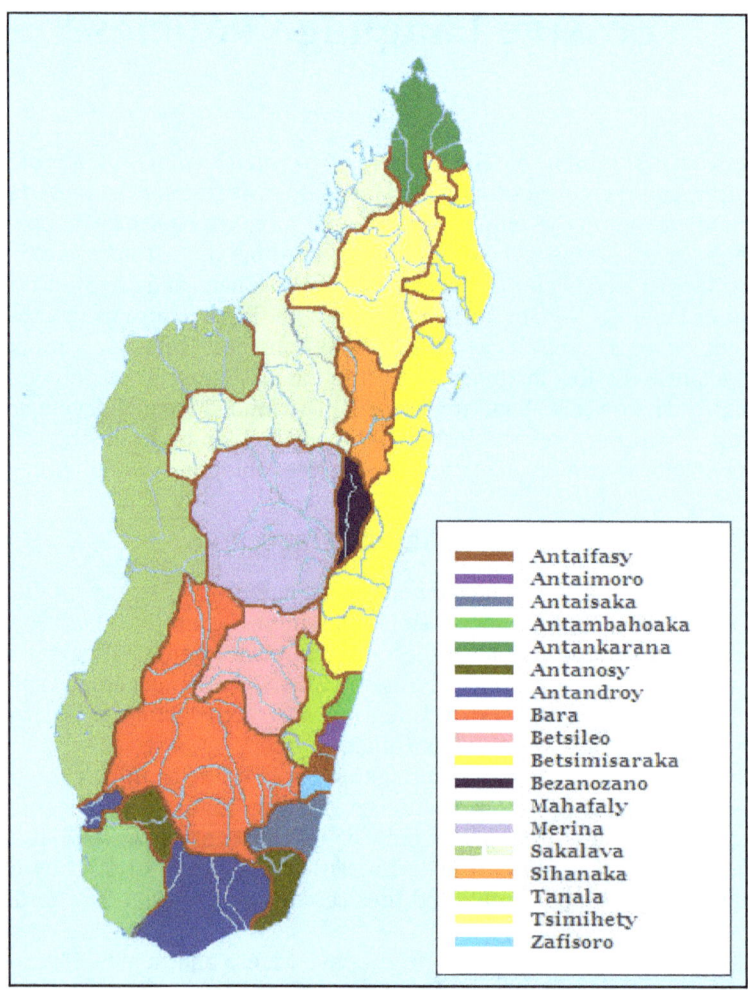

© 2010. Lemurbaby. From Wikimedia Commons, used under CC BY-SA 3.0 license. commons.wikimedia.org/wiki/File:Ethnic_groups_of_Madagascar_Map.png/

The ambitious Merina King Radama was recognised as king of Madagascar (Radama I) by the emissaries of the Kingdom of Great Britain. The historically older Sakalava Kingdom of the west coast of Madagascar and the Betsimisaraka Kingdom of the east coast, and numerous smaller entities with their own system of governance and way of life, local languages, and needs were not considered significant to the endeavor. Severe persecution of Christians followed soon after the death of Radama in 1828, even as the first Merina Bibles came off the press, and lasted for most of the rule of more than three decades of his successor, Queen Ranavalona I. Religious freedom returned after her death. The Merina conquests of Madagascar continued.

Norwegian and other Scandinavian missionaries soon joined the English, contributing significantly and consistently to the spread of Protestant Christianity in Madagascar, to education, research and documentation. Catholics also started schools and did their own Bible translation and research, recording valuable information about Madagascar and supporting French influence across the island in opposition to the Protestant English. Part of this heritage is how the name of Jesus was translated and how different versions of this name resulted in different Christian identities today. Each wave of development during the nineteenth century and each new foreign involvement continued to implement and impose this dominant language of the Hauts Plateaux region, the missionary-standardized form of Merina Malagasy—apparently without imagining the need to acknowledge or develop other varieties of Malagasy.

The Merina Kingdom of the central plateau, empowered by Great Britain, continued making inroads to subdue more of Madagascar under its flag and even the Christianization of the island was openly likened to *Tafika Masina* 'Holy War'. Merina dominance and influence was most successfully expanded to the other peoples of the central plateau, the Vakinankaratra and the Betsileo, but was also imposed on a number of other groups. France, which had gained and lost small territories in Madagascar since the sixteenth century, became a strong factor towards the end of the nineteenth century, succeessfully colonizing Madagascar in 1896. All these factors set the scene for modern Malagasy language matters and for deep conflict in the domain of language policies. The historical layer of colonialism created new problems in Malagasy society and accentuated existing ones, none of which were necessarily resolved by the subsequent achievement of independence, judging by how much economic and political influence the previous colonial power still has in postindependence Madagascar.

18.2 Language development in Madagascar

During the sixty years prior to independence in 1960, the Merina government lost their ruling power to a French administration, but not their position of domination. Their language, standardized through the Bible translation of the 1820s and taught in schools, continues in its dominance to this day as the language of government, school, and church. It has become the face of indigenous language in Madagascar, even assuming the role of "national mother tongue" vis-à-vis French. Being the only Malagasy language variety to have been standardized, the assumption became embedded that Merina Malagasy [plt], which became "Official Malagasy," is the only language in Madagascar that is called "Malagasy." Foreigners have not always understood that the term Malagasy is used generically, describing anything or anyone that is "of Madagascar" (similar to the generic terms African or Japanese or Indian)—for instance, Malagasy language(s), Malagasy economy, the Malagasy people. To "be" Malagasy means to be an indigenous person or a national from Madagascar. To "speak" Malagasy means that one is a mother-tongue speaker of a language variety of Madagascar or has learned a language variety of Madagascar.

Standardized Merina, institutionalised as Official Malagasy, remains inadequately accessible to much of the population outside the Hauts Plateaux region. Empirical studies show poor proficiency in and understanding of Official Malagasy (Bouwer 2003). This language hegemony partly results from a strong Merina backlash to French colonialism, leading to the powerful ethic of unity-no-matter-what, and partly is due to lack of means and motivation to invest in developing every regional language variety for the benefit of native speakers of the respective regions.

The possibility of experiencing greater Malagasy unity by acknowledging the regional diversity of Madagascar seems to be conceptually irreconcilable with the political ideology of unity. This has led to a subsequent devaluing of the significance and implications of language variation, and, with a lack of consideration of empirical evidence, to the detriment of development and education. Diversity has not been democratized in Madagascar.

Giles and Johnson (1987:95) hold the perspective that

> a society which supports an ideology of cultural and social diversity encourages the development of bicultural individuals who can participate in the activities of more than one ethnic group while still maintaining their ethnic identity.

To the contrary, the ideology of unity or "unicity" still generally dictates the focus of governance and language research in Madagascar. Malagasy linguist Tsimilaza writes that refusing to admit to the diversity of Malagasy is refusing to study how language functions and is a denial of the very object of linguistic study:

> The dialectal variations of Malagasy should be considered for their intrinsic value. ... Support of the unity of the Malagasy language, for example, should not result in the mopping up of dialectal variations, in particular that of the concrete implementation of the respective languages. ... It is feared that linguistic fragmentation will lead to political fragmentation. ... It seems therefore that Malagasy linguistics, especially concerning dialectology, aims to blur differences to protect unity. ... We believe that such an attitude is unscientific. (Tsimilaza 1992:35–36, personal translation)

An empirical study of language attitudes, language choice, language use, intelligibility factors, and proficiency in Official Malagasy (Bouwer 2003) reports evidence of strong ethnolinguistic vitality among the diverse language communities around the island. The study suggests that the official position on Malagasy language unity is exaggerated and does not acknowledge the significance of variation in Malagasy society and language. The official view holds that Official Malagasy (the standardized Merina language of the Hauts Plateaux region, developed and promoted by missionaries of the nineteenth century) is the optimum medium of communication for all Malagasy citizens in all salient domains. The ideology of government that Official Malagasy is the language of all Malagasy people, and that everyone in Madagascar understands it and is able to use it effectively, was never based on empirical research. It lives on largely as a received policy, as an enforced viewpoint, the validity of which is rarely questioned, especially among the ruling population of a certain age.

The ethnolinguistic vitality of Official Malagasy cannot be denied: it has status, institutional support, and demographic support, but remains limited in where it is effectively used—not enjoying insider status outside of its immediate power base of the central plateau where most people understand and speak it and identify it as their language. Official Malagasy can be viewed as the successful and accepted language of wider communication of the central plateau of Madagascar and of governmental institutions across the island. In spite of being a national language, it does not enjoy the function of language of choice outside of its region of origin. Outside the plateau area, it is acknowledged as having power, but is regarded with suspicion and as foreign in every local context investigated across more than twenty other regions (Bouwer 2003).

Even where understanding is required in order to develop, process, reason, and respond, this language of the central plateau, Official Malagasy, has been maintained for multiple generations as the only language of education except for French (Babault 2006; Clignet and Ernst 1995; Koerner 1999; Schmidt 1997). The intrusive events of the nineteenth and twentieth centuries have caused a dichotomy of response to communication and to governmental institutions. All that is communicated in and that functions through Official Malagasy and French—namely, in church, school, the legal system, health system, and government—is tolerated as foreign, nonessential and potentially threatening to the life of local communities. While all minority peoples are familiar with these institutions, they mainly live in and are sustained by their own trusted traditional belief systems, their traditional legal system, their traditional ways of transferring knowledge, and their traditional local economies— all of these domains expressed through their mother-tongue varieties (Bouwer 2003). Much-needed development in education, administration, health, environment, and other domains is perceived to be foreign by the targeted grassroots constituency because it is communicated in an outsider language. The default response to perceived intrusion among the receptor communities seems to be conservatism, holding on to the safety and familiarity of the traditional ways.

The other dominant language of the island is French [fra], with which most Malagasy have a love-hate relationship, but which has been in a continuous duel and duet with Official Malagasy for the primary role in education in Madagascar. French is significantly more foreign than Official Malagasy to the majority of Malagasy people and is often incompetently taught and inadequately assimilated by learners, so that Madagascar is far from functionally francophone in daily practice. (Some attempts have been made over the years to bring English [eng] into more prominence as there is need of international languages, but this has never succeeded.) French is not only the most politically powerful foreign language in Madagascar, but is also powerfully linked with the Malagasy economy. Various Indian and other Asian languages are used in Madagascar, but are limited to the Asian (*Karana* "Indian" and *Sinoa* "Chinese") communities. Some pockets of Swahili [swh] speakers and Comorian speakers are found, particularly in the West. Some Arabic [acq] is used, especially in religious contexts.

18.3 Language ecology

Ecolinguistic theorists (Nettle and Romaine 2000; Michalopoulos 2011; and others) show that the greatest ethnolinguistic diversity is found where difficult terrain makes contact problematic and rare. Madagascar certainly qualifies as difficult terrain, an ecological contributor to linguistic diversity.

The island supports a unique ecology of multilingualism, but has been widely described as monolingual for a number of reasons, and by a variety of authors. Since the first contact of Europeans with the island and particularly since the nineteenth century, the tendency has been to underestimate linguistic variation. Language diversity in Madagascar had been mentioned sporadically since the sixteenth century, but not described in any detail apart from a few isolated cases. Language has typically been dealt with as if every visitor anywhere in Madagascar encounters one and the same language or as if the language encountered in Antananarivo is the same language spoken everywhere else on the island. Missionaries and colonial agents, nevertheless, have collected data on a number of Malagasy language varieties, preserved for the most part in archives located in Madagascar, Mauritius, England, France, and Norway (e.g., Richardson 1877).

Vérin, Kottak, and Gorlin (1969) did a glottochronological study for archeological research and found that Malagasy varieties have a percentage of cognates with Official Malagasy ranging between 61% (e.g., for Ntandroy, a southern variety, and for Sakalava, a western variety) and 92% (for Betsileo, a plateau variety). Bouwer (2003) did extensive lexicostatistic studies and found similar results, incorporating a larger selection of language varieties.

Research indicates that around twenty significant language varieties exist around Madagascar today with multiple variations of each (Vérin, Kottak, and Gorlin 1969; Bouwer 2003) (see map 2). Doctoral- and Masters-level linguistic studies have been written or are in progress on numerous varieties of Malagasy languages, including: Bara (Rabenilaina 1983), Masikoro (Erasmus 2015), Northern Betsimisaraka (O'Neill 2015), Northern Sakalava (Thomas-Fattier 1982), Ntandroy (Ratsima 1981), Sakalava (Bare-Thomas 1976), Sihanaka (Ranjivason 1985), Southern Betsimisaraka (Dez 1960), Tsimihety (Tsimilaza 1981), and many more. The anthropological and ethnological studies on the diverse identities of Madagascar are also very numerous.

Map 2. Languages of Madagascar

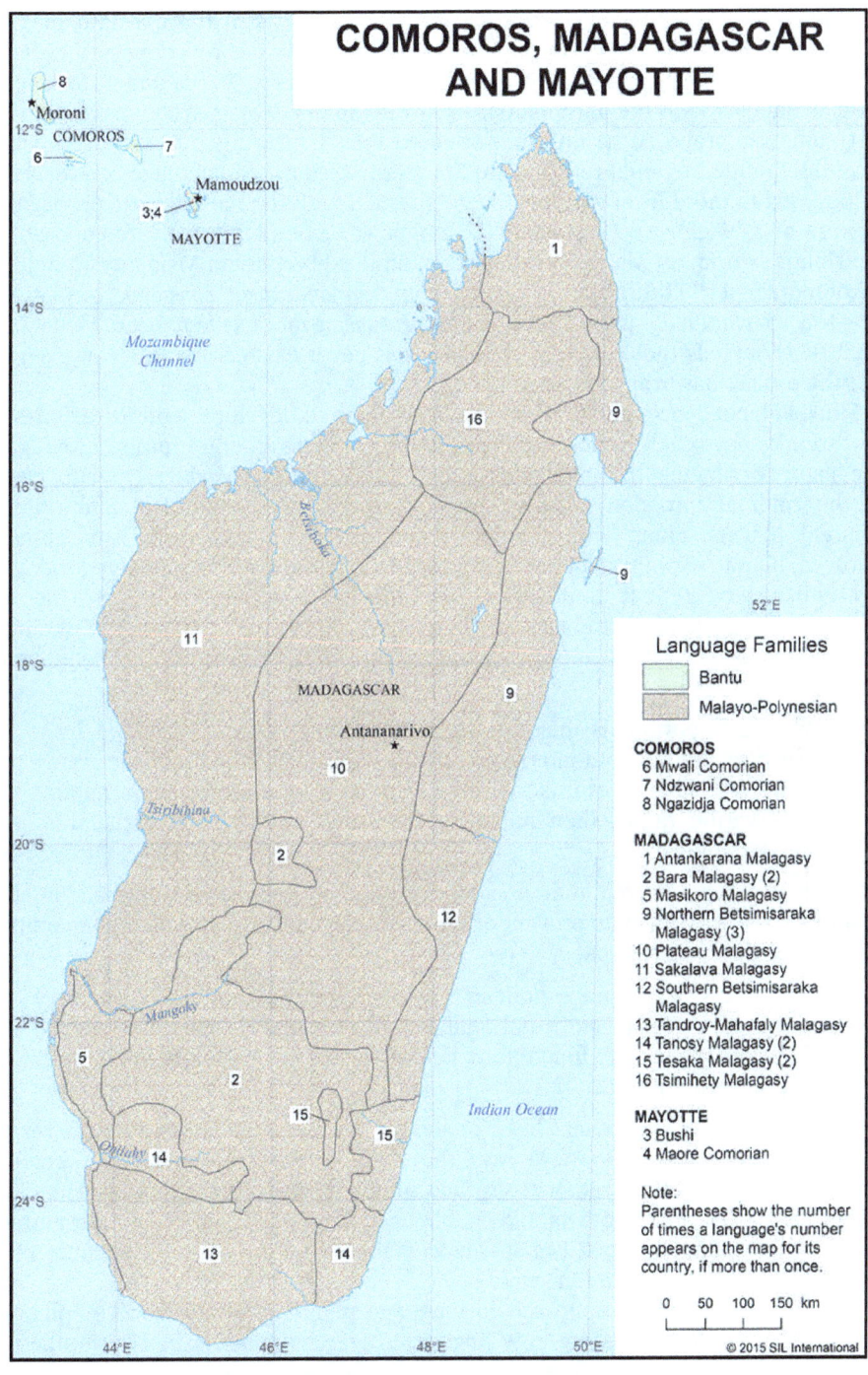

Ironically, it was the French colonial government that first positively acknowledged a distinction between Official Malagasy, the standardized Merina language, and "other dialects" of Madagascar. They decreed twice during their rule that children would initially be taught in their mother tongue (as opposed to Official Malagasy) and slowly be brought into French so that they could learn through that medium (Schmidt 1997). This policy may partly be blamed for the reactionary legislation during the postindependence Malagasization period of the 1970s and 1980s, when Official Malagasy was the only standardized version of a Malagasy language (Merina) that could be proposed as an alternative to French. During this Marxist-Socialist Second Republic, regional reactions to Standard Merina as a language of instruction (as opposed to more local varieties) were quashed with the nationalistic propaganda promise of a "*Malagasy Iombonana*" (a language to be deliberately "composed" of contributions from all Malagasy "dialects"), an ideal "Common Malagasy" language. Rakotondrabe (1993:38) states "*Ce que tout le monde peut constater, c'est que ce malgache commun n'a pas vu le jour, et l'on peut même dire que le projet a été perdu de vue.*" [It is obvious that common Malagasy has never existed and one can even say that the project has dropped out of sight.]

Since independence, no attention has been given to developing other varieties for education or any other purposes, politically minoritizing all other forms of Malagasy. The history of nineteenth century missionary intervention in Madagascar, superseded by the colonial intrusion, against the background of the political ambitions of different players, along with the interacting linguistic and social environments involved, help to explain the underlying conflicts that are still not resolved today.

Mühlhäusler (2002:4) emphasizes that language planning should provide "the support system needed to sustain (language) diversity," that would maintain "cooperative rather than competitive links with a wide variety of other languages." He says:

> What is important is that the diversity of languages is sustained by a structured habitat and interrelationships with other inhabitants. In trying to preserve languages it is therefore important to concentrate on habitat preservation rather than narrowly focussing on the empowerment of individual languages.

Mühlhäusler points out that one of the hidden agendas of political language planning has always been to prevent or reduce social conflict by reducing the number of languages. He stresses that

> the success of language policies has been greatly limited by the very notion of a nation and a national language itself. Nations may not be ideal habitats for any functioning language ecology, certainly not nations in a modern sense. (2002:12)

Joshua Fishman and others have analysed the factor of nationhood in respect to language. Fishman (1968:44) says that "the distinctions made . . . between sociocultural integration (nationalism) and political integration (nationism) and the successive transitions of both should enable us to examine the internal, intranational consequences of multilingualism in the developing nation as well as some of its external, international consequences."

A language ecological approach to language planning would involve "planning for diversity"—"understanding how linguistic diversity is structured" (Mühlhäusler 2002:13) without creating (more) conflict. In the case of Malagasy this approach would imply freeing up the harmonious diversity of language systems in Madagascar which would positively affect the preservation of the very threatened natural environment. In harmony with the Whorfian premise that, "We dissect nature along lines laid down by our native languages" (Whorf 1956:213–214), Mühlhäusler (2002:5) evokes the two-way relationship between language and environment and poses the question of "to what extent the well-being of the habitat depends on the well-being of the languages spoken therein." He argues that "the diversity of languages [is] a vast repository of accumulated knowledge about the environment and environmental management." From a preservation perspective it would thus be important to preserve each different "world view" as it is represented by a particular "language."

While Madagascar is known for its diversity, recent satellite footage shows how illicit logging and dubious agricultural methods have already destroyed 90% of the indigenous forest. If the human, linguistic, and natural ecologies of Madagascar can be managed as the valuable assets that they are, the tragic erosion might be halted and partially reversed, even at this late stage (Kaufman 2018).

18.4 Sociolinguistics and language policies in Madagascar

Language policies during the colonial period, continuing since independence, have been very unstable for early learners (primary school) and for most of school education in Madagascar, switching back and forth between French and Official Malagasy as medium of instruction. Teachers of the 1990s had to teach using French, a language in which they were not at all competent (Koerner 1999), because their own education took place during the era of Malagasization, when French was out of favor in this domain.

There has been a moderate interest in Malagasy academic circles about how sociolinguistic theory and empirical study could inform the case of Malagasy language realities. Some Malagasy work seeks application in the area of language policies, but still strongly holds to the "one nation, one language" paradigm. But Rabenoro and Rajaonarivo (1997), in their practical and well-reasoned sociolinguistic paper, recognize that all Malagasy varieties should be considered when language of education is planned. They also touch on the problem of misunderstanding the language situation because of partial information and erroneous assumptions on the part of foreign parties. The same misconception unfortunately rules within Madagascar: the one standardized variety of Malagasy (the Merina variety) is assumed to be *the* language of Madagascar. All the other language varieties of Madagascar are then called dialects, giving the impression of there being a spoken language called "Malagasy" along with minority dialects of that language.

> It is customary to call "language" what is actually varieties of a language—socially or geographically. It is the variety with an official status, perceived by foreigners as the only language of a country, which usually benefits from the category "language" while the remaining language varieties are qualified as "dialects," "variants," or "varieties." (Rabenoro and Rajaonarivo 1997:1, personal translation)

Their paper is a somewhat refreshing and less biased treatment of the subject of language in Madagascar, and needs to be relaunched into the public discourse after being forgotten for twenty years. The field of sociolinguistics yields some actionable understanding of the particular case of multilingualism found in Madagascar, where a number of related language varieties vitally coexist but only one of these has been developed for official use and for education. This situation has not been optimally successful for development, because of many factors, including the inadequate understanding of the dominant variety in areas outside of its main constituency.

18.5 Diglossia

Multilingualism in Madagascar could be described as a case of diglossia, by adapting the concept to the particularities of its situation. Ferguson's description (1959) works for understanding numerous stable bilingual situations in the world, where the High prestige variety and the Low prestige variety are two divergent forms of the same language, as in the case of Switzerland with High German [deu] and Swiss German [gsw]. "Diglossia" to Ferguson refers to more than some standard form with its dialects, because typically in this view the High variety is never used in ordinary conversation. Joshua Fishman (1967) expanded the definition of diglossia to cover situations in which the High and Low varieties used within a community are unrelated languages. He distinguishes clearly between *bilingualism*, which is the use of two or more languages by an individual, and *diglossia*, which refers to the use of two or more languages within a society for functionally distinct purposes. Fishman expands the term diglossia to refer to both situations of multilingualism at the societal level as well as to the differentiation of functions for each of the languages. Another point stressed by Fishman (1968:45) is that "conscious and even ideologized language differences need not be divisive," as in the case of diglossia, where a single society recognizes two or more languages as their own, each with its own domains. Both divisiveness (which can magnify minor differences) and unification (which can minimize or totally ignore major differences) are to him ideologized positions. Thirdly, Fishman (1968:46) points out that "most 'new nations' of Africa and Asia are not yet ethnic nations" and this strengthens the value of his diglossic approach. A problem arises with these views of diglossia when considering less stable language situations, like those in Spain (with Spanish [spa] and Catalan [cat]) or in Haiti (with French and Haitian Creole [hat]) or with most postcolonial African language situations. Madagascar is one such case where the diglossia is unstable because of unresolved underlying conflicts.

Brann (1990) proposes the term "triglossia," for such postcolonial situations, where speakers use an official language (the foreign imposition) and a local language of wider communication for public domains (a national imposition) and an ethnic variety for insider domains and intimacy (my interpretation). This is somewhat helpful for understanding a case like Madagascar, where language conflict remains threefold, between French and Official Malagasy and both with the various "dialects," prestige depending on the domains of use. Official views of the language use situation in Madagascar have usually been unrepresentative of the true regional reality, due to the political imposition of Official Malagasy and French as rival High status languages.

Numerous authors have struggled to apply models of diglossia to situations under study. Babault (2006:35–36) mentions Philippe Gardy (1985) who formulated the term "diglossic complex" to represent the multiple diglossic functions that can be found in language communities. Babault describes the case of Madagascar as a "diglossic complex … characterised by a latent instability, due to an undeniable dimension of conflict."

Malagasy linguist Michel Rambelo (1981:15) attempted to apply diglossia theory to the Madagascar situation by interviewing Malagasy speakers on their preference of language medium for radio programs they listen to. His study suggests that a dual diglossia exists in Madagascar in many situations, which to him consists of, on the one hand, Official Malagasy (OM) versus French (F), and on the other hand, OM and F versus the local dialect (D). He found that in Madagascar, where the French language (F) was imposed and coexists with Official Malagasy (OM) and the regional dialects (D), preference and status of language varies according to the situation and function. In a diagram, he shows the relative prestige relationships to be as follows:

Either	F > OM > D	(in rural areas, among illiterates)
Or	OM = F > D	(in rural areas, among illiterates)
Or	OM > F > D	(in urban areas, among the politicized middle class)
Or	D > OM > F	(in purely rural, traditional contexts, where one D variety has H status above the rest)

Both French and Official Malagasy are outsider languages of literacy. Among rural illiterates, there are differences in perceptions of status, depending on the exposure in the region to the competing dominant languages. The above schema summarizes the status assigned to the different languages in Madagascar, and also hints at the attitudes encountered towards the language varieties available to Malagasy speakers.

We have found in situations of prolonged participant observation and from responses to language attitude interviews, that in rural Madagascar, the ranking relationship is own D to neighboring D for ingroup communication, as against OM, F, and all other languages—with everything not one's own language being viewed as foreign, suspect, and far away. Malagasy speakers often accommodate the status quo by displaying appropriate attitudes of cooperativeness, a respect which does not show in practice. A rural community might agree with an official delegation that "it is a good thing not to burn the mountain flank," but in practice they have no intention to obey.

While the Madagascar situation does not fully satisfy standard diglossia models, valuable additional perspectives might be found through an Ethnolinguistic Identity Theory (ELIT) evaluation of the language situation of Madagascar.

18.6 Views of ethnicity, ethnolinguistic vitality, and Ethnolinguistic Identity Theory

Joshua Fishman (1980:16) understands ethnicity to be

> rightly understood as an aspect of a collectivity's self-recognition as well as an aspect of its recognition in the eyes of outsiders. Ethnic recognition differs from other kinds of group-embedded recognition in that it operates basically in terms of paternity rather than in terms of patrimony and exegesis thereupon.

To Fishman ethnicity rests on three factors. The first factor is *paternity*, in that language is often seen as a biological inheritance, which explains why language is often regarded as the primary symbol of ethnicity (Fishman 1977:25). The second factor is *patrimony*, which explains the history of ethnic groups and of ethnic membership (1977:20). The third factor is *phenomenology*, which accounts for the interpretation of members of ethnic groups concerning ethnic heritage and ethnic behavior (1977:23).

To Giles, Bourhis, and Taylor (1977:307), "ethnic groups are an example par excellence of linguistic categorization since they are often found to manifest their distinctiveness from each other by means of separate languages and dialects." Mann also names four critical attributes regarding the relationship between ethnicity and language (from Giles and Coupland 1991:96), namely, that language is "a marker of group membership," "an important cue for ethnic categorization," "an emotional dimension of ethnicity," and "a means of facilitating ingroup cohesion." Mann (2000:460) then summarizes ethnicity, language, and intergroup relations as follows:

> every ethnic group usually possesses a language, which is fashioned by and conveys its origins, history, traditions, values and world view; language can be used, and is used, for intergroup distinctiveness (i.e. as a boundary marker); language can serve as a symbol of ethnic identity and loyalty; and the relationship between language and ethnicity is, however, mutable.

Ethnolinguistic vitality is the function of a combination of factors. These have been discussed and summarized by numerous authors. For instance,

> Ethnolinguistic vitality is a group's ability to maintain and protect its existence in time as a collective entity with a distinctive identity and language. It involves continuing intergenerational transmission of a group's language and cultural practices, sustainable demography and active social institutions, social cohesion and emotional attachment to its collective identity. (Ehala 2015:553)

> Ethnolinguistic vitality theory asserts that Status, Demographic, Institutional Support, and Control factors make up the vitality of ethnolinguistic groups. An assessment of a group's strengths and weaknesses in each of these dimensions provides a rough classification of ethnolinguistic groups into those having low, medium, or high vitality. (Yagmur 2011:111)

The Malagasy language communities we have had opportunity to investigate demonstrate most of these vitality factors. In the course of ongoing language assessment in different regions of Madagascar, data was obtained which yields an understanding of ethnolinguistic vitality for those communities (Bouwer 2003). Such findings could provide an unthreatening handle on the conflicted situation of language use in Madagascar, especially for language policy makers. The minority languages of Madagascar are alive and well and are being maintained in their local contexts.

Note that most of the ethnic names in Madagascar were assigned to groups by outsiders. For discerning the role of identity, it is particularly useful to obtain the subjective identities from individuals and groups, rather than to base research findings on the assumed ethnonyms assigned over many years and to which the people themselves have accommodated. Poirier and Dez (1963) found that Malagasy respondents reported adherence to over sixty respective subjective ethnic identities in Madagascar. Unfortunately their study had little impact in an environment of Malagasization. Most literature reports the official opinion that there are eighteen ethnic or cultural groups in Madagascar, which is very much an outsider assessment and simplification of complex realities.

Landry and Allard (1994) investigate the relationship between ethnolinguistic vitality and diglossia. They conclude that, "Ethnolinguistic vitality and diglossia may be incorporated within a single conceptual framework by treating ethnolinguistic vitality predominantly as a between-group effect and diglossia as a withingroup effect" (1994:38).

18.7 Applying Ethnolinguistic Identity Theory to the case of language maintenance in Madagascar

Ethnolinguistic Identity Theory (ELIT) could be a helpful tool to combine with sociolinguistic research as Malagasy policy makers hopefully reconsider their options concerning language planning in Madagascar. ELIT captures language choices as *group beliefs* among individuals who belong to a specific ethnic grouping and is useful for showing up differences in linguistic identity across cultural communities, or ethnicities.

ELIT (Giles and Johnson 1987) is an application to language and a further development of the social identity theory by Tajfel and Turner (1979), who studied intergroup behavior and how we differentiate between ingroup and outgroup and formulate belonging. The research is largely done through interviews and questionnaires. The resulting strategies of language choice and language use demonstrate language attitudes and perceptions of high and low status and affect language maintenance or loss. Giles and Johnson (1987:71) found that an individual's sense of belonging depends on the three variables of perceived vitality, perceived group boundaries, and a small number of group memberships. Social boundaries result from how individuals perceive of and define ingroup and outgroup behavior. Ethnolinguistic belongingness would be stronger in individuals who identify with fewer group memberships.

Giles and Johnson propose that minority ethnic groups with the above-mentioned characteristics would be likely to maintain their ethnolinguistic identity, being deliberate in using their heritage language, demonstrating divergence from the outgroup, and not achieving native-speaker ability in L2. When applied to situations in Madagascar, this is found to be the case in varieties of coastal (that is, non-plateau) Malagasy. Ethnolinguistic identity is definitely strong among the Merina for Official Malagasy (Standardized Merina, Plateau Malagasy) in the Hauts Plateaux region.

As for the first variable of *perceived vitality*, the ethnic identity profiles obtained through the author's research around Madagascar yield a perception of certain vitality. To a discussion question about their opinion concerning the sustainability of their way of speaking ("what would you predict for the future of your language? When your six-year-old has his own children, what language do you think they will speak in their home?"), about 90% of participants indicated with confidence their belief that their language will continue into future generations. When asked about which language(s) parents would like their children to learn at school, they answered *"Ambaniandro"* (name for Official Malagasy in the south) or *"Hova"* (name for Official Malagasy in the north). The reason consistently given was, "Because our children already know their own language." The perception of vitality of their own language was found to be strong in every location interacted with, except in the case of the Southern Betsimisaraka, where participants in the discussions were less hopeful of the longevity of their language. It is being used by all generations, but the persons who raised doubts observed that "Official Malagasy is intruding everywhere and maybe the young people will change" under the pressure. At the same time, reported use of their own language is a given in all domains except school, church liturgy, and government. Notices are done in the mother tongue; when asked why this is, they replied, "So that people will understand."

As for *perceived group boundaries*, they are consistent across ethnolinguistic groupings. Ingroup versus outgroup identification is very strong and specific. Children from mixed marriages identify with the father's identity, regardless of which variety they speak most (e.g., the Bara Zafindravola of the Mikoboka, who often marry Masikoro women, but whose identity is strongly Bara). As for *number of group memberships*, there is generally single group membership with a strong sense of ethnolinguistic belongingness to that group. Thus the three factors in ELIT indicate that minority ethnic groups in Madagascar are likely to maintain their distinct ethnolinguistic identities along with their distinct languages.

There is no institutional support for any Malagasy language variety except the Official Malagasy (standardized Merina), but ingroup support is strong and the reported use and expectation of sustainability is positive. Status factors are not as clear, but Official Malagasy is allocated to very specific domains, holds the status of language of education and is perceived as a threat to the local language. In the northwestern royal village of the Antakarana, it is taboo to speak the Merina (Official Malagasy) language and on the Antakarana island of Nosy Mitsio, Merina people and their language are taboo. For the rest of Madagascar, this distinction is more subtle, but it is always present.

Data obtained through personal and group interviews across ecolinguistic communities outside the central plateau in Madagascar (Bouwer 2003, and unpublished survey work in 2017) indicate that the heritage language or mother tongue remains the encyclopedia Malagasy ethnic communities live by, in that local knowledge and local systems are expressed in local language for communication, for understanding, and for successfully interacting with the environment. In a few cases, the factor of "sustainable demography" has been problematic, as where entire families have moved away from the traditional language area, but social cohesion has usually been retained (e.g., Bara who have lost their village, or Ntandroy who migrate in search of pastures or cash) together with the other factors mentioned previously. Institutional support is local and group-specific: for all important events, religious, and other, mother tongue is used. In some cases this shows even in how dramatically people's lifestyles changed through the intervention of *malaso* "bandits', who caused the displacement of, for example, whole communities of Bara, but that the ethnolinguistic identity remains strongly Bara, regardless of the forced demographic changes to which speakers must accommodate.

Another situation is how prolonged *kere* "famine' in the south has inspired migrations of Ntandroy communities across Madagascar, but they seem to maintain their group identity and language as they also keep village life intact. Atesaka, Betsileo, and Mahafaly people have moved in search of food and income, resettling their villages, sometimes changing their subsistence economy, but maintaining their customs and language. The Mahafaly who are forced further north, outside of their traditional territory, resettle in typical Mahafaly villages but have to find new ways of making a living, so instead of cattle-raisers they become charcoal makers and sellers and such. But, they keep using their own language and they build Mahafaly-style houses. The family tomb remains in the home territory in most cases of community displacement.

18.8 Conclusion

I have tried to sketch here some landscapes of the language ecology of Madagascar. These are healthy outside of official policies and perspectives that do not take care of preserving diversity. Rural life sustains diverse ethnolinguistic identities, but schoolgoers in Madagascar do not have equal access to viable education, even though schools are everywhere and most children attend school, at least for a few years. Speakers of language varieties other than Official Malagasy are disadvantaged in exposure to development and are often harassed and taken advantage of by politicians, police, and military, especially when *taratasy* "paperwork' and *fanjakana* "government' are involved. In matters of justice, people usually rely on their local structures, rather than calling on the authorities, who are called *vazaha* "foreigners'. Much useful information is inaccessible to villagers, because it is often communicated in the Official Malagasy, as in the case of elections and referendums.

There are numerous examples in the literature citing nations where governments faced the inadequate educational policies of their past, and bravely planned to include all ethnolinguistic communities. Nepal is one such example where in 1995, there was an official move towards mother-tongue primary education. Nepal has great ethnolinguistic diversity, with more than 100 languages from four different language families. But having a favorable policy is only part of the story, as the case of Nepal illustrates—rioting, murder, and unrest obscured the application of those plans for more than a decade. The example of language planning problems in Nepal, described by Eagle (1999) and Burnett (2012), and a study of ethnolinguistic identity in Nepal (Sonntag 1995) show similarities with numerous cases in less developed economies of the world. The government of Nepal made bold strides to break away from the philosophy of monolingualism, but in practice education still continues mainly in English and Nepali. Papua New Guinea decided on multilingual education some decades ago (Malone and Paraide 2011). Zimbabwe has moved from "uniting" all Shona dialects into one, to giving official status first to three languages, and then to sixteen languages in the 2013 Constitution, though in practice, the decision to recognize all mother tongues of Zimbabwe has not been fully put into educational practice (Hungwe 2007; Ndlovu 2013). In Madagascar, education policies have mostly avoided the issue of mother-tongue education, keeping the discussion in the arena of French versus Official Malagasy (Dahl et al. 2005).

The mother-tongue debate continues in the economically vulnerable areas of the world. So many things can go wrong—funding, the distraction of a natural disaster, elections—that are detrimental to consistency and sustainability, but there is at least more information available now than two or three decades ago. It seems that in sociolinguistics we keep wrestling with the heritage of colonialism, a form of planned migration of power for economic benefit—the unresolved pain of borders being drawn through the homelands of people exploited by foreign powers. UNESCO's 1960 *Convention against Discrimination in Education*,[1] which declared the universal right to mother-tongue education, has never been universally fulfilled and implemented. In numerous multilingual situations around the globe, mother-tongue education only sporadically reaches the debates and work sessions of politicians, language planners, and educationalists.

---

[1] portal.unesco.org/en/ev.php-URL_ID=12949&URL_DO=DO_TOPIC&URL_SECTION=201.html/

It is hoped that Malagasy government, health care, education, church, and legal institutions would take advantage of empirical evidence and seek to include minority groups around Madagascar in their best interest, respecting their ethnolinguistic communities and values—not solely for the sake of preserving diversity, but rather for the sake of combating the resistance of what is perceived as outsider and foreign, non-essential to survival and prosperity. Likewise, recognizing and accommodating to the linguistic diversity that exists in Madagascar would facilitate greater accessibility to life-enhancing choices and enable all communities to participate in planning the national future. These minority groups account for more than seventy-five percent of the total population of twenty-five million people.

References

Babault, Sophie. 2006. *Langues, école et société à Madagascar: normes scolaires, pratiques langagières, enjeux sociaux* [Languages, school and society in Madagascar: school standards, language practices, social issues]. Paris: L'Harmattan.

Bare-Thomas, Dominique. 1976. Le dialecte Sakalava du Nord-Ouest de Madagascar: Phonologie, grammaire, lexique [The Sakalava dialect of northwestern Madagascar: Phonology, grammar, lexicon]. Thèse de doctorat de 3e cycle. Université de Paris.

Bouwer, Leoni E. 2003. The viability of Official Malagasy in the language ecology of southern Madagascar with particular reference to the Bara speech community. PhD dissertation. University of South Africa, Pretoria.

Brann, Conrad Max Benedict. 1990. Pour une métalangue du multilinguisme [For a metalanguage of multilingualism]. *La Linguistique* 26(1):43–51.

Burnett, Robert Griffiths. 2012. Mother tongue education: Nepal's educational dilemma. Honors thesis. Franklin and Marshall College, Lancaster, PA.

Clignet, Rémi, and Bernard Ernst. 1995. *L'école à Madagascar: évaluation de la qualité de l'enseignement primaire public* [School in Madagascar: assessment of the quality of public primary education]. Paris: Karthala.

Dahl, Øyvind, Marie Ange Andriamanantenasoa, Irène Rabenoro, Malalatiana, Rafam'Andrianjafy, Roselyne Rahanivoson, and Suzy Rajaonarivo. 2005. Redéfinition de la politique linguistique dans le système educatif à Madagascar: Rapport du task force [Redefinition of the policy of linguistics of the educational system of Madagascar: Report of the Task Force]. *SIK-Rapport* 2005-3. Stavanger, Norway: Misjonshøgskolens forlag.

Dez, Jacques. 1960. *Le dialecte Betsimisaraka du Sud (région de Nosy Varika)* [Southern Betsimisaraka dialect (Nosy Varika region)]. Antananarivo, Madagascar: Académie Malagasy.

Eagle, Sonia. 1999. The language situation in Nepal. *Journal of Multilingual and Multicultural Development* 20:272–327.

Ehala, Martin. 2015. Ethnolinguistic vitality. In K. Tracy, T. Sandel, and C. Ilie (eds.), *The international encyclopedia of language and social interaction*, 553–559. Hoboken, NJ: Wiley. DOI:10.1002/9781118611463.wbielsi046/.

Erasmus, Beverley. 2015. Demonstratives in Masikoro oral narratives. MA thesis. University of Gloucestershire, UK.

Ferguson, Charles A. 1959. Diglossia. *Word* 15:325–340.

Fishman, Joshua A. 1967. Bilingualism with and without diglossia; diglossia with and without bilingualism. *Journal of Social Issues* 23(2):29–38.

Fishman, Joshua A. 1968. Nationality-nationalism and nation-nationism. In Joshua A. Fishman, Jyotirindra Das Gupta, and Charles A. Ferguson (eds.), *Language problems of developing nations*, 39–51. Hoboken, NJ: Wiley.

Fishman, Joshua A. 1977. Language and ethnicity. In Howard Giles (ed.), *Language, ethnicity and intergroup relations*, 15–58. London: Academic Press.

Fishman, Joshua A. 1980. Bilingualism and biculturalism as individual and societal phenomena. *Journal of Multilingual and Multicultural Development* 1(1):3–17.

Gardy, Philippe. 1985. Langue(s), non-langue(s), lambeaux de langue(s), norme [Language(s), non-language(s), language flaps, standard]. In André Winther (ed.), *Problèmes de glottopolitique*, 60–63. Mont-Saint-Aignan, France: Publications de l'Université de Rouen.

Giles, Howard, Richard Yvon Bourhis, and Donald M. Taylor. 1977. Towards a theory of language in ethnic group relations. In Howard Giles (ed.), *Language, ethnicity and intergroup relations*, 307–349. London: Academic Press.

Giles, Howard, and Patricia Johnson. 1987. Ethnolinguistic identity theory: A social psychological approach to language maintenance. *International Journal of the Sociology of Language* 68:69–100.

Giles, Howard, and Nikolas Coupland, eds. 1991. *Language: Contexts and consequences*. Brooks/Cole Mapping Social Psychology Series. Buckingham, UK: Open University Press.

Hungwe, Kedmon. 2007. Language policy in Zimbabwean education: Historical antecedents and contemporary issues. *Compare: A Journal of Comparative Education* 37:135–149.

Kaufman, Mark. 2018. Space photo shows forests devastated by logging. *Mashable*, 13 July 2018. mashable.com/2018/07/13/nasa-space-photo-madagascar/.

Koerner, Francis. 1999. *Histoire de l'enseignement privé et officiel à Madagascar (1820–1995). Les implications religieuses et politiques dans la formation d'un peuple* [History of private and official education in Madagascar (1820–1995). The religious and political implications in the formation of a people]. Paris: L'Harmattan.

Landry, Rodrigue, and Réal Allard. 1994. Diglossia, ethnolinguistic vitality, and language behavior. *International Journal of the Sociology of Language* 108:15–42.

Malone, Susan, and Patricia Paraide. 2011. Mother-tongue based bilingual education in Papua New Guinea. *International Review of Education* 57:705–720.

Mann, Charles C. 2000. Reviewing ethnolinguistic vitality: The case of Anglo-Nigerian Pidgin. *Journal of Sociolinguistics* 4(3):458–474.

Michalopoulos, Stelios. 2011. The origins of ethnolinguistic diversity. Ms. Tufts University, Medford, MA.

Mühlhäusler, Peter. 2002. Language as an ecological phenomenon. *The Linacre Journal: A Review of Research in the Humanities* 5:61–68.

Ndlovu, Eventhough. 2013. Mother tongue education in official minority languages of Zimbabwe: A language management critique. PhD thesis. University of the Free State, Bloemfontein, South Africa.

Nettle, Daniel, and Suzanne Romaine. 2000. *Vanishing voices: The extinction of the world's languages*. Oxford: Oxford University Press.

O'Neill, Timothy. 2015. The phonology of Betsimisaraka Malagasy. PhD thesis. University of Delaware.

Poirier, Jean, and Jacques Dez. 1963. *Les groupes ethniques de Madagascar* [The ethnic groups of Madagascar]. Antananarivo, Madagascar: Université de Madagascar, Faculté des Lettres et Sciences Humaines.

Rabenoro, Irène, and Suzy Rajaonarivo. 1997. A l'aube du 21e siècle, quelle politique linguistique pour Madagascar? [At the dawn of the 21st century, what language policy for Madagascar?] *Mots* 52:105–119.

Rabenilaina, Roger-Bruno. 1983. *Morpho-syntaxe du malgache: Description structurale du dialecte Bara* [Morpho-syntax of Malagasy: Structural description of the Bara dialect]. Societe d'Etudes Linguistiques et Anthropologiques de France 189. Paris: SELAF.

Rakotondrabe, Modeste. 1993. Malgachisation de l'enseignement et Francophonie [Malagasy teaching and French]. In Rabezafy, Emmanuel (ed.), *Recherches et Documents*, 28–71. Antsiranana, Madagascar: I.S.T.P.M.

Rambelo, Michel. 1981. Contribution à l'étude de la situation linguistique à Madagascar: les rapports entre le malgache officiel, le malgache dialectal et le français dans une situation de diglossie [Contribution to the study of the linguistic situation in Madagascar: the relations between Official Malagasy, Malagasy dialect and French in a diglossia situation]. Thèse de 3e cycle. Aix-Marseille I, France.

Ranjivason, Jean Théodore. 1985. Morpho-syntaxe du malgache: étude des formes prédicatives verbales du sihanaka [Morpho-syntax of Malagasy: study of verbal predicative forms of Sihanaka]. Thèse de 3e cycle. Université de Paris VII.

Ratsima, M. 1981. Etude sociolinguistique chez une colonie Antandroy [Sociolinguistic study at an Antandroy colony]. *Omaly sy Anio (Hier et Aujourd'hui)* 13–14:319–327.

Richardson, James. 1877. *Lights and shadows, or, chequered experiences among some of the heathen tribes of Madagascar with notes geographical, political, social and religious, also on the Bara, Tanosy and Vezo dialects and itinerary*. Antananarivo, Madagascar: London Missionary Society Press.

Schmidt, Bernd. 1997. *Madagaskar. Zur Geschichte seiner Sprache und Kultur* [Madagascar. The history of its language and culture]. Aachen, Germany: Shaker Verlag.

Sonntag, Selma K. 1995. Ethnolinguistic identity and language policy in Nepal. *Nationalism and Ethnic Politics* 1:108–120.

Tajfel, Henri, and John C. Turner. 1979. An integrative theory of intergroup conflict. In William G. Austin and Stephen Worchel (eds.), *The social psychology in intergroup relations*, 33–47. Monterey, CA: Brooks/Cole.

Thomas-Fattier, Dominique. 1982. *Le dialecte sakalava du Nord-Ouest de Madagascar: Phonologie, grammaire, lexique* [The Sakalava dialect of northwestern Madagascar: Phonology, grammar, lexicon]. Societe d'Etudes Linguistiques et Anthropologiques de France 185. Paris: SELAF.

Tsimilaza, Alphonse. 1981. Phonologie et morphologie du Tsimihety (Madagascar) [Phonology and morphology of Tsimihety (Madagascar)]. Thèse de 3e cycle. Université de Nancy II, France.

Tsimilaza, Alphonse. 1992. La notation de l'accent en Malgache: Réflexions sur quelques questions de transcription et d'orthographie [The notation of the accent in Malagasy: Reflections on some questions of transcription and orthography]. *Etudes Océan Indien* 15:33–48.

Vérin, Pierre, Conrad P. Kottak, and Peter Gorlin. 1969. The glottochronology of Malagasy speech communities. *Oceanic Linguistics* 7:26–83.

Whorf, Benjamin Lee. 1956. *Language, thought, and reality: Selected writings of Benjamin Lee Whorf*, edited by John B. Carroll. Cambridge: Technology Press of MIT.

Yagmur, Kutlay. 2011. Does Ethnolinguistic Vitality Theory account for the actual vitality of ethnic groups? A critical evaluation. *Journal of Multilingual and Multicultural Development* 32(2):111–120.

19
Multilingualism, Urbanization, and Identity among the Ejagham Speaking People

John R. Watters

Abstract. This case study explores the nature of multilingualism and urbanization among the people who speak the Ejagham language [èyŭm éjáyám] and how these phenomena correlate with their identity as Ejagham people [ànè éjáyám]. I identify the state and trends in multilingualism and urbanization in the Ejagham homeland in southwest Cameroon and southeast Nigeria, as well as those in diaspora, as observed over more than forty years. Two major features mark the urbanization experience among the Ejagham. One is its historical time depth, in particular regarding the development of the city of Calabar over the past four centuries. The second feature is its two-way nature. In addition to the expected form of urbanization, in which Ejagham speakers move from rural homelands to urban centers (whether in Nigeria and Cameroon or North America, Europe, and elsewhere), there is also an opposite process whereby the Ejagham region becomes more urbanized itself through the immigration of non-Ejagham speakers to participate in the mining and agricultural enterprises. Identifying these trends should feed into the planning of language programs to meet the language-related needs of those who speak Ejagham or self-identify as Ejagham, regardless of where they reside.

19.1 Introductory and theoretical comments

In terms of shifts in language use and identity, the Ejagham [etu] tend to shift first in the use of their language before they shift in their identity. Language shift is most clearly observable between generations in diaspora situations, since the dominant language of the diaspora location usually becomes the main language of the child as he or she matures in the educational and social situation of the given location. They may still identify as being Ejagham in origin but not speak any of their heritage language.

Bucholtz and Hall (2004:369–394) provide an overview of a variety of issues in the literature on identity and propose a model that provides analytical tools for further research. They refer to the model as "tactics of intersubjectivity." It recognizes the social (i.e., status) and political (i.e., power) relations that contribute to the construction of identity through a variety of symbolic resources that include language as a major one. They argue that "the interconnections between language and identity are multiple, complex, and contextually specific." Other claims include:

- Anthropology concerns identity "since cultural processes are intimately bound up with socially located cultural subjects" (375).
- Identity is not an attribute of individuals or groups but of situations (376).
- Language practices are reflective of social identities, not constitutive of them (376).
- "The extent to which identities are forged in action rather than fixed in categories is evident in studies of status" (376).
- "[H]igh-status identities are not entirely given in advance but are interactionally negotiated" (376).
- "Semiotics, or the study of systems of meaning, offers a valuable perspective from which to view identity" (377).
- "Language has both social meaning (pragmatic or contextual) and referential (semantic) meaning (377)."

These claims can no doubt be contested, but they provide an informative set of claims with which to analyze identity and language. The authors go on to note that a working model of identity must be able to "accommodate such issues as markedness, essentialism, and institutional power as central components of identity"(387). They define identity as follows:

> *Identity:* an outcome of cultural semiotics that is accomplished through the production of contextually relevant sociopolitical relations of similarity and difference, authenticity and inauthenticity, and legitimacy and illegitimacy. (Bucholtz and Hall 2004:382)

Such a general claim about their theory of "tactics of intersubjectivity" is notably reminiscent of Pike (1967). Pike's primary analytical tools for human behavior were the concepts of contrast, variation, and distribution. In the analogy to Bucholtz and Hall, *contrast* could relate to *essentialism* in that it is derived from categories of sameness and difference, markers that distinguish one item from another, identifying what a given item essentially is in contrast to others. As for *variation*, it could relate to *markedness* in that some items are marked relative to other items because they vary in their essential nature with allo-forms. Finally, the *distribution* of items concerns the actual situation in which the given item and its variations are used, and in the case of identity it involves social situations in which relations of *institutional power* and personal status, i.e., legitimacy and illegitimacy, can be at play. Whether these analogies would hold up under further analysis, on first reflection there seems to be a good analogue in categories between Bucholtz and Hall's essentialism, markedness, and institutional power, and Pike's contrast, variation, and distribution. At a more general level it could be said that all of them are concerned about human behavior in social situations.

What follows is a case study of the Ejagham language and people and their relationship to identity. It involves issues of essentialism, markedness, and power, both institutional and interethnic. In some contexts, the Ejagham relationship to others seems to be more peaceful and open, and in other contexts the Ejagham relationship is one of resistance in which they struggle with the power of the other by choosing English or Pidgin English over the language of the more powerful or more numerous, such as the Ibibio [ibb]-Efik [efi] and Igbo [ibo]. But an even more powerful dynamic than resistance is involved. It is a pragmatic one in which future economic success is more probable if one learns English than if one learns another African language. Of course, this involves them in choosing the language of those even more powerful, namely the Anglo-Saxon world, but this contrast positively shows that a key element of identity is the local, existential situation and not a merely international, abstract, and distant one.

19.2 Profile of the Ejagham community

The homeland of the Ejagham[1] speaking people is found in the rainforest of southwest Cameroon and southeast Nigeria (see map 1).[2] Rainfall is around 120 inches (3,000 mm) or more per year and falls mostly in the months of May to October, with dry season being November to April.[3] However, Calabar and its environs, near the Atlantic Ocean, receive rain up to ten months of the year.

The Ejagham rainforest lies within the Cross River Basin of Cameroon and Nigeria and forms a continuous territory within a triangle-like shaped region formed by the city of Calabar, Nigeria, at one point and the towns of Ikom, Nigeria, and Mamfe, Cameroon, at the other two points (see map 2). The territory comprises approximately 1,800 square miles (4,660 square kilometers), most of it sparsely populated. The distance north to south is about 68 miles (109 kilometers); the distance east to west is about 85 miles (137 kilometers). The international boundary between Cameroon and Nigeria divides their territory into two. In Cameroon, they live in the administrative subdivision of Eyumojok within the Manyu Division in the South-West Region. In Nigeria, they live primarily in four Local Government Areas (LGAs) of the Cross River State: Calabar Municipal LGA, Akamkpa LGA, Etung LGA, and Ikom LGA.

---

[1] Simons and Fennig (2018) list Ejagham as ISO 639-3 code [etu] with a language vitality rating of EGIDS 5 (Developing).
[2] Most of the material in this section derives from Watters 1981.
[3] See the website of the United Councils and Cities of Cameroon, cvuc.cm/national/index.php/fr/carte-communale/region-du-sud/145-association/carte-administrative/sud-ouest/manyu/407-eyumojock/.

Map 1. Location of Ejagham homeland

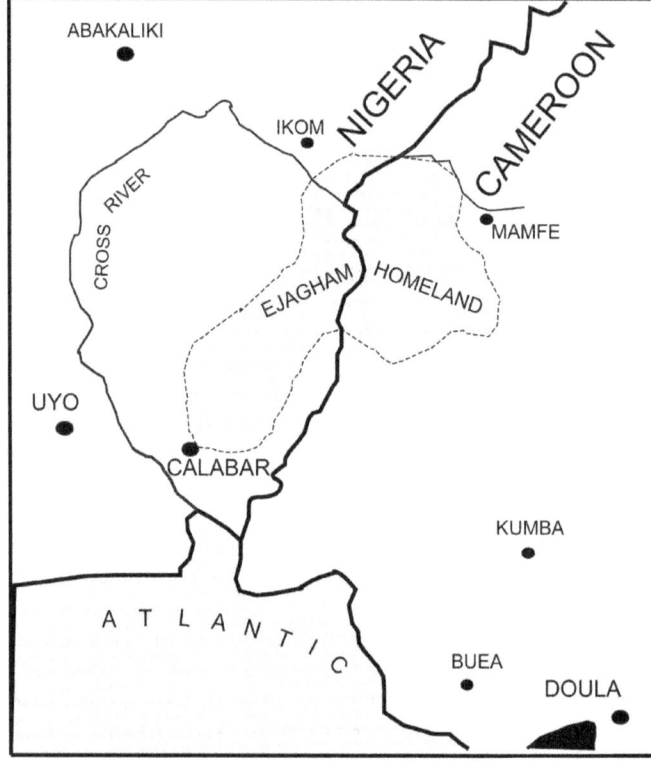

Based on estimates from the year 2000, Simons and Fennig (2018) report that the Ejagham language has approximately 116,700 speakers (67,300 in Nigeria and 49,400 in Cameroon).[4] Approximately 140 villages are clustered in various areas, not spread out evenly throughout the region. There are approximately 80 villages in Nigeria and 60 in Cameroon.

The dominant second language used in southwest Cameroon and southeast Nigeria where Ejagham is located is Pidgin English (Cameroon Pidgin [wes]), but in more formal contexts it is a form of Standard English [eng]. Pidgin English is the lingua franca. It is also a creole (i.e., a first language) for many in the younger generation in towns and cities in Cameroon and Nigeria.

Ejagham consists of three major dialects: Western Ejagham (WE), Eastern Ejagham (EE), and Southern Ejagham (SE). The WE dialect has about 75,000 speakers, the EE dialect 35,000, and the SE dialect 10,000. Of the WE dialect, 60,000 speakers are in Nigeria and 15,000 in Cameroon. The EE dialect is spoken only in Cameroon and the

---

[4] The Nigerian growth rate according to the World Bank is currently 2.62%. If we use that growth rate for the years 2001 to 2018, the Ejagham would number 185,886. Whether this is accurate or not, I have observed on visits to Cameroon in 2009 and 2012 and to Nigeria each year from 2012 to 2016 that the Ejagham villages seem more full of children than I remember from the 1970s and 1980s. See: google.com/publicdata/explore?ds=d5bncppjof8f9_&met_y=sp_pop_grow&idim=country:NGA&dl=en&hl=en&q=nigeria+population+growth/. Accessed 3 May 2018.

SE dialect only around Calabar, Nigeria. WE consists of five subdialects: northern, eastern, southern, western, and southwestern. EE consists of two subdialects, northern and southern.

Map 2. Ejagham language area

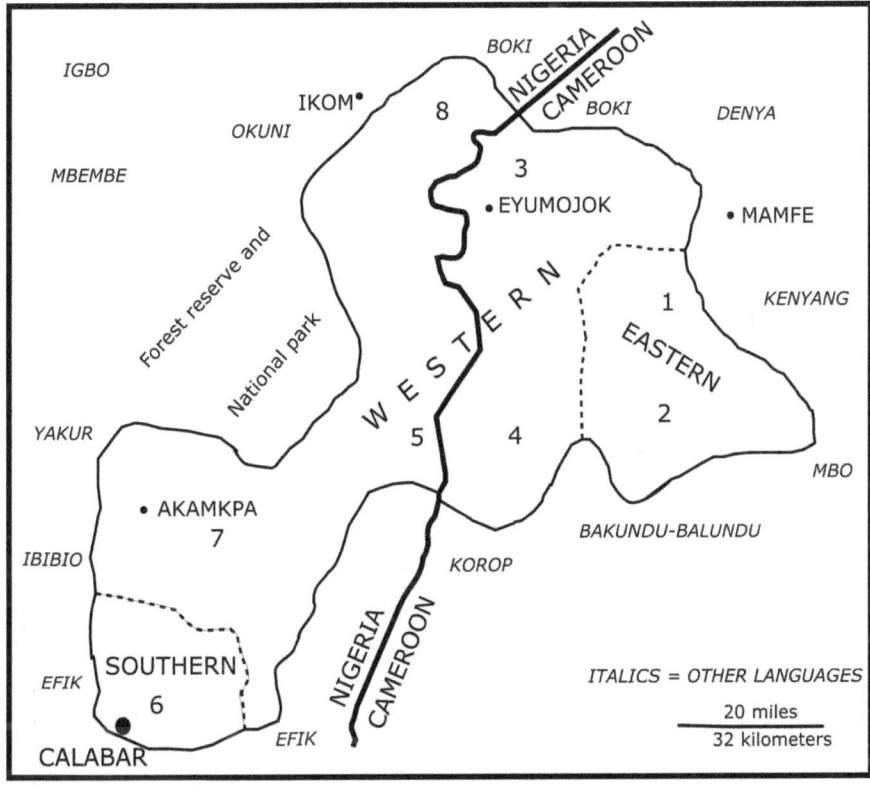

1. Kembong and environs
2. Obang
3. Eyumojok and environs
4. Upper Ekwe
5. Northeast Akamkpa LGA
6. Calabar and environs
7. Akamkpa town and environs
8. Ikom-Etung commercial center

The Ejagham share a common inheritance in both material and social culture. They do not have a centralized paramount ruler except in Calabar among the SE where the Ndidem rules. This institution is likely a borrowing from other coastal West African communities. Most villages consist of a set of extended families with the family elder of each extended family providing leadership for the given village. The notion and practice of chieftainship among the Ejagham is a complicated reality that goes beyond this study. Its history lies in the institution of the Leopard Society whose chief historically was also the village chief. This tradition was complicated by the arrival of the British colonial administration and its demand for a chief that had some aptitude in reading and writing English. This left many villages with two chiefs: the traditional chief and the "white man's chief."

There are four primary economic centers and one secondary economic center that draw Ejagham speakers to their markets. In Cameroon, the town of Mamfe with a population of 36,500 (2017 estimate)[5] is the primary economic and government center. It lies about ten miles (16 kilometers) outside the eastern region of Ejagham. But the Ejagham in Cameroon also have a secondary center in the town of Eyumojok, well within the WE area and about ten miles (16 kilometers) from the Nigerian border. It provides government administrative leadership and services for the entire Cameroon Ejagham area. Economically it serves the more local region in that Ejagham from the Kembong area generally look to Mamfe for their commercial activities. Kembong, with a population of more than 6,350 and Afap, both in EE, have sizeable market days serving the local region. In Nigeria, three economic centers are found: the municipality of Calabar which has a population of 371,000 (2006 census)[6] where the SE have their paramount ruler, the Ndidem; Akamkpa LGA which has a population of 151,125 (2006 census)[7] and was originally an Ejagham area but now filled with outsiders; and Ikom town which is the center of the Ikom LGA and its population of 162,400 (2006 census).[8]

Each of these three Nigerian cities present the Ejagham people with the challenge of urbanization. Languages with smaller populations like the Ejagham do not fare well in urban environments. Calabar is the capital of the Cross River State, and serves as its political, economic, and cultural center. It is also the center of the SE where their paramount ruler serves as the traditional chief for the northern half of the municipality. In the past, the northern part of Calabar consisted of a few (Ekin) Ejagham villages and the southern part was Efut-speaking. Calabar now is filled with tens of thousands of speakers representing the scores of languages of the state and the neighboring state. It is especially populated by Efik-Ibibio speakers. The traditional Ejagham village areas can generally be identified by those who know the city, but they are surrounded by and have merged with the larger population. Calabar is the location where the British established their power in eastern Nigeria. This took place in the 1800s and the British favored the Efik during their colonial rule.

Akamkpa to the north of Calabar was a quiet Ejagham village just a few decades ago, but it is now an industrial center with some sixteen granite quarries operating in its LGA. Some of the best granite in the world, reported to be 97% pure, is found in these quarries, and it is desired by the Gulf States for their building projects. This demand for quality granite has brought a large influx of Ibibio and other workers from the neighboring state as well as heavy equipment and hundreds of trucks and truck drivers onto the roads. Calabar and Akamkpa thus represent significant points where the forces of urbanization and globalization have become realities inside the Ejagham geographical region.

Further to the north, the town of Ikom is more distant from the urbanization and globalization dynamics of Calabar and Akamkpa. It serves as a regional economic center for trade in central and northern Cross River State and trade between Nigeria and Cameroon. As such, it represents an economy impacted by urbanization more than globalization. The urban influx comes from the Igbo population just to the west of Ikom. Speakers of Olulumo-Ikom, an Upper Cross River language, are found largely in Old Ikom, down from the upper plateau, beside the Cross River. Many Ejagham also live in Old Ikom town, but others live on the upper plateau. Over the past few decades the upper plateau has become a vigorous market area with mostly

---

[5] en.wikipedia.org/wiki/Mamfe/. Accessed 3 May 2018.
[6] en.wikipedia.org/wiki/Calabar/. Accessed 3 May 2018.
[7] en.wikipedia.org/wiki/Akamkpa/. Accessed 3 May 2018.
[8] en.wikipedia.org/wiki/Ikom/. Accessed 3 May 2018.

Igbo traders involved in the running of the local economy that serves the center and north of the state. It also serves as the trading center for goods traded by land with Cameroon. The Pan-African Highway that is planned to connect Lagos, Nigeria, to Mombasa, Kenya, includes the road that runs between Ikom, Nigeria, and Mamfe, Cameroon.

Education has been available to the Ejagham for decades, brought by the German Catholic mission in Cameroon before World War I and by the Scottish Presbyterian mission in Nigeria in the late 1800s. In those early years it was specific to certain locations. It expanded significantly after World War II and independence in the 1950s and 1960s. The Ejagham have been known in Cameroon as "book people" because of the success of their brighter young people in school over the past decades. Primary education today is problematic though available, with teacher absenteeism in Cameroon a major problem. Absenteeism does not seem to be as big a problem in Nigeria, at least in the urbanized areas. There are secondary schools in the economic centers, and universities in each of the states: the South-West Region of Cameroon has the University of Buea and the Cross River State of Nigeria has the University of Calabar. Among the Ejagham there are a number of people with doctor's, master's, and bachelor's degrees today. They serve in various roles almost exclusively in the urban centers within their nations or in the wider Ejagham diaspora. A number have received tertiary education in Europe and the United States.

In terms of religion, more than 80% of the population would probably identify as Christian. The presence of a Christian identity has increased significantly over the past thirty years. The Catholic Church is the most prominent among the Ejagham in both Cameroon and Nigeria, apart from Calabar, due to the engagement of German Catholics in early years in Cameroon and then the work of the Mill Hill Missionaries after World War I in both Cameroon and Nigeria from 1922. The Calabar area is predominantly Presbyterian due to the work of Scottish Presbyterian missionaries beginning in 1846. Other Protestant denominations with Western roots are found in the Ejagham area today as well as churches of African origin such as the Deeper Life Bible Church. Traditional religion is also practiced, including by some who identify as Christian.

There is a diaspora Ejagham community in the cities of Nigeria. Calabar serves as a location of choice for those who come from the northern area of Western Ejagham in Nigeria. Other cities include Abuja, Port Harcourt, and Lagos. The diaspora community in Cameroon are commonly found in the cities of Kumba, Buea, Limbe, Bamenda, Douala, and Yaounde. Ejagham diaspora are also found in Europe and North America.

19.3 Nodes of convergence

There are significant locations within the Ejagham region in Cameroon and Nigeria where various parameters converge. I will refer to these as "nodes of convergence." The parameters that form these nodes of convergence include speech varieties, accessibility to market towns, media, government, education, and churches. These form a composite that relates to the issues of multilingualism and urbanization in notable ways. These nodes include the following: Calabar and environs, Akamkpa town and the quarries, Etung-Ikom commercial center, northeast Akamkpa LGA, Eyumojok and environs, Upper Ekwe, Kembong and environs, and the Obang area (see map 2).

Each of these locations is identified with certain developments relative to multilingualism, urbanization, and their identity as speakers of Ejagham. Each node has its particular speech form, economic dynamics, government services, educational services, media, and church institutions. These are the most important domains and institutions that impact the language habits and identity of the Ejagham.

The nodes of convergence divide into two major regions. The eastern region includes all of the Ejagham villages in the nodes within Cameroon (Kembong, Obang, Eyumojok, and Upper Ekwe) and those in the northeast of Akamkpa LGA in Nigeria. The western region includes most of Nigeria Ejagham (Etung-Ikom commercial center, Akamkpa and the quarries, and Calabar and environs). Consideration will be given first to the eastern region. The eastern region is more traditional while the western region is noticeably more affected by urbanization and globalization.

19.4 Eastern Ejagham region relative to multilingualism and urbanization

The eastern Ejagham region comprises all the Ejagham speakers in Cameroon and a small number that live in northeast Akamkpa LGA, Nigeria, near the Cameroon border. This includes the following nodes of convergence: Kembong and Obang, comprising all of the Eastern Ejagham dialect; and Eyumojok, Upper Ekwe, and northeast Akamkpa, all of which are part of the Western Ejagham dialect.

The eastern region is less urbanized than the western. In fact, it basically consists of rural villages apart from the administrative center that has been located in Eyumojok. Eyumojok also has a secondary school and a small medical center. Because of these institutions, it has the largest concentration of non-Ejagham speaking persons anywhere within the eastern region. With those additions, Eyumojok probably has changed from a village to a very small town.

The language repertoire in the eastern region consists of Ejagham, Pidgin English, and, in more formal contexts, Standard English. At the more local level, it also includes whatever neighboring language or languages are spoken. The Ejagham often learn something of the language or languages of their immediate neighbors. The neighboring languages to the eastern region along with their number of speakers are: 106,000 Bakundu-Balundu to the south, 65,000 Kenyang [ken] to the east, 11,200 Denya [anv] to the north, and 3,700 Boki [bky] to the north in Cameroon (with the larger population of 140,000 Boki being found in Nigeria).[9] The eastern Ejagham region may include 55,000 to 60,000 Ejagham speakers, using the population estimates from 2000 cited by Simons and Fennig (2018).

In Cameroon, Mamfe is the closest urban center, with a population of around 36,500. It is outside the Ejagham area, being entirely within the Kenyang speaking area, to the east of the Kembong node of convergence and the Ejagham area in general. Those living in Mamfe are largely from the Manyu Division, including speakers of Kenyang (the predominant group), Ejagham, and Denya. Eyumojok and Kembong are the largest population centers in the Ejagham area in Cameroon, but Kembong remains a large village.[10] None of the neighboring languages listed above present an urbanizing force but are as rural as the Ejagham villages of the eastern

---

[9] These population figures are found in the *Ethnologue* (Simons and Fennig 2018).
[10] It is reported that Kembong actually consists of fourteen villages that the Germans forced to move together before World War I.

region. The closest urban environment to northeast Akamkpa is Akamkpa town, some distance from northeast Akamkpa both in terms of kilometers and in terms of accessibility due to poor roads.

Low urbanization means the eastern region is more traditional, reflecting inherited, local values and the primacy of the Ejagham language. The dominant lingua franca is Pidgin English. As for the role of neighboring languages, the Kembong convergence area is bordered on the east by the Kenyang. Many who live close to this border area understand and even speak Kenyang. The village of Ossing is divided into two; one section speaks Ejagham and the other Kenyang. Residents can speak to one another in their own language and be understood. Up the road are two villages, Ntenako and Ndekwa. They identify as Ejagham villages but residents use Kenyang as their language of choice. So the notion of a border between Ejagham and Kenyang refers to a very porous, fuzzy border without a hard line between the two.

In the village of Ogomoko in the Kembong convergence node, one section of the village traces its origin some generations ago to the Kenyang speaking area. Today they are fully Ejagham in terms of language and culture. In another case, in the Obang convergence node, some people have migrated from the Balue section of Oroko to the south into Obang. Today they are fully Ejagham, but I was told that the Balue immigrant families could be identified even today by the shape of their toes. So the symbols of identity can include more than language.

These examples of the Ejagham relationship with the Kenyang and Balue-Oroko do not demonstrate a lack of identity boundaries among the Ejagham. Instead, they demonstrate a lack of hard boundaries. For the Ejagham, this means immigrants are welcome. One of the likely major contributors to this openness toward immigrants is the fact that the Ejagham have never, up to now, lacked for land to assign for farming to new arrivals. This openness to immigrants also means that men can search for wives among villages of neighboring language groups and over time experience a shift in their language use to the neighbor's language as in the switch from Ejagham to Kenyang in the villages of Ntenako, Ndekwa, and half of Ossing.

A similar situation holds in the northern side of the Kembong convergence area. There the neighboring languages are Denya and Boki. They are spoken on the north side of the Manyu River, which is referred to as the Cross River in Nigeria. So there is a physical boundary, but this does not serve as a hard border relative to language. The Denya and Boki have frequent contact with the Ejagham villages closest to them.

One of the unusual features of the eastern region are the two main roads constructed by the British, both of which have been unpaved since they were built. The more important of the two roads is the one that runs from Ikom in Nigeria, through Eyumojok, and on to Mamfe in Cameroon. The other road runs from Calabar through northeast Akamkpa to Eyumojok. The more important road was designated over fifty years ago to be part of the Trans-African Highway network, specifically part of the Pan-African Highway linking Lagos, Nigeria to Mombasa, Kenya. However, it was unpaved and remained almost impassable during much of the rainy season. In the 1980s, Nigeria paved its short section from Ikom to the border with Cameroon, but the Cameroon portion remained unpaved until about 2013 or 2014. The Chinese built a new road bed and paved it from Mamfe to the border with Nigeria to connect with the Nigerian pavement.

The impact of this road relative to urbanization remains unclear, but it probably does not signify great changes in the next decade. Most traffic will travel straight through the Ejagham area traveling between Mamfe and Ikom. The significant trade does not lie along the road but at the towns of Mamfe and Ikom and beyond. The road will, however, provide an easier way for the Ejagham in the eastern region to get their food products to larger markets. If the food, agriculture, and timber industry develop along the road in Cameroon, they could lead to the development of internal urbanization as has happened in Akamkpa town and the Etung-Ikom areas in Nigeria.

Access to media is provided to the residents primarily via radio. Broadcasts are in English or Pidgin English. Radio Calabar does broadcast periodically in Ejagham because Ejagham was chosen back in the 1970s or 1980s as one of the three Cross River indigenous languages to be broadcast. Any television viewing is usually of English programs from Nigeria and French and English programs from Cameroon. Some also pick up video newscasts on their cell phones. These are also in English.

The Ejagham region is largely Christianized and Christianity provides the largest forms of institutional religion. The eastern region is most heavily influenced by the Catholic Church, but there are various Protestant denominations, some being imported through the work of missionaries from Europe and others being indigenous denominations. The primary language of choice in most of these churches is English. The primary reason for this is that priests and pastors are often not speakers of Ejagham. Those Ejagham consecrated as priests and pastors serve elsewhere, outside the Ejagham area. However, the churches in the eastern region often make an effort to include Ejagham language in their worship through songs, Scripture readings, and sometimes sermons. At one point I was told by leaders of the Ejagham Language Development Association that 75% of the churches in the Ejagham region of Cameroon used the Ejagham New Testament in some way in their services and church life.

19.5 Western Ejagham region relative to multilingualism and urbanization

The western Ejagham region is found entirely in Nigeria. This includes the following nodes of convergence: Calabar and environs, Akamkpa town and the quarries, and the Etung-Ikom commercial center. It is composed of an estimated 10,000 to 15,000 Ekin Ejagham speakers in the convergence node of Calabar and environs, as well as some 50,000 to 60,000 Ejagham speakers distributed within the convergence nodes of Akamkpa town and the quarries, and the Etung-Ikom commercial center.[11] The Southern Ejagham dialect is spoken in the Calabar LGA, while subdialects of the Western Ejagham dialect are spoken in the Akamkpa LGA and the Etung LGA. At the same time, many from the Etung LGA have moved to the nearby Ikom commercial center, and many from both the Etung LGA and the Akamkpa LGA have migrated to Calabar.

---

[11] The population numbers of the Ejagham in Nigeria are more difficult to determine than those in Cameroon. The Ekin Ejagham population numbers here are deduced from the overall estimate of Ejagham speakers in Nigeria of 70,000. If there are 10,000 to 15,000 Ekin Ejagham speakers then there would be 55,000 to 60,000 in the combined regions of Akamkpa and Ikom-Etung. These numbers seem low. Footnote 39 concerning population growth suggests there might be 50% more present than the numbers from 2000 found in Simons and Fennig (2018). Therefore, the number of Ekin Ejagham speakers may be between 15,000 and 20,000, and the number of speakers in Akamkpa and in the Etung-Ikom region are likely greater than currently stated.

The western region is the most urbanized and urbanizing region within the Ejagham homeland. It is in this region that urbanization has both historical and bidirectional features. The historical feature concerns the development of Calabar over the past four centuries, and probably most markedly, the past century. The bidirectional feature of Ejagham urbanization first involves Ejagham speakers moving into urban centers such as the cities of Calabar and Ikom and beyond. Secondly, it involves speakers of other languages who have moved and are moving into the Ejagham western region. I will start with the Calabar and environs node and then move on to Akamkpa and Etung-Ikom nodes. For a more in-depth historical view of the Ejagham and their expansion within the rainforest of Nigeria and Cameroon, see Watters (2001:57).

19.5.1 The urbanization of Ejagham in Calabar and environs

Calabar became an international trading port in the sixteenth century, trade revolving around palm oil and slaves. The earliest documentary evidence of Ejagham in Calabar is found in Ardener (1968:126 "Postscripta") which places Ejagham probably being spoken in Calabar in 1668. This reflects a likely migration of Ejagham from what is today the Kembong convergence node in the Eastern dialect in Cameroon to the region of the trading post of Calabar. This migration may have taken place 400 years ago, motivated by the earlier forms of globalization involving the trade of palm oil and slaves with European nations. They likely formed the core of what became the Southern Ejagham dialect around Calabar. The Ejagham in Calabar today maintain the oral tradition that traces their origin to Mbakang [m̀bá àkâŋ] 'the road of salt', a village in the Kembong convergence node in Cameroon. A variety of Ejagham villages were established in the area of the Calabar trading center. These include Big Qua Town, Akin Qua Town, and Ekot Ansa that now form neighborhoods within Calabar, as well as other villages outside Calabar.

Three language communities formed the core of the early Calabar. The Southern Ejagham villages were inland, away from the Cross River, in the forested area. The Ejagham as a whole have lived primarily in the rainforest and practiced farming and hunting. The second language community, the Efut-speaking people of the Cross River linguistic group, established themselves to the south of the Ekin Ejagham. The third group, the Efik-speaking people also of the Cross River linguistic group, were along the banks of the Cross River and practiced fishing. These three groups provided the core around which the town and now the city of Calabar grew. At least three of the Southern Ejagham villages became embedded within the larger city and are still identifiable as neighborhoods within the city—Big Qua Town, Akin Qua Town, and Ekot Ansa. Today, the Southern Ejagham dialect, Ekin Ejagham, is spoken to some extent in these neighborhoods within the Municipal LGA of Calabar, one of two LGAs that make up the city of Calabar. It is also spoken in Southern Ejagham villages outside Calabar city. Calabar has a population of 371,000 people drawn from all over the Cross River State. A reasonable estimate of the number of speakers of the Southern dialect in the Municipal LGA would be 15,000 to 20,000.

Calabar has served as a regional and state capital for decades. On our first visit in 1975 its population was much less and it covered much less territory. It was made up primarily of the Ekin Ejagham, the Efut, and the Efik, each with their own rulers, as well as a growing number of Ibibio and Igbo speakers. Already in 1975, one could hear many of the Ejagham youth speaking Efik rather than Ejagham. This was due in part to Efik being taught in school at the time along with English.

Today as the capital city of the Cross River State, the city has speakers representing every language spoken within the state as well as representatives from languages spoken in neighboring states as well as Cameroon. So the Ejagham community is dwarfed by this massive population, most using English or Pidgin English, or Efik to communicate across their linguistic boundaries. Some might use Ekin Ejagham with their language-mates.

As noted above, the Ejagham villages of Big Qua, Akin Qua, Ekot Ansa, and so on are all swallowed up in the municipality of Calabar. One can find speakers of Ekin Ejagham in these locations, but most are of the older generations. There have been attempts to teach children their heritage language. In one meeting a woman in her sixties testified that when she was young her mother did not teach her to speak Ekin Ejagham. Instead her mother used Ejagham as a secret language to be used among her mother's age group. Her mother instead used English or Efik with her. So among the Ekin Ejagham, a strong sense of being Ekin Ejagham still exists, but the use of the language is lost for many and at risk for others. The identity of the Ekin Ejagham continues beyond the issue of language in that they have a paramount ruler, the Ndidem, who is recognized as the traditional chief of the northern part of the municipality. In addition, they have a strong oral history as being very early residents of the Calabar region. Even in speaking with a leader of the Efut community in Calabar, the Secretary of the Apostolic Church, he said all the Efut speak Efik and English today like many Ejagham, but they are trying to revive their lost Efut language. So both of these groups in Calabar have maintained their identity, either as Ekin Ejagham or Efut, in the face of the Efik-Ibibio population, while the use of their heritage language is either dying or has completely disappeared.

A closing remark regarding the power of institutions: in a conversation with the Secretary of the Catholic Archbishop of Calabar, he told me that the official languages of the diocese were English and Efik. He informed me of this church policy even though Ejagham speakers likely make up a larger population within the diocese than the Efik. This choice reflects the colonial choices made decades ago under the British. So institutions like the Catholic Church seem to maintain colonial language practices. A more favorable solution for Ejagham within the Catholic Church may not be possible since the Ekin Ejagham are largely Presbyterian through the efforts of the Scottish Presbyterian mission. As one observes language use in the region around Calabar, and further afield in the areas around Akamkpa and Ikom, there is the strong possibility that in the next generation or two the use of Pidgin English and English will be established not just as the lingua franca but also as the main language of the youth and others, possibly impacting language and identity issues of half a million people. In fact, the BBC in 2018 opened a Pidgin English digital service for West Africa audiences and gave the first prize for an essay contest in which texts were written in Pidgin English. This will be a continuing endeavor by BBC, and it certainly raises the stakes for African languages like Ejagham in the southern half of Cross River State.

19.5.2 The urbanization of Ejagham in Akamkpa and the quarries

Moving from the node of Calabar and environs to the node of Akamkpa and the quarries, the Ejagham speakers in this node use a subdialect of Western Ejagham. They probably number no more than 25,000 to 30,000 (or perhaps 35,000 to 45,000). The Akamkpa LGA overall has a population of 151,125. Until some thirty years ago, Akamkpa LGA was a quiet, rural, primarily Ejagham-speaking area.

However, some of the highest grade granite was found in its forests, offshoots of the Cameroon Volcanic Line. Out of this discovery, sixteen granite quarries have opened and they have drawn many non-Ejagham speakers—Ibibio, Efik, and others into the LGA. The Ibibio to the west of Akamkpa LGA number over five million (Simons and Fennig 2018) as first language speakers. The granite industry is tied to globalization processes in that some of the most interested consumers of this granite are found among the Gulf States. High quality granite is sought for their significant building projects. The effect among the Ejagham of Akamkpa is that rather than having migrated to an urban area, their very region has become increasingly industrialized and the majority of the residents do not appear to be Ejagham.

In the convergence node of Akamkpa and the quarries, Ejagham is still spoken, even in the town of Akamkpa. Back in 1970s and 1980s when I visited Akamkpa, the town was small and Ejagham widely used. The population was largely Ejagham. One teacher was using Ejagham materials produced in the Cameroon program in his classes in Akamkpa. More recently in 2013, while visiting a family and their neighbors in Akamkpa, there appeared to be a healthy intergenerational use of Ejagham between parents and children. Also, in 2013 I visited a church in the village of Obung, about a fifteen-minute drive east of Akamkpa. Perhaps more than half of the approximately 1,000 people in attendance were Ejagham speakers. The Scriptures were read in Ejagham and English, the sermon given in Ejagham and English, and multiple songs sung in Ejagham. When I stood to introduce the Ejagham New Testament and other Ejagham materials, I read some of the New Testament and also read a traditional folk tale. As I read the tale of the Stink Bug and the Chameleon, the parishioners dissolved into loud laughter. So I knew many still understood and responded to the deeper cultural meaning of their Ejagham language and its literature.

However, I was told the catechist in Obhung was not supportive of the use of the Ejagham language in the church, even though he is Ejagham. This is representative of many Ejagham speakers who are leaders in institutions. It apparently is more acceptable or respectable to use English than Ejagham, likely as a marker of progress and education. As explained by Karan's (2011) Perceived Benefit Model, the perceived benefit of using English appears to be supporting potential language shift. It also represents the reality that English has greater status and represents more power than Ejagham to many individuals like the catechist. Yet, at the same time, there was great enthusiasm in the materials that were made available in Ejagham. In conclusion, as Akamkpa increases in urbanization, Ejagham is still spoken, but in a context where the more prestigious language is English.

Moving north toward Ikom town from the Akamkpa LGA, it is possible to find over twenty different languages spoken. These belong to the Cross River group of languages. Like Ejagham, these languages tend to have smaller populations compared to the Ibibio and Igbo. They are mostly separated from the majority of the Ejagham by a sparsely inhabited portion of rainforest. Like the Ejagham, they primarily reside in rural villages, though a couple of these villages are more like towns or developing cities. The languages and their speakers are found on both sides of the Cross River.

19.5.3 The urbanization of Ejagham in the Etung-Ikom commercial center

On the other side of these Cross River languages one finds the town of Ikom. Ikom serves as a commercial center for central Cross River State and is part of the Etung-Ikom convergence node. Ikom LGA has a population of 162,400 and the Etung LGA has over 80,000. The Etung LGA is primarily an Ejagham government area, but numerous non-Ejagham live in the area as resident laborers for cocoa farms owned by Ejagham speakers. Ejagham is primarily associated with Etung LGA, but many Ejagham have moved into the urban environment of Ikom LGA. Given the population numbers, it is possible that 40,000 to 50,000 Ejagham live in the two LGAs, most of them in the Etung LGA, numbers again not supported by population reports for the Ejagham.

The upper Ikom town has developed into the most dynamic commercial town north of Calabar and Akamkpa. This is a significant change compared to my first experiences there in 1975 and 1976. It was a quiet town with the main town down by the river and mostly open fields on the upper plateau and government offices up on the plateau. Today some would refer to it as a city. The upper Ikom town is populated primarily by Igbo. The Igbo homeland lies to the west of Ikom town where most of their population of about 27 million live. They have easy access to the Ikom area. The urban population of Ikom impacts the Ejagham who live in the Ikom and Etung LGAs. This includes all of Ikom town as well as the Ejagham villages along the Cross River to the east of Ikom and those inland to the north of the river. They do their primary trading with the markets in Ikom, which are primarily in Igbo hands.

In the Ikom-Etung convergence node, other than the leading role of Igbo speakers in the commercial life of Ikom, another dynamic that impacts the Ejagham of the Ikom-Etung area is the farming of cocoa. The Ejagham have been successful in planting large farms of cocoa. In many cases, they have hired non-Ejagham speaking personnel to farm the cocoa for them so the Ejagham of this area have become relatively wealthy. These laborers come with families and have ended up living in the area with their families, some for three generations now. An example of the result of this immigration of non-Ejagham speakers is the village of Agbokem. Down by the Cross River, where the tourists go to see the waterfalls, the traditional village is thoroughly Ejagham. However, up the hill at the level of the farms is a larger village of "outsiders" who are hired farm labor. The local priest told me that 90% of his parishioners are not Ejagham. The sustained presence of outsiders strengthens the use of Pidgin English in the area, even more so among the children as they attend school together with the children of the farm laborers. I have observed the same situation in other Ejagham villages of the Ikom area. Yet in each village Ejagham is clearly being taught to children at this time. Whether this continues as a stable situation of diglossia between home and the daily life of the larger community remains to be seen.

In the Ikom-Etung convergence node the presence of geographically close linguistic neighbors has an impact similar to that seen in the eastern Ejagham region where, for example, some Ejagham have daily contact with their Kenyang neighbors and can intermarry. The largest Ejagham village in Nigeria is Bendeghe. It is similar in size to Kembong in Cameroon and is the most northern of all Ejagham villages. The Ejagham practice exogamy in which the social group is defined as any blood-related person, either maternally or paternally related. So it is common for men to look for wives in neighboring villages. In the case of Bendeghe, some of the larger neighboring villages consist of Boki speakers. The result has been that many women in Bendeghe are Boki and still speak Boki to one another and to those in their close-by home village. An example of their presence is the choice for the word "God'. Bendeghe and Abia are the only villages in which one will hear from many Ejagham speakers that the true word for "God' should be ɔsɔ́wɔ̀, even though there are those who still use the traditional Ejagham word ɔ̀bhàsì. All of the other 130 plus Ejagham-speaking villages use the word ɔ̀bhàsì. This is another example of the Ejagham preference for fuzzy borders (Smalley 1994:300–331).

One practice that challenges the use of the Ejagham language within institutions in both the eastern and western regions of Ejagham is that in the educational sector and the religious denominational sector local leaders, whether teachers or pastors or priests, are changed every two or three years. Most of these local leaders in the two sectors are sent to places outside their home area so they are always strangers. In the case of the Ejagham, these leaders are always left with English or Pidgin English as the shared language with the local community. This practice exists in both Cameroon and Nigeria, and it undermines the sustainable use of Ejagham in schools and churches. One leader may support the use of Ejagham in the schools or churches, and the next leader may withdraw support. The support or lack of it may be active or passive. This disparity among leaders and their orientation to local languages, following LePage and Tabouret-Keller (1985), can be explained as "acts of identity." The choice to prefer or demote the local language is a message of identity and power on the part of the leader, priest, or pastor. It was clear that with the Ejagham in a church in the Etung LGA in the village of Bijang and another church in the village of Etome in the Ikom-Etung area, there was strong displeasure among those in attendance because the leader did not give space for the use of Ejagham other than in songs. Meanwhile, a church in Bendeghe and another in Abia were more pleased because space was granted for the use of Ejagham. In fact, what was an almost extreme level of emotional response to my presentation of Ejagham materials in churches in Bendeghe, Bijang, and Obung seemed to signal a deeply felt threat to a possible waning use of their language in these institutions and a strong desire to support its use in the institution of the church.

19.6 Ejagham and education

Language and education have a significant relationship, particularly with regard to the language used as the medium of instruction. Over the past sixty years or more, English has been the medium of instruction for those fortunate enough to attend school. However, Ejagham-speaking children in the Calabar and Akamkpa area have often been required to also learn Efik in school. That requirement did not seem to reach into the Etung-Ikom area or Cameroon. A primary question is: how does the Ejagham-speaking community view the relationship between Ejagham and English in the formal education setting?

As mentioned in section 19.1, Ejagham express and display resistance to the (potential) dominance of the Ibibio-Efik and Igbo in their lives, and this includes the possible use of one of those languages as the medium of education. At the same time, there is more than resistance involved; there is a pragmatic element in the choice of English over Ibibio and Igbo that probably is more powerful than the inter-ethnic dynamic. From my first visit among the Ejagham in 1973, two themes were clear about the relationship between Ejagham and English. When I would bring up the possibility of Ejagham being taught in primary schools with parents many would ask a mostly rhetorical question: "Will teaching them to read Ejagham get them a job?" The economic incentive among the Ejagham to learn English in order to secure employment has been strong probably since the 1950s or 1960s. On other occasions the conversation about Ejagham being taught in schools would lead to discussion of the possibility of multilingual education in which Ejagham and English would both be taught. Some parents would respond with something like, "If it's English and

Ejagham, that would be all right, but never English and Douala [dua]. Teach our children their own language and English, or just give them English." Apparently, as early as the 1960s there had been discussion about choosing seven regional languages among the 273 indigenous languages of Cameroon as those to be taught in school. In the eastern Ejagham area located in Cameroon, the proposal was to require the learning of Douala. I never found any Ejagham person who was positive about Douala being taught to Ejagham children. So, in education, Ejagham could possibly have a place as long as English was also taught, but no other Cameroonian language should be imposed on them.

In later years, I found similar attitudes among the Ejagham of Nigeria. Among those in Calabar and environs and the Akamkpa LGA, some had been required to learn Efik in school. But today it appears that Efik is no longer taught in schools in the Cross River State. Even though communities in Nigeria are allowed to teach their own language to their children during certain school hours if they have the curriculum and materials prepared, no community has succeeded in doing so and the institutional education authorities are moving ahead with an English-only program.

In fact, for about a decade in the late 1990s and early 2000s, Ejagham was taught in some form in primary schools in Cameroon. A few thousand children were at least introduced to the reading of Ejagham. Currently this has been halted. In Nigeria, the teaching of Ejagham in primary schools on such a grand scale has never occurred. However, for a few years in the 1990s, a Cameroonian taught Ejagham to secondary school students in Bendeghe in Nigeria. Also, in the 1980s, a primary school teacher in Akamkpa town taught Ejagham at the final level of elementary education and required students to pass the Ejagham exam before they could graduate. That experiment only lasted a few years.

19.7 Diaspora relative to multilingualism and urbanization

Whether the diaspora is within Cameroon and Nigeria, or in Europe and North America, Watkins' (2007:282) insight is observable: the "continued existence of a partial body of speakers ... appears to be sufficient to satisfy the linguistic aspect of the maintenance of a separate ethnic identity." In both forms of diaspora, whether within the given nation or overseas, because of technology in this day and age, speakers of Ejagham are able to keep contact with relatives, friends, and colleagues in the homeland via cell phone, Skype, email, and other electronic means. They often speak Ejagham with those people in the homeland with whom they connect by voice. The result is that what were once great distances of separation in decades past have now become relations close at hand, and their shared identity as Ejagham speakers is maintained in ways that were not possible in the past.

19.7.1 Diaspora in Cameroon and Nigeria

The Ejagham diaspora in Cameroon includes speakers residing in Kumba, Buea, Bamenda, Douala, and Yaounde. In Nigeria it includes speakers residing in Calabar from the Akamkpa and Ikom areas, and in cities such as Abuja, Port Harcourt, and Lagos. I am most aware of the situation with the diaspora in Cameroon.

The diaspora usually involves the educated elite among the Ejagham, who are able to find employment in urban centers. They usually begin their life in this new residence when still young, such as just out of university or advanced training centers. At times they marry spouses who speak other languages than Ejagham, but many times they come already married to an Ejagham speaker.

In observing the behavior of Ejagham speakers who take up residence in cities outside the Ejagham homeland, I have noticed that they face two fundamental challenges relative to their language and identity. First, they have needs as adults to find and maintain relationships with other Ejagham speakers, preferably from their own dialect and subdialect area. Second, if they have children, their children are uprooted from the language and culture in which they were raised, and it causes dissonance in their lives but without any good resolution.

In the case of the first challenge, Ejagham speakers address their need in at least three ways. One strategy is for them to seek individuals who come from the same village or neighboring villages. These friendships provide opportunities to use Ejagham rather than Pidgin English or English or French spoken in the wider urban setting. Their common identity also provides a greater sense of trust in sharing their experiences, successes, and failures in living in the urban environment. Another strategy is to join up with a "family" group that meets at regular intervals. The family may consist of those from the same extended family or the term "family" may serve as a metaphor for the meeting of those who come from the same village or set of villages. A third way to build connections with other Ejagham speakers is to join a larger association that meets regularly, such as the Ejagham Cultural Association that meets monthly. This allows for an evening of hearing and speaking Ejagham and reinforcing their common culture and identity within the larger urban and national context.

In some cases, identifying with other Ejagham speakers in the above groupings is not sufficient or possible for the given individual. In these cases, individuals might participate in larger groupings that allow them to associate with others from the same geographical area, as with the "Manyu Elements." Its meetings include Kenyang and Denya speakers as well as Ejagham speakers—people from the same administrative division. Beyond the local geography, associations may be formed around a common national grouping such as those from Cameroon, both anglophone and francophone. I know of some in the diaspora in the USA who join in monthly meetings with others from Cameroon. The participants can come from both the anglophone and francophone regions of Cameroon. Perhaps because of its multilingual context and more diffuse identity, the Manyu Elements did not seem to attract as many Ejagham speakers as the Cultural Association. The Manyu Elements also did not meet as regularly as the Cultural Association.

In the case of the second challenge, namely how to pass Ejagham on to the younger generation in the urban setting, there are fewer solutions. In these Ejagham marriages there is little to no intergenerational passing of the language. I have had a number of these parents ask me if I would teach their children Ejagham. I explained to them in each case that I would not be able to do so, but if they sent their children for a year back to their grandparents in the home village their children would learn Ejagham. No one that I know took me up on this suggestion. Apparently in each case it was too much of a cost to have their children miss a year of school in the urban environment. They would likely fall behind a grade in the competitive urban environment. The result is that these children growing up in the diaspora in Cameroon (and Nigeria) no longer speak Ejagham, even if they might maintain an identity as being Ejagham because of their parents' identity with their heritage language and culture. They usually end up speaking the official or national language, and the language of education in the two countries. So the heritage language may fade away, but identity is maintained even if to a lesser intensity than that of their parents. Whether the children of these children will maintain any sense of being Ejagham remains to be seen.

19.7.2 Diaspora in Europe and North America

The same holds true in the case of the diaspora in Europe and North America as the description of the diaspora within Cameroon and Nigeria in the preceding section. I have had the privilege to follow closely some Ejagham friends who moved to the USA in 2002. They arrived with all their children and a fourth one was born a year after they arrived.

The parents did not find other speakers of Ejagham where they first resided but instead built friendships with the other foreign students at the seminary and African immigrants at a church. There was an occasional meeting of Manyu peoples from Cameroon, but not enough to find fellow Ejagham speakers or build relationships. After graduation they moved to another state to an area that has many residents from Africa. They also found a number of Ejagham speakers with which they could meet and discuss issues concerning their homeland and share a meal of *ḿfúní* and pounded yams.[12] However, the day-to-day life demanded English. In the past four years, in search of cheaper rent, they moved to another state. They have settled and even purchased a house. But, as they put it, they really have no friends. They are deeply involved in the ministry of a local church, but the father and mother work long hours to support their children. Three sons are now in university, with the oldest now hired and being promoted by his employer. They are all hard working, bright, and industrious like their father and mother. But what of their Ejagham language and their Ejagham identity? The father and mother have strong Ejagham identities.

As for the children, the parents committed themselves early to speak only Ejagham at home with the goal of building their children's fluency over the years. They appeared to be meeting their goals over the first couple years. However, as their sons moved into higher grades, English became the preferred language since their entire life in school and out of school required English. Three of the four are now in university and the fourth will soon be in university. They still know a few Ejagham phrases, but when I greet them in Ejagham our conversation quickly moves into English.

It seems the general rule is: if children immigrate to the continents of Europe or North America and they already have fluency in Ejagham relative to their age level, over the years their Ejagham does not develop and the dominant language of the

---

[12] *Mfúní* and pounded yams is the meal of choice among speakers of Ejagham. It is also a special meal among the speakers of Kenyang. *Mfúní* refers to the leaves of a vine that grows on trees in the rainforest. It often requires someone to climb into the trees to bring the vines down so the leaves can be plucked. The leaves are a key ingredient of the sauce that includes palm oil and some type of meat or fish. It is commonly known outside the Ejagham and Kenyang area of Cameroon by the Kenyang term "*eru* and pounded yams." It is now recognized as a special meal in southwest Cameroon and southeast Nigeria, and more broadly in West Africa. It is also found abroad where West African diaspora communities are present. However, other leafy vegetables may substitute for the authentic *ḿfúní* leaf. An Ejagham proverb states: *Ó kumi ka njəm njok, o bhôŋ ḿfúní na nnyô*. 'If you sit on the back of an elephant, you can pick *ḿfúní* with your mouth.' One interpretation: "If you have a wealthy or powerful relation or friend, you can get the good things in life with little effort."

given country becomes their own. Even as they lose or never gain fluency in their heritage language, they will still have an identity as an African and usually more specifically as an Ejagham, an identity passed on to them by their parents. The loss of the use of Ejagham in-country or abroad seems to support Dorian's (1999:31) conclusion that a language is one of "an almost infinite variety of potential identity markers" and can easily be replaced by other languages that are more effective in the new reality. So the children of Ejagham speakers in North America become Ejagham who speak English but are conscious of their African and Ejagham roots through other markers that point to the Ejagham part of their new identity.

19.8 Conclusion

Urbanization is impinging on the Ejagham people, particularly on the western front in Nigeria, where languages with large populations such as the Igbo and Ibibio pose a homogenizing force. However, instead of adopting these major languages, the Ejagham and their neighboring languages who also have fewer speakers, resist the cultural centric forces of the Igbo and Ibibio and adopt Pidgin English and English as a leveling mechanism. A young man I often traveled with inside the Cross River State was a native speaker of the Yala language in Nigeria. He was on equal footing with the Igbo in the Ikom markets and the commercial ventures in Calabar because he could speak English. He also had learned some Efik while a student at the University of Calabar, which helped him in various street-level contexts in Calabar. However, it is English that has the greatest power in the context. It provides a doorway into the more urban world of paid employment, in commerce, education, government services, mass media, and the church.

The long-term sustainability of the Ejagham language will exist in the homeland in Cameroon and Nigeria, not in the diaspora in Cameroonian and Nigerian cities nor in the countries of Europe and North America. The younger generation in the homeland grows up in a community that uses Ejagham orally on a daily basis in all types of social situations, while the younger generation in the diaspora moves out of that community into ones that use different languages. Their fluency and experiences as they move toward adulthood demand that they master the languages of their new city or country of residence.

At the same time, one question remains outstanding: do the parents who have moved into the diaspora need or want language materials in Ejagham or do they become sufficiently fluent in the language of the city or country of residence to meet their social and spiritual interests? From the few I know, their fluency in the language of the diaspora seems to surpass that of their heritage language. Yet, they still have a latent Ejagham proficiency which allows for an affective and cognitive response to material produced in Ejagham.

References

Ardener, Edwin. 1968. Documentary and linguistic evidence for the rise of trading policies between Rio del Rey and Cameroons, 1500–1650. In I. M. Lewis (ed.), *History and social anthropology*, 81–126. London: Tavistock Publications.

Bucholtz, Mary, and Kira Hall. 2004. Language and identity. In Alessandro Duranti (ed.), *A companion to linguistic anthropology*, 369–394. Oxford: Blackwell.

Dorian, Nancy C. 1999. Linguistic and ethnographic fieldwork. In Joshua Fishman (ed.), *Handbook of ethnic identity*, 25–41. Oxford: Oxford University Press.

Karan, Mark E. 2011. Understanding and forecasting ethnolinguistic vitality. *Journal of Multilingual and Multicultural Development* 32:137–149.

Le Page, Robert B., and Andrée Tabouret-Keller. 1985. *Acts of identity: Creole-based approaches to language and ethnicity*. Cambridge: Cambridge University Press.

Pike, Kenneth L. 1967. *Language in relation to a unified theory of the structure of human behavior*. Second edition. Janua Linguarum, Series Maior 24. The Hague: Mouton.

Simons, Gary F., and Charles D. Fennig, eds. 2018. *Ethnologue: Languages of the world*. Twenty-first edition. Dallas, TX: SIL International. Online version: ethnologue.com/.

Smalley, William A. 1994. *Linguistic diversity and national unity: Language ecology in Thailand*. Chicago, IL: University of Chicago.

Watkins, Justin. 2007. Burma/Myanmar. In Andrew Simpson (ed.), *Language and national identity in Asia*, 263–287. Oxford: Oxford University Press.

Watters, John R. 1981. A phonology and morphology of Ejagham, with notes on dialect variation. PhD dissertation. University of California, Los Angeles.

Watters, John R. 2001. Some phonological characteristics of Ejagham (Etung), and Ekoid Bantu language of Cameroon and Nigeria. In Ngessimo M. Mutaka and Sammy B. Chumbow (eds.), *Research mate in African linguistics: Focus on Cameroon*, 55–78. Cologne: Rudiger Koppe Verlag.

20
Ethnologue as a Sourcebook for Mapping Multilingualism: The Case of Sango

Kenneth S. Olson and Gary F. Simons

Abstract. The focus of *Ethnologue* has been on first language (L1) use. This is reflected in the maps currently included in the resource, which show locations and boundaries corresponding to the distribution of L1 speakers. The location of second languages (L2s) is only occasionally represented by maps. Recent restructuring of the *Ethnologue* database provides a pathway for the production of L2 maps. As a test case, we produce a map of the geographic distribution of Sango [sag] in Central African Republic. Using available census data, we include on the map an estimate of the percentage of the population of each language community that uses Sango as an L2. We also discuss how the map sheds light on the identities associated with the use of Sango as an L2.[1]

20.1 The changing role of *Ethnologue* in a multilingual world

When the first edition of *Ethnologue* appeared in 1951, it consisted of ten mimeographed pages describing only forty-six languages. It opened with these words:

> Elaborate descriptions and classifications of the world's fauna and flora have been published in countless books and articles. Similar undertakings for the languages spoken in the world today have lagged far behind—only a few relatively rare and inaccessible lists and descriptions being available for many language areas. For the Christian who feels burdened with the urgency of giving the Word of God to every man in his own tongue, this want is most distressing. (Pittman 1951:1)

At the outset, the fundamental research question for *Ethnologue* was: What are all the distinct languages being used in the world today? The frontiers of knowledge involved identifying and describing thousands of previously unknown languages. The fifth edition in 1958 listed 2,360 living languages; the sixth edition (1965) listed 3,164; the seventh edition (1969) listed 4,493; the ninth edition (1978) listed 5,103; the eleventh edition (1988) listed 6,140; and the threshold of 7,000 living languages was crossed in 2005 with the fifteenth edition.[2] Once a language was identified, the

---

[1] We wish to thank William Samarin, Christoph Müller, Mark Karan, and Elke Karan for helpful comments and suggestions.

most basic questions for describing it were things like: What is it called? Where is it located? How many people speak it? What other languages is it related to? What are its major dialects? Does it have the Bible or any other literature?

After seven decades the situation has changed dramatically. When *Ethnologue* began, the local languages of the world were largely unknown, and their users were thought to be basically monolingual. Today the languages are basically known, and their user communities are known to be largely multilingual. The trend of adding about a thousand languages every ten years has ceased with the number of living languages leveling off at around 7,100 during the 2010s. Today the fundamental research question for *Ethnologue* has become: What is the global language ecology? Language ecology is "the study of interactions between any given language and its environment" (Haugen 1972:325). That environment includes other languages—not just neighboring languages in a peer relationship, but also regional and national languages that may be in a dominant relationship. The description of a language within its environment must therefore include information about language use and language policy relative to the L1 and all the other languages its speakers may use. Haugen (1972:337) closes his article by listing ten basic questions (quoted verbatim below, including his use of italics) that are essential to answer in describing the ecology of a language:

1. What is its *classification* in relation to other languages?
2. Who are its *users*?
3. What are its *domains* of use?
4. What *concurrent languages* are employed by its users?
5. What *internal varieties* does the language show?
6. What is the nature of its *written traditions*?
7. To what degree has its written form been *standardized*, i.e. unified and codified?
8. What kinds of *institutional support* has it won, either in government, education, or private organizations?
9. What are the *attitudes* of its users towards the language?
10. Finally, we may wish to sum up its status in a *typology* of *ecological* classification, which will tell us something about where the language stands and where it is going in comparison with the other languages of the world.

The *Ethnologue* database has fields for addressing all of these questions; it is the editorial objective of the overall effort to complete this level of basic description for every known language.

20.2 Mapping the range of L2 use

The *Ethnologue* description of a language seeks to document its use both as a primary language (L1) and as a secondary language (L2). For given individuals, L1 is the language they are most comfortable using in the domains of everyday life. It is typically the first language they learn, but that is not necessarily the case. And a person typically has one L1, though in the case of someone who has grown up using

---

[2]The fifteenth edition (2005) reports the number of living languages as 6,912. However, with the introduction of EGIDS in the seventeenth edition (2014), 126 languages that were previously described as extinct were reclassified as 9 (Dormant) and thus newly counted as living. Therefore, in terms of the current method for counting living languages, the 7,000 threshold was actually surpassed in the 2005 edition.

more than one language from infancy, there is the possibility of more than one L1 (see Harris, chapter 12 this volume, and Kim et al. 1997:174). In *Ethnologue* usage, an L2 is then any other language that a person might use.

Ethnologue has become known for its color map plates, which number 236 in the twenty-second edition (Eberhard, Simons, and Fennig 2019). These maps show the range of territory in which languages are used as an L1. The absence of maps showing the range of use as an L2 can lead to misinterpretation of the resource. We recently encountered a scholar from another academic discipline who was researching how language use in Africa interacted with his field of study. His impression from *Ethnologue* was that Africans could choose between only two languages: (1) the L1 or (2) the national language (that is, French, English, Portuguese, etc.). He was unaware of the existence of lingua francas and the important role that they play in the life of Africans across the continent. In dialoguing with him, it became clear that the maps were foundational in forming his understanding of the language situation in Africa, so that the absence of L2 maps in *Ethnologue* is what led to his inaccurate impression. Although information about L2 use is present in the text, introducing maps showing the range of L2 use could be a more impactful way of conveying such information—not just to the public at large, but especially to educators, development workers, government workers, church workers, and others who are serving in the midst of societal multilingualism.

Recent additions to the structure of the *Ethnologue* database provide a straightforward path for the generation of L2 maps. Specifically, the database has added a new intersection table to record the many-to-many relationship between language communities and L2s—that is, a single language community may use many L2s, and many language communities may use the same L2. In *Ethnologue* products,[3] this information appears in the "Language Use" section of a language entry. The use of another language as an L2 by the language community in focus is indicated by the phrase, "Also use *Name of L2* [*ISO code*]." If they use multiple L2s, a list of second languages is given. If such use is limited to a particular domain or age group or gender, a brief remark about this may be added.

This information can be used to create a range map for a particular L2 by coloring in the regions corresponding to all the language communities that use it as an L2.[4] Map[5] 1, first published in Olson and Lewis (2018), is an example of this. Lingala[6] [lin] and Bangala [bxg] are used as L2s across the northern and western regions of the Democratic Republic of the Congo (DRC), as well as the northern part of the Republic of the Congo (RC). Although it arose as a lingua franca in the late nineteenth century in the mid-river region—about halfway between Kinshasa and Kisangani (Meeuwis 2010, 2013)—Lingala has more recently emerged as an L1 in and around Kinshasa.

---

[3] ethnologue.com/products/.

[4] We are indebted to our colleague, Marcus Love, who used information we provided from the *Ethnologue* database.

[5] We thank the following people for help in producing the Lingala/Bangala map: Douglas Boone, Annette Harrison, Wendy Atkins, Maryanne Augustin, William Gardner, Bettina Gottschlich-Modibale, Constance Kutsch Lojenga, Rob McKee, David Morgan, Salikoko Mufwene, Cami Robbins, Larry Robbins, Paul Thomas, Angela Williams-Ngumbu, and Doug Wright.

[6] A succinct overview of Lingala is given in Meeuwis 2013.

Map 1. Geographic distribution of Lingala and Bangala (Olson and Lewis 2018)

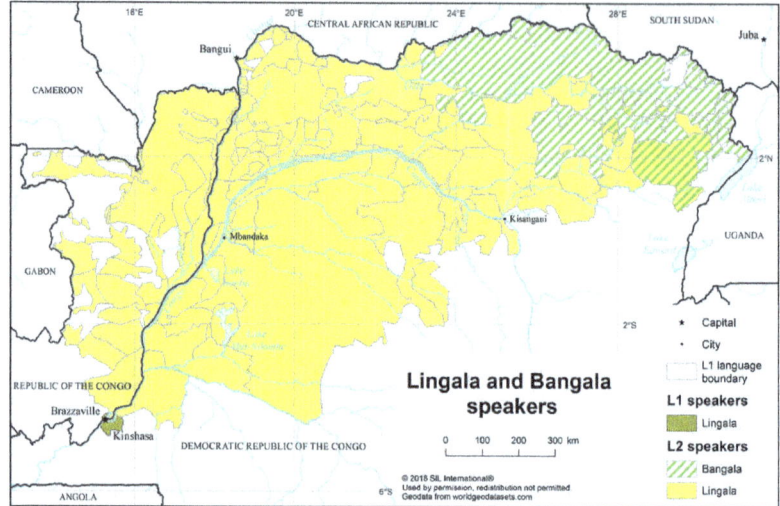

Note: White areas within the Lingala/Bangala region are sparsely populated or uninhabited.

In map 1, the boundaries of Lingala/Bangala L2 use are shown to coincide with the boundaries of the local language areas. This should be construed as an approximation. For example, along DRC's northern border with CAR, Lingala is used on *both* sides of the Ubangi and Mbomou Rivers, though its use tapers off quickly as one travels north.

In some cases it is necessary to distinguish the L1 and L2 boundaries. For example, for the Komo [kmw] community, Lingala is the primary L2 used west of the Lualaba River (the region directly south of Kisangani on the map), while Congo Swahili [swc] is used east of the river. As a result, we have included only the part of the Komo region west of the river in the Lingala L2 area in map 1.

20.3 Mapping the degree of L2 use

Ethnologue further refines the "Also use" phrasing by the use of a set of quantifiers that provide rough estimates of the degree to which an L2 is used, as shown in table 1 below. As an example of the use of quantifiers, the "Language Use" field for Buduma [bdm] of Chad lists three L2s—two using a quantifier to estimate the degree of use, while the third provides no estimate of the degree to which the language is used:

> Most also use Kanembu [kbl], especially those living near Bol. Many also use Yerwa Kanuri [knc]. Also use Chadian Spoken Arabic [shu].

Table 1. Quantifiers describing the extent of L2 use in a language community (Eberhard, Simons, and Fennig 2019)

Quantifier	Criteria
All	At least 95% of the ethnic population use the reported language as L2
Most	At least 65% but less than 95% of the ethnic population use the reported language as L2
Many	At least 35% but less than 65% of the ethnic population use the reported language as L2
Some	At least 5% but less than 35% of the ethnic population use the reported language as L2
Few	Less than 5% of the ethnic population use the reported language as L2

Using this picklist of quantifiers to estimate the degree of L2 use is a recent innovation in the *Ethnologue* database introduced for the nineteenth edition (2016). Prior to this, the database required the amount of L2 use to be reported as the estimated number of bilingual speakers, but it had proven virtually impossible for the contributors to provide information of that precision. The editors thus introduced the picklist of quantifiers in hopes of making it feasible for contributors who have firsthand familiarity with a situation to provide an impressionistic estimate of the extent of bilingualism without needing to do research to establish an exact number.

When all of the "Also use" statements for a particular L2 within an area include a quantifier, it is possible to use the information in the *Ethnologue* database to create a more nuanced range map that uses shading to represent the degree of L2 use. As a test case, we developed such a map for the use of Sango[7] [sag] as an L2 in Central African Republic (CAR).[8] The result is shown in map 2.

---

[7] A succinct overview of Sango is given in Samarin 2013.
[8] Due to lack of data, we did not attempt to map the distribution of Sango in adjacent countries.

Map 2. L2 use of Sango in Central African Republic

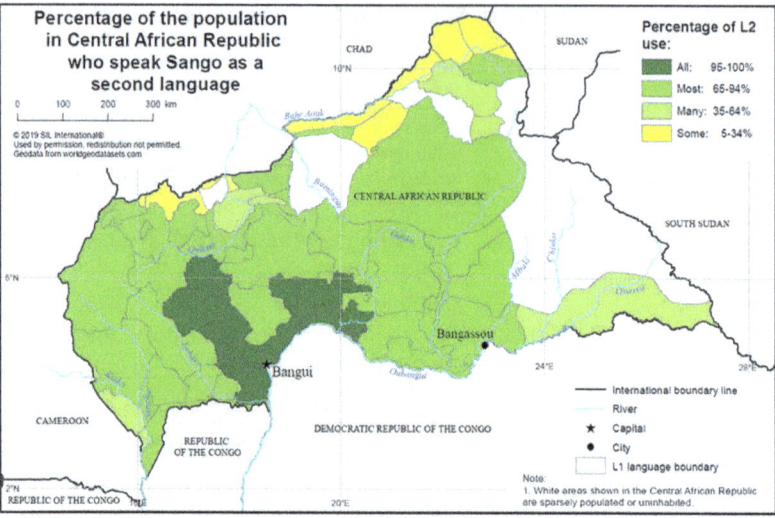

We made use of data from the 1988 government census in CAR (Karan 2001:89-90) to select the appropriate quantifier for the use of Sango as an L2 for each language community in the country. One of the questions asked during the census was whether or not each person spoke Sango (Karan 2001:89). The census compiled the data for each region and reported a percentage of Sango use for each region.

For most language communities, the conversion of the data from political region to language region was relatively straightforward, with a single quantifier value being assigned to each language. However, it was necessary to assign different quantifiers to some geographic subregions of three languages: West Central Banda [bbp], Banda-Banda [bpd], and Manza [mzv]. Further modifications may be necessary to the *Ethnologue* database to accommodate such cases.

Before discussing the results, a few comments about the methodology are in order. On the positive side, the census question that was asked directly corresponds to the information encoded in the quantifiers—the percentage of a population that uses Sango. Also, every household was interviewed, so the data are quite complete.

At the same time, the results need to be qualified. The census interview is an *indirect* measure of language use, rather than a direct measure of language use itself. Mark Karan (2001:89) suggests that several factors may have led to the over-reporting of Sango use: the question was asked by a government employee, the head of the household provided the information on behalf of the entire family, and use of Sango is considered prestigious in CAR (cf. Samarin 1955:262–263). Sango's status as a symbol of national identity (see below) was likely also a significant factor (Mark Karan, personal communication). That being said, Samarin (2007:352–353) reports that in a 1962 survey of Sango use in the rural Gbeya [gbp] area, he found that the average percentage of Gbeya-Sango bilinguals was 66%, which was close to the number reported in the 1988 census for that region.

In much of the country, either all or most people report speaking Sango. The most concentrated areas are in and around the capital Bangui, north and east of Bangui along the Ubangi River, and inland to the northwest and northeast of Bangui. The places where use of Sango is more limited are in the eastern, northern, and southwestern edges of the country. The regions in white on the map are generally uninhabited.

20.4 Identity and the spread of Sango

Sango is the main lingua franca in CAR. The generally accepted view is that it developed on the Ubangi River in the late nineteenth century as a pidginized[9] form of one of the speech varieties from the Ngbandi group[10] (Lekens 1951, cited by Samarin 1955:256; Samarin 1986:382; Boyeldieu and Diki-Kidiri 1988:31; Karan 2001:6). The source variety is often identified as "Sango Riverain," an appellation that corresponds to one of the extant varieties [snj]. However, the term is sometimes used in a broader sense to refer to all the riparian varieties of the Ngbandi group. Hence some uncertainty remains about the exact source variety.

Sango has spread extensively, particularly to the north of the river, so that it is now used throughout most of the country. It is also spoken to some degree across the borders in northern DRC, northern RC, eastern Cameroon, and southern Chad (Samarin 2007:347, Meeuwis 2013). It has also emerged as an L1 (Karan 2001:5), with roughly 500,000 L1 speakers (Eberhard, Simons, and Fennig 2019). Jacquot (1961:163) describes the creolization of Sango in Bangui among children from various language groups using Sango as a common language in school (cf. Samarin 2001). In 1964 it was named the national language by constitutional law no. 64/37—the same law that made French the official language. Then in 1991 it became an official language of CAR alongside French by constitutional law no. 91/001 (Koyt 1994:503).

Karan (2001:92–93) offers two key factors in explaining the areas of high Sango use. First, these regions correspond to major transportation arteries—the Ubangi River (navigable up to Bangassou), the Lobaye River, and the Ouaka River. Considering Sango's history as a lingua franca, this is not unexpected.

Second, the region also generally corresponds to the location of the two major Protestant church communities before independence—the churches connected to the Baptist Mid-Mission (BMM) and the Grace Brethren International Mission (GBIM, now called Encompass World Partners). Both missions began work in CAR in the early 1920s, and both made administrative decisions early on to use Sango exclusively. The BMM adopted Sango in 1923, and the GBIM somewhat later following World War II, after initially focusing on the local languages (Samarin 2007:351). This was mainly for the pragmatic reason of facilitating mission work across each respective region. The entire Sango Bible was published in 1966—a collaboration between the two communities. The Roman Catholic Church initially used the local languages in its work but later switched to Sango, likely for the same reason (Karan 2006:239).

---

[9] Diki-Kidiri (1986) and Morrill (1997) hold a different view, arguing instead that Sango did not undergo pidginization as it emerged from its source language.

[10] Eberhard, Simons, and Fennig (2019) consider the Ngbandi group to consist of several distinct languages. However, Boyeldieu (1982) finds minimal linguistic variation between the varieties in CAR: Sango Riverain, Yakoma [yky], and Dendi [deq]. Buchanan (2007:11) reports, "Les Dendis comprennent bien le yakoma, le ngbandi et le sango, c'est-à-dire qu'il existe une bonne intercompréhension entre ces parlers" [The Dendis understand Yakoma, Ngbandi, and Sango well, that is to say there is a good intercomprehension between these dialects], but earlier (p. 8) he notes that Dendi speakers have some difficulty understanding Ngbandi [ngb] from DRC.

Identity issues come into play in explaining the spread of Sango. First, it is not coincidental that the spread of the language reached—and was generally attenuated by—the international borders. Sango was not used by the French colonial government (Le Page 1997:60), but Central African recruits in the French Army promoted Sango use for interethnic communication (Karan 2006:239, cf. Samarin 1955:256–257). Subsequently, the language became associated with the independence movement (Le Page 1997:60). When William Samarin conducted a sociolinguistic survey in a Gbeya [gbp] village, the residents considered Sango to be "the language of the Central African Republic" (Samarin 1986:379). With factors like these in the background, the language gradually became a symbol of national identity in CAR (Karan 2001:12, 18; Koyt 1994).[11]

Identity issues also came into play in the adoption of a new official Sango orthography in 1984. This orthography was seen as reinforcing an independent national identity for two reasons: (1) It was created by Central African linguists, and (2) it intentionally distanced itself from the previous orthography, which was based extensively on the French orthography (Karan 2006:269–270, 307).

Second, while the use of Sango in the major church communities started for pragmatic reasons, it has now taken on a function of building church unity (Karan 2001:108). Samarin (1955:256) states, "Some Africans feel that the native languages tend to divide the people whereas Sango unites them all into one Christian body. Moreover, there is some evidence to indicate that Sango has come to be identified, at least among the Protestants, as the Christian language." The churches encourage the spread of Sango because they see it as a way to more efficiently carry out their ecclesiastical functions and also unite the various ethnic groups.

20.5 Conclusion

In summary, the inclusion of L2 maps in *Ethnologue* would help it to reflect better the realities of our multilingual world. This in turn would benefit users of this resource by giving them a better understanding of the linguistic realities on the ground. Such maps would not simply portray the geographic range of use for languages of wider communication, but also of the identities their users could share.

References

Boyeldieu, Pascal. 1982. Structures sociales et particularismes linguistiques en pays de langue 'Ngbandi': Éléments pour une étude [Social structures and distinctive linguistic identities in the Ngbandi language region: Data for a study]. In Pascal Boyeldieu and Marcel Diki-Kidiri (eds.), *Le domaine ngbandi*, 13–80. Bibliothèque de la SELAF 93. Paris: SELAF.

Boyeldieu, Pascal, and Marcel Diki-Kidiri. 1988. Le group ngbandi-sango-kpatiri [The Ngbandi-Sango-Kpatiri group]. In Yves Moñino (ed.), *Lexique comparatif des langues oubanguiennes*, 31–33. Paris: Geuthner.

---

[11] In additional to a national identity, Samarin (1955:259–260) suggests that additional factors may have contributed to the attenuation of Sango at the borders. These include competition with other lingua francas (e.g., Lingala in DRC, Chadian Spoken Arabic in Chad) and economic isolation from its neighbors.

Buchanan, Michael. 2007. Rapport d'enquête sociolinguistique: Première évaluation parmi les Dendis [Sociolinguistic survey report: Initial assessment among the Dendis]. *SIL Electronic Survey Reports* 2007-001. sil.org/resources/publications/entry/9152/.

Diki-Kidiri, Marcel. 1986. Le sango dans la formation de la nation centrafricaine [Sango in the creation of the Central African Republic]. *Politique Africaine* 23:83–99. Paris: Karthala. politique-africaine.com/numeros/023_SOM.HTM/.

Eberhard, David M., Gary F. Simons, and Charles D. Fennig, eds. 2019. *Ethnologue: Languages of the world*. Twenty-second edition. Dallas, TX: SIL International. ethnologue.com/.

Harris, Kyle. 2021. L1 and L2 comprehension and emotional impact among early proficient bilinguals. In J. Stephen Quakenbush and Gary F. Simons (eds), *Language and identity in a multilingual, migrating world*. Publications in Sociolinguistics 9. Dallas, TX: SIL International.

Haugen, Einar. 1972. The ecology of language. In Einar Haugen, *The ecology of language: Essays by Einar Haugen*, 325–339. Language Science and National Development. Stanford: Stanford University Press.

Jacquot, André. 1961. Notes sur la situation du Sango à Bangui: Résultats d'un sondage [Notes on the status of Sango in Bangui: Results of a survey]. *Africa: Journal of the International African Institute* 31(2):158–166. DOI:10.2307/1158103/.

Karan, Elke. 2006. Writing system development and reform: A process. MA thesis. University of North Dakota, Grand Forks. commons.und.edu/theses/3004/.

Karan, Mark E. 2001. *The dynamics of Sango language spread*. Publications in Sociolinguistics 7. Dallas, TX: SIL International.

Kim, Karl H. S., Norman R. Relkin, Kyoung-Min Lee, and Joy Hirsch. 1997. Distinct cortical areas associated with native and second languages. *Nature* 388(6638):171–174. DOI:10.1038/40623/.

Koyt, Michel M. 1994. Situation et politique linguistiques en République Centrafricaine [Language status and policy in the Central African Republic]. In Pierre Martel and Jacques Maurais (eds.), *Langues et sociétés en contact: Mélanges offerts à Jean-Claude Corbeil*, 503–516. Canadiana Romanica 8. Berlin: De Gruyter.

Le Page, Robert B. 1997. Political and economic aspects of vernacular literacy. In Andrée Tabouret-Keller, Robert B. Le Page, Penelope Gardner-Chloros, and Gabrielle Varro (eds.), *Vernacular literacy: A re-evaluation*, 23–81. Oxford Studies in Anthropological Linguistics 13. Oxford: Clarendon Press.

Lekens, Benjamin. 1951. Nota over het ngbandi als voertaal in Ubangi [Note on Ngbandi as the language of wider communication in the Ubangi region]. *Kongo-Overzee* 17:162–164.

Meeuwis, Michael. 2010. *A grammatical overview of Lingála*. LINCOM Studies in African Linguistics 81. Munich: Lincom Europa.

Meeuwis, Michael. 2013. Lingala. In Susanne Maria Michaelis, Philippe Maurer, Martin Haspelmath, and Magnus Huber (eds.), *The survey of pidgin and creole languages. Volume 3: Contact languages based on languages from Africa, Asia, Australia, and the Americas*. Oxford: Oxford University Press. apics-online.info/surveys/60/.

Morrill, Charles Henry. 1997. Language, culture, and society in the Central African Republic: The emergence and development of Sango. PhD dissertation. Indiana University.

Olson, Kenneth S., and M. Paul Lewis. 2018. The *Ethnologue* and L2 mapping. In Ericka A. Albaugh and Kathryn M. de Luna (eds.), *Tracing language movement in Africa*, 45–65. New York: Oxford University Press. DOI:10.1093/oso/9780190657543.003.0003/.

Pittman, Richard S. 1951. *Missionary Ethnologue for intercessors, translators, missionaries, and mission councils* [Ethnologue. First edition]. Berwick, Australia: Wycliffe School of Linguistics. 10 pp., mimeo. First page reproduced at sil.org/history-event/first-edition-ethnologue/.

Samarin, William J. 1955. Sango, an African lingua franca. *Word* 11:254–267. DOI:10.1080/00437956.1955.11659562/.

Samarin, William J. 1986. French and Sango in the Central African Republic. *Anthropological Linguistics* 28:379–387. jstor.org/stable/30027964/.

Samarin, William J. 2001. Explaining shift to Sango in Bangui. In Robert Nicolaï (ed.), *Leçons d'Afrique: Filiations, rupture et reconstitutions de langues: Un hommage à Gabriel Manessy*, 351–391. Louvain-Paris: Peeters.

Samarin, William J. 2007. Review of *The dynamics of Sango language spread*, by Mark Karan. *Journal of Pidgin and Creole Languages* 22:347–366. DOI: 10.1075/jpcl.22.2.08sam/.

Samarin, William J. 2013. Sango. In Susanne Maria Michaelis, Philippe Maurer, Martin Haspelmath, and Magnus Huber (eds.), *The survey of pidgin and creole languages. Volume 3: Contact languages based on languages from Africa, Asia, Australia, and the Americas*, 13–24. Oxford: Oxford University Press. apics-online.info/surveys/59/.

Afterword

21
The Research Agenda Going Forward

Gary F. Simons and J. Stephen Quakenbush

As Isaac Newton famously wrote in 1676, "If I have seen further, it is by standing on the shoulders of giants." This has come to be a metaphor for how scholarship works. The authors of the papers in this volume, to help them see what they have been able to see in their contributions, have stood on the shoulders of over five hundred works cited in all of their lists of references. But the process does not stop there; as the future unfolds, others will stand on the works collected in this volume to see further yet.

It is built into the format of a Pike Center symposium that the participants take time to peer ahead and think together about priorities for follow-up research. During the course of the symposium, presenters and discussants alike were asked to make note of open research questions arising out of the various presentations. In the closing session, the collected questions were discussed and rated. The following paragraphs describe the open research problems that were identified as most significant.

Understanding patterns of societal multilingualism. A theme that consistently emerged throughout the symposium is that "multilingualisms vary." One of the main contributions of this collection of papers is the window it gives on patterns of language and identity in communities associated with smaller, local languages. The authors make use of a number of theories and models to gain insight into how issues of identity help to explain observed patterns of language use—Communication Accommodation Theory (Giles 2016), Ethnolinguistic Identity Theory (Giles and Johnson 1987), Perceived Benefits Model (Karan 2001), Social Capital Theory (Coleman 1988), Sustainable Use Model (Lewis and Simons 2016). Can we synthesize the most insightful components from these models to achieve a more cohesive and comprehensive understanding of how identity issues explain patterns of societal multilingualism? Is there a basic taxonomy of possible configurations of multiple languages in relation to multiple identities? How might such a taxonomy help us to understand and describe basic patterns of societal multilingualism?

Understanding individual multilingualism. The papers in this volume by Kyle Harris and Daniel Paul talk about the situation in which people are so proficiently bilingual as to not have a single dominant language (or "heart language"). Research is needed to better understand this phenomenon. How prevalent is it among local language communities around the world that the majority of speakers could be characterized as "balanced bilinguals"? Or, as discussed in the papers in this volume by Sangsok Son and Maik Gibson, how often do dynamic, emergent language practices prevail such that reference solely to a distinct set of "named languages" is inadequate to describe how people communicate? How strong is ethnic identity versus national identity in these situations?

Late acquisition of heritage language. The typical model for intergenerational transmission of local languages is that they are passed from parents to children as a first language. However, there are situations (particularly in multilingual urban settings) in which young people are known to learn their language of heritage identity as a second language, even learning it from their peers rather than in the home. Research is needed to understand this phenomenon. How does late acquisition of the "mother tongue" work? Is it as effective as transmission in the home? How prevalent is it?

Understanding identity shift. Some ethnic identities are strong and resist shift, while others are not and succumb to shift along with the language associated with that identity. But even when an ethnic identity resists shift, the language associated with it may not. We need a model for understanding the dynamics of identity shift in relation to language shift. Such a model would help us to identify situations in which both ethnic identity and language use are sustainable, only ethnic identity is sustainable, or neither is sustainable. (The fourth possibility of sustaining language use without sustaining the associated ethnic identity is not thought to be possible; see Lewis, chapter 3 this volume.) The insights of the Identity Construction Factors (Eberhard chapter 2, this volume) seem promising in this respect, but will require empirical testing against many case studies in order to grow into something with demonstrable explanatory and predictive power. Once we have a model that works, a methodology for applying it in the assessment of situations in the field should be developed.

Scale in language development. How can insights related to language and identity help us in determining the appropriate scale for language development efforts? Small-scale efforts (such as at a dialect level) result in products that are most closely matched to the variety of language that is used by the local community. Large-scale efforts, on the other hand, seek a wider audience for their products and thus attempt to establish an orthography intended for use on a pan-dialect or even cross-language level. While efforts aimed at the small scale may result in literature that is easier for its intended audience to read, such efforts are not likely to encompass a large enough user community to be sustainable in terms of the ability to produce a growing literature. The Magar Kham case study (Stephen Watters, chapter 15 this volume) involves the trade-off between following localized language practices in language development versus trying to forge a shared language practice for an overarching ethnic identity. Research is needed to develop strategies for dealing with situations like this. When is a local identity with its associated local language practice too local to serve as the basis for effective language development efforts? Where are actual case studies in which a shared language practice covering variation across an entire ethnic identity has been successfully developed? What would be indicators for choosing small-scale development over large-scale development and vice versa?

Language development for sustainable identity. The Sustainable Use Model (Lewis and Simons 2016) posits that EGIDS level 9 (Dormant), in which "the language serves as a reminder of heritage identity for an ethnic community, but no one has more than symbolic proficiency," can be a stable and sustainable outcome of language shift. But it is not an inevitable outcome; language shift with identity shift could result in the complete loss of the ethnic identity. Research is needed to develop strategies for helping language communities to achieve sustainable identity. For communities that remain in their homeland but have shifted language, what mechanisms do they use to maintain heritage identity and how does language fit in? What mechanisms do displaced peoples use? What kinds of language development activities are appropriate in situations where language has shifted but identity is holding strong?

Closely related to this is the need for **evidence about the impact of language development on strengthening identity.** Anecdotes abound about how language development efforts have had a positive impact on a group's self perception or sense of self esteem. But these have never been compiled into an organized collection. Research is needed to collect such stories and to turn them into a collection of evidence. What kinds of activities have been demonstrated to have what kinds of impacts? What is the prevalence of these positive impacts on group identity—are they typical or exceptional? What are the common factors in situations that result in positive impacts versus those that do not?

Of the many open problems for further research that were proposed and discussed during the symposium, the above are the ones that were judged by the participants as being the most significant. We hope that this listing will serve to inspire follow-up research that builds on the work in this volume to help us all see even further.

References

Coleman, James S. 1988. Social capital in the creation of human capital. *American Journal of Sociology* 94:95–120.

Giles, Howard, ed. 2016. *Communication accommodation theory: Negotiating personal relationships and social identities across contexts*. Cambridge: Cambridge University Press.

Giles, Howard, and Patricia Johnson. 1987. Ethnolinguistic identity theory: A social psychological approach to language maintenance. *International Journal of the Sociology of Language* 68:69–100.

Karan, Mark E. 2001. *The dynamics of Sango language spread*. Publications in Sociolinguistics 7. Dallas, TX: SIL International.

Lewis, M. Paul, and Gary F. Simons. 2016. *Sustaining language use: Perspectives on community-based language development*. Publications in Ethnography 42. Dallas, TX: SIL International.

Contributors

Leoni Bouwer is a Senior Language Assessment Consultant for SIL International and coordinator of a Malagasy Bible translation project for Wycliffe South Africa. She holds a PhD in Linguistics from the University of South Africa, Pretoria. She has been involved in linguistic fieldwork in Madagascar since 1999.

John M. Clifton is a Senior Consultant in Linguistics with SIL International, and an Adjunct Professor of Linguistics at the University of North Dakota. He holds a PhD in Linguistics from Indiana University. Most of his fieldwork has been in Papua New Guinea and Central Asia; his main research interests are sociolinguistics, orthography, and language documentation.

Marlute van Dam is a linguist and translation consultant-in-training for SIL in Romania. She holds an MA in Linguistics from the University of Leiden and an MA in Ecumenical Theology from the University of Bonn. She has more than three years of experience in conducting fieldwork among the Roma people. Her main interests are sociolinguistics and semantics.

David Eberhard is the General Editor of *Ethnologue*. He holds a PhD in Linguistics from Vrije Universiteit, Amsterdam. He has conducted fieldwork among Amazonian communities in Brazil for twenty-two years, and led training events on community-based language development for local speakers of over sixty minority languages in twelve countries. His passion for minoritized communities and their languages drives his interest in language shift, maintenance, and development, as well as the phonology and morphology of Nambikwara languages and the learning of vernacular languages.

Jaap Feenstra is serving in SIL as a strategy consultant and has held other strategic leadership roles in the organization. He holds an MA in Leadership from Trinity Western University. He grew up bilingually in the Frisian part of the Netherlands. He has worked nearly twenty-five years as a field linguist and translation facilitator among the Tlicho people in subarctic Canada. He is also serving as a translation consultant.

Maik Gibson is the International Sociolinguistics Coordinator for SIL International. He holds a PhD in Linguistics from the University of Reading. He has done fieldwork in Tunisia and Kenya; he also does research on linguistic diversity in cyberspace.

Kyle Harris is the Area Director for Asia/Pacific Islands Region and the International Scripture Engagement Coordinator for Pioneer Bible Translators. He holds a PhD in Leadership Studies from Johnson University. His PhD research focused on the development of attitudes of Indonesian seminary students towards the use of vernacular languages and vernacular Scriptures in their future ministries and his primary interest is in factors affecting Scripture engagement in highly multilingual contexts. Kyle served as a Bible translator in Papua New Guinea and is now based in Indonesia.

Sunny Hong is an anthropology consultant for SIL International and an adjunct professor at the Dallas International University. She holds a PhD in Intercultural Studies from Biola University. She is particularly interested in multicultural and refugee issues.

Mark E. Karan is a Language Strategy Consultant and Senior Sociolinguistics Consultant for SIL International, and an adjunct professor at the University of North Dakota. He holds an MA in Linguistics from the University of North Dakota and a PhD in Linguistics from the University of Pennsylvania. He is particularly interested in the dynamics of language shift.

M. Paul Lewis is a Senior Sociolinguistics Consultant for SIL. He holds an MA in Linguistics from the University of Texas at Arlington and a PhD in Sociolinguistics from Georgetown University. He did fieldwork in Guatemala and has taught or consulted in many other parts of the world.

Janet McLarren is an anthropology consultant with SIL Eurasia. She holds an MA in Anthropology from California State University at Los Angeles. She conducted her MA fieldwork among North African immigrant women in southern France, looking at how they adapted and integrated into French culture. She has taught national and mother tongue translators and is interested in understanding biblical cultures from an anthropological perspective.

Mary McLendon works in diaspora engagement with JAARS (Waxhaw, North Carolina). She completed graduate studies in linguistics and translation with SIL and holds a Bachelor of Science degree in Nursing from the University of Vermont. Her interests include assisting diaspora peoples to engage with the Scriptures and in Bible translation.

Kenneth S. Olson is a Senior Linguistics Consultant for SIL International. He holds a PhD in Linguistics from the University of Chicago. He has done fieldwork in the Democratic Republic of the Congo and elsewhere. He currently serves on the International Phonetic Association Committee on Alphabet, Charts, and Fonts.

Daniel Paul is a translation and linguistics consultant with SIL. He holds an MA in Linguistics from the School of Oriental and African Studies, University of London, and a PhD in Linguistics from the University of Manchester. He has done fieldwork in Tajikistan, Iran, and Azerbaijan.

J. Steve Quakenbush holds a PhD in Sociolinguistics from Georgetown University and is a Fellow of the Pike Center for Integrative Scholarship. He has held various academic and administrative positions in SIL International. He was directly involved in translation and language development work in the Philippines over a thirty-year period and has published on Agutaynen and Austronesian linguistics, language development, and language endangerment.

Gary F. Simons is SIL's Chief Research Officer. He is also Director of the Pike Center for Integrative Scholarship and the Executive Editor of *Ethnologue*. He holds a PhD in Linguistics from Cornell University and has done fieldwork in the Solomon Islands and Papua New Guinea. He has also done significant work in linguistic computing and is a co-founder of OLAC, the Open Language Archives Community.

Scott Smith is a sociolinguistics consultant for SIL's Africa Area; he is also Regional Manager for SIL in Equatorial Guinea. He holds a DEA in Applied Linguistics from the Autonomous University of Madrid. He has done fieldwork in Africa for twenty-three years, and has taught undergraduate and graduate linguistics courses in three continents. He is a consultant-in-training in sociolinguistics and translation.

Sangsok Son is a literacy and education consultant for LEAD Asia and South Asia Group of SIL. He holds an MA in Applied Linguistics from Charles Darwin University, Australia, an MPhil in Linguistics from Delhi University, and a PhD in Education from Jawaharlal Nehru University, India. His research interests include multilingualism and trans-languaging in education. He is involved in developing trans-languaging methods for linguistically heterogeneous classrooms and multilingual students in Thailand after having worked in India for fifteen years.

Calvin Tiessen is a Facilitator for Partnerships and Advocacy with SIL International. He holds an MA in Linguistics from the University of North Dakota. He is currently pursuing a doctoral degree in Anthropology through Middlesex University in London, UK.

John R. Watters is Senior Advisor to the SIL Executive Director. He began as a researcher of the Ejagham language in 1973. Since 1981, he has held various types of SIL leadership roles: technical, executive, and governing. He holds a PhD in Linguistics from UCLA. He has focused on the Bantoid languages of Cameroon and Nigeria, engaging more particularly with Ekoid languages within Bantoid, specifically Ejagham and Mbe. His research interests include information structures, morphology and tone, tense-aspect-mood, comparative-historical topics, and language and society.

Stephen Watters is a linguist and translator with SIL International working in the Himalayan region. He also has an adjunct faculty position with the linguistics program at Baylor University, and is a fellow at the Institute for Studies of Religion, Baylor University. He holds an MA in linguistics from the University of Texas at Arlington and a PhD in linguistics from Rice University. He has done fieldwork throughout South Asia and the Himalaya with interest in many aspects of linguistics and translation.

SIL International® Publications
Publications in Sociolinguistics Series
ISSN 1091-9074

8. **Borrowing versus code-switching in West Tarangan (Indonesia)**, by Richard J. Nivens, 2002, 230 pp., ISBN-10 1-55671-134; ISBN-13 978-1-55671-134-3.
7. **The dynamics of Sango language spread**, by Mark E. Karan, 2001, 151 pp., ISBN-10 1-55671-122-0; ISBN-13 978-1-55671-122-0.
6. **K'iche': A study in the sociology of language**, by M. Paul Lewis, 2001, 261 pp., ISBN-10 1-55671-120-4; ISBN-13 978-1-55671-120-6.
5. **The same but different: Language use and attitudes in four communities of Burkina Faso**, by Stuart Showalter, 2001, 261 pp., ISBN-10 1-55671-092-5; ISBN-13 978-1-55671-092-6.
4. **Ashéninka stories of change**, by Ronald James Anderson, 2000, 245 pp., ISBN-10 1-55671-102-6; ISBN-13 978-1-55671-102-2.
3. **Assessing ethnolinguistic vitality: Theory and practice, selected papers from the Third International Language Assessment Conference**, edited by M. Paul Lewis and Gloria Kindell, 2000, 205 pp., ISBN-10 1-55671-087-9; ISBN-13 978-1-55671-087-2.
2. **The early days of sociolinguistics: Memories and reflections**, edited by Christina Bratt Paulston and G. Richard Tucker, 1997, 362 pp., ISBN-10 1-55671-253-7, ISBN-13 978-1-55671-253-1.
1. **North Sulawesi language survey**, by Scott Merrifield and Martinus Salea, 1996, 322 pp., ISBN 1-55671-000-3.

SIL International Publications
7500 W. Camp Wisdom Road
Dallas, TX 75236-5629 USA

General inquiry: publications_intl@sil.org

Pending order inquiry: sales@sil.org
publications.sil.org

www.ingramcontent.com/pod-product-compliance
Lightning Source LLC
Chambersburg PA
CBHW060418300426
44111CB00018B/2889